SHELLS

Cheryl Claassen

CAMBRIDGE
UNIVERSITY PRESS

PUBLISHED BY THE PRESS SYNDICATE OF THE UNIVERSITY OF CAMBRIDGE
The Pitt Building, Trumpington Street, Cambridge CB2 1RP, United Kingdom

CAMBRIDGE UNIVERSITY PRESS
The Edinburgh Building, Cambridge, CB2 2RU, United Kingdom
http://www.cup.cam.ac.uk
40 West 20th Street, New York, NY 10011-4211, USA   http://www.cup.org
10 Stamford Road, Oakleigh, Melbourne 3166, Australia

First published 1998

Printed in the United Kingdom at the University Press, Cambridge

Typeset in Times 11/13 pt [VN]

A catalogue record for this book is available from the British Library

Library of Congress Cataloguing in Publication data

Claassen, Cheryl, 1953–
Shells / Cheryl Claassen.
    p. cm. – (Cambridge manuals in archaeology)
Includes bibliographical references and index.
ISBN 0 521 57036 0 (hbk.). – ISBN 0 521 57852 3 (pbk.)
1. Fish remains (Archaeology).   2. Shells.   3. Molluscs.
I. Title.   II. Series.
CC79.5.A5C58   1998
930.1 – dc21   97-35274 CIP

ISBN 0 521 57036 0 hardback
ISBN 0 521 57852 3 paperback

**This book is dedicated to my parents
Harold F. Claassen and Dorothy Buchanan Claassen
of Tulsa, Oklahoma**

they took an undisciplined 7-year-old girl and, through their
example, taught her the value of discipline

CONTENTS

FIGURES

TABLES

ACKNOWLEDGEMENTS

I have written this book after years of reading and conversing about shell matrix sites, making it difficult to sort out influences. Bibliographies have often been as useful as the actual articles and are even more quickly forgotten. I certainly need to acknowledge those articles of the latter half of the 1970s and of the early part of the 1980s which I read while preparing my 1982 dissertation – writers such as Mellars, Bailey, Rowley-Conwy, Ambrose and Binford. More specifically I acknowledge the writings and references of Rollins et al. 1990, references of Waselkov 1987, the taphonomy bibliography of Koch (1989), and references in Kidwell and Bosence 1991. I want to thank an anonymous reviewer for important details in Chapters 2 and 3, as well as Frank McKinney, Appalachian State University, for reviews of sections of Chapters 2 and 3. Dena Dincauze reviewed the manuscript on two occasions and provided moral support to me and verbal support to Cambridge. Jessica Kuper, editor at Cambridge, was quick to respond to my enquiries, and hopeful of my perseverence. I should also acknowledge those authors who encouraged my skeptical attitude about dietary reconstruction, and generated my enthusiasm with their non-dietary innovations – Elsie Begler and Richard Keatinge, Sarah Campbell, Julie Stein, Dolph Widmer, Ken Sassaman, Betty Meehan, Jon Ericson and Joel Gunn. I admire greatly the imaginations of each of these individuals. Several people also have been instrumental in facilitating my field experiences with shell matrix sites and I wish to acknowledge them: Alan McCartney for the Aleutian exposure, when I first encountered the shell matrix in the early 1970s, Patty Jo Watson for the Green River experience, Mary Jane Berman and Perry Gnivecki for the Bahamian experience, Stuart Fiedel for the Dogan Point experience, and Joan Gero for nudging me toward an explicit statement of my thinking about gender in shellfish societies. It is obvious in the text how these key experiences have shaped my perspective. The outline of the book at the chapter level has been influenced by the perception and organization of Reitz et al. 1996.

My department has paid the bill for illustrations in this volume and time off from teaching to research this and earlier shell projects. The National Science Foundation, the American Philosophical Society, the Appalachian State University Research Council, and the undergraduates of the archaeology program at Appalachian State have funded my analyses over the past fifteen years.

Permissions to reprint the following tables, illustrations and quotes are gladly acknowledged: Academic Press for Figures 17, 24; *American Midland Naturalist* for Figure 26; Chacmool Association of the University of Calgary for Figure 29, 30; *Florida Wildlife* for Figure 16; Geological Society of America for Figure 10, *Lethaia* and Scandinavian University Press for Table 4; Quaternary Research for Figure 27; Rochester Museum and Science Center and Charles Hayes for Figure 31; Routledge Press for Table 6; University of Alabama for Figure 38 reprinted from Introduction by Ken Carstens in *Of Caves and Shell Mounds*, University of Alabama Press, 1996; University of Cambridge Press for Figures 1, 37; University of Chicago Press Figure 25; University of Queensland for Figure 12, 13, 14; Jean Andrews for Figures 4, 5, and 6; Pam Ford for Figure 17; William Marquardt, publisher for the Institute of Archaeology and Paleoenvironmental Studies, University of Florida for Figures 33, 34, 38; Jerry Milanich and the Department of Anthropology, University of Florida for Figure 20, 21; Michael Russo for Figure 28; Ken Sassaman for supplying Figure 3; Gary Wessen for Table 7.

1

THE ARCHAEOLOGY OF SHELL MATRIX SITES

Molluscs have served humans in numerous ways for thousands of years. Many gastropod and bivalve species have been modified into ornaments, tools, and money. Shells left in archaeological sites attest to the use of the flesh for human food and for bait, and to the search for pearls. Shells have been used as fill, building material, burial layers, and containers; they have been treated to extract their color; cut up for inlay, cameos, buttons, beads, trinkets, pearl nuclei; and crushed for pottery temper, poultry feed, medicine, and fertilizer. Archaeologists have been interested in shell artifacts and shell matrix sites for over 200 years. We have determined when the shells were harvested, the growth environment, past cataclysmic environmental events, the stretch of coastline whence trade shells originated, the contribution of shellfish to the diet, and human competition with other predators, by analyzing shells. In this chapter, I will explore anthropological and archaeological knowledge about human use of shellfish by presenting archaeological data on the antiquity of shellfishing and the uses of shell and flesh, and by presenting the history of archaeological interest in this material. I will also present a number of different research topics that shells can be used to address and the potential shells have for generating research topics as well.

1.1   A brief archaeological history of human use of molluscs

Although hominids have been present on earth for over 3 million years, our interest in shelled creatures appears to be relatively recent. The 300,000-year-old French site of Terra Amata has the earliest evidence both of housing and of shell collecting (Lumley 1972:37) but shells at even this relatively late date in human development are uncommon elsewhere in France and the world. Several South African cave and open air sites have a shell matrix dating from 130,000 to 30,000 years ago (Singer and Wymer 1982, Volman 1978). Spain's Cantabrian coast has deposits of shells as do several locales around the Mediterranean (Gibraltar, Haua Fteah in Libya) dating to the period 50,000 to 40,000 years ago. There are numerous deflated sites with freshwater shells in southern Egypt as early as 22,000 BC (Gautier 1976). In Asia, the earliest shell matrix sites are to be found on the Viet Nam coast, part of the Shonvi culture, dated 33,000 to 11,000 years ago. In the Lake Mungo area of Australia (western New South Wales), piles of freshwater shells associated with human occupation are as old as 35,000 years (Meehan 1982).

The majority of shell-bearing sites worldwide – freshwater or marine – appeared during the Holocene (the past 10,000 years), when sea level rise, which eroded and inundated earlier shell-bearing sites, slowed considerably and modern shorelines were established allowing for quiet water habitats to form and river siltation to slow. The Hoabinh culture of Viet Nam is notable for its shell heaps of 11,000 to 7,000 years ago. China's earliest shell matrix sites appear along with the earliest farmers, ca. 13,000 to 10,000 years ago in the provinces of Kwangsi and Yunnan. Early pottery, some of which is shell tempered, is found in the series of freshwater shell matrix sites along the Yung-chiang River, in Kwangsi (Chang 1986:85–86). Shellfishing appears to have greatly intensified at 9,000 years ago along a 60-km section of the Cantabrian coast of northern Spain (Bailey 1983c).

It is after 10,000 years ago that shell matrix sites are preserved in the Americas. The earliest dated Pacific marine shell matrix sites in the western hemisphere are currently found in Peru (Quebrada Jaguay 280 site, 8250 BC, Ring site, 8,575 BC) and California (a site on San Miguel Island, 8300 BC) and on the Atlantic are found in New York (Dogan Point site – 5000 BC). Increased sea level, erosion, and storms are responsible for the loss of sites older than 5,000 years along much of the Atlantic. For instance, the several hundred sambaquis of Brazil (particularly from the states of Espírito Santo and Santa Catarina), exhibiting a range of shapes and sizes and containing five dominant species, are no older than 5,250 years (Suguio et al. 1992:92).

1.2   Shells and archaeologists

Large piles of shell on land were clearly in need of explanation. Early speculators attributed their creation to wind, water, and humans, with geologists and natural scientists often the last people to credit them to humans (Christenson 1985). Recognition of these sites as the product of human activity proceeded rapidly throughout the nineteenth century. Japetus Steenstrup in 1837 (Morlot 1861:291), and later Charles Darwin (1839:234), specified criteria for human made shell heaps observed in Denmark and Chile. Vanuxem talked about oyster deposits in New Jersey (US) in 1843, Gunn discussed the shell heaps on the shores of Tasmania in 1846, and the Danish government assembled the famous kjokkenmoddings (kitchen middens) study group in 1848. By the publication of Morse's Omori (Japan) report in 1879, human made shell heaps had been identified in England, Scotland, Ireland, France, eastern US, Mississippi Valley (US), California, British Columbia (Canada), Aleutian Islands, Chile, Ecuador, Australia, Tasmania, Malay archipelago, and Japan. But the concerns of these investigations during the nineteenth century were more sophisticated than simply questioning the source of their accumulation.

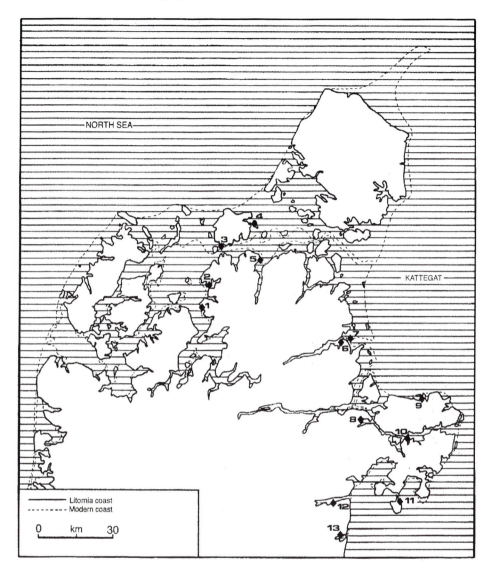

Fig. 1 Ertebølle site distribution in Jutland, Denmark.

Toward the goal of examining the human adaptation to and any changes in the paleoenvironment, the Danish government sponsored an interdisciplinary project, beginning in 1848, with three professors from the University of Copenhagen: Steenstrup, a biologist; Worsaae, "the most celebrated prehistoric archaeologist in Europe" (Trigger 1986:xii); and Forchhammer, a geologist. The project studied the shell matrix sites of Jutland (Figure 1) and published six annual reports (Forchhammer et al. 1851–1857). Its summation in German by Morlot and then translation into English in 1861 had several impacts (after

Christenson 1985:239): (1) awareness on an international scale of this type of site and its probable great age, (2) elevation of the explorations of and conversations about this type of site to a higher status in science, and (3) shift from interest by geologists and natural scientists to interest by archaeologists. Trigger (1989) sees a stark contrast between the archaeological concerns of the Danish in the mid-nineteenth century and Paleolithic archaeology as practiced in England and on the Continent. The Paleolithic archaeologists working at the same time in Europe recognized in artifacts only dating capabilities.

Many investigators saw obvious implications for sea level changes and climate changes in shell matrix sites evident in their location and in their fauna. Morse, excavating the Omori mound near Tokyo, typed the species, recorded abundance, size changes, and changes in metric proportions. To complete his examination he made collections of living fauna as well as making market purchases to identify the edible species. He linked the differences noted between the site fauna and the modern fauna with environmental alterations, in one case specifically naming a change in salinity (Morse 1879:24). Fifteen years earlier he had turned to a study of the land snails in a shell matrix site in Casco Bay, Maine to reconstruct the surrounding local environment. His mentor, Jeffries Wyman, had similarly discussed the paleoenvironment for the Florida freshwater molluscan deposits using snails (Wyman 1875).

Within the US, archaeologists working on shell matrix sites were largely following the example set by the Danish project and the review of that project supplied by Morlot (1861), which were steeped in the perspective of evolutionary change. The model of European evolutionary thinking presented in the Danish investigation predisposed its US readers to a precocious recognition (within North America) of the significance of stratigraphy as well. With a recognition of stratigraphy came a recognition of sequential changes in stone and ceramic technology, and an early use of typology as a basis for understanding micro-changes. In fact, Wyman produced the first ceramic typology in North America utilizing the sherds from the Florida freshwater shell heaps. Shell mound interpretation within the US was the one area of archaeological interpretation before 1900 where native peoples were credited with a history of progressive change (Trigger 1986:xxii).

Dating was of concern for the early shell-heap studies and was attempted during the period 1840–1920 using deposit stratigraphy, shell characteristics, and artifact attributes. Wyman employed a crude form of dendrochronology to assess the passage of time since the heaps in Massachusetts and Florida had accumulated. He also noted the poor preservation of shells in the lower levels of Massachusetts sites and thought it indicative of advanced age. Morse imputed significant time depth to the appearance of the shells at Omori – he commented on their yellowness, chalkiness, and the "characteristic appearance of the nacreous portion, generally seen in shells long buried in the ground" (Morse 1879:36). He made estimates of the age of the Omori heap from species ratios and shell metrics assuming that changes in ratios could be rapid while changes in metrics would require greater time. To quantify the amount of time, he examined shells from a 250-year-old dredge spoil and found many more similarities in condition, species ratios, and metrics with a modern assemblage than with the archaeological assemblage.

Other aspects of these early studies demonstrate concern with native processing techniques, accidental inclusion of specimens of some species, and the geographical distribution of heaps. Dall, Morse, Matthew, and the Danes before them, recognized that artifacts were essential clues to the past lifestyles of a mound's creators. Matthew (1884) noted ceramic ornamentation, recognized house pits, defined the types of tool in each stratum, the distribution of chips and house pits, and even offered an estimation of the population that generated a heap in New Brunswick, Canada (Trigger 1986). He and others also noted the environmental information implied by the land snails (Bobrowsky 1984:78).

Shell heaps were also subjects for early attempts at estimating the rate of garbage accumulation. Dall (1877) may be the earliest to have estimated the number of years (Waselkov 1987:140) over which a mound built up. Statham (1892) calculated the quantity of oyster shells (*Saccostrea commercialis*) in a mound in Australia and then predicted that the mound was 1,770 years old based on oyster yields garnered in the 1880s. Subsequent radiocarbon dates were remarkably similar in estimate (Bailey 1993:2). The California school of shell-heap quantification (1940s) elaborated on the work of Dall, to calculate not just total time of mound accumulation but also length of each occupation, number of occupants, and the relative contribution of foodstuffs to their diet. Experiments were occasionally employed to derive numerical solutions for some of the variables. In spite of obvious stratigraphic subdivisions, the California school workers steadfastly viewed the 425 San Francisco Bay sites as homogeneous and employed small samples for their investigations.

But for many decades following this early period little attention was paid to the shells in sites. Species identification was rare and the recognition of strata or microstrata was virtually absent. Arbitrary levels reflected a belief that there was no meaningful internal stratification in a shell matrix. A remarkably sophisticated study was produced around the end of the era, that by Willey and McGimsey (1954) of the Mongarillo Culture of Panama. These authors devised a relative chronology based on species ratios, argued that the greater the variation in the contents of a heap the larger and more frequent the samples needed to be, and targeted the single stratum of refuse as the appropriate sampling universe in addition to addressing the culture history of this little-known area.

1.3   Contemporary research

The languid interest in the shells themselves dissipated under the influence of the writings of three authors in the late 1960s. From New Zealand Wilfred Shawcross in 1967 initiated a second wave of quantitative research in shell matrix sites. A publication by William Ambrose (1967) specified the research potential of these sites for dietary information, relative chronology, paleoenvironmental reconstruction (specifically water temperature estimates and terrestrial environment), and information about collection strategies. Ambrose urged readers to consider the shell matrix as a research domain and to sample at the level of a single dump, lens, or scatter, while disapproving of Shawcross' (1967) revival of the California school with all its unsupportable assumptions.

Research concerns 1968–1990

The greatest impetus for a renewed interest in dietary reconstruction and shells in sites, however, came from Lewis Binford's (1968) hypothesis that the late Paleolithic population in coastal and riverine areas of the eastern Mediterranean incorporated first shellfish and then grass seeds into the diet because of a scarcity of both land and preferred foodstuffs. Binford's hypothesized relationship between coastal and inland ecology, carrying capacity, human diet, and agriculture ushered in three decades of research into ecology and human population pressure. This hypothesis gave shellfish and shell matrix sites a central role in the argument and a research agenda (e.g. Bowdler 1976, Voorhies 1976, Waselkov 1987, Yesner 1981).

Binford (1968) posited that the increased harvesting of molluscs evident in the tremendous number of new shell heaps created during the Holocene was triggered by population pressure brought about by either restriction in territory or reduction in the quantities of foodstuffs. This argument was predicated on the archaeological record of eastern Mediterranean cultures at the Pleistocene–Holocene transition, and, in subsequent applications by other authors, on the record in Mexico, Europe and Japan (see presentation and evaluation in Waselkov 1987). In those cases the coincidence of shell matrix sites and the appearance of domesticates is potentially explained by population pressure. But the mounds of shell (Figure 2) and rings of shell (Figure 3) elsewhere in the United States suggest other hypotheses, as does the coincidence in Australia, and in several American countries, of initial human occupation and the oldest shell matrix sites, far earlier than population pressure on resources or domesticates can be posited. The search for a single explanation for the appearance of large numbers of shell heaps after the Pleistocene or for the domestication of plants had ended, by 1990, in failure.

The research concerns for excavators of shell matrix sites in the 1970s–1980s period were:

Fig. 2 Upper strata in shell platform mound at Pineland, Florida, Calusa culture.

(1) dietary reconstruction – nutrition, meat weights, vertebrate proportions
(2) seasonality of shellfishing
(3) paleoenvironmental reconstruction
(4) variation in types of shell-bearing sites
(5) forager or collector settlement patterns
(6) formation processes

Once again Lewis Binford stimulated much research at shell matrix sites during this era with his distinction between forager and collector exploitative patterns (Binford 1978, 1980), evident in research collections such as that edited by Bailey (1983a). Another important stimulus to work in the New World was Michael Moseley's thesis that maritime resources underwrote complex civilization in the Andes (Moseley 1975).

New techniques attended the new research questions. Before the decade of the 1960s was over growth lines in shells were being examined to determine activity and site seasonality, and methods of sampling were being compared (see Ambrose 1967). In the 1970s column sampling was popular in shell matrix sites (often to the exclusion of any other type of exposure), and screening became common. Site catchment analysis was being applied to shell matrix sites throughout Europe (e.g. Rowley-Conwy 1983, numerous chapters in

Fig. 3 Shell ring, coastal South Carolina.

Bailey 1983a). In the 1980s, "new" techniques included the use of natural levels (although arbitrary levels remain the norm even in the 1990s) and the recognition of microstrata, the use of multiple exposure types, coring to determine original topography and component distribution, and various types of geophysical sensing devices. Throughout the 1970s and 1980s it was common to identify shells to species, predict dietary contributions of various taxa, examine shells macroscopically for environmental information as well as to assay amino acids for predicting temperature and/or age. Soil chemistry and soil texture analyses informed on formation processes. Radiocarbon dating of marine shell became more controversial as did growth line and oxygen isotope estimates of harvest time. Experimentation reappeared as a technique to investigate formation processes. Dozens of researchers took up land snail analysis to reconstruct local and even regional climate and vegetation. The landmark book for this endeavor was and is still John Evans' (1972) *Land Snails in Archaeology*.

For the English-reading world, the exemplary shell matrix site study prior to 1990 was Paul Mellars' (1987) *Excavations on Oronsay*. This project on Oronsay Island, Scotland exemplifies many of the concerns of researchers working in the 1970s and 1980s. Five shell heaps were excavated from 1970 to 1979 under the direction of Paul Mellars with publication in 1987. Motivating Mellars' interest in these sites was his interest in coastal adaptations of hunter-gatherers within one region. He wanted to gather information about the subsistence strategies, the size of the human group(s) and their frequency, and duration on these mounds, the distribution of these sites, and what caused the abrupt end to their accumulation after 700 years of use. The report begins with five chapters on the present and past environment drawing on land mollusc data in part, and on radiocarbon-dated shells from beach sediments. One chapter each is devoted to sampling concerns, to a presentation of macro-stratigraphy at each of four sites, to human, and to non-human bone. Curiously, shells figure little in the data or conclusions presented in this volume but are discussed in earlier reports (e.g. Mellars 1978).

Dietary reconstruction
Articles written during this period concerning excavation at sites with at least some shell are replete with questions and assumptions about gathering behavior, consumer behavior, systemic types of shell-bearing deposits, and uses for shells. It was to wildlife conservation and ethnoarchaeology – the study of living peoples by an archaeologist – that we began to turn for information on these topics. Why we have done so little ethnoarchaeology may be due to the normative assumptions that pervade research centered on shell-bearing sites: there is so much uniformity in systemic context that little could be learned through observation. The handful of projects that were conducted in this era, however, invite the reader to question much of what has been assumed in archaeological reconstruction (e.g. Bigalke 1973, Durán et al. 1987, Kayombo and Mainoya in Msemwa 1994, Meehan 1982, Moreno et al. 1984, Msemwa 1994).

The most significant advance in the reconstruction of diet came from the various ethnographic accounts of modern shellfishers. These studies identified and examined the variables involved in dietary reconstruction. For anyone working with shell matrix sites, the single most important publication to appear in the period 1970–1997, based on citations, was Betty Meehan's ethnoarchaeological account of the shellfishing activities of Anbarra women of north Australia (Meehan 1982).

Like all early works of ethnoarchaeology, Meehan's ethnography served as a cautionary tale to those who would depict shellfishing as drudgery, its nutritional value as negligible, and its participants as desperate. This report, more than any piece of archaeological detective work, contradicted the voices from the "why-would-anyone-have-ever-started-shellfishing?" school. Meehan detailed the amount of time Anbarra women spend shellfishing, why they do and do not shellfish, the calories consumed, including when and where, shellfishing as a route to high social status, and other topics.

The most extensive project undertaken to date to understand human adaptation to and utilization of shellfish is that on the Transkei coast of South Africa. For two decades archaeologists, anthropologists, and ecologists have studied the past and present patterns of exploiting the intertidal molluscan resources of this 260 km long shoreline. These papers present ethnology (Bigalke 1973, Hockey and Bosman 1986, Mills 1985, Siegfried et al. 1985), ecological studies (Hockey et al. 1988, Lasiak 1992, Voigt 1975), nutritional studies (Bigalke 1973), and excavations in modern sites (Voigt 1975). The ecological studies present data on intensity of harvest, recovery rates for prey species, and numbers, gender, and age of gatherers.

Msemwa (1994) sought to understand the constraints under which both urban and rural shellfishers worked on the coast of Tanzania. Urban women of three ethnic groups collected shellfish on as many days a month as possible for sale to city restaurants. Msemwa investigated when shellfishing occurred and who did it, transportation distance, tidal height influence on gathering and discard, ownership of shells and hearths in common processing stations, and some formation processes of the processing midden.

My own work among fishermen of San Salvador Island in the Bahamas demonstrated the important role of shellfish, both flesh and shells, as fish bait. Conch (*Strombus gigas*) offal, chitons, bleeding teeth (*Nerita* sp.), top shells or magpie shells (*Cittarium pica*), land crabs, and hermit crabs were all used when angling for bait fish and for table fish. Large numbers of conch, top shells, and land crabs were used to bait fish traps. At one boat landing, five fish traps awaited cleaning and use. They contained eleven top-shell shells, twelve conch shells, eleven triggerfish skulls, four triggerfish post-cranial skeletons, one boxfish, eleven crab carapaces, and one *Thais* shell. It is easy to imagine a sizable shell "midden" containing numerous shells and fish bones accumulating as fish traps are emptied of their spent bait on land, which is done when the traps are brought ashore, yet none of the contents of that "midden" would represent human food debris.

Types of shell-bearing sites

In northwestern Mexico, in Marismas Nacionales, there are four types of shell-bearing sites: 48 linear mounds dominated by *Ostrea corteziensis* and devoid of artifacts, 20 *Tivela* deposits (*Tivela byronensis*), 557 oyster piles found inland with sherds, bone, charcoal, etc., and 2 *Anadara grandis* mounds, one of which is a pyramidal temple mound (Shenkel 1974:59–60). Each of these site types may be related to different types of human behavior, not simply the daily accumulation of food debris discarded at home. Variation in the shell-bearing sites in Peru has been interpreted as different classes of sites: casual, habitation, processing, workshops, and secondary (Sandweiss 1996:130), meaning that the human behavior responsible for the accumulation of shells differed in each place.

The ethnographic record provides many examples of systemic uses for discarded shell and reasons for intentionally accumulating shells in one place. These reasons include industrial waste (e.g. shell button, cameo, dye, porcelain, lime manufactures), architectural features (e.g. bleachers, breakwaters, flooring, graves, mounds, retaining walls, foundations for roads), and waste from fish bait production (Onat 1985). Furthermore, several species of birds and terrestrial mammals, such as the scrub fowl in Australia or the oystercatcher in eastern North America, are known to mound shells, and modern ocean-dredging operations have created shell-bearing sites in dredge-spoil areas. In short, not all shell-bearing sites are simply the visible elements of meals.

Until the archaeologist can determine the formation processes of individual shell accumulations, functionally neutral terms such as "shell-bearing site" or "shell matrix site" are preferred to "shell midden" which implies a pile of food refuse shell. For this reason, the term "midden" only appears in this book when food refuse disposal is the known purpose of a shell deposit. Widmer (1989) has pointed out that our failure to identify classes of shell-bearing deposits has led to misinterpretation of sites and the failure to recover numerous classes of data. Normative thinking has reduced all archaeological shell and associated animal and plant debris to food debris and, consequently, all forms of shell-bearing deposits to secondary refuse deposits. The assumption that basketsful of secondary refuse are being excavated has governed excavation and sampling strategies.

In archaeological context, systemic deposits of industrial waste, garbage, and architectural features take the form of shell-filled pits, scatters, lens, and mounds, to name just a few possibilities. Any one of these classes of deposits might have been used by one social group to hold shell for architectural use or to dispose of subsistence or industrial waste. Any one of these classes of deposits or combinations might appear at a dinnertime camp, or a short-term or long-term residential base. Any one of these classes of deposits could be created by women or men, state or band members, farmers or habitual gatherers, urban dwellers or nomads. A shell deposit classificatory scheme based on archaeological criteria is the most direct way to elucidate variation in the archaeological record (Shenkel 1974).

Classification schemes proposed by McManamon (1984) and Widmer (1989) began with the archaeological characteristics, and sorted deposits into kinds of archaeological deposits. Based on density indices for lithic tool types, lithology, fire-cracked rock, fauna, and flora, in sites on Cape Cod, Massachusetts, McManamon detected four classes of deposits: primary refuse, limited activities; primary refuse, wide range of activities; secondary refuse, shell midden; secondary refuse, general midden. Widmer (1989) developed a classification based on his excavation experience in southwest Florida. The underlying organization to this scheme is a distinction between site and deposit:

(1) Shell midden site – secondarily deposited shell from food consumption with no other activities evident at the site.

(2) Shell midden – discrete lens or deposit of shell only.

(3) Shell-bearing midden site – a site composed of secondary refuse of many kinds of remains, including shell, generated by a wide range of activities.

(4) Shell-bearing habitation site – primarily shell debris in site matrix but used for architectural needs; the shell may or may not have originated as food debris.

Perhaps the greatest service this classification does is to acknowledge that shell may be present in a specific locale for some reason other than as food debris. Assuming all shell debris equals human food debris, we make further assumptions about the gender of the collectors and the site's place in the settlement system: where there is much shell and there are few artifacts, the shell debris is a women's dinnertime or processing camp; where there is much shell and there are many artifacts, the site is a base camp or aggregation point for many ages and both sexes. These assumptions are wrong in some situations and are explored in Chapters 7 and 9.

Research concerns 1990–1998

Work at shell matrix sites in the 1990s remains heavily influenced by the concerns of 1980s researchers in some countries, and slightly less so in other areas. Notably different is the greater emphasis placed on site formation processes and the diminished interest in dietary reconstruction. For the latter, the requisite assumptions are now recognized as many, cumulative, and untestable. Instead, the current interests can be summarized as

(1) formation processes of shell-bearing sites
(2) culture history
(3) paleoenvironmental reconstruction
(4) social aspects of the use of shell matrix sites

Formation processes
After 150 years of archaeological conception of shell as a ecofact, shell has recently taken on new import as a sedimentary particle. Most noteworthy and portentous has been Julie Stein's sedimentological approach to the British Camp shell deposit on San Juan Island in the Pacific at the Canadian–US border.

The motivation for excavating the British Camp shell heap and its contiguous areas was to explain the depositional and postdepositional processes which had configured the site up to 1983 when the excavation began (Stein 1992c). Stein began by determining the original surface topography and the accretional direction of the deposits using extensive augering. Geophysical methods were used to explore an area of the site larger than that excavated to delineate further the geomorphology of the site. Then excavation proceeded through the identification and removal of dump episodes, or facies, each facies described by the quantity of shells and their fragmentation, the quantity of rocks and their angularity, and the color of the matrix. Smaller sediments were analyzed in the lab for grain size and carbonates. Shell and fire cracked rock were treated as clastic sediments, matter that has been subjected to transport mechanisms. Facies were then grouped into larger lithostratigraphic units to correlate excavation units, into postdepositional weathering units, and into ethnozones based on relative abundance of chipped stone. The lack of coincidence of these three types of zone across and within the excavated units revealed clues to site formation processes. The shifts in zonation were related to the action of ground water, the amount of shell, and the depositional history. Other chapters in the book present data on historical disturbances, on postdepositional effects on plant remains and on bone, grain sizes, and lithics. Clearly, this study focused on site history, on explaining the archaeological record, rather than on the anthropology of the occupants, and it promises to alter significantly the way shell matrix sites will be excavated in the future. The profession-wide interest in formation processes merits the largest chapter in this book.

Culture history
Shell matrix sites and shell deposits have a reputation for providing much better preservation of ecofacts than do non-shell sites. For this reason shell sites have been favorite places for answering culture-history questions and remain so. For much of South America, Asia, and Africa, basic culture historical information has yet to be collected for many classes of site and the identification of settlement patterns which might combine site classes is even more neglected. Even within areas where archaeological chronologies are well developed, cultures with conspicuous shell matrix sites often have underdeveloped culture histories (e.g. the Shell Mound Archaic in the south-central US, the Channel Islands off California, the western coast of Australia), a legacy of the assumption that there is little to be learned about culture change from a shell deposit. Active research projects involving site identification, testing, and dating are under way around the world.

Social organization and shell matrix sites
Many authors have acknowledged that women's labor is largely responsible for the accumulations of shells which attract archaeologists. Shell matrix sites then, are drawing the attention of a number of researchers who identify gender as an important axis of human interaction. That these sites could also manifest a spiritual world view and constitute a spiritual or ritual landscape is a recent idea occupying several researchers in at least the US (Chapter 9).

   Shellfish have been more than food. Shells can tell us more about their human users than their diet and health. Their potential for generating research questions and for elucidating human social and spiritual behavior is often overlooked. Take, for example, the shell mound sites on the Green River in

Kentucky (US), part of the Shell Mound Archaic culture. These sites are mounds of freshwater bivalve and univalve shells with burials containing grave goods fashioned from marine bivalve shells. Data typically gathered by archaeologists are the identification of the freshwater and marine species, their quantities and proportions, and the time of year they were harvested, leading to deductions about the diet and the adjacent river at the time of occupation tucked into assumptions about site function and basic social characteristics of the village population. All reporters failed to problematize the high incidence of bivalves still paired, which suggests that these mounds of shells are not villages at all. At one of these shell mounds a contradiction between the river reconstruction based on shell species and that based on geomorphology was taken to mean that one or the other researcher was wrong. But if both are assumed correct then the evidence indicates that the shells did not come from that place in the river, again calling into question the function of the presumed village site. Furthermore, the actual distribution of these mounds, assumed to be ubiquitous across the mid-south of the United States, was never correlated with the distribution of naiads in eastern US rivers which is and was ubiquitous. As for the marine shells, several writers had queried which coastal area they come from, but unproblematized were which mechanism(s) of human interaction are suggested by the quantities of exotic shell in these sites and why these people needed to import marine shells for beads, cups, atlatl weights, and pendants, when local freshwater shells were being used for beads and could have been used for the other items as well. Why did they make a distinction between marine and riverine shells and how was that distinction defined? While noting that shell items were associated with the dead, no one had asked why this would be so. What symbolic role did shell play, did beads play, did pendants play? Finally, beads, thought to be ubiquitous throughout the eastern US and of few styles, are neither, raising questions about fashion provinces, sources of shell, and a lack of interaction between regions (Claassen 1996b). What shells can tell us about social organization is the least tapped aspect of their research potential.

Suggestions for future research

Research is still hampered by the lack of experimentation and ethnoarchaeological observations on topics such as shellfishing, shell use, shell symbolism, midden collapse, and plant colonization of shell deposits. Even small campus-bound projects can make inroads into these areas.

Ethnoarchaeology projects that have addressed shellfishing and shell middens have looked at their role in both agricultural and hunting-gathering communities. However, subsistence base is only one of many variables suspected to influence the role of shellfish in prehistoric societies and consequently the types of shell-bearing deposits. Future ethnoarchaeological projects should be planned so as to explore other variables such as duration of habitation, length of harvesting season, and economic use. Even within the variable "subsistence base," we lack comparable studies necessary to make cross-cultural comparisons.

Paleoenvironmental reconstruction projects of this decade required the use of multidisciplinary teams of investigators who analyze marine sediment cores, terrestrial sediments (chemistry, texture), geomorphology, samples of wood charcoal, pollen, accidental invertebrate inclusions, etc. Many earlier projects, using only macroscopic analyses of molluscan species diversity and metrics, are now known to be quite simplistic in their interpretations.

The topics for further research which are immediately apparent are:

(1) Redo earlier studies of environmental reconstruction with more sophisticated analyses and questions. Employ terrestrial land snails in these analyses, as well as conduct studies of amino acid racemization, isotopes.
(2) At many shell matrix sites the fundamental question of when the shell accumulated has not been addressed.
(3) Conduct much more experimentation on formation processes.
(4) Conduct much more ethnoarchaeology for information on formation processes, social context of shell-bearing sites, and shell use.
(5) Address more imaginative hypotheses about shell and shell-matrix sites – revisit "closed cases" with new hypotheses about social organization.

In this book I will present these and other research questions and the means by which archaeologists can address them. In Chapters 2 and 3 the reader will find the biology of molluscs and the taphonomy of shell and shell piles. In subsequent chapters I will explore the techniques of use to archaeologists pursuing questions about ancient environments and human behavior. Chapter 4 presents issues of sampling and quantification. Chapter 5 is an exploration of how shells can inform on their aquatic and terrestrial habitats, and even on global weather patterns. Nutrition and subsistence are the topics of Chapters 6 and 7, including information on shell seasonality techniques and bone chemistry. Shell artifacts play a significant role in many cultures. Their variation and analysis are the focus of Chapter 8. Finally, Chapter 9 looks at how shell analysis can lead to an investigation of issues in social complexity, issues such as settlement patterns, religious symbolism and landscapes, and human interaction along the axes of gender, social ranking, and corporate group identity.

2

SHELLED ANIMALS:
BIOLOGY AND PREDATION

Shelled organisms frequently encountered in archaeological sites include molluscs, barnacles, and echinoderms. This chapter will explore the biology and ecology of molluscs as well as predation. Reproduction, feeding, shell formation, and diseases are highlighted. Predation, by and upon molluscs (including historical modes of human predation), is discussed at length for it is this relationship that typifies the role of humans in molluscan populations. In the following discussion, and in the chapters to follow, it is often most efficient to refer to entire groups of molluscs at the level of order or family such as the cerithiids, muricids, pulmonates, etc. These groups have been elaborated upon in Table 1.

2.1   The biology of shelled organisms

Molluscs are invertebrate animals, most with a calcium carbonate exoskeleton called "shell." Five classes of molluscs have external shells: the chitons, most univalves (snails), tusks, bivalves (clams, oysters, mussels, unios), and some cephalopods. Molluscan classes which do not produce a shelly exoskeleton (Aplacophora) or which live in extremely deep water (Monoplacophora) are not treated in this volume. A biology text such as that by Hughes (1986) or Solem (1974) is recommended for more information on many of the topics to follow.

Chitons, which constitute the class Polyplacophora, are made up of eight plates on a fleshy girdle. They have an adherent foot that is almost as wide as the shell, a head, no eyes or tentacles, and gills on each side of the foot. All chitons occupy marine habitats and crawl over rocks and shells searching for seaweed, or sponges and other sedentary animals to eat.

The class Scaphopoda, the tuskshells and toothshells, consists of species with long tapering slightly curved shell tubes open at both ends. They have a wedge-shaped foot and a mouth, and no eyes or gills. It is the wide end that protrudes into the substrate and out of which comes the foot.

Most snails, of the class Gastropoda, have a spiral growth pattern that forms as either a cone or a disk. The central column around which gastropod shell spirals is known as the columella which can be either solid or hollow. The final shell whorl ends in an aperture through which the animal's foot and head are extended. In many species the foot has attached to it a calcified plate, the

Table 1. *Family names used in the text, with example* Genera *following (after Emerson and Jacobson 1976 and Rehder 1981)*

Cerithiid snails – (Cerith horn snails). Genera: *Cerithium, Bittium, Finella, Erithiopsis, Alaba, Triphora, Diastoma.* Moderate to quite small in size, short siphonal canal, flaring lip, elongated. Live in mud and grassy marine areas.

Chamid clams – (Chamidae, jewel box shells). Genera: *Chama, Arcinella.* Almost circular, thick shells which cement to rocks or reefs or single shells in intertidal or shallow water. Strongly sculptured shell.

Corbiculacea clams – (superfamily for Corbiculidae family, marsh clams). Genera: *Corbicula, Polymesoda, Pseudocyrena.* Live in brackish and fresh water in warmer climes. Burrow in mud or other soft substrate.

Dreissenacea clams – (superfamily for family Dreissenidae, false mussels). Genera: *Mytilopsis.* Triangular-shaped shells found in fresh and brackish water.

Hydrobiidae snails – (hydrobia and faucet snails). Genera: *Bithynia, Lyogyruus, Amnicola, Hydrobia.* Inhabit brackish water but mostly freshwater species. Tiny to small in size.

Littorinid snails – (Littorinidae, periwinkles). Genera: *Littorina, Tectarius.* Some species have short spires, usually a smooth shell, round to ovate in form. Cling to rocks and grasses near the tide line.

Lymnaeidae – (pond snails). Genus: *Lymnaea.* Species without operculum, and aperture opening to the right when spire up. Pulmonate (air breathing) aquatic snails. The shell is so variable as to make identification by it almost useless, except in US.

Muricid snails – (Muricidae, rock shells). Genera: *Murex, Hexaplex, Purpura, Thais, Nucella.* Heavy, thick shells with elaborate decor – spines, knobs, ridges. Siphonal canal is very long, often lined with spines. Typically three varices (ridge or vein) to a whorl. Carnivorous; some with a gland producing purple dye. About 100 genera and over 700 species world-wide.

Muricinae snails – (subfamily of Muricidae). See above.

Mytilidae mussels – Genera: *Mytilus, Brachidontes, Lithophaga, Modiolus.* Fan-shaped shells with umbo at narrow end. Some live attached to rocks or wood, others bore into corals or rocks or burrow in sand or gravel. All have byssus for anchoring to a surface.

Naticid snails – (Naticidae, moon and ear snails). Genera: *Polinices, Lunatia, Sinum, Natica.* Carnivorous, plow through sandy bottoms.

Neritid snails – (Neritidae, nerites). Genera: *Nerita, Puperita, Neritina.* Globular gastropods with a large body whorl and a short apex. Cling in great numbers to wave-washed rocks. Live in marine, brackish, and fresh water.

Nuculanidae clams – (elongated nut clams). Genera: *Nuculana, Yoldia.* Most abundant in cold water and moderately deep water. Lack pearly inner surface.

Nuculidae clams – (nut clams). Genus: *Nucula.* Living mostly in water greater than 9 ft. deep. Small, roughly triangular shell that is inflated. Shallow burrows, nacreous interior.

Opisthobranchs – marine gastropods constituting 4 percent of molluscan species. Have no operculum.

Pectinid bivalves – (Pectinidae, scallops). Genera: *Pecten, Chlamys, Hinnites.* Shells with "ears" at umbo end. Can swim, have light-sensitive eyes, and byssus.

Planorbidae snails – (planorbid, ram's horn snails). Genera: *Helisoma, Gyraulus, Planorbula.* Unbanded, flat, disk-shaped shells with deep umbilicus and all orbits on one plane. Spiral to the right (when umbilicus down).

Prosobranchs – largely marine but with terrestrial and freshwater representatives. Constitute 53 percent of extant molluscan species. Divided into archaeo- and Caenogastropoda. Littorinoidea, Cerithioidea, Buccinidae, Muricidae, Calyptraeidae, Eulimidae, and Trochoidea are some representative superfamilies.

Table 1. (*cont.*)

═══

Pulmonate snails – a subclass of terrestrial, freshwater gastropods, plus a few marine littoral
  snails. Forty-three percent of extant molluscs.
Strombidae snails – (true conch, winged conch). Genera: *Strombus*. Tropical snails of five
  genera, seventy species world-wide. Live among marine grasses in sand or rubble.
  Herbivorous, exuding tubes of eggs.
Trochid snails – (Trochidae, top shells). Genera: *Margarites, Solariella, Calliostoma*. All have a
  pearly interior and operculum. Herbivorous heterosexuals.
Unionid clams – (Unionidae, freshwater mussels, naiads). World-wide but greatest speciation
  in Mississippi River valley. Tremendous morph formation. Practically immobile once
  settled. Eggs hatch into glochidia, parasitic on fish skin, gills, fins.
Venerid clams – (venus clams). Genera: *Gemma, Chione, Arctica, Mercenaria, Antigona*. Oval
  or heart shaped with pronounced umbo. Marine dwellers.
Vermetid worms – (Vermetidae, worm shell). Genera: *Spiroglyphus, Serpulorbis*. Found in
  warm water. Begin life tightly coiled then grow straighter with maturity. Attach to rocks,
  shells, wood.

═══

operculum, which fills the aperture when the animal withdraws but which rarely is preserved. Most gastropods have a foot, head, eyes, tentacles, and gills. Gastropods occupy fresh and salt water and are the only molluscan class with members adapted to land. Gastropod shapes and terms can be found in Figures 4 and 5.

Bivalves (Class Bivalvia) have symmetrical or asymmetrical paired shells or valves. The body of many bivalved animals has a wedge-shaped foot, no head, a pair of siphons, and gills. The valves are joined by a springy ligament. Articulating shelly "teeth" on both valves are an important taxonomic feature. The adductor muscle pulls the valves shut. Scallops and oysters have only one such muscle, mussels have a large one posteriorly and a small one anteriorly, and clams have two equal sized adductor muscles, toward the front and the back. The adductor muscle scars are visible on the shells. The edge of the valve is called the "margin," the apex or beak where the teeth are to be found is called the "umbo" (plural "umbones"). Other shell terms are included in Figure 6. Bivalves are found in both fresh water and salt water. Freshwater bivalves sometimes are called naiads and unios.

The Cephalopods (octopi, cuttlefish, squids) include both shelled and un-shelled predatory molluscs exclusively marine in habitat. The shelled members are the *Nautilus* and the argonaut whose shells are coiled. The argonaut shell is actually an egg case, not an exoskeleton, and therefore found only in females. Arms (ninety arms in *Nautilus*) surround a mouth and a beak, and the eyes are well developed. The animal occupies the most recent chamber.

Guidebooks for general molluscan identification are indispensable for archaeological work. One should strive to use the most recent text available because the scientific names of molluscs often change and have a torturous history. The names of molluscs found in North American waters were system-

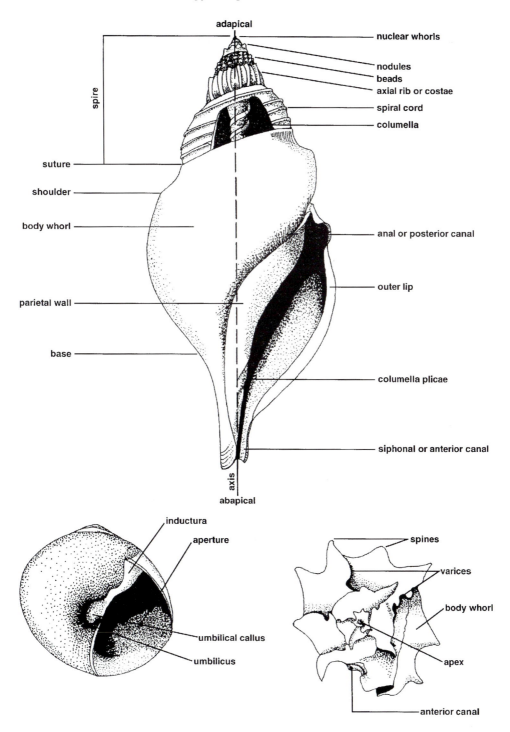

Fig. 4 Gastropod terms.

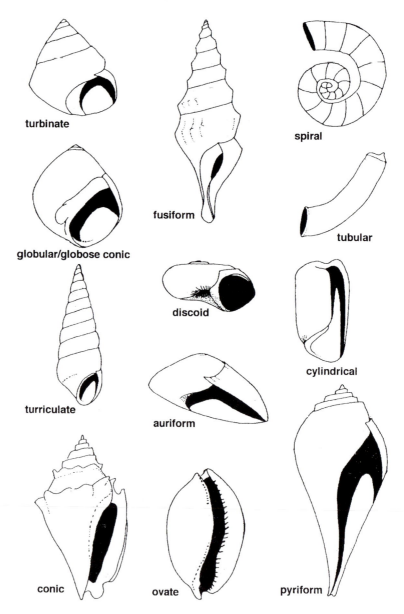

Fig. 5 Gastropod shape terms.

atized in 1988 (American Malacological Union 1988) and Vaught (1989) updates the systematics of all living molluscs. As is customary in taxonomy, molluscan orders end in "-oda," suborders in "-ea," and superfamilies in "-ae." Presentations of molluscan taxonomy offered by archaeologists or malacologists familiar with archaeological problems and species can be particularly useful. Among these publications are Evans (1972) for British land snails, Allen

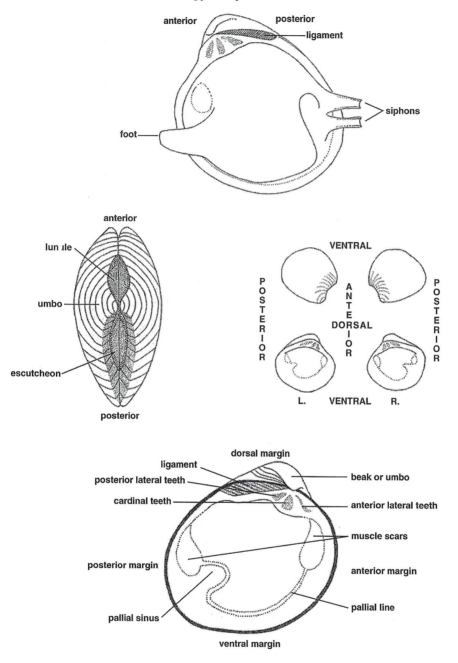

Fig. 6 Bivalve terms.

and Cheatum (1961) for Texas land snails, Vokes and Vokes (1983) for Yucatan bivalves, and Wells and Bryce (1985) for Australian marine molluscs.

Shell formation

The mantle is the tissue responsible for depositing "shell." The mantle covers the inner surface of the shell and in some species is reflected onto the outer surface at the growing margin. In other species – olives, cowries, etc. – the mantle completely covers the exterior of the shell to create a slick shell surface. There are three major aspects of shell formation: (1) the metabolic reactions associated with calcium carbonate formation and the synthesis of the organic matrix, (2) the secretion of components of the shell by the mantle, and (3) crystal growth and the formation of the crystalline layers (Wilbur 1964:245).

The extrapallial fluid, which is enclosed between the mantle and the inner shell surface, is the medium in which form the organic matrix and the crystalline components of shell. Calcium carbonate deposition is a function of the calcium ion concentration in the extrapallial fluid, which is a result of the amount entering the body. A marked reduction of the calcium concentration of sea water may reduce or even prevent calcification (Wilbur 1964:245).

(1) A specialized area of the mantle area secretes a sheet of protein (the periostracum), which becomes tanned and is the substratum on which the outer crystalline shell layer is deposited.

(2) Calcium, bicarbonate, and CO_2 passes [sic] through the mantle epithelium to the extrapallial fluid between the mantle and the inner shell surface. Crystals of calcium carbonate are formed.

(3) The mantle secretes organic material, largely protein, into the extrapallial fluid between the mantle and the shell or directly onto the inner shell surface. This provides the organic matrix of shell.

(4) Crystal nucleation occurs on the organic matrix or on the surface of crystals previously deposited.

(5) Oriented crystal growth takes place on and within the organic matrix. Lateral crystal growth displaces the surrounding matrix which becomes sandwiched between crystals as they grow toward each other and form a single layer. (Wilbur 1976:91)

Structural layers

There are two crystalline forms of calcium carbonate in shells: aragonite and calcite. If aragonite the crystals can occur in three microstructural types: prismatic, nacreous, and porcelaneous. Calcitic crystals occur in only two microstructural types: prismatic and foliated (Carter 1980). Calcitic shell is harder, less dense, and less soluble than aragonitic shell and is, therefore, more likely to fossilize. Calcitic shell occurs in very few freshwater molluscs (Vermeij 1993:45, 47), some cold-water molluscs, and is the main shell form in oysters. Aragonite is the shell form of the unionids and land snails, as well as the marine gastropods of genera *Haliotis* and *Nerita*. Layers of calcite and aragonite alternate in *Patella* limpets.

The microstructural types of crystals are combined in different ways by different taxa. (Herein lies the potential to determine the family of shells used as ceramic temper.) Many molluscs have three structural layers. These are the periostracum, prismatic, and homogeneous layers (Figure 7). Some have a fourth layer, the cross-lamellar layer. Different parts of the mantle are responsible for depositing each layer (Carter 1980).

The outer surface layer of many living shells is the pigmented, organic periostracum (Figure 7b) which is rarely encountered on archaeological specimens. The periostracum is the first layer secreted and is oriented along the growing edge of the shell. It may be leathery or hairy. It isolates the shell edge during calcification and prevents dissolution of the shell in cold or acidic water. It is typically much thinner in marine bivalves than in the unionaceans which inhabit more acidic water.

Below the periostracum is the prismatic layer. Here, closely fitting columnar crystals sit either vertically or obliquely to the direction of growth (Wilbur 1964:253; 1976). The growth layers are steeply inclined to the shell surface and crop out at the exterior surface forming surficial growth lines (Barker 1964:70). Daily lines are visible. In cross-section this layer extends less than one-fourth of the way into the profile and has a brown tint (Figure 7a).

The prismatic layer is bounded by the homogeneous layer (in *Mercenaria* and some other genera), a muscle-scar shell layer (Pannella and MacClintock 1968:67), and the myostracum, a line arching from umbo to margin. Below this layer is the inner homogeneous layer. Under magnification there is a visible pattern of alternating opaque and translucent growth layers which are parallel to the growth direction for most of their length beginning at the umbo, until they turn rapidly and sequentially upward widening as they approach the prismatic layer. This homogeneous layer has a nacreous structure of closely packed horizontal or oblique layers of crystals in tabular form (Wilbur 1964:253). During times of stress such as spawning, the structural elements in the outer part of the middle homogeneous layer are rearranged as they are being deposited, into a crossed-lamellar structure. This altered area extends into the lower part of the prismatic layer.

The nacreous unionaceans living in freshwater habitats have a very primitive, simple, shell structure. A periostracum of medium thickness covers the prismatic layer which overlies the nacreous layer (Figure 7b). Slightly more complex microstructure can be found in freshwater molluscs of the Corbiculacea and Dreissenacea superfamilies which have developed crossed-lamellar microstructure. This is the innermost layer. In these groups, calcite lamellae oriented perpendicularly give a dull finish.

The nacreous layer in *Haliotis*, *Nautilus*, some other marine species, and most unionids is made up of 450 to 5,000 very fine layers in every 1 mm of

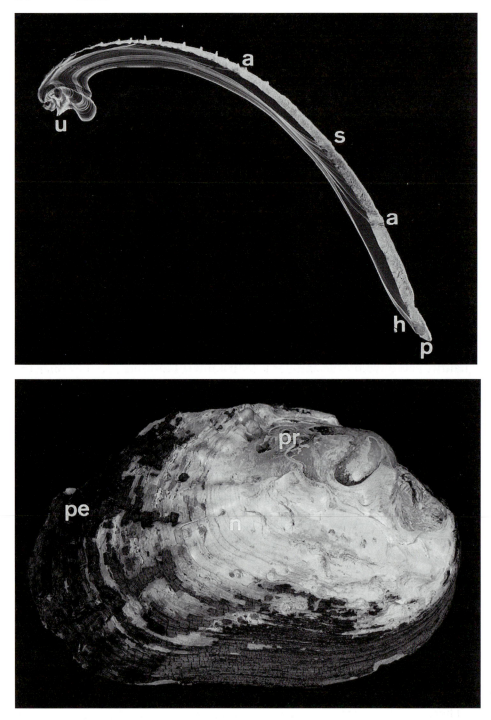

Fig. 7 a. Structural layers of marine bivalve *M. mercenaria.* a = annulus; h = homogeneous layer; p = prismatic layer; s = slow growth; u = umbo. From s to a is
the width of slow growth. From a to s is the width of fast growth.
b. Structural layers of naiad. n = nacreous layer; pe = periostricum; pr = protein
layer.

aragonite (Solem 1974:10). These crystals are deposited parallel to the surface, in plate form. Erosion or dissolution of the periostracum and prismatic layers is typical in stream-dwelling Unionacea (Figure 7b) which burrow quite shallowly. It is thought that the nacreous layer provides more protection to the soft tissue in these cases than would crossed lamellar and homogeneous microstructure (Tevesz and Carter 1980:310). In a large number of unionaceans horizontal sublayers of conchiolin can be found interspersed in the nacreous layer with heavier concentrations in the umbonal region, particularly in genera *Alasmidonta*, *Elliptio*, and *Margaritifera*. These patches of conchiolin appear to be laid down for both reinforcement and repair of the shell (Tevesz and Carter 1980:315).

Growth rate
The growth rate of shell is influenced by water temperature, salinity, sediment type, currents, valve opening times (availability of food, duration and frequency of disturbances), and possibly photoperiod (Wilbur 1976:100, 102). Spawning also causes a slowing of the growth rate. Water temperature, along with salinity, seems to set the upper and lower limits of the growth rate (Ansell 1968).

Calcium carbonate can only be deposited when the mantle is extended. The quantity and quality of the available food control how long and how often the animal extends. Pratt and Campbell (1956:9) found that the average growth rate of filtering bivalves increased with an increased concentration of phytoplankton, but at a steadily diminishing rate.

Unionacean growth has been studied by several workers. Negus (1966) found a general positive association between coolness of the growing season and width of the annual increment. Animals living in deep water and fine grained sediments in lakes tend to show less change in growth rate over the course of their lives, live longer and grow more slowly than animals living in rivers and streams (Stansbery 1970). Annual bands in lake dwellers are more distinctive and more regular in their spacing as well (Tevesz and Carter 1980:308).

Duration and frequency of disturbance decrease calcium carbonate deposition. Long periods of retraction can be caused by several environmental events such as hurricanes or predation. During biological events such as spawning, shell growth slows down drastically. Some of these events happen daily, such as exposure during low tide, and predation, while hurricanes and spawning are seasonal. During closure, the extrapallial fluid dissolves the carbonate to release oxygen for breathing and, consequently, dissolves shell recently accumulated.

There are three growth stages visible in the bivalved shell cross-section: juvenile, mature, and senile. During each stage the animal experiences a different overall growth rate. Juvenile animals grow slightly more quickly than do mature animals, and respond to environmental factors differently (Eldredge et al. 1976). Growth during the juvenile and mature stages accounts for the majority of the shell length at death. The senile animal is very slow growing and that region on the shell consists of numerous annual marks closely packed together. Although there is a decrease in the growth rate with age, a condition characteristic of organisms generally, growth marks remain rhythmic temporal markers.

Incremental growth lines in temperate bivalves correspond to sub-daily, daily, fortnightly, monthly, seasonal, and annual increments of shell. Stress marks occur irregularly and irrespective of any specific amount of elapsed time. These incremental marks are visible because of variation in the relative proportions of organic material (conchiolin) and calcium carbonate. Freshwater bivalves do show incremental growth structures but their variety and significance have received little attention. The stimuli for the occurrence of annuli in tropical molluscs are presumed to be different than those for species in temperate waters. Daily and annual growth increments are treated in detail in Chapter 6.

As for shell shape, a change in the physical and "social" environment of a mollusc can cause change in the shape of the shell as subsequent shell material is deposited. For instance, the shape of the eastern oyster (*Crassostrea virginica*) is broad when living in coves, long when living in deep channels, and variously shaped when living in high density reef communities. Shape may also change as the animal ages. Many naiad species can be sexed based on differences in the shell shape. These alterations are discussed further in Chapter 6. The geometry and economics of shell construction are detailed in Vermeij (1993).

Reproduction

Understanding how molluscs reproduce is essential for understanding changes in population numbers, an area often explored by archaeologists. Unfortunately, reproduction is quite complicated and highly variable among the molluscs. There is considerable variation between and even within species in growth rates, sexuality, fecundity, egg protection, and life cycle. Some textual sources which offer discussion of reproduction are Russel-Hunter (1978) for marine invertebrates and Hughes (1986) for marine snails. At each stage in life, a specific range of environmental requirements govern survivorship. In general, adults can tolerate a wider deviation in environmental requirements than can, for instance, larvae.

Sexuality and eggs
Many species have fixed sexual expression, either male or female (such as the gastropod whelks and the *Nautilus*), and copulation is heterosexual. Many other species are hermaphroditic, where any adult pair can copulate (opistho-

branchs); fewer species can self fertilize (e.g. *Odostoma modesta*). Some species change sexual expression over time, such as many of the patellid limpets (e.g. *Crepidula fornicata*). These limpets usually are first male, then female.

Some molluscan species prepare for reproduction by building up protein energy reserves immediately before the reproductive period (e.g. muricid snails, *Nucella lamellosa*) while other species derive the energy for reproduction from lipids and carbohydrates (e.g. *Littorina littorea, Patella vulgata*). Tropical species have breeding periods that generally synchronize with the rainy season. Temperate species tend to breed in late spring or early summer. Species in stable freshwater environments, such as are found in caves, may have individuals breeding throughout the year (Russel-Hunter 1978:359).

When the necessary environmental and physical prerequisites are achieved by the adult, eggs and sperm can be produced. Fecundity (the number of eggs produced per clutch) is directly related to the volume of the gonads which increases with age (Hughes 1986:125). Fecundity is also fixed by ecophenotype and genes as well as being environmentally stimulated by factors such as length of photoperiod (Russel-Hunter 1978:358). There are molluscs that are short-lived, experiencing only one reproductive phase before death, and molluscs that experience more than one reproductive phase. Females in short-lived species produce multiple clutches that grow increasingly larger in number of eggs; then they abruptly die. Females in longer-lived species become more fecund with each reproductive phase.

Spawning is to produce or deposit eggs or discharge sperm. Fertilization may occur internally or externally depending on species. In gastropod whelks and the *Nautilus*, fertilization is internal. Many bivalved (particularly New World naiads) and most univalved species eject sperm and eggs into the water at spawning time with fertilization left to chance. Eggs may number in the millions, and are most numerous among the bivalves, or may be produced singly, as is the case with the abalone (gastropod).

In addition to a spray of eggs, eggs may be found in jelly masses, in horny cases, or attached to shells, seaweed, intertidal rocks, or the substrate. The jelly masses and hard capsules confer various benefits to the eggs (see Hughes 1986). Dogwhelks will congregate during winter and deposit egg cases in large communal clumps. Other gastropods hold, or brood, their encapsulated or jellied eggs (e.g. Littorinids). Still other species create eggs with yolks inside capsules.

Embryos and larvae
A minute portion of the eggs spawned eventually hatch. In some species the egg passes through an embryo stage, completed inside the capsule or jelly mass, and hatches as a juvenile. The jelly mass or yoke provides the energy necessary for development until the individual is capable, as a juvenile, of obtaining food on its own. This direct development into a juvenile is character-

istic of chitons, some opisthobranchs, and most cephalopods. In many other molluscs, however, larvae hatch from the eggs to spend a few hours as tro- chophores and then weeks either as free-swimming veligers or as parasitic glochidia, depending on the species. The time spent in this stage is species specific but metamorphosis into a juvenile can be delayed by some species.

With metamorphosis the new juvenile experiences "substantial changes in diet, locomotion, predators, and other demands" (Jablonski 1985:36). It is possible that the juvenile stage is even more difficult to survive than was the previous stage. The successful settlement of juveniles onto a substrate is known as recruitment.

Dispersal of adults, larvae and eggs
Veligers feed on planktonic life forms while drifting in the plankton zone at the top of the water column for varying lengths of time. They are vulnerable to predation, starvation, and desiccation. They are equipped with a tiny shell, a foot, eyes, mantle, and tentacles. Many tropical bivalves and gastropods have larval stages lasting at least six months. During this stage the veligers may drift across the Atlantic Ocean or travel the length of an island group in the Pacific. It takes but seventy-seven days to drift from Japan to Hawaii. Many temperate water veligers are viable for three to six weeks. In currents as slow as 0.5 km/hour, veligers can drift up to 500 km before they settle (Schellema in Jablonski 1985:35). Only a tiny proportion of the larvae which hatch survive the veliger stage.

When the larva is ready to metamorphose, it becomes photonegative and sinks near to the bottom which it can explore by touch and scent as it seeks a place to settle. If the substrate is suitable for settling, the larva will settle, metamorphose, and be counted among the new recruits. If the substrate or hydraulic conditions are not suitable, the veliger may delay settlement and metamorphosis for a while longer depending on nutrient availability and genetic determination of larval period. A delay period of 200 days has been recorded in *Aplysia juliana* (Hughes 1986).

Larvae of most freshwater bivalves and mytilid clams differ from those of most saltwater molluscs in that they are parasitic on fish gills rather than free swimming. Some species of glochidia parasitize specific fish species, others are generalists. At metamorphosis the larva changes into a juvenile and drops from the gill to settle. Only a small portion of the glocidia will successfully settle and be recruited into the population.

For larvae, embryos, and glochidia that are dispersed by currents, tides, and fish, the location of an adult breeding population is often irrelevant to recruit- ment and the establishment of new populations. Observations of modern El Niño events in Peru indicate that the sand-dwelling clam *Mesodesma donacium* may take a decade or longer to recolonize its habitat while the rock-dwelling mussels *Perumytilus purpuratus* and *Semimytilus algosus* can recolonize in six months or less (Sandweiss 1996:137). The naiad community in a shallow-water section of a river could be completely eradicated and yet new individuals could be growing there the next year. Only the absence of host fish or appropriate habitat can explain the lack of naiad communities in a specific stretch of river, never human exploitation.

For the addition of recruits to an established population, however, the size of the breeding population can impact on recruitment, usually to depress it. For marine epifauna that affix eggs to rocks or substrate or bear live young, the distance between adult populations and juveniles will be small and thus determine the population size of embryos and larvae. A very successful recruitment can significantly depress recruitment in subsequent years due to crowding.

Changes in floral communities, including changes in sunlight exposure, humidity, and quantity of decaying matter, stimulate the extirpation and immigration of land snail species. Snails catch on to the hair of passing guanacos to be transported across barren areas between lomas communities in Peru (Craig 1992:128). Planorbid snails are also dispersed by winds as demonstrated by capture at elevations of 10,000 ft. In order for aquatic snails to colonize new habitats, adults, eggs, or larvae must be introduced from a nearby source. A common vector of introduction is mud carried on the feet of amphibians, insects, livestock, humans, or birds. During wet weather aquatic pulmonate gastropods can even disperse overland, particularly if that land is well vegetated. Flood water, floating ice, and floating timbers are other means of dispersal for gastropods (Bobrowsky 1984:82, O'Connor 1988). Bobrowsky (1984:82) reports that adult snails have appeared in newly created ponds one day after inundation.

Demographics

Some species are opportunists (r selecting). They succeed in rapidly colonizing new areas or devastated areas through rapid life-stage development and a single reproductive phase. They typically have a short life (less than twelve months), small body size, and catastrophic mortality. Their survivorship curve typically is positively skewed with high mortality in the youngest growth stages (Cerrato 1980:453). Exemplary species are *Mulinia lateralis*, *Donax* spp.

Specialists are those species adapted to stable environments. They have populations close to carrying capacity, long life spans, larger body size, and since specialization comes at the cost of reproduction, a lower reproductive capacity (k selecting). Their survivorship curves are diagonal or negatively skewed, with mortality being density dependent (e.g. *Nucula annulata*). Demographics are further treated in Chapter 4.

Feeding

Within the saltwater habitat can be found feeding and dwelling zones such as subtidal, intertidal, etc. Zonation of the coastline is frequently recognized in human predation studies. (The reader should consult Newell [1970] or other texts on shore ecology for an in-depth discussion of zonation.) Different species have adapted to different zones. Individuals of one species living in different zones often constitute different morphological types (morphs). Significant ecological variation across zones occurs in salinity, moisture, water pressure, etc.

The food preferences of terrestrial gastropods are poorly understood. Some are herbivores, a few are carnivores, and most are omnivores, living on detritus. There is some evidence that food would rarely be a limiting factor for these gastropods – land snails feeding on deciduous litter consumed less than one percent of the annual litter production (Mason in Thomas 1985).

Factors leading to qualitative differences in feeding are "organic matter in relation to grade of deposit, the source of organic matter in deposits, seasonal variations in the potential food of deposit feeders and the role of micro-organisms in the nutrition of deposit feeders" (Newell 1970:238). Feeding in shelled animals occurs in one of five ways. These are browsing, predation, scavenging, suspension, and deposit feeding (Newell 1970:168–230).

Browsing is the mode of feeding for most chitons, and many gastropods. The browse is vegetative matter, commonly algae, which is consumed in several feeding steps.

Predation characterizes gastropods in particular. In carnivorous species of gastropods the anterior end of a snout on the head has the mouth, the cavity which contains the rasping tongue (radula), and other organs. The radula is different than that in browsers, and in some molluscs jaws have developed. Some molluscs specialize on soft tissue, others, particularly those in the orders Mesogastropoda and Neogastropoda, can penetrate thick shells of bivalves, gastropods, and barnacles. This ability is especially well developed in the Muricinae and Naticidae. The creatures in these families possess both an accessory boring organ which secretes a chemical solvent, and a proboscis for drilling into the shell of the prey. The resulting hole shape is often identifiable to species.

Scavengers eat the flesh of fish and many invertebrates. Well-known scavengers are gastropods of the genus *Nassarius*, the whelk *Buccinum undatum*, and sea urchins.

Suspension feeding is a common strategy of intertidal invertebrates (some gastropods, the majority of bivalves). Mucus nets, strands, or bags are often used to trap suspended food. A ciliary mechanism (hundreds of threads of cytoplasm projecting from a row of cells which thrash in one direction) in the mantle intercepts suspended food. A mucus screen removes particles too large to be handled, and a ciliary tract moves particles out of the mantle into the digestive system.

Deposit feeding is feeding directly on the deposit upon which the creature lives. Among the creatures which feed in this manner are bivalves of the families Nuculidae and Nuculanidae and the carnivorous *Dentalium*.

Infaunal (living in the sediment) bivalves which are suspension feeders or deposit feeders bring water in through a tube-shaped inhalant siphon. Water drawn in is passed over the gills. Mucus strands in the gills entangle diatoms and other microplankton and transport them to the small mouth. Flap-like palps push the food into the esophagus. An exhalant siphon expels water and wastes (Abbott 1977). A continuous supply of water is passed across the gills for both feeding and respiration. A burrow may be maintained for this purpose which leads from the buried animal upward to the surface of the sediment. The siphons extend just to the surface of the substrate in most suspension feeders but the inhalant siphon of deposit feeders is longer and lies upon the surface of the substrate. The degree of maintenance of the burrow and the depth of burial are related to the type of bottom and to the species (Newell 1970:219).

Diseases

Diseases in molluscs or hosted by molluscs impact on their population numbers and human health, both of anthropological relevance. Here, the reader will find separate treatments of diseases impacting on molluscs but harmless to humans, and diseases hosted by molluscs which afflict humans.

Molluscan diseases harmless to humans

There are numerous microbes and parasites which sicken molluscs and sometimes result in shell modification and mass die-offs. Lest these shell-modifying diseases be confused with human shell alteration, and in order to help archaeologists to understand better the growth environment of the archaeological shells, a review of these diseases is offered now. These diseases are caused by bacteria, fungi, protozoans, trematodes, cestodes, and parasitic crustaceans (Sindermann 1970:109). (Viral infections are rare in molluscs.) Not all of the named offenders are problematic in all their various life forms nor do the offending organisms uniformly afflict molluscs in all their life stages. For instance, larval microbes more typically afflict larval bivalves. The disease literature is largest for oysters, less frequent for clams and mussels, and scant for economically important gastropods.

Fungi can invade the shell and the soft tissue and are particularly troublesome in warm water and salinities lower than 15 ppt. Fungi commonly degrade the calcium carbonate structure in dead shells. The fungus *Ostracoblabe implexa* invades the living shell to extract the organic compound. This fungus caused "shell disease" (as does *Monilia* spp.) in living oysters in the

Black Sea and may be responsible for the death of the commercial industry there in the early part of the twentieth century. Shell disease creates fragile shells which exfoliate in flakes and "reddish-brown branched filiform structures" in the inner nacreous layer of *Ostrea edulis* (Naydenova and Zakhaleva 1993:1). Foot disease (which may be the same as shell disease but caused by a different fungus) causes blistering of the shell around the adductor muscle (Sindermann 1970:114). Both shell and foot diseases are common in European oysters and mussels but rare in US and Indian bivalves.

Protozoa parasitize oyster eggs and adults. Protozoa are responsible for several major molluscan diseases: SSO (*Haplosporidium costalis*) or seaside disease, MSX (*H. nelsoni*), Dermo (*Perkinsus* [= *Dermocystidium*] *marinus*), and Aber (*Marteilia refringens*) which was first reported in Brittany in 1968 killing *Ostrea edulis*. Molluscan mortality can exceed 90 percent in newly exposed populations but survival of resistant individuals eventually results in resistant populations. Greenish rubbery warts and knobs form on the inside surface of shells in the region of the muscle attachments when the invader is *Perkinsus marinus*, common in the Gulf of Mexico.

MSX is characteristic of mid-Atlantic US waters. As of 1992, it had afflicted only the eastern oyster (*Crassostrea virginica*) (S. Ford 1992). The infective spore can live outside a host for years. Dermo has caused mass mortalities in bay scallops, eastern oyster, and many other bivalved species. It is found principally in southern US waters. Both Dermo and MSX are found in water with a salinity greater than 15 ppt up to 30 ppt but Dermo is more tolerant of low salinities.

Trematodes are parasites which long have been known to stimulate pearl production. Larval trematodes sterilize their host and eventually kill it. They infect soft shelled clams (*Mya arenaria*); oysters in Europe, Gulf of Mexico, New Zealand, and Taiwan; mussels in California, England, Wales, Japan, and the Gulf of Mexico; *Donax* spp. in California, Gulf of Mexico, France, and *Tapes* spp. in Japan. Alternating ratios of hosts, trematode parasite, and a hyperparasite cause dramatic fluctuations in numbers of *Donax* spp. The trematodes may pass from birds, fish, stingrays, and crabs to molluscs or vice versa.

Gastropods are frequently intermediate hosts of trematodes that attack marine fish. While resident in the gastropod the trematodes sterilize the host and inhibit its seasonal migration. "The pervasive and, at times, severe effects of larval trematode infection on abundance and reproduction of marine snails and snail populations must not be underestimated" (Sindermann 1970:145). For instance, 52 percent of the periwinkle *Littorina littorea* population at a US study locale were infected with trematodes. Pink abalone (*Haliotis corrugata*) in California can have blisters and foot damage caused by a larval nematode, which weakens the animal's hold on rocks. A trematode using *Lymnae* and *Physa* of the Great Lakes (US) causes "swimmer's itch" (Emerson and Jacobson 1976:304).

Other organisms also afflict molluscs. Parasitic cestodes stunt growth and have led to widespread mass die-offs in oysters of Hawaii, Florida, North Carolina, Japan, and Taiwan, in little-neck clams (*Protothaca staminea*) in Humboldt Bay, California, and in gastropods which feed on the body fluids of bivalves, as well as crustacea. Tumors have been observed in oysters and clams. *Polydora* worms cause "mud blisters" on the shell interior. *Cliona* sponges bore tunnels through shells weakening them and allowing bacteria and fungi to invade the animal and shell more readily. A viral disease known as gill disease afflicted *Crassostrea angulata* in southwestern France after *C. gigas* was introduced in 1966.

Infestations of molluscs which afflict humans
Of concern here are the various organisms causing paralytic shellfish poisoning (PSP), diarrhetic shellfish poisoning (DSP), and several diseases in which molluscs act as the invertebrate host to trematodes in a complex life cycle such as schistosomiasis and fascioliasis. Much lore about paralytic shellfish poisoning and red tides, or algal blooms, can be found in the archaeological literature.

Anthropologists and archaeologists as well as shellfishers are usually aware of PSP which can be fatal in humans but often is not. Coincident with the attention to shells from shell matrix sites since 1970, has been a world-wide increase in the geographical scope, intensity, and frequency of the red tide phenomenon (Anderson 1989) which may make it seem that PSP had as great a potential for human harm in the distant past as it does today. This uniformitarian analogy is most probably invalid. Many reports document the first cases of PSP and DSP in their respective regions in the 1970s and 1980s (Europe 1968 [Wyatt and Reguera 1989:33], Philippines 1983, and India and Australia, 1985) pointing to the spread of the various responsible dinoflagellates and diatoms (photoplankton) from customary areas to new areas, the occurrence of unusual environmental circumstances, global environmental trends, evolving new toxicity, and, of certain relevance, increased human activities in the coastal zone (see papers in Okaichi et al. 1989). Of the latter cause, increased soil erosion, increased organic wastes, and increased culturing of bivalves which greatly elevate the levels of certain key chemicals in the water, are prime reasons for newly occurring algal blooms.

The geographical areas where red tides and PSP are common and have temporal depth apparently are only the northwest coast of the US and New Guinea. In 1793 and 1799 large numbers of Koniag sea otter hunters died of PSP off the coast of Vancouver and Alaska (Abbott 1972:216; Moss 1993:640). PSP is today principally confined to the northern mainland coast of British Columbia, and the southwestern and northeastern shores of Vancouver Island (Moss 1993:644).

PSP is not usually fatal. "Within historic medical times, there have been 957 cases of bivalve paralytic poisoning [in the United States], 222 of which have resulted in death" (Abbott 1972:216). As of 1972, all but three of those deaths had occurred in Pacific coast residents. Dozens of diatoms and dinoflagellates bloom in colored masses and are harmless to humans eating fish and shellfish from those waters. Spain has annual red tides as does the east coast of India but without toxicity. Conversely, harmful quantities of algae can infiltrate fish and shellfish yet not discolor the water.

Several steps are involved in the generation of PSP or DSP. Environmental conditions trigger the seeding of plankton. The seeds of many plankton species form cysts which can lie dormant in marine sediments for thousands of years. A separate suite of conditions governs the transformation from cyst to vegetative state and the simultaneous bloom of millions of individuals. Filter-feeding marine molluscs ingest the plankton and accumulate their toxins in their own bodies. Generally the peak toxicity of molluscs occurs after the peak bloom. Different individual molluscs in the same population will accumulate different quantities of toxins. The human predator must harvest these molluscs within several months of the bloom to be endangered. Cooking methods such as boiling and broiling have rendered the toxins harmless (Gonzales et al. 1989:48) while bivalves steeped in vinegar retained their toxicity. The toxicity of the particular molluscs consumed can mean that human individuals in the same collecting party will show no sickness, be slightly ill, very ill, or die. Human body size is relevant as well in mortality from PSP, with children succumbing to toxicity levels not lethal to adults.

PSP is a highly seasonal sickness, although the season varies around the world. In Taiwan PSP occurs during April while in the Philippines it occurs during mid-summer. Sickness begins with consumption of about 4,000 MU (mouse units)/400 g of shellfish meat. Paralytic shellfish poisoning affects the central nervous system. Within five minutes of ingesting the 4,000 MU a tingling sensation is felt in the lips, the neck, arms, fingertips, and feet. Paralysis follows in fifteen to twenty minutes. In severe cases headache, thirst, nausea, vomiting, ataxia, and aphasia may be experienced. Deaths occur as a result of respiratory paralysis, as quickly as four hours after ingestion. The milder cases recover completely within forty-eight hours.

There are a number of other sicknesses (Table 2) caused by trematodes and nematodes which afflict humans, domesticated and wild animals, and which are parasitic in gastropods. Probably for much of human history trematodes have used snail (among them eighty-seven Planorbidae, seventy-one Lymnaeidae, forty-two Hydrobiidae species [Brown 1978:290]) and vertebrate hosts in their life cycles. Today these infections can be found over much greater geographical ranges, and hosted by larger numbers of gastropod species. Unlike the shellfish poisonings these infections are seldom the ultimate cause of death in vertebrates but they do take their toll. The offending trematode parasites pass one or more preadult stages in a (usually freshwater) gastropod and their adult life in a vertebrate. They are free-swimming larva when outside a host.

Table 2. *Trematode diseases afflicting humans*

Disease name	Affects human	Found in	Genera of snail hosts	Source
Schistosomiasis	blood	tropics	*Bulinus*	Stephenson 1987
S. haematobium	urinary tract	Africa, Mediterranean	*Bulinus*	Stephenson 1987
S. mansoni	intestines	Africa, Middle East, Brazil	*Biomphalaria*	Stephenson 1987
S. japonica	intestines	China, Indonesia, Philippines	*Oncomelania*	Stephenson 1987
Fascioliasis	liver	Chile, Peru	*Lymnaea*	Malek 1985
Paragonimiasis	lungs, muscles brain, spine	Far East, Egypt South America	*Melanoides*	Malek 1985
Angiostrongyliasis	brain	Pacific, SE Asia	*Prosobranchiata*	Malek 1985
Heterophyiasis	intestines	Egypt	*Polamidida*	Brown 1994
Paramphistomatidae	stomach	Africa, Near East, SW Asia	*Bulinus*	Brown 1994
Echinostomiasis	intestines	Asia	*Biomphalaria*	Brown 1994

Like red tides, these trematodes recently have been transported around the globe and new habitats are being created in ancient homelands particularly through irrigation projects. The use of fresh water for latrines is a constant source of eggs, invertebrate hosts, and the cercariae–skin contact for all the affected vertebrates.

Schistosomiasis, or bilharziasis, is a blood disease of tropical regions infecting over 200 million people in 71 countries, primarily in Africa, the Orient, Middle East, and on a lesser scale in South America and the Caribbean. Its transportation from the Old World to the New World occurred with the African slave trade (Brown 1978). In the New World its hosts are all species of *Biomphalaria*.

Eggs of these blood flukes hatch in fresh water. The larva must find an aquatic snail host within a few hours. There, two generations of sporocysts emerge which eventually leave the snail host after a minimum of three weeks as "cercariae" in numbers far exceeding the number entering as larvae. These cercariae may exit from a snail host for months. Still living in fresh water, they are free swimming until invading a vertebrate host (cattle, sheep, dogs, mice, rats, antelopes, and hippos) through its skin or digestive tract. They migrate through the circulatory system while becoming adults, then produce eggs in the new host which pass out through urine and feces.

Fascioliasis is a trematode disease of the liver. Human fascioliasis is known from several countries in the Americas, especially Chile and Peru, and in Old World sheep and cattle cultures (Brown 1994:338). The snail hosts belong exclusively to the family Lymnaeidae (*Fossaria*, *Stagnicola*, and *Pseudosuccinea*) which inhabit all types of water bodies, from stagnant to large lakes, and are common in pet shop aquaria. Lymnaeidae graze on algae, decaying vegetation, dead fish, and watercress plants. The liver fluke *F. hepatica* was introduced into Australia during European colonization there. A recent introduction of the North American snail *Pseudosuccinea columella* to a number of Old World countries provides a potential host for a dramatic enlargement of the range of *F. hepatica* (Brown 1978:295).

Non-predator causes of death

In addition to death from some of the infestations just described, there are other, non-predatory, causes of molluscan death. Fresh water kills marine molluscs as the cells of the mollusc fill, expand, and rupture (osmotic pressure). For genera whose shells do not completely close, such as *Barnea* (angel wing), there is little chance of avoiding increased osmotic pressure.

Soft shell clam (*M. arenaria*) mortalities have been observed in association with high water temperatures and low salinities. Normal Gulf of Mexico salinity is usually 36 ppt but variation is the rule. Heavy rains and flooding will cause salinity to decrease rapidly. "It is usually about eighteen months after the water returns to its normal salinity before the bottom fauna becomes reestablished" (Andrews 1971: 19). When the decrease in salinity is gradual some molluscs can stay closed for several weeks, liberating oxygen from the calcium carbonate of their shells. Several studies have shown that gradual reduction or increase in salinity has little effect on marine molluscs.

El Niño storms bring about the catastrophic death of cold-water species by warming the water in estuaries. Hurricanes can scour the bottom of estuaries destroying beds and communities.

Mass mortality or die-off in a single species is known to occur among bivalves, although no satisfactory explanation has been found. Both saltwater and freshwater species are affected. Since the late 1970s, major die-offs of freshwater naiads have been reported, apparently occurring at a greater frequency than in the past (Neves 1986). Only a few cases since 1955 can be linked to drastic physical perturbations or gross industrial pollution. In many other cases a wide variety of commensal ecto- and endoparasitic species, diagenetic trematodes, and pathogens have been suggested but research has failed to confirm these explanations (Bates 1986). Five percent of all naiads in a river in Virginia (US) died in June 1983; no environmental or histological factor could be pinpointed and no other forms such as fish were affected, eliminating a toxic spill explanation (Ahlstedt and Jenkinson 1986). Die-offs in 1985 and 1986 on the Tennessee River (Alabama) occurred without any sign of accompanying fish death, obviously abnormal water-quality conditions, or other apparent correlates (Jenkinson 1986). Histological assay of dead naiads from a die-off which claimed 50 percent of the naiads in an Oklahoma river indicated no abnormalities (Zale 1986). Many more examples of the phenomenon could be given but none can be explained.

This phenomenon creates community-wide deaths in riverine settings, not species specific deaths. Die-offs then would have most explanatory relevance to freshwater prehistoric situations where shellfishing ceases or greatly diminishes. However, species specific die-offs are more common in the marine setting. Among the saltwater bivalves observed to suffer mass die-offs are clams, oysters, and mussels of many species.

Archaeologists have made use of several aspects of molluscan biology. r and k selection, demography, and shell growth have been fruitfully employed. Commonly misunderstood by archaeologists are the aspects of fecundity, larval life stage, algal infestations, growth rates, and the place of molluscs in the food chain.

2.2   Predation

Predation is a contest between prey and predator, both equipped to survive. Molluscs prey on each other and on non-molluscan species and are the prey of creatures as different as beetles, octopods, and humans. Much of the architecture of shell is generated by the alternating predator and prey roles of shelled organisms. Molluscs in their shells are in danger of "being swallowed whole, enveloped and suffocated, trapped, thrown to the ground from the air, cut open, hammered, crushed, drilled, speared, poisoned, parasitized, nibbled, or killed by forced entry" from non-human predators (Vermeij 1993:98). Generally speaking as salinity increases the number of species increases while the number of individuals within a species decreases (Andrews 1971:20). As a consequence, the numbers of different types of predators increase. In warm water, metabolisms are faster so that encounters between members of different species increase in number (Vermeij 1993:110).

Molluscs do have senses which help in locating prey and in avoiding predation. Touch is well developed in a few species, with tentacles and the foot being the most sensitive areas. Taste is present in all species with heads. Sight ranges from none to light sensitivity in some clams to eyes that actually observe in the cephalopods. Sight is most important for tidal species; deep-water and infaunal species lack sight. Bivalves with eyes may have light-sensitive spots scattered on the mantle, concentrated around the siphon, or on the edge of the mantle (Andrews 1971:35). Smell is quite important to the carnivorous gastropods (e.g. *Natica*) for locating prey and is nonexistent in bivalves. Hearing ability is unknown.

Attachment mechanisms play a dual role in permitting feeding and in resisting predation by preventing dislodgment. Chitons, limpets, and coiled snails produce mucus from the foot which holds the animal to the rock, weed, or other surface. Some bivalves, such as the mussels (Mytilidae), adhere to a place by secreting from the foot a large number of proteinaceous filaments known as byssus. Oysters and chamids cement one valve to the substrate and vermetid snails cement their tubes with calcium carbonate. Some chitons and limpets protect themselves from dislodgment by sitting in self-made depressions. Predators capable of dislodging molluscs are muricid snails, crabs, urchins, herbivorous fish, and birds (Vermeij 1993:73–76).

Shells protect their inhabitants. Protection is afforded by the strength of the shell, its resistance to dissolution, its thickness, projections, coloration, narrow apertures, interdigitating hinge teeth and crenulations on margins, and the animal's ability to repair holes and cracks with calcium carbonate patches. Some species even affix stones, shells, and other detritus to their shells to provide camouflage.

When an entire mollusc is ingested, the flesh is consumed and the shell expelled. Some prey species can close up tightly and pass through the digestive tract to emerge weeks later undamaged. Ingestors are sea stars, sea anemones, segmented worms, gastropods, fishes, leeches, and birds. Other predatory species consume only the flesh by invading the valve(s). Predatory snails (e.g. *Polinices* and *Thais*) insert their proboscis between the valves or into the aperture and poison or anesthetize the victim before consumption. Beetles and snakes insert mouthparts into snails as do birds and fish. The gastropods *Busycon* (Figure 8), *Busycotypus*, and *Fasciolaria* use the lip of their own aperture to wedge apart closed bivalves (Vermeij 1993:101).

Crabs, lobsters, turtles, sea otters, lizards, crocodiles, puffer fish, porgies, triggerfish, rays, drums, some sharks, beetles, and snails crush the shells of molluscs. Crabs and spiny lobsters break small increments off the bivalved margin or the snail aperture until the animal is exposed or crush the spire of a gastropod. Some shrimp hammer shells to break them, as do thrushes and mongooses. Gulls, vultures, and crows drop shells from the sky to shatter them.

Breakage is the most common cause of death in tropical molluscs. Beach collections made by Vermeij (1993:10) on western Pacific beaches contained 20 percent broken shallow-water shells, while other collections found 10 percent of North Pacific snails, 42 percent of shells on beaches of Hokkaido Island, and 10 percent of tropical Atlantic snails were broken. On the beaches of Guam 96 percent of the *Strombus gibberulus* specimens were broken. Also commonly found broken as a result of predation are other small conchs (Strombidae), horn shells (Cerithiidae), and moon snails (Naticidae).

Some resistance to breakage derives from shell shape, size, and thickness as well as shell microstructure. Shell is stronger when compressed than when tensed and nacre is the strongest microstructure as long as the animal is alive

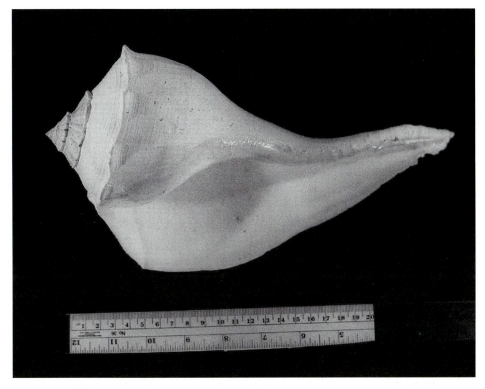

Fig. 8 *Busycon perversum.*

to repair its shell. Nacre fails in compression by crack formation and growth in an irregular manner through the organic matrix, not through the inorganic mineral tablets. In prismatic and porcelaneous shell microstructure cracks grow through and between mineral tablets. Strength in crossed-lamellar structure is greatest in the direction in which the shell layers were laid down (Vermeij 1993:50).

Shell wall thickness is another, often final, defense which is compromised if cracks are present in the shell. Breakage can also be thwarted by a shell that is stiff. Stiffness can derive from folds, corrugations, ribs, knobs, spines, overlapping whorls, all of which are especially prominent in warm-water species where encounters with predators are more frequent than in cool water (Vermeij 1993:126). Shells with an umbilicus have exposed coils; the walls are, therefore, poorly buttressed. Most umbilicus-bearing shells are found in fresh water and on land where breakage agents are fewer than in the marine setting and where whole ingestion is quite common.

In addition to the deterrents offered by a calcium carbonate structure, other aspects of the shell can thwart predators. Projections on shells deter whole consumption (but are lacking on land snail shells). Irregularities in the mantle edge produce corresponding sculpture on the shell, such as spines and fluting. (At the time of formation, all shell ornamentation followed the edge of the outer lip [Andrews 1971:33].)

The slick shells of cowries, olives, and marginellas are difficult to grasp and turn. Thickness is often greatest at the lip which may deter predators who "peel" back shell at the aperture. Several species have a thickened, slick area, known as the callus, to the inner side of the aperture which increases compression strength at that point and helps resist cracking.

Drilling of shell is done by gastropods, particularly naticid and muricid snails who produce neat, slightly conical or straight sided holes (Carucci 1992); octopods equipped with a radula secrete an enzyme which softens the shell during drilling. Drilling by a snail can take up to four days, but only thirty minutes for octopods. The goal of drilling is to reach the enclosed meat. Drilled clam shells are frequent on Japanese shores. In collections of Pacific beach debris in Panama every articulated pair of *Chione subrugosa* valves was edge drilled (Vermeij 1993:109).

Other organisms tunnel or excavate in shell for non-predatory reasons and are known as bioeroders (algae, fungi, foraminiferans, polychaete worms, phoronids, sponges, bryozoans, barnacles, bivalves, gastropods). The organic sheet between the prismatic and the homogeneous layers may deter some predators and bioeroders as do the mineralized layers in oysters, basket clams (Corbulidae), and freshwater clams (Unionidae, Margaritiferidae). Calcitic shell structure and very hard aragonitic shell also deter some predators and bioeroders (Vermeij 1993:47–48). Encrustation by coralline seaweeds prevents bioerosion in reef building gastropods (Smyth cited in Vermeij 1993:47–48) and other epibionts can serve the same function. Encrusters are absent on freshwater and terrestrial molluscs.

In addition to the senses, attachment mechanisms, and the shell, molluscs have other means of avoiding capture. Locomotion, ink ejection (cephalopods), opercula, nests of refuse held together with byssus threads, camouflage (detritus on shell, ink), toxins, mucus, mimicry, leaping, rapid burrowing, rolling into a ball (chitons), cover of sponges (effective against sea stars), and parasitism or commensalism on other species with better defenses are ways molluscs enhance survival in a shell armor.

Chemical or mechanical receptors are borne by most molluscan predators. The marine molluscan prey often releases a chemical cue to its presence detected by predatory snails and echinoderms. Crabs detect movement with receptors in their antennae and hairs on their claws. Other predators detect vibrations and changes in pressure caused by movement. Tightly shut clams and snails sealed behind seated opercula escape chemical detection. Therefore, shells whose margins or apertures are damaged or never close completely are at great risk of chemical detection and invasion (Vermeij 1993).

For some species escape is passive. Responses to predators or danger may be to let loose of a hold and fall off rocks, or sink silently through the water column. Freshwater molluscs are very poor burrowers and swimmers and lack speed or sustained locomotion ability (Vermeij 1993:115–116). Once uprooted from the substrate, many naiads cannot rebury themselves.

Human predators

Predation techniques used by native peoples against shelled creatures have been discussed frequently (e.g. Jones and Richman [1995:41–42], California; Meehan [1982], northern Australia; Waselkov [1987:166–170], worldwide). Instead of recounting the various native ways of harvesting and preparing shelled animals I want to introduce the reader to a number of techniques utilized in historic times for harvesting bivalves primarily. While innovation has had a role in the equipment employed in harvesting, many of these techniques are, no doubt, centuries old among African, Asian, New World, and European peoples but largely undocumented until commercial exploitation evolved. Following that section I will turn to a discussion of human predation strategies. The data presented are gleaned from the few ethnoarchaeological and ethnological projects to study shellfishing and from records of various food and manufacturing industries which have been based on shell or shellfish flesh. Overexploitation is frequently raised as an explanation for changes in shell sizes, changes in species ratios, and the presence or absence of a species or of molluscs in general, and it is discussed at some length.

Capture techniques for bivalves

For the purposes of this presentation, I have divided human predatory techniques into those that allow the person to stay dry and those that require getting wet.

Wet techniques   Native populations the world over have been observed collecting shellfish by hand or by toe, whether the goal was the meat, the shell, or a pearl. Hand collecting has often been embellished by simple equipment such as the use of a lever to pry an epifaunal species free, or a stick to dig out infauna or to put between the gaping valves of clams and lift the creature to the surface.

Diving for shells is an ancient practice. Until the middle of this century women dove in Japanese waters to retrieve shells and pearls. In the months of March through June men dove in the southwestern Pacific to recover pearls or pearl oyster shells. They descended to depths as great as 110 feet holding their breath for up to two minutes dozens of times daily (Williams 1962). Men and women dive for freshwater mussels in Ghana's Volga River (Waselkov 1987:97). Diving as a gathering technique in the US mussel industry appears to have begun in an Arkansas river about 1920 employing used appliances (e.g. a hot water tank). SCUBA gear is used today.

Dry techniques   Much of the equipment that has been developed for shellfishing has allowed the human predator to stay dry and, in most cases, to harvest greater quantities of shells in a given unit of time than is possible when harvesting by hand in the water.

There is some evidence that the Indians of the US and Canada dragged branches across shoals to capture naiads of the Mississippi River watershed, capitalizing on the naiad's closure response to anything touching its mantle. One simply had to lift the branch and pull off the clinging bivalves. French Canadian loggers and women harvesting from Chinese rivers were observed utilizing branches in the same technique (Claassen 1994:15–16). This capture technique – known as brailing – was improved upon by several individuals in the 1890s. It consists of multiple crowfoot hooks on multiple chains suspended from a horizontal bar that is tossed out the stern of a boat and dragged across the river bottom (Figure 9).

A non-hinged form of a long-handled rake was used from medieval times into the twentieth century to gather pin shells (Abbott 1972:185). Waselkov (1987:97) describes the Maori use of long-handled scoops and rakes to harvest naiads. The clam tongs probably derived from earlier equipment and may have been the next piece of apparatus modified for commercial musseling in the US. Two rakes with exceptionally long handles were hinged together like a pair of scissors giving rise to the name "scissor fork." The tongs were lowered into deep water, the two forks forced together and sediment, debris, and shells lifted to the surface. These tongs were still in use on the Wabash River (US) in the 1960s.

Rakes and rakes with baskets were common tools of pearlers in the US in 1895. The shellers' dip-net drag was reportedly invented in the spring of 1911, in the US. The apparatus appears to have been a combination of the fishermen's dip net and the clam rake and was sometimes called a dredge. No two dip nets were alike, varying in size of the hoop and length of the net (Claassen 1994). The shoulder rake, in use by 1918, was a metal rake 1 ft in breadth with ten to twelve tines as much as 9 in. long, fitted with a wooden handle 15 or 20 ft long. The boat was anchored above a bed and the rake "walked back," bow to stern, lifted and emptied. It was best used in swift water on beds with abundant shells and was the favorite implement to use through ice to harvest shellfish.

Of the 51,571 tons of shells taken in selected portions of the US from 1912 through 1914, crowfoot hooks captured 70 percent of them, forks 10.5 percent, tongs 7.8 percent, hands 5.3 percent, dip nets 3.3 percent, dredges 1.2 percent, and rakes 1.2 percent (Smith 1898:59). Although mussels are essentially immobile (they can move distances of up to 100 ft), their capture is not certain. Not all species are equally capturable by all techniques (details in Claassen 1994).

Fig. 9 Braile boat and equipment on Kentucky Lake 1987.

Human predation strategies

The most extensive project undertaken to understand the human adaptation to and utilization of shellfish was that on the Transkei coast of South Africa. For two decades archaeologists, anthropologists, and ecologists have studied the past and present patterns of exploiting the intertidal molluscan resources of this 260-km shoreline.

The distance that people travel to collect shellfish is no greater than 11.26 km (7 mi). Women, girls, and very young boys are the consumers of shellfish and are the primary collectors, but men have been observed collecting (Bigalke 1973). Most of the bivalves collected are taken home in the shell, but chitons are shelled at the waterfront. Shellfish flesh is never mixed with other foods, but the liquor (extrapallial fluid) is mixed with maize. Newly circumcised boys and newly married women are to refrain from consuming oysters or crayfish, because these foods will enhance sexual appetite.

After six months of monitoring the shellfishing of 230 collectors, Tregoning and van der Elst (in Buchanan 1985:213) learned that the average harvest was 4 kg to 6 kg of limpets and mussels. Each collector could provide the entire community with enough shellfish meat by collecting three times her own daily caloric need, requiring her to cover about 12 m² to collect 9,000 kilojoules of limpets or 1 m² for mussels. Shellfish flesh is a major meat complement to the agropastoral-based diet of these peoples (Bigalke 1973).

In 1986, during spring tides, Hockey et al. (1988) performed a two-day airborne survey of the Transkei coast, recording people in the intertidal zone, their activities, shore type/geology, house density, land use, and livestock. They counted 1,447 women older than thirteen years, 84 men, and 257 children shellfishing in the intertidal zone. The estimated annual removal of mussels, chitons, and other shellfish from the 99.2 km of rocky shore south of Port St. John was 552,835 kg, and that from the 66.4 km of rocky strip north of the city was 2,183 kg, where shellfish contributed little to the diet of coastal peoples. In the southern area, the harvest represented over 5.09 million kilojoules and 159.9 kg of protein per year. This intense shellfishing activity is changing the species configuration of the intertidal communities while improving nutrition, argued the authors, as is evident in the lower incidence of kwashiorkor close to the coast.

Lasiak (1992) reported on seasonal variation in harvesting along the Transkei coast in the Ngomane area over a period of eighteen months. Eighteen species were taken regularly, with more than 60 percent of the individuals in any month being the brown mussel (*Perna perna*). Four species of limpets (*Patella*), *Haliotis spadicea* (abalone), and *Burnupea cincta* (whelk) were frequently collected. Only 6 percent of the molluscs came from the intertidal zone, the majority coming from the infratidal zone. When a closed area of the coast was opened to exploitation, the mussels collected in the first month differed significantly in size from those made at the end of the open period. The specimens of abalone and *Patella longicosta* collected in the preserve were smaller than those in the long-exploited area, specimens of *Patella miniata* and *P. oculus* were larger than those taken outside the preserve, and those of *Turbo sarmaticus* were of equal size.

Both Lasiak (1992) and Meehan (1982) found that collectors in South Africa and in north Australia targeted single species during harvest episodes. The target species varied from day to day in the Australian case and showed a long-term preference for brown mussel in the Transkei case. Lasiak attributed the preference for mussels to their immobility and large aggregations, palatability, and digestibility. Informants told Bigalke (1973) and Lasiak that they gathered limpets when mussels were difficult to get due to storm conditions. They also reported reduced collecting during the winter because the flesh was less tasty. Lasiak found that their gathering only four to six days a month resulted in 284 to 426 kg/yr/gatherer, significantly higher than Elizabeth Voigt's (1975) estimates of 71 to 107 kg/yr.

Epifaunal mussel species are harvested by humans either by plucking the larger individuals from the mass or by stripping the entire mass from its substrate. Experimental harvesting has sought to establish criteria for distinguishing the two strategies. That by Jones and Richman (1995:46–48) was conducted with *Mytilus californianus* in an unexploited setting and an exploited setting on the Santa Cruz County California coast. They found distinctive cumulative proportion curves to indicate each harvest strategy regardless of prior exploitation and that the plucking strategy produced a greater yield of kilocalories per hour of work. However, in habitats of ongoing mussel exploitation by humans the distinctions between strategies were less marked.

Overexploitation by humans
Overexploitation by humans is commonly thought to account for changes in species ratios or in the mean or modal size of a species. The test implications for the hypothesis of overexploitation of a species as they have appeared in the literature are four:

(1) Mean shell length will decrease from the bottom of a deposit sample to the top.
(2) The modal size of the archaeologically derived population of a species, when examined against figures for an unexploited population of the same species, will be significantly smaller.
(3) Less easily procured individuals or species will increase in number from bottom to top of the deposit.
(4) Less easily processed individuals or species will increase in number from bottom to top of the deposit.

None of these test implications is adequate for identifying a shellfish population overharvested by humans. Each implication individually, as well as the four collectively, can result from environmental change. The first and second implications are relevant to the hypothesis of intensive exploitation of molluscs by other predators, and the third and fourth implications are relevant to yet another hypothesis evoking technological innovations. None is applicable to recruitment success or failure, or juvenile mortality.

How likely is it that humans can significantly reduce population sizes and alter demographics? There is some literature that observes age, size, and species changes in areas harvested by humans, such as that reviewed above for the Transkei coast. A summary of these observations and additional ones for Papua New Guinea, Queensland, Australia, New Zealand, central Chile, and the US follows.

Transkei Coast: Hockey et al. (1988) assert that the annual harvest as estimated at 552,835 kg is "changing the species configuration" along the coast. Lasiak (1992) observed that at the opening of a previously closed collecting area, abalone and limpet were smaller in size than those in the long-harvested area, that other limpet species were bigger inside the preserve than outside, and that individuals of the genus *Turbo* were of the same size inside and outside of the preserve.

Papua New Guinea: Swadling (1977; 1980) writes that although there is no evidence for prehistoric harvesting pressure on shellfish over 2,000 years, shellfish resources are today greatly reduced near those villages which have experienced the largest population growth since European contact. Because the molluscs now collected are small, she asserted that the reduction in shell size was due to heavy human exploitation (1977:186) and recommended closing some beds.

Exploited regions exhibit higher population densities of *Strombus luhuanus* than those in unexploited regions (Catteral and Poiner 1987).

Queensland, Australia: Two beach areas were sampled at six sites and five sites respectively (Catteral and Poiner 1987). *Anadara trapezia* individuals were significantly larger in the intertidal than in the subtidal zones and were most dense in the subtidal area. Longer individuals (> 50 mm) were more likely to be found on the surface of the substrate and shorter ones to be buried. Thirty percent of the intertidal animals were buried. Reproductive activity was greatest in those shorter than 50 mm. *Saccostrea commercialis* individuals were predominately located on the surface of the substrate in the intertidal zone. Few *Pyrazus ebeninus* individuals were buried and none was found in the subtidal zone. *Strombus luhuanus* were distributed equally between the intertidal and subtidal. In the intertidal population between 10 and 30 percent of the sexually mature animals were buried, as were the majority of juveniles. All of the venerid bivalves were encountered in the subtidal zone and were buried. The presence of buried adults ensures that eggs and larvae will be produced as do the adults located in the subtidal zone. Larvae of three of these species are viable for up to four weeks which means that recruitment from distant populations is possible.

New Zealand: A modern human can collect $27\,m^2$ in one hour. The estimated standing crop at Black Rocks of four molluscan species could therefore be depleted in 1,000 to 1,200 hours of collecting or a few seasons (Anderson 1981:117–118).

Chile: Catches of limpets by hand pickers were smaller in mean size than those gotten by skin divers (Durán et al. 1987).

US: Commercial harvesting records indicate declines in shellfish populations after several to many years of harvesting. The razor clam (*Siliqua patula*) industry of the Washington–British Columbia area increased from 2.7 million to 11 million pounds of meat in twelve years of hand picking and then declined until commercial interest was lost over several more years (Ritchie 1977:5). Soft-shell clams were extensively harvested off the coast of New England from 1850 to 1958, when they were apparently depleted, then harvested primarily from Maryland from 1951 to 1970. When that fishery was declared overfished, attention returned to New England. From 1919 until 1976 clam (*Saxidomus giganteus* and *Protothaca staminea*) production by hand harvesting in west-central Puget Sound (Washington, US) was stable at 1 million to 2 million pounds of meat per year, except during the late 1930s when landings peaked at 3.5 million pounds. Poundage was declining in the 1970s (Ritchie 1977:75). There are dozens of other examples.

In every case cited above, the assumed cause of decline in shell size or shellfish quantities is human collecting. In no case cited above has that explanation been proven; it is rare that multiple hypotheses are even tested. There are numerous other biological relationships capable of explaining these phenomena.

Things that cause changes in mean shell size and species proportions Predation by animals other than humans is usually far more intense than that by humans. Recruitment and juvenile survival may be even more influential on population sizes and their demographics than is predation. In many species, different habitats generate different morphs (a local population distinguishable from others by morphology or behavior) often varying in shell size. Seasonal changes in estuaries produce a different mean size and proportions for populations. Changing environmental conditions can impact on mean size. Finally, archaeological sampling strategies have been shown to be the culprit behind data that demonstrated declining frequencies and sizes in several cases. Each of these potential solutions to archaeological findings of decreasing sizes and numbers of molluscs will be discussed in turn.

While it is easy to imagine the impact of animal predation on an individual animal, the impact of populations of predators on populations of molluscs is even more dramatic. *Mytilus trossulus* (= *M. edulis*) experiences as much as an 80 percent attrition rate in some populations due to predation by diving ducks and other waterfowl. Sea stars tend to consume mussels shorter than 10 cm at the rate of about eighty mussels per year per individual star. Colonizing sea otters rarely eat mussels (0.8 percent of diet) but when abalone are absent, mussels can constitute up to 40 percent of their diet (Jones and Richman 1995:37).

Birds are voracious consumers of molluscs (as are fish). For instance, the oystercatchers off a section of England's coast were seen to consume 32 to 64 cockles (*Cerastoderma* [= *Cardium*] *edule*) per hour per bird in one setting and 200 per hr in another, and 400 $\frac{5}{8}$–$\frac{7}{8}$-in. mussels (Drinnan 1957:454–457). Given that there were an estimated 400,000 oystercatchers in the observation area, 6.4 *million cockles per day* were consumed, a daily predation rate of only 0.2 percent of this commercially harvested cockle population. The mortality of that cockle population was estimated at 74 percent in the winter of 1955, with oystercatcher predation responsible for 22 percent, fish predation *more than double that*, and human commercial activity insignificant even though active. Human harvesting at any point in the past was insignificant in the face of these figures.

Several Pacific coast investigators have considered predation by animals other than humans, even the competitive exclusion of humans, as an explanation for decreasing and low numbers of a molluscan species in sites. Conversely, the demise of the other competitor has been used to explain a surge in the number of molluscs present in a site. The sea otter, predator of sea urchins, abalones, Pismo clams, and numerous other shellfish, has been held responsible for the number of shellfish in at least four prehistoric cases (Clarke and Clarke 1980; Davis 1981; Simenstad et al. 1978). Davis (1981) has developed test implications for this hypothesis focusing specifically on the sea otter. Similar work needs to be undertaken for other predator–prey relationships.

The major factor contributing to juvenile survival of soft-shell clam populations is the population size of the predatory green crab. Warm water during winters increases the green crab population. In the Gulf of Mexico, cycles of green crab abundance have roughly paralleled the serious depletion of soft-shell clam, and the abundance of green crabs in Massachusetts waters since 1940 has undoubtedly played a large role in the decline of soft-shell clam stock there (Claassen 1986b). Predators take a tremendous toll on molluscan populations.

Recruitment/juvenile survival. In Massachusetts, tidal flats that produce large numbers of soft-shell clams and quahogs yearly may suddenly become barren, while other flats are consistent producers for commercial harvesters year after year (Belding in Claassen 1986b).

Why intense recruitment occurs in certain areas and not in others that appear to be ecologically similar is not understood. Low recruitment is usually attributed to environmental conditions that adversely affect success in spawning, larvae survival, juvenile survival, and growth. It is in this situation that a reduced breeding population exacerbates the population size. Low levels of recruitment are usual in heavily harvested areas but high recruitment does occasionally occur. One year of high recruitment can sustain a sizable fishery for several years.

In New England and Maryland, the lack of adequate brood stocks for soft-shell clams is not likely to be the cause for major fluctuations in population abundance because a significant portion of the population is located in beds not open to either commercial or recreational shellfishing and, therefore, ample spat is produced. Instead, as with quahogs, inadequate *juvenile* survival appears to be one of the major factors involved in the relative abundance of soft-shell clam populations. Efforts at restocking barren flats have been tried for more than seventy years with varying results.

Morphs. In many species, different shore zones or different sections of rivers are marked by populations of molluscs of one species that differ in average size. In the Chilean example above, the limpets were larger in the subtidal zone than in the intertidal zone, not because humans had less access to the subtidal and the population was less heavily exploited, but because subtidal individuals of that particular limpet species are always larger than intertidal ones of the same age, a result of the better growing conditions in the subtidal zone. Subtidal individuals of *Anadara trapezia* and *Saccostrea commercialis* had an average mean size smaller than the intertidal individuals in all collections made by

Catterall and Poiner (1987). A change in collecting locale or the proportion of individuals extracted from multiple locales could significantly alter the size profile of an archaeological deposit.

Seasonal impact. Neither the habitat configurations nor the molluscan communities living in them are necessarily stable. Estuarine communities are characterized by short-term and long-term fluctuations in taxonomic composition and in numbers of individuals. The research of Staff et al. (1986) demonstrates that even bivalved species are unstable in number of individuals month to month (Figure 10). A change in the season of collection could account for changes in relative proportions. In short-lived species, the mean size of the population changes with each month in the life cycle. A change in the season of collection of these species *will* account for changes in mean size.

Environmental changes. Changes of substantially different types, from increased sedimentation, decreasing water temperature, decreasing dissolved oxygen, a retreating saltwater boundry, to industrial pollutants, increased sea birds attracted to garbage dumps, artificial warming of water, etc., can and do cause changes in the sizes and proportions of species available to the collector. Hurricanes and heavy freshwater loads in estuaries often account for the sudden disappearance of a species and for the success of restocking efforts. Devastated areas improve with time as do areas where human harvesting has been continuous. Intensively harvested soft-shell clam beds declined in production by 8 million pounds of meat in ten years and then increased by 5.5 million pounds of meat in the next seventeen years while harvesting continued (Ritchie 1977).

One can also look to restocking efforts to see the fallacy in assuming that all of God's dangers for molluscs involve humans. In acreage closed to human harvesting, spat and juveniles are often released or planted, with varying success. The recruitment of spat can be insufficient to re-establish a population and juveniles can die at high rates, months after planting.

Finally, it is within the nature of science that accidents can account for the specifics of a data set. Sampling of sites is often not based on random selection of units or subsamples but on factors such as time and money. Upon closer scrutiny, some temporal patterns in species proportions or size changes often dissolve into statistical artifacts (e.g. Russo 1988; Campbell 1981; Mackay and White 1987). Two examples of reanalysis are given below.

At the Duwamish No. 1 shell matrix site in Seattle, Washington (US) initial testing seemed to reveal decreasing proportions of native little-neck clam (*Protothaca staminea*), rocksnail (*Thais* spp), and particularly edible blue mussel (*Mytilus edulis*), and increasing proportions of butter clam (*Saxidomus giganteus*) and moon snail (*Polinices* sp.) through time (Campbell 1981:215). Campbell, who conducted the subsequent excavation, found the manner in which the percentages had been calculated to be responsible for this impression.

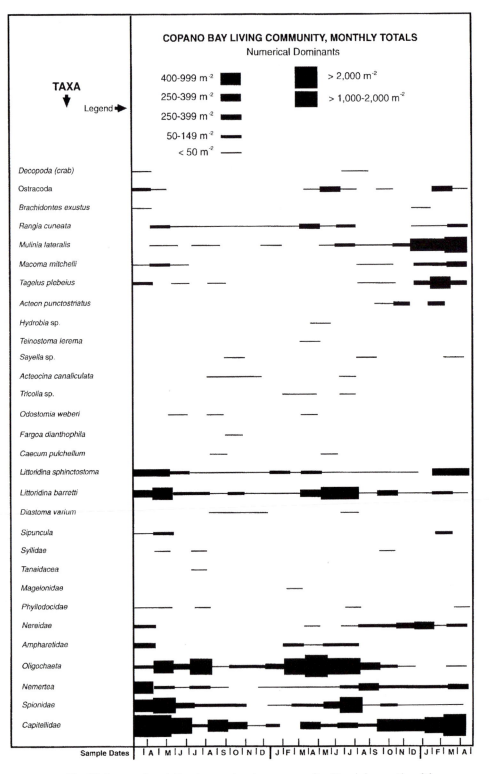

Fig. 10 Seasonal variation in an estuarine community. X-axis is months of the year.

The initial percentages were calculated by taxon, not by stratum. If the species composition of the site is to be examined, which is what the interpretation of decreasing or increasing species proportions implies, then each stratum must be treated as a separate case. It is necessary to know what proportion of a given stratum each taxon represented. Standardization for differing sample sizes (not thickness of natural stratum) should be conducted within the case, not across cases.

> The correction for differing thicknesses of strata is an additional, unnecessary, and unjustified step which distorts the numbers intended to represent the species proportions. When natural strata are used, differences in thickness are part of the variability of the record itself. Differences in absolute sample size resulting from the use of naturally bounded samples may present problems in analysis, but in this case they can be dealt with by using percentages calculated within the strata. (Campbell 1981:217)

When Campbell recalculated the percentage of species *within each stratum* trends dissolved and were replaced by a picture of great variation in species distribution horizontally and an insufficient number of levels to assess vertical changes. Reworking of this data before excavating led Campbell to design her project to study the horizontal variability in species distribution in order to "establish parameters against which the significance of vertical differences could be assessed" (Campbell 1981:219).

Sullivan (1984) argued that for sites on the coast of New South Wales, there was a marked increase in the human exploitation of mussel (*Mytilus planulatus*) in late prehistory. The representativeness of her samples was unspecified. Mackay and White (1987) challenged that claim on three points. One was the issue of sample representation with these authors pointing out that at most of the sites implicated, site samples of less than one percent had been examined. Their second point of contention was the attribution of the pattern to more sites than could support the claim and overly precise dating of those sites. Their re-evaluation found only one site which showed greater collecting of mussel, and much variation in mussel percentages in the late prehistoric zone at the other sites. Their third point was the natural variation in recruitment rates and sets that could cause a heavy set over a period of years and a light set or no set over a period of years.

Both the Seattle and New South Wales cases indicate the same analytical problem, the failure to consider multiple hypotheses for observed statistical trends, in this case the hypothesis of statistical artifact. Numerous other cases of presumed temporal changes have entertained only one hypothesis for species and size changes. The mistake of assuming that decreasing shell size or numbers is the result of human exploitation is more than bad science, it is unfortunate public policy. Closing shellfish beds near villages means that people are denied a free foodstuff and that traditional practices are branded illogical, environmentally unsound. Closing shellfish beds, miles of river, or entire lakes to shellfishers has substantial economic impacts. Time and time again, human harvesting is being blamed for declines in poundage and numbers of shellfish – in the rivers of the interior eastern US, in the oyster and clam beds of the two coasts of the US, along the shores of Chile, South Africa, Tonga – and the disruptive activities of shellfishers for declines in game fish (particularly in the US), as well as for the more familiar declines in marine turtles and fish. While humans are, indeed, most likely to be responsible for all these declining fisheries, it is not their harvesting activities that are responsible. Blaming the collector delays or prevents agencies from uncovering the real pathogens making our oceans sick.

The manner in which ecological aspects of any species interact in the natural environment and cause population fluctuations in abundance is poorly understood. Humans are not the only significant predator in a molluscan food chain and are often quite insignificant. Archaeologists can contribute to a greater understanding of the interactions of prey, predators, environment, even survivorship, with studies of molluscan assemblages, but only if multiple hypotheses are entertained and adequate test implications are derived.

3

TAPHONOMY OF SHELL AND SHELL ASSEMBLAGES

An interest in how shell matrix deposits form has been present for over one hundred years. Early investigators of shell piles such as Brinton (1867), Chadbourne (1859), Lyell (1849), Morlot (1861), and Vanuxem (1843) (all articles reprinted in Trigger 1986) questioned the formative agent, recognized stratigraphy, and studied sea-level changes from the location of deposits.

Storms, animals, even earthquakes were thought capable of creating or elevating natural shell deposits. Subsequent research has demonstrated that all of these phenomena can and do create dry-land accumulations of shelly skeletons. In the late twentieth century archaeologists are again struggling to distinguish natural from cultural accumulations, and even prehistoric from historic accumulations. Classifying and characterizing types of natural accumulations in marine settings engage a large number of paleontologists in the study of taphonomy, studies which are also informative for archaeologists.

With few exceptions archaeologists have not conceptualized shells as sedimentary particles. In the presentation to follow, I have adopted the shell-as-sedimentary-particle viewpoint for a discussion of natural taphonomic processes and include relevant information on cultural processes which transform shells into sedimentary particles. Prior summations of formation processes can be found in Waselkov (1987) for bivalves and Bobrowsky (1984), Carter (1990), and Thomas (1985) for gastropods.

It is important to understand the taphonomic processes at work on shell and shell deposits for many reasons – to evaluate the integrity of a specimen or deposit, to stabilize shells in curated collections, to understand how a deposit was created, to assess the fidelity of the assemblage to the molluscan community nearby, to understand how the archaeological deposit has been/is being modified, and to recognize natural deposits. The taphonomic pathways for shell deposits can serve as a classification scheme for shell-bearing sites. The taphonomic histories of individual and groups of shells in the ground prior to excavation are fundamental to all subsequent analyses yet our understanding of these processes is the most underdeveloped of any topic discussed in this book. That knowledge that has accumulated is far greater for aquatic molluscs than for terrestrial snails. Actualistic studies have proven to be the key to elucidating these processes in paleontology and, although rare, have been very useful in archaeology as well.

53

Taphonomy encompasses those processes which modify or transform individual shells – perforation, fragmentation, abrasion, encrustation, dissolution, heating – and which work at the level of the taxon and in groups of shells to bring about disarticulation, sorting, orientation, transportation, burial, exhumation, and concentration. While these processes do not compromise the integrity of a shell chosen for analysis as long as the concentrators of the shells have been human, they do compromise the integrity of *provenience* for individual shells and for bulk shell samples. But more positively, their study potentially will reveal much about physical changes in the site's setting and integrity, and in human behavior.

In the discussion of taphonomy to follow, I recognize that there are different types of settings for shell-bearing sites. For many terrestrial sites, the only shell present may be land snails. They are best preserved in calcareous soil although Bobrowsky (1984:83) maintains that terrestrial gastropods "preserve very well in many deposits." While some information is presented here on processes of dissolution, breakage, and concentration of land snails, it pales by comparison to the amount of information available for marine shelled animals. Paleontologists have little to say about the taphonomy of dry shell exposures but archaeologists have begun to explore their taphonomy with experiments. The paleontological literature is most applicable to deciding whether or not a shell deposit or portions of a shell deposit are natural or cultural in origin and to the submerged or uplifted shell deposits and those cultural deposits being eroded by sea water. It is less useful for dry shell deposits impacted by high water tables.

3.1   Taphonomic processes active on individual shells

Shells are not impervious to weathering and other destructive forces. The decay of shell is familiar to many archaeologists and curators. Chemical and mineralogical alteration impacts on chemical and growth line studies, the lack of coloration frustrates symbolic archaeologists, and fragmentation creates piles of "shell hash" in the lab.

For shells which rest under water at least daily in an ocean setting, the taphonomic sequence often appears to begin with perforation, to proceed through corrosion, abrasion, encrustation, then fragmentation, and to end with dissolution and chemical conversion. For shells which have been brought onto land and accumulated by humans, away from the influence of boring and eroding aquatic taxa, the sequence is quite different. Encrustation and perforation by bioeroders are absent. Dissolution and chemical conversion are often the only processes at work.

Shell in culturally created concentrations impacted by water – either salt or fresh, wholly or partially – will experience a sequence more complex than the shell in a dry deposit. It is possible to distinguish shells brought to the deposit dead from those collected alive and to determine where the dead shells came from by the recognition of taphonomic sequences. Actualistic studies with modern assemblages in the site's setting will facilitate these efforts.

Types of processes

Taphonomic processes are distinctive in their physical impact and often easily recognized in the field. Their order of discussion will be encrustation, perforation/fragmentation, abrasion, dissolution and chemical conversion. The cultural process of heating will complete the review. Useful review articles by paleontologists are those by Kidwell and Bosence (1991) and Parsons and Brett (1991).

Encrustation

Numerous aquatic animals seek out a hard surface (or substrate) to support their skeletons, and shells are often chosen. Coastal archaeologists are familiar with oyster attachment to each other, as well as encrustation by barnacles. Bryozoa, corals, and algae also attach to shells both when the mollusc is alive and when dead (Figure 11). The activities of these creatures erode the periostracum and erode and pit the surface of the shell. One study found the average bare space in dead *Crassostrea virginica* valves to be only 14 percent, 30 percent on *M. mercenaria*, and 40 percent on *Chlamys* valves (McKinney 1995). Heavy encrustation occurs on dead shells exposed at the water–sediment interface in quiet or low-energy water habitats. Shell ornamentation increases surface area available for settling. Shell mineralogy also influences encrustation levels.

Perforation/fragmentation

Numerous animals bore into living shell for calcium or through shell to reach the soft tissue on the other side. Those in pursuit of calcium continue to bore the dead shell. Umbones and apices may be completely breached as may the shell at the margin, by boring sponges, foraminifera, bivalves, barnacles, gastropods, worms, octopods, and others. Perforation increases the surface areas which admits additional abrading, boring, and encrusting organisms, and facilitates fracture of the shell (Figure 11).

Within calcareous soils destruction of snails and bivalves will involve fragmentation more frequently than dissolution since the soil is approaching calcium supersaturation. Fragmentation increases the susceptibility of the particles to size sorting and transport in general. The rate of fragmentation will be highest in the A horizon (Carter 1990:498).

There are five typical structural types of shell – prisms, nacre, crossed-lamellar, foliated, and homogeneous, often in combinations. Most bivalves build a shell with one of three combinations: (1) prisms without, nacre within,

Fig. 11 Shell degradation: from left to right, top to bottom, perforated, eroded, encrusted, and drilled shells.

(2) foliated with a little crossed-lamellar, or (3) crossed-lamellar only or with some homogeneous structure. Families, typically, and superfamilies, occasionally, have the same structural type. Each structural type has specific mechanical properties, examples of which are given in Table 3.

"Nacre is in general considerably stronger in tension, compression, and bending than the other [forms of microstructure]" (Currey 1980:80). Not only does nacre offer the strongest structure, it is stronger than jade, flint, slate, chalcedony, or granite. Homogeneous structure is very weak in tension for it has very little protein content. Foliated shell is the weakest type in compression. Crossed-lamellar structure is stiffest, while the "prisms of *Pinna* [are] very compliant" (Currey 1980:80). Very little is known about the fracture behavior of prismatic structure.

Breakage occurs most readily at structurally weak points. Locations of dramatic changes in shell shape, ornamentation, and growth lines are just such points and contribute to species specific fracture patterns. In general, gastropods will break at their apertures and the spire will separate from the body whorl. If breakage is to be quantified and typified it will be necessary to compare a single species across taphofacies (Parsons and Brett 1991:41).

Within marine settings fracturing of whole shells after death occurs most often in shallow water impacted by waves and strong currents and results from

Table 3. *Mechanical properties of bivalve shell structure (each Mega Newton and Giga Newton per meter squared value is mean for species). (Adapted from Currey 1980:79.)*

	Tensile strength (MNm^2)	Compression strength (MNm^2)	Bending strength (MNm^2)	Modulus elasticity (GNm^2)
Nacreous				
Hyria ligatus	79	382	211	44
Anodonta cygnaea	35	322	117	44
Pinctada margaritifera	87	419	208	34
Atrina vexillum	86	304	173	58
Modiolus modiolus	56	416	199	31
Crossed-lamellar				
Hippopus hippopus	9	229	35	50
Mercenaria mercenaria	22	336	95	66
Egeria sp.	43	163	106	77
Ensis siliqua	–	196	85	55
Chama lazarus	–	222	36	82
Prisms				
Pinna muricata	62	210	–	12
Foliated				
Ostrea edulis	–	82	93	34
Pecten maximus	42	133	110	30
Saccostrea cucullata	40	74	44	29
Homogeneous				
Arctica islandica	30	248	60	60

particle-on-particle impact (Chave 1964). Chave conducted three experiments using tumbling barrels. After 183 hours of tumbling shells with chert pebbles, *Nerita* snails showed some wear and the bivalves, other gastropods, and echinoids were fractured. After 40 hours of tumbling with sand the urchin (*Strongylocentrotus*), *Piaster*, and algae were completely reduced to particles smaller than 2 mm but the molluscs were only slightly abraded. After 183 hours the mussels (*Mytilus*) were nearly whole but with perforations near the hinge, a gastropod (*Aletes*) was reduced to half its size but both it and a *Tegula* were still identifiable, the abalone (*Haliotis*) was fragmented, and limpets were worn but identifiable.

Turning to terrestrial contexts for shells, there are several physical processes which can fracture valves. Roots penetrate thinner portions of valves and follow their crevices generating fracture by the increase in their diameter during growth; they also exude chemicals which dissolve the shell. Overburden causes compression and can cause compression fractures, slumping, and creep.

Freeze–thaw cycles will accelerate valve degradation by separating growth increments, particularly in coarsely laminated species such as oysters.

Coutts (1969) found that wind action could easily fragment shells of *Notohaliotis* and those of *Cellana, Subninella, Brachidontes,* and *Plebidonax* to a lesser extent. In a comparison of *Subninella* shells and opercula he found that twice as many opercula as whole shells were recovered suggesting a loss rate for the shells of 50 percent (but see opercula discussion under bird accumulators, this chapter). Koike (1979:72) estimated that 70 percent, 58 percent, and 49 percent of the *Meretrix lusoria* shells originally deposited in three Jomon house pits had survived, using the Feller formula and valve pairing. (Wild and Nichol [1983] discuss the Feller formula as well as others for predicting original population size.)

Muckle (1985) examined fragmentation of shells tossed, poured, and trampled. Initial deposition resulted in either no fragmentation or breakage into only large pieces. Shell species (*Protothaca staminea, Mytilus edulis,* and *Venerupis japonica* – all eastern Pacific) was an important determinant of fragmentation but height of discard, the number of valves discarded together, and the age of the shells appeared to be insignificant variables. Highly fragmented deposits are probably the result of activities subsequent to initial discard.

Fragmentation of oysters (*C. virginica*) at the oyster matrix site of Dogan Point, NY, was quantified as the ratio of shell weight retained in the half-inch mesh screen divided by that in the quarter-inch mesh screen (Claassen and Whyte 1995). A backdirt pile of oyster shell and sediment from excavation in 1969, when half-inch screens were used, proved to have fragmentation ratios of .59 to 1.96; surface levels elsewhere in the site had ratios of 3.76 or less. Areas of deep shell (1 m thick) had ratios ranging from 13.20 to 47.76, where presumably little postdepositional disturbance had occurred other than that by worms and rodents. The widely differing fragmentation ratios in a pit feature from the Osprey Marsh site, South Carolina (Chapter 4) led to the recognition of a complex history of the pit fill.

Abrasion

Abrasion refers to the removal of calcium carbonate by physical processes or bioeroders. Its signs are muted shell sculpture, polished surfaces, and rounded edges (Parsons and Brett 1991:44). Abrasion is most intense in the near-shore wave, current, or tidal zones (Parsons and Brett 1991). For bivalves the sequence of abrasive damage to the shell is generally the umbo, then the posterodorsal margin, and then the post-umbonal slope. Shell ornamentation is particularly susceptible. Extensive rolling will create a horseshoe-shaped shell fragment. The speed and intensity of abrasive damage on an abandoned shell depends on the grain size of the surrounding sediment, and the surface area per unit weight of the shell. Larger light shells (such as *Argopecten irradians irradians, Mya arenaria*) will abrade more rapidly than heavy smaller shells, such as *M. mercenaria*, in the surf zone but this is not the case in embayments.

Bioeroders also create abrasive damage to a shell both when it is occupied and when it is abandoned. Bioerosion is the work of animals seeking food and shelter. Algae grow on calcium carbonate skeletons digesting the organic matter that binds the crystals below the surface of the shell. Grazing predators scour the shell's surface taking calcium carbonate and algae away. Borers are looking for a home in the shell and do less abrasive damage than do grazers. Hermit crabs, also looking for a home, drag a gastropod shell over the sediment surface abrading the aperture and ultimately wearing away that face of the shell.

Several archaeologists and zooarchaeologists have recognized the information potential of abraded archaeological shell. Frank Dirrigl (1995) calculated roundness and sphericity for freshwater and marine bivalves recovered at the Goldkrest Site in New York, favoring the visual comparison chart of Powers (1953) for roundness. He qualified the sphericity by indexing the greatest width to greatest length. A ratio of .80 or higher was a highly spherical specimen. Specimens of the same age and taphonomic history should show equivalent roundness and sphericity, while intrusive specimens will differ in one or both measures.

Acid dissolution
Calcium carbonate ($CaCO_3$) is more resistant to corrosion than many other materials found in animals and therefore is an excellent material with which to build a shell. Corrosive resistance is compromised by cold water, acidic water, and high pressure. There are several ways to buffer the shell living in cold water and high pressure which many species have adopted: the calcite shell, the periostracum, shell-encrusting epibionts, and shell walls separated by protein sheets (Vermeij 1993:45–49).

Calcium carbonate skeletons "dissolve" in the presence of either freshwater (ground water, streams) or saltwater. Dissolution is greatest in high salinity, low temperatures, and areas of much bioturbation. Water that is undersaturated with calcium dissolves calcium more readily than does water that is oversaturated (i.e. tropical waters).

The dissolution of aragonite provides calcium cement which can shore up the aragonite shell. In the prismatic layer each calcite prism is encased by an organic sheath or conchiolin. The conchiolin can be removed by algae, "oxidation by gaseous oxygen, or oxygen dissolved in water or combustion during heating" (Kent 1988:12), the latter being the quickest and the most serious. The elimination of the sheaths allows calcite or silica crystal cement to occupy the now empty space around the prisms. Without cementation or in undersaturated water, shells ultimately disintegrate into their microscopic structural elements – the sedimentary needles, fibres, flakes, and granules. Nacre falls into aragonitic flakes, calcite falls into flakes, crossed-lamellar aragonite crumbles into granules. First color and lustre are lost, then the shell acquires a chalky appearance and feel (Alexandersson 1979:847). Oysters become lustrous as exterior calcitic layers fall away to expose fresh calcite. Surfaces become pitted. (Shells in contact with *Thalassia* grass rhizomes have linear white traces of dissolution.) Etching can accentuate ornamentation. As dissolution progresses shells get thinner overall, particularly at the edges, and perforation of a bivalved shell often appears first at the muscle scar. In tropical water shell remains hard due to a magnesium calcite support (Alexandersson 1979:851).

Acids dissolving shells in a terrestrial setting are carbonic acid, calcium bicarbonate, ammonium nitrate, sulfuric acid, nitric acid, and others. Rain combines with atmospheric carbon dioxide to form a weak carbonic acid that intensifies in strength as soil carbon dioxide joins the solution. Calcium carbonate from shell in the moist soil reacts with the stronger carbonic acid forming calcium bicarbonate, which is water soluble. "Shell" is thus dissolved. Ammonium nitrate is formed by lightning and dissolved by rain water. Sulfuric and nitric acids are exuded by plant roots or formed during the decay of organic matter in soil, and are carried in acid rain (Kent 1988:14).

The rate at which these acids dissolve $CaCO_3$ is governed by the acidity of the ground water and the duration of exposure to the acids, among other factors. $CaCO_3$ reduces acidity so that large concentrations of shells experience leaching at a slower rate than do thin scatters or the margins of deposits (Kent 1988:15). In addition to the influence of shell mineralogy on dissolution rates are the factors of surface areas to weight, and skeletal porosity. Shells with a high surface area to weight dissolve more rapidly, as do more porous skeletons such as those of barnacles or those that are extensively bored or drilled (Parsons and Brett 1991:43).

Calcium carbonate can also be dissolved by fluids associated with predators. For instance, terrestrial and semi-terrestrial hermit crabs are responsible for dissolving or breaking away the internal architecture of the gastropod shells they inhabit for long periods of time (Carucci 1992).

Chemical conversion

Calcite skeletons high in magnesium chemically are the least stable (echinoderms), aragonitic skeletons more stable, and calcitic skeletons low in magnesium ($< 4\%$) the most stable. Aragonite is unstable at hydrostatic pressures less than 4 kb (at 25 °C or 16 kb at 600 °C). After death, the unstable aragonite skeleton can (1) undergo spontaneous inversion to calcite at temperatures at or below 30 °C, (2) dissolve, or (3) recrystallize, or be replaced by another mineral such as dolomite, silica, hematite, or pyrite (Land 1967).

Most eastern oyster (*C. virginica*) valves from archaeological sites have lost most of their aragonite but the spaces have not yet filled with calcite (Kent

1988:13). Most frequently, aragonite converts to calcite by first the complete dissolution of aragonite with the mold later filled by calcite, or by inversion or calcitization. In archaeological settings with mixed soil and shell, conversion is most likely to occur if the ground water is undersaturated with calcium carbonate. If it is just below saturation then calcitization will occur (Tucker 1991:100). However, "the pressure of certain metal ions [rare in *C. virginica*], such as Mg^{2+}, Sr^{2+}, or Ba^{2+} stabilizes aragonite and decreases the transformation rate" (Kent 1988:14).

Recrystallization occurs most often in alkaline soils, and in shells as they dry in the lab. Salts that commonly recrystallize within shells are sodium carbonate and sodium chloride (Kent 1988:11). Permineralization is the result of ground water, laden with dissolved ions, penetrating the interior of the shell and occupying the space previously occupied by conchiolin. Calcite or silica crystals typically form, the former in alkaline and the latter in acidic environments. Permineralization consolidates the exposed prisms and slows dissolution (Kent 1988).

Heating
Heating shell physically alters the crystallography and compromises the internal cohesion of the structure. Burned shell fractures more easily and weighs less than does unburned shell. Chemists working with shell samples should suspect a sample with greater than 43 percent calcium to have been subjected to heat or other taphonomic processes. (Experimental error in shell calcium was 38 percent to 43 percent in Claassen and Sigmann [1993].) Three shell-burning experiments provide useful information on the transformations which occur (Linck and Modreski 1983; Robins and Stock 1990; Spennemann and Colley 1989).

Robins and Stock (1990) manipulated several southwestern Pacific bivalve species in campfire and furnace at temperatures from 200 to 1,000°C. The campfire burned between 600 and 850°C. Linck and Modreski (1983) burned shells from the northwestern Atlantic in a wood stove and furnace, with temperatures ranging from 650 to 1,900°F (343 to 1,038°C).

Calcium carbonate loses crystalinity between 500 and 700°C, with aragonite converting to calcite at 520°C (968°F). As temperature increases the protein components oxidize progressively faster. At lower temperatures, "carbonized films, streaks and nodules would be left as residue" (Robins and Stock 1990:87). At the highest temperatures in an oxidizing atmosphere, the carbon will oxidize to leave a sulfur-rich ash.

There is significant breakdown and weight loss in *Plebidonax deltoides* beyond 800°C as demonstrated by Figure 12. Upon agitation (by forced vibrator) in nested geological sieves for thirty seconds, heated shells of various species broke into smaller particles (Figure 13). The higher the temperature, the more readily most shells fragment (Figure 14) (Robins and Stock 1990).

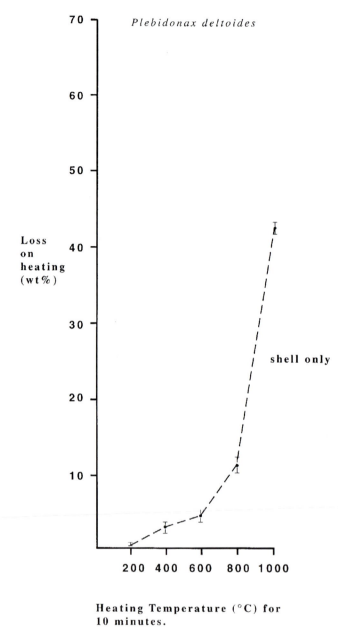

Fig. 12 Shell weight loss with heating.

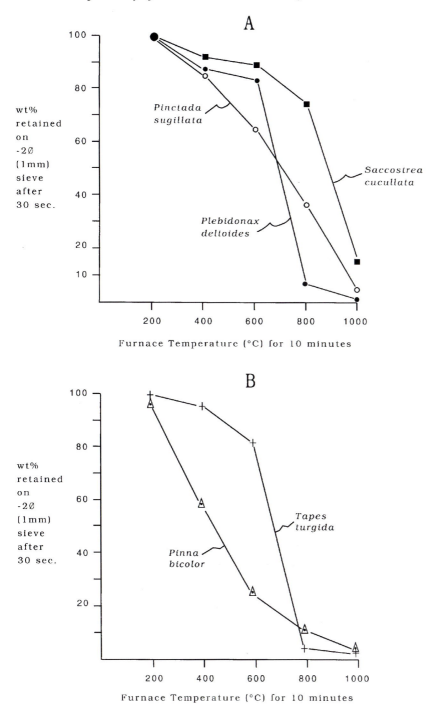

Fig. 13 Particle size distribution after mechanical destruction.

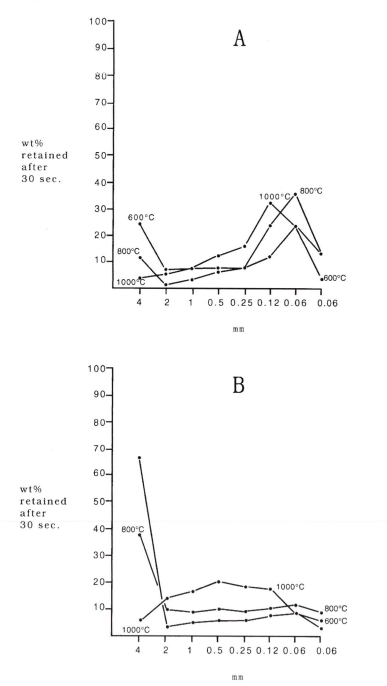

Fig. 14 Mechanical destruction of shells heated at different temperatures. Particle size distribution after mechanical destruction of (A) *Pinna bicolor*, (B) *Pinctada sugillata*, (C) *Fragrum unedo*, (D) *Anadara trapezia*.

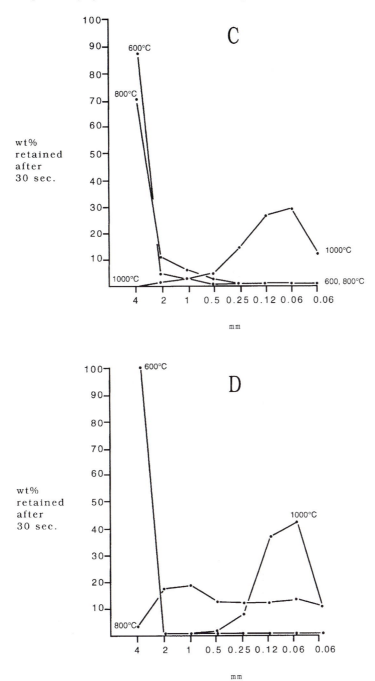

Oysters (*Ostrea*) with their lamellar structure exfoliate completely upon extended contact with fire. "Exfoliation does not occur with certain venerids and
pectinids, which are so hard that when kept on the fire for a prolonged time,
instead of being destroyed they acquire a greater hardness to the point of
vitrification" (Lima et al. 1986:87).

Burning of shell has been a common source of lime throughout the world.
Quicklime production from clam (probably *M. mercenaria* or *Mya arenaria*)
and oyster (*C. virginica*) shells requires heating to 1,517°F or 825°C (Linck and
Modreski 1983). In addition to burned shells, unburned shells were often
added as binder or filler. Linck and Modreski found that "clam" and oyster
shells heated to different temperatures fluoresced different colors under short-
wave ultraviolet light even though the physical changes in the two species were
identical.

Unburned clam and oyster fluoresce a mild bluish color. At lower heats in a
furnace, a dull yellow appears and at higher heats a dull gray. At 1,200°F
(649°C), oyster shows a dull orange, clam a dull bluish. At 1,400°F (760°C)
oyster fluoresces a vivid yellow, like the fluorescent color of historic mortar,
and continues to be yellow at higher heats until the shell is reduced to powder.
This powder is white in daylight but fluoresces dark bluish to maroon or
bluish-white.

The color sequence is different for clam at 1,400°F and higher. At 1,400°F
clam is moderately bluish with flecks of faint green and yellow. There is no
green tint above 1,400°F, and no color at 1,700°F (927°C) and higher.

Within the heating environment of a wood stove (greater than 900°F or
482°C) the two species fluoresce more similarly. Oyster yields a vivid yellow
color with scant orange, light and dark green, purple, and violet flecks, while
clam is predominantly dull gray with vivid orange, aqua, and traces of yellow
in about a third of the shell.

Some concretions of shell in sites may be due to burning. Palmer and
Williams (1977:25–26) outline a process whereby shell is converted to calcium
oxide by heat, which, when it contacts solutions of calcium bicarbonate, would
precipitate calcium carbonate, a binder for shells, artifacts, and ecofacts (also
Kent 1988:15).

Issues of taphonomy and individual shells

A number of issues arise as a result of the processes just presented. What
sequences of taphonomic processes are known? How can various types of
processes be distinguished? How long, on average, do shells last when not
fossilized?

Sequences of taphonomic processes
A unique study of biofacies (fauna composition) and taphonomic processes

along Massachusetts' Cape Cod (Meldahl and Flessa 1990) is illustrative of the potential for archaeologists to identify shells collected dead from different environments and to recognize patterned taphonomic sequences. Collections of twenty modern dead surface shells in eighteen tidal-flat and salt marsh locations were examined for taphonomic traits. For *Spisula solidissima* collected on the outer tidal flats, five of six collections displayed the sequence fracture, abrasion, corrosion, algal bioerosion, barnacle encrustation, and algal encrustation. For middle tidal flat collections, the sequence was fragmentation and corrosion, followed by either encrustation or algal bioerosion. For the inner tidal flat, corrosion was the first stage in four cases followed by barnacle and then algal encrustation; some shells lacked fragmentation and corrosion. For *M. mercenaria* on the salt marsh fragmentation preceded corrosion, usually to be succeeded by abrasion then by algal bioerosion on the outer flats, or by algal bioerosion and then barnacle encrustation. The two pathways identified were (1) an encrustation/bioerosion dominated pathway in the low-energy upper intertidal and deeper subtidal zones and (2) an abrasion dominated sequence in the high-energy lower intertidal and shallow subtidal zones.

Dirrigl (1995) has proposed six stages of shell deterioration for shells in an acidic soil matrix. These stages are (1) periostracum intact; shell not cracked, (2) superficial flaking of periostracum, observable growth lines well defined, (3) periostracum absent; growth lines less defined, dorsal surface of shell smooth, (4) shell worn; no growth lines observable, (5) shell layers separated and flaking, and (6) shell falling apart *in situ* and fragile; may have chalky appearance. Stratigraphically associated shells can be expected to show the same stage(s) of deterioration regardless of mineral structure.

Distinguishing types of processes

Valves that are found in terrestrial settings and have exposed calcium carbonate prisms or deeply incised growth lines on the hinge (oysters) or on the dorsal surface (clams) have lost their conchiolin. Severe alteration of the calcite structure is indicated by visible cement and increased luminescence (Pirrie and Marshall 1990:340).

Several authors indicate that distinguishing the several processes can be difficult. For instance, it is easy to confuse dissolution with algal microboring. "Individual algal borings on *M. mercenaria* are too small to be seen without high magnification but multiple borings produce a green tinted pitted texture on shell surface distinct from corrosion textures under $10 \times$ magnification" (Meldahl and Flessa 1990:53). Pirrie and Marshall (1990:344) found that a combination of cathodoluminescence and geochemical studies is useful for distinguishing degree of diagenetic alteration but that SEM observation was not sufficient.

Perseverance of shells

It is clear from geological deposits that aquatic shells can last millions of years when burial is rapid. Left exposed, however, to oceanic processes and to terrestrial ones, the survivorship of individual shells is much reduced.

> The nacreous shell of the trochid [snail] *Calliostoma ligatum* deteriorates very rapidly... The rapid decay of the matrix, coupled with the high surface area of the remaining mineral component ensures that the shell loses about half its original strength in compression after only 3 days. The thick shells of other molluscs also weaken after death, but this deterioration is probably slower because of the lower organic content. (Vermeij 1993:50–51)

Vermeij adds that "because decay is temperature dependent, deterioration after death may be especially rapid for warm water shells."

After three years of observation of *M. mercenaria*, *Argopecten i. irradians*, and *Mya arenaria*, submerged in a shallow, low-energy, sub-littoral environment, Driscoll (1970) found that valves with greater surface area per unit weight displayed a greater weight change, broke more frequently, and were more heavily encrusted than were those with less surface area per unit weight. The periostracum of all three species was damaged in the first year and missing by the end of the second year. The interior nacreous luster was duller after two years except for the luster retained by *M. mercenaria* at the adductor muscle scar. The hinge ligaments of *M. mercenaria* survived all three years and none of its shells was completely perforated. At the end of two years, 88 percent of the scallop and 56 percent of the *Mya arenaria* had been perforated and after three years all of the scallops and 86 percent of the *M. arenaria* were breached. Furthermore, after three years there were chipped ears and margins on the scallops and chipping or breakage of half of the margins of *M. mercenaria*. Driscoll concluded that when compared to low-energy muddy habitats, shell destruction is 150 times more rapid in surf zones with fine sand and one thousand times more rapid in surf zones with coarse sand because of abrasive action. Shells with less surface area per unit weight are buried more rapidly where dissolution is the chief taphonomic process at work.

After 307 days, over 50 percent of all newly dead shells in Texas lagoons were missing but the losses were greatest among juveniles and "poorly calcified opportunists" under 3 mm tall. Nevertheless, "The temporally persistent core of the community is captured by the shelly death assemblage," concluded Kidwell and Bosence (1991:126).

Estimates of the actual number of years shells of different California species can survive buried in 50 cm of submerged sandy sediment are offered by Peterson (1976) based on weight losses in seven and one half months of burial (Table 4). A survey of the radiocarbon literature indicates that shells on the continental shelf can survive upwards of 10,000 years while those from shallow, near-shore environments are typically hundreds of years old (Flessa and Kowalewski 1994:162). The difference in survival rates is attributable to

Table 4. *Dissolution of shells buried for $7\frac{1}{2}$ months under 50 cm of sediment in* Mugu Lagoon. (*Peterson 1976; reproduced with permission from* Lethaia.)

Species	Sand substrate % loss	Muddy sand substrate % loss	Average persistence (yrs)
Cryptomya californica	.99	.23	102
Sanguinolaria nuttallii	.66	.23	141
Prothothaca staminea	.14	.00	894
Dendraster excentricus	20.56	15.15	4
Bulla gouldiana	11.65	8.87	6
Macoma secta	.44	.20	191
Chione undatella	.36	.54	139
Diplodonta orbellus	3.92	–	18
Olivella biplicata	–	.70	53
Tresus nuttallii	.86	–	160
Macoma nasuta	.47	.20	187
Apolymetis biangulata	1.69	–	51
Donax gouldi	.27	00	463
Nassarius fossatus	12.01	–	6
Tagelus californicus	1.48	–	62
Polinices reclusianus	1.24	.49	73
Polinices lewisi	–	.24	88
Cerithidea californica	13.16	13.07	5
Heterodonax bimaculata	.24	–	521
Tivela stultorum	.41	.00	305
Trachycardium quadragenarium	–	.47	66
Argopecten circularis	–	.14	103

greater attrition in shallow waters, post-glacial sea-level rise (there has been less time for shells to accumulate in new areas), and sampling bias.

Chave (1964:380) concluded after several experiments that shell durability, which varies more than for any other type of sedimentary particle, was most governed by microarchitecture of the shell and little conditioned by skeletal mineralogy. "Dense, fine-grained skeletons are the most durable ... least durable are those with much openwork and organic matrix" (1964:381). However, "chemical durability ... is controlled mainly by mineralogy and the chemistry of associated waters; microarchitecture is of secondary importance" (Chave 1964:382).

A combination of processes such as abrasion and dissolution contributes to the perseverance period of less than 1,000 years for land snails in actively weathering soils (Evans 1972:228). For chalk soils, Evans specifies a gastropod faunal record no longer than 300 years. Buried soils are where one must look for older gastropods. A gradient in numbers of individuals from few to many (moving downward) in a soil profile is probably due to dissolution of shell in the upper few centimeters of soil while a decrease in species diversity from top to bottom is due to factors governing preservation.

Color preservation depends largely on the chemistry and stability of the pigment, taphonomic processes, and shell mineralogy. Color is most frequently preserved in gastropod fossils. "Melanins are generally insoluble in organic and acid-based solvents" (Hollingworth and Barker 1991:106) while tetrapyroles are soluble in most liquids. Since pigments are deposited in the prismatic layer and periostracum, bioeroders and abrasion commonly eliminate them. Prolonged exposure to sunlight will fade pigments while fluorescence will illuminate the reds. Color in calcitic outer layers of shell will preserve the longest. Neritid snail fossils have notoriously long-lasting color.

3.2   Taphonomy of groups of shells

Various natural and cultural processes create and disturb shell clusters to produce the time-averaged deposits usually encountered by archaeologists. Eventually, these taphonomic processes completely eliminate shell matrix sites. In this section, the formative agents of sites (storms, water, animals, and humans) are explored as are their role in disturbing deposits. Several regions of the world which lack shell-bearing sites although rich in molluscan fauna focus our attention on the possible taphonomic impacts on regional prehistories.

Formative agents for shell deposits

Deposits of marine and terrestrial shells can be created by waves, currents, fluctuating lake levels, fluvial redeposition, mass movement of sediment, wind deflation, eroding beaches, colluvium, animals, and humans, both prehistoric and historic. Here I examine the characteristics of the various formation agents.

Storm-created shell accumulations
Storms were once thought to have generated large numbers of shell accumulations (e.g. Bartram in Wyman 1875:14–15). Since the acceptance of humans as shell accumulators, the role of storms in accumulating shells has largely been forgotten, although by several modern accounts (e.g. Bird 1992) they both build and destroy shell deposits.

Storms transport shells via wind and water movement. Little has been written about wind transport of shells while much has been written about water transport and is reviewed in the section on shell transport below. Storms in many localities create shell deposits on coasts by pulling up shell detritus and living populations of molluscs from the intertidal and shallow subtidal zones and sweeping this material shorewards into a beach ridge ("chenier").

Depending on the sediment load and its speed of deposition, the shellfish beds may not be re-established. If they are not, a subsequent cyclone or hurricane can not generate subsequent cheniers (Chappell 1982).

Storms can also appear to create sites by removing sediments which had buried a shell deposit, or deflating cultural deposits perhaps making them more conspicuous. In addition to forming cheniers, storms can erode and redeposit shell from cultural collections. Bird (1992) observed that one cyclone which hit the Queensland coast of Australia significantly reduced and/or modified, twenty-three sites. Up to 5 m of shoreline recession, beach erosion, and dune scarping was observed. "The seaward margins of numerous sites were clearly wave-reworked" (Bird 1992:79). Sites which survived were either well inland of the storm surge or sheltered behind foredunes, but even they were deflated.

A very few modern archaeologists have considered the role of storms in creating or modifying terrestrial shell deposits. Hughes and Sullivan (1974) reported on storm wave shell deposits on the southeastern coast of Australia. These deposits consisted of redeposited human debris including charcoal and stone artifacts, as well as molluscs of sizes and species not usually found in human middens, sub-rounded to well-rounded shell grit less than 5 mm across, water-worn shell larger than 5 mm, much rounded gravel less than 5 mm across, and pumice.

The large numbers of drilled bivalves and gastropod shells in a Micronesian site led Carucci (1992) to the conclusion that storms had deposited beach and intertidal material in the human-created shell deposits. He also interpreted the unusually high numbers of crushed and cut shells in a site to indicate re-deposited beach shell mixed with human-deposited shells.

Animal accumulators of shell
There are a number of animals that concentrate shells such as several aquatic mammals (e.g. mink, muskrat), rodents, worms, and birds. There is little readily available literature on the mammals and rodents, but much on the worms and birds. The worms are the most significant concentrators of land snails, more so than humans, while birds may well be the most significant concentrators of marine bivalves and gastropods after humans.

Birds are voracious consumers of molluscs (data in Chapter 2). What is often unappreciated about birds by archaeologists is their shell-fracturing capabilities. Molluscs are opened along stretches of beach by many species of birds such as gulls, rooks, crows, ravens, and oystercatchers. The middens of Pacific gulls "could be confused as marine shell beds," warned Teichert and Serventy (1947:322) to geologists, or as short-term human camps (Jones and Allen 1978). Teichert and Serventy observed a high density of broken turbo shells (*Turbo stamineus*), with whole limpets, chitons, and other molluscs undamaged generally. Often the *Turbo* opercula outnumbered all other items. Jones and Allen

(1978) further observed bird middens containing mutton bird bones, crab parts, *Modiolus pulex* and *Brachidontes rostratus* shells, as well as large numbers of opercula of *Subninella undulata*. Other authors have reported bird predation of whelks, sea urchins, and *Haliotis*.

These prey and the mixture of bones, crabs, bivalves, and gastropods, are suggestive of human activities. Similar associations of biological items which do not occupy the same habitat were advanced as evidence of their human accumulators by Vanuxem in 1843. Other aspects of this phenomenon are not, however, suggestive of human activities – their small size, their thinness, and their topographic location. Pacific-gull middens often occupy a small area (200 cm^2), are quite thin (0–3 cm), are found from just above high tide up to 70 feet above sea level (asl), and are often situated on prominent points, rock ledges, and limestone. The accumulations can be expected to lack artifacts, charcoal, and manuports.

Many birds prey predominantly on one molluscan species in a particular habitat. Examples are the concentration by gulls and crows on the gastropod *Thais lamellosa* or oystercatchers on the bivalve *Cerastoderma* [= *Cardium*] *edule*. Bird middens are also found on lagoons and river banks of inland Australia, the latter composed principally of the freshwater naiad *Velesunio ambiguis* (Jones and Allen 1978). In many coastal settings, particularly along the Pacific coast line, the human accumulations are marked by multiple species of molluscs such that single-species accumulations are suspect bird middens, possibly reworked by waves.

Birds also concentrate shells in nests. Scrub-fowl (*Megapodius reinwardt*) and Mallee-fowl (*Leipoa ocellata*) in Australia scrape together mounds of debris insulated with a layer of sand or earth and other materials to incubate their eggs. Some of these mounds exceed 10 m in height, 12 m in diameter (Bailey 1993:Fig. 8; Stone 1989). These egg mounds are quite variable in size and shape, often merge through connecting ridges into a horseshoe shape, and are located at spots between coast and woodland (Stone 1989). These birds may choose to create their nests at the edge of human shell discard areas in order to utilize that material.

The brown noddy tern lines its nests with marine shells and debris. Ten tern nests on a Gulf of Mexico island contained 12,435 g of shell, principally *Codakia orbicularis*. Two nests had over 2,200 g each (Wright and Kornicker 1962).

In addition to the *C. orbicularis* in each brown noddy tern nest, *Lucina pennsylvanica*, *Barbatia cancellaria*, other bivalve fragments, whole gastropods *Acmaea iamaicensis*, *Diodora listeri*, and fragments of *Busycon* sp. and *Scaphella* sp. were found in nests. Fish bones were also deposited there. This variety of material again suggests a human hand. With over 4,000 terns on the island, making approximately 2,000 nests, several with more than 2,200 g of shell within, the potential for the creation of archaeological "hot spots" from fallen nests is great.

The density of shells on a beach must be high in order to confuse paleontologists or archaeologists and density is controlled less by flock size than by water activity. On prograding beaches each high tide will bury the shells with sediment, and separate that tidal accumulation from earlier ones, as is the case in the oystercatcher example. In eroding beaches, each high tide will bury the shells by scouring and then redepositing less sediment which leaves little sediment separation between tidal cycles, concentrating shells rapidly. These shells become vulnerable to transport by wave or current activity and may accumulate in large numbers elsewhere on the waterfront, where they become candidates for archaeological sites or marine shell beds.

While the human versus bird origin for whole sites may present only minor problems for archaeologists to resolve (although see the debate in *Archaeology in Oceania* volume 26 which queries whether *all* of the mounded sites on the north Australian coast were created by scrub-fowl, and follow-up by Bailey 1993), the mixing of shells harvested by birds with those harvested by humans may be a rather significant formation process.

Several authors have noted the high proportion of *Turbo* opercula in Australian human shell deposits (e.g. Coutts 1969). In the two studies of Pacific-gull middens cited above, both noted the predominance of *Turbo* opercula while offering two different explanations. Teichert and Serventy (1947) reasoned that the cat's eye operculum was the densest part of this gastropod so that sites with a predominance of opercula and rare *Turbo* shells had weathered for a long time. Jones and Allen (1978) posited that *Turbo* meat adhered to the operculum after the shell had been smashed and was thus transported by the bird to the eating site with the meat. Either explanation could also explain the high number of opercula at human consumption sites, but the predator could be either bird or human. Birds may also be adding shells with particular fracture patterns to human sites, particularly those birds that drop shells from on high to crack them. Several studies have shown that the birds are nonspecific in their drop targets. White shell deposits may be attractive to them or the human deposits may sit sufficiently near to the surf zone to have accidental association with the dropped shells.

Formation of shell accumulations in marine settings
Both *in situ* shell beds and zones of shell are created underwater. Wave action in lakes has occasionally created gastropod zones at a depth of 8 to 10 m below the surface (Bobrowsky 1984).

In situ shell beds form during the rapid burial of living molluscan communities or through the accumulation of dead shells and sedimentation. There are several aspects of bed formation that serve to identify natural beds: shell articulation, orientation, sorting, and transport. It is not uncommon for archaeologists to report difficulty in determining the natural or cultural origin of a shell deposit (e.g. Watters et al. 1992). The following paleontological observations should offer some guidance.

Shell articulation   One of the earliest criteria for determining a natural shell deposit from a human-created one was the incidence of paired valves. For instance, Vanuxem (1843) reported that the total lack of paired valves in several large Chesapeake Bay oyster shell heaps was clear indication of human intervention. Articulation of valve pairs is a phenomenon thought to be a common occurrence in natural marine shell deposits but is, in fact, by no means a frequent phenomenon and varies according to the habit of the bivalve. From observations made in accumulations below the storm wave base in the northwestern Gulf of Mexico, 44 percent of the dead infauna were still paired while only 4.6 percent of the dead epifauna were (Callender et al. 1990). The high disarticulation rate could be the result of high water energy, scavenging at the time of death, or bioturbation of the sediments.

Side Sorting   Side sorting in marine shell deposits is indicative of the amount of shell transport. Albertzart and Wilkinson (1990:350) offer an equation for determining a significantly sorted assemblage. That equation is

$$P(L) = n!/(L!)(r!) \bullet 0.5^L \bullet (1 - 0.5)^r$$

where:

P = percent
L = number of left valves
n = number of total valves
r = number of right valves

Their procedure is first to calculate cumulative probability and then to determine the number of left valves in a sample of a given size which corresponds to that probability.

The side sorting of disarticulated bivalves is little influenced by habitat, abrasion or transport by littoral currents but is influenced by shell shape. Along the outside of Padre Island (Texas), the waves approach from the southeast carrying the "right valves toward the top of the swash zone and left valves at the toe of the forebeach slope" (Albertzart and Wilkinson 1990:354). If the wind direction changes, however, so will the direction of transport of the two valves. Twenty-five bulk samples of shells from the central Texas coast revealed that only *Anadara ovalis*, *Crassostrea*, *Noetia*, and *Rangia* valves side sorted. Right valves were more common in only eight samples for oyster and *Noetia* and in only eight samples for left valves for *Anadara ovalis* and *Rangia*. The authors concluded that sampling strategies are largely responsible for the illusion of a missing valve side.

A number of researchers have concluded that a significant number of one side in a deposit of bivalves indicates uneven hydrodynamic properties in the water body, such as beaches with a swash zone, or tides. Shimoyama and Fujisaka (1992:299), using a simulation, found, however, that small sample sizes and sample areas are responsible for this impression. They used identically shaped valves and found that valve side approached equity as shell diffusion increases and does so to an even greater degree when shape differences are allowed.

Shell orientation   Shells orient during growth in particular ways for differing reasons, e.g. infaunal bivalves must orient with siphons upward, epifaunal gastropods with opercula downward. The growth of subsequent generations of individuals upon older individuals will cause some reorientation of the dead shells (Callender et al. 1990). Molluscs preserved in their life position must have been covered with sediment very rapidly and then experienced little or no bioturbation.

Once dead, shells are subject to many reorienting processes. Shells in a wave system will come to orient perpendicular to the direction of water flow while empty shells will orient with their long axis parallel to the current direction. Paleontologists record the inclination to the bed and the azimuthal orientation of the long axis of individual shells. In land snails, several observers have recorded a random orientation of shells suggesting that a patterned distribution represents a disturbed deposit (Bobrowsky 1984:84).

With respect to the orientation of bivalved shells concave side upward or downward, strong currents, waves, and migrating ripples cause shells to orient predominantly concave down. In quiet water below storm wave base, concavity ratios are close to equity. Claims that shells in quiet water will rest concave up are probably reflecting the impact of commercial fishing, concluded Callender et al. (1990). On eroding or prograding back beaches along the central Texas coast, most shells are concave down (Albertzart and Wilkinson 1990). Resuspended shells, in either stagnant or moving water, will settle concave up. As the effective density of shells in water decreases so does the frequency of the concave up position, such that 50 to 69 percent of shells will settle concave up (Kidwell and Bosence 1991:156). Ronen (1980:167) dumped baskets of *Glycymeris* shells on a beach finding that 60–75 percent of the shells rested concave up.

Shell transport   The transport of exotic species from adjacent environmental zones is minimal in low energy settings such as lagoons, subtidal shallows, or tidal flats. Transport of shells through adjacent zones is a significant source of shells in high-energy settings such as barrier islands, shoals, and tidal inlets (Parsons and Brett 1991:28). Vermeij (1993:11) observed that "Drag, lift, and acceleration reaction in a sea coast setting have greater impact on larger and longer objects. Small/short objects are less impacted by water movement and forces."

The degree to which exotic shells contaminate geologic shell beds and skew efforts to reconstruct the past habitat has been explored by paleontologists. In a survey of this literature, Kidwell and Bosence (1991) report that transported

Table 5. *Characteristics of shell deposits accumulated by various agents*

				Type of accumulation				
Author	Human Gill	Human Bailey	Human Attenbrow	Redeposit H&S	Redeposit Attenbrow	Lake H&S	Gull Various	Marine Gill
Characteristic								
Gradual date sequence	x		unre					
Charcoal			x	x	x			
Blackened shell		x		x		no		
Stratigraphy	x		x	x	no	x		x
Flakes	x	unre	unre	x				
Tools	x	unre	unre					
Pebbles	x		unre	small	unre			
Fauna	x		unre		unre		x	
> 2 habitats			poss					
Inedible sizes	no	x	x	x	x		x	x
Single species	x	unre			unre		x	
Unworn shell	x		x	no	no		x	no
Broken shell	x		no		x		x	x
Paired shell			unre		unre		x	x
Shell grit				x	x			
Gravel				rounded				
Pumice	no			x	x	x		

Key: unre = unreliable characteristic; no = not present; poss = possible characteristic.
References: Gill 1954, Hughes and Sullivan 1974, Attenbrow 1992, Bailey 1993.

exotics were infrequently encountered in submerged deposits. Only 9 percent of the species in an ebb dominated tidal sound were exotics. Examining tidal flats, Frey and Dorjes (1988) found 8 to 25 percent of the species and 5 to 8 percent of the individuals to be exotic to the inner flats, 38 to 50 percent of the species and 6 percent of the individuals exotic in the middle flats, and 17 to 67 percent of the species in the outer flats, or 1–5 percent of the individuals. Greater than half of the individuals in the death assemblages were from the most common live species. Kidwell and Bosence concluded that differences in the death assemblage from the ordering of live species abundance are more likely to be the result of taphonomic processes than of ecologic ones. They found that water transport favors small shells of free-living epifauna and very shallow-burrowing infauna (1991:138).

Time averaging   Of greatest significance to paleontologists who attempt to reconstruct ancient or recent environments is the phenomenon of time-averaging. A survey of data from natural shell accumulations revealed that the longer a shell deposit has been accumulating, the greater the probability that shells from successive generations and habitats have been mixed and age–size class relationships modified by taphonomic processes. This situation worsens as distance from shore and depth of water increase such that near-shore deposits are a mixture of shells over several thousands of years and off-shore deposits accumulate shells over considerably longer periods. Testifying to the former estimate is that twelve *Strombus gigas* shells collected from the beach of Barbuda (West Indies) showed a range in radiocarbon dates of 5,480–1,755 rcy (radiocarbon years, Watters et al. 1992:39). Time averaging is created by biological, sedimentological, and taphonomic processes. It is also caused by modern human activities such as dredge spoil deposition and many sampling strategies used by archaeologists and paleontologists (Fursich and Aberhan 1990:143).

A mixture of shell preservation stages is a principal clue to identifying the reworked deposit. So is the presence in cultural deposits of predator-drilled and broken shells (Carucci 1992, Spanier 1986).

Comparison of the agents of accumulation
Table 5 summarizes characteristics of wave redeposited shell, marine shell beds, gull accumulations, lake deposits, and human accumulations evident in the literature from Australia. Similar characteristics are discussed in Verger (1959).

Some shell matrix sites along the Israeli coast contain *Glycymeris* valves primarily in the concave side down position, intermixed with rounded pot-sherds, and are found on a wide range of elevations. Because of the concave side down position and rounded sherds several investigators have interpreted these accumulations as natural shell accumulations, being either *in situ* beds or shells deposited by tsunami. Nevertheless, a basal layer of sharp angled sherds, a higher stratum of sandstone slabs supporting two (collapsed) storage jars whose sherds were sharp angled, and sherds coated with a lime solution indicated to Ronen (1980) that much of one Israeli deposit had never been in water, and was, instead, a carefully engineered platform with the valves intentionally turned concave side down. Further experimentation found that a sweeping motion, done three or four times, created a concave side down percentage similar to the proportions of undisturbed beds and of the contested deposits. Ronen recounts the use of shell as building material during various historic periods in Israel: in cement, as foundations, and as pavements.

It is clear that few of these characteristics in Table 5 are unique to humans or nature. Proportions and conditions of edible and inedible shells, pebbles, and shell grit, concave up or down ratios, as well as sizes of shells and their condition (e.g. Carucci 1992), can help to establish an argument for a primary or secondary deposit of shells. Archaeologists should endeavor to identify commensal and accidental species, as well as shells collected dead. The fragmentation, abrasion, corrosion, bioerosion, encrustation, drilling, and even species proportions contain valuable information which can reveal time-averaged samples, postdepositional impact on shell deposits, and taphofacies. Attenbrow (1992) considered the geographical setting and the distance of the deposit from the shore, as well.

Disturbance processes in shell deposits

Faunalturbation
Hundreds of plant and animal species are capable of disturbing archaeological stratigraphy and creating it. Among the animals of concern are those as tiny as termites, ants, crabs, and voles, and those as large as dogs and humans. The impact of a few of these bioturbators is explored below.

Earthworms   Earthworms process soil through their bodies and then cast (exude) processed dirt either below the surface in their tunnels or on the surface. Items 0.8 mm or smaller in greatest dimension, including many species of land snails, can be ingested as a consequence, to be fragmented or transported upward or downward by the worm. The voids created by tunneling worms also allow downward displacement of molluscs. While most worms work the A horizon, *Lumbricus terrestris*, a common worm in Europe and North America, works the A and B horizons. In rendzina soils of the British chalklands, earthworms create a stone-free zone 20–25 cm thick and lower the now temporally mixed snail assemblage to the bottom of that zone (Evans 1972:228). *L. terrestris* actually carries gastropod shells and seeds down to its aestivation chambers for lining. Carter (1990:499–505) states that rapid cast accumulation at the surface (5–10 mm/yr) results in upper A horizon assemblages of snail shells being a twenty- to thirty-year mixture. At this rate of casting a surface shell will be at the bottom of the A horizon in fifty years. Shells recovered in the B horizon must have fallen or been carried to that depth and, consequently, represent a time-averaged collection of much greater duration. A strongly positive gradient of many gastropods high in the stratigraphy and few at the bottom is probably due to rapid burial by worms (Evans 1972:211).

Stein (1983) provides a detailed study of earthworm bioturbation in a 4,000-year-old naiad shell mound in the US. The shell deposit is some 2 m deep but the resident earthworms (*Aporrectodea trapezoides* and two species of *Diplocardia*) can work soil to a depth of 6 m. They overwinter by moving away from the surface. This shell deposit and many others provide ideal habitat: porous silt-loam texture, moist soil, frost penetration to only 37 cm, and a slightly alkaline pH. Stein estimated that in this site of 1,345 m³ matrix volume, subsurface-casting earthworms completely digest that matrix every fifty-one years. The effects of this activity have been to obliterate features, alter and homogenize the soil chemistry and texture, reduce the vegetable and other biological matter to sizes less than 2.0 mm, and displace small items.

Hermit Crabs   Hermit crabs take up, move, and discard gastropod shells on a land surface. They cannot dig the dirt out of a shell nor can they dig very deep into the ground or into a deposit of shells (Carucci 1992). A microstratum of hermited, burned, and broken shells in association led Carucci to identify a buried floor or stable paleosurface in a site on Rock Island, Micronesia.

Terrestrial rodents   A number of rodent species bring land snails to their burrows. The pattern of predation on terrestrial snails – how the shells are bitten through – is unique to each individual rodent and provides evidence that burrows are filled with the snails collected by one rodent in its lifetime (Goodfriend 1991a:418).

In addition to fracturing and storing gastropod shells, rodents disturb the stratigraphy of shell matrix sites. Mole tunnel systems run up to 36 linear km quite near to the surface while their chambers are somewhat deeper. Their prey is earthworms (Bocek 1986:590). These and other burrowing animals create a zone of disturbance about 30 cm thick within which plant matter is moved downward and soil and objects from 0.6 cm to 5 cm in size are transported to the surface. Because burrowers tunnel under objects larger than 5 cm, those objects, and smaller ones, fall into the tunnels and settle out below the 30-cm earth-moving zone. This action creates what is known as "cobble zones." Bocek's study indicated that rodents create artifact frequency peaks above 30 cm, cobble zones below 30 cm, but impact on horizontal distributions insignificantly. The bones of recent burrowers should be found at the surface or at 30–50 cm in their chambers (Bocek 1986).

Fig. 15 Rodent tunnels in wall profile of the shell matrix Dogan Point site.

Rodent tunnels were seen during excavation at the 7,000-year-old Dogan Point site (Figure 15). Groundhog bone was found on the surface, vole at 35 cm, moles at the surface and at 30 cm, and shrew at 20 cm, suggesting that all the individuals were recently reworking the site. Rodents are probably responsible for the finding of 64 percent of the cobbles deeper than 30 cm (Claassen 1995b). A tunnel created a false humus zone in one wall at a depth of 45 cm; other tunnels passed under the shell deposit. Heavy tremolite boulders sat on top of shell in several locations. While humans could have placed these boulders on top of the shell, it is more likely that shell slumped into rodent tunnels passing under the boulders.

Marine Animals   Marine animals either tunnel through the sediment or over-turn sediment during feeding. Shell pockets are produced by the feeding activity of rays, shell concentrations by the burrowing activity of crustaceans, and shell layers by the feeding activity of worms such as *Arenicola* (Fursich and Aberhan 1990:143). The mixing by marine faunalturbators can extend 75 cm deep into the sediment of shallow water bodies with the most rapid mixing – movement of shells up to 30 cm per year – occurring in the upper 18 cm. A simulation of these mixing activities demonstrated that while it was "relatively easy to mix a sequence by introducing reworked fossils," it was difficult "to disorder a sequence by mixing fossils in place" (Cutler and Flessa 1990:231). In the former case, just a few reworked shells could significantly degrade the stratigraphic integrity. Shells up to 4,000 years old, eroded from a beach deposit, accounted for up to 85 percent of the surface shells in tidal channels in Bahia la Choya in the Gulf of California. Cutler and Flessa and other authors conclude that the effects of disorder can be minimized by increasing sample size at each horizon and increasing sample spacing.

Humans   Disruptions of shell deposits by humans can be as subtle as walking across surfaces or as obvious as mining the shell. I suspect that far more humans have considered the shells in heaps to be in storage than have considered them to be discarded, at the end of their usefulness.

Robert Muckle's (1985) trampling experiments were designed to examine fragmentation and vertical displacement of fragments. After 80, 160, 320, and 640 walking passes over *Saxidomus giganteus*, *P. staminea*, and *M. edulis*, the debris was screened through nested sieves to measure reduction. Particle size and rate of reduction varied by species. After 1,000 walks over shells resting on a loam substrate, 96 percent of the shell was found in the top two centimeters of loam, 3 percent 2–4 cm deep, and 1 percent 4–6 cm deep.

Msemwa (1994) observed activities on a modern shell heap in Tanzania, Africa. A hearth located in shade was periodically re-excavated by local people to lengthen its uselife. There resulted a ring of removed shells surrounding the hearth that slumped back into the excavation. Shells were also quarried from this shell processing site for flooring and supplemental chicken feed.

Shell from archaeological sites has been mined for industry and construction materials throughout history. Ancient ceremonial mounds of shell found along the Gulf of Mexico coast and bulk heads of shells fronting Pacific coastal sites give the appearance of secondary shell deposits. US colonial records indicate the practice of ringing apple trees, fertilizing fields, producing quicklime, and forming tabby and bricks with shells, often with instructions to get the shells from Indian sites. Live oak trees are an indicator plant for prehistoric shell deposits along the coast of the southeastern US. These trees – needed in boat building – were probably intentionally planted in shell matrix sites.

Lynn Ceci (1984) has ably reviewed many uses of archaeological shell (Table 6) and concluded that there are three economic motivations involved: to retrieve objects within the matrix, to reclaim the land surface under the deposit, or to harvest the shells themselves. In all three cases, the result is severely disrupted stratigraphy in at least a portion of the site or total destruction of the site (e.g. Figure 16).

The impact of taphonomy on regional histories
It should be obvious by now that the taphonomic processes described above will ultimately result in the visual disappearance of the exoskeletons of

Table 6. *Summary of the uses of "discarded" shell. (Modified with permission of Routledge Press, after Ceci 1984.)*

Agriculture	Construction	Commerce	Decor
midden farming	foundations	lime	walls
fertilizer:	fill	maize processing	graves
coarse aggregate	roads	oyster spat beds	yards
chemistry	parking lots	recreation – tourism	gardens
garden topsoil	track beds	shell temper	jewelry
golf course greens	sidewalks	betel and pinang nut quids	
tennis courts	effluent lines		
poultry feed	cisterns		
	tombs, cemeteries		
	sea walls		
	bleachers		
	mounds		
	flooring		
	platforms		
	building material:		
	coarse aggregate		
	quicklime		
	land fill		

molluscs. It is quite possible then that shell matrix sites and lenses of shell were once located in places and associated with cultures for which there is now no visible record of this site type. Archaeologists have credited rising sea level with obscuring Pleistocene-aged sites, but few archaeologists have credited calcium carbonate dissolution, abrasion, storms, sand incursion, or human removal with the ability to destroy vast numbers of sites and affect the record of shell exploitation in a region or for creating a record falsely credited to human accumulators. Just such possibilities exist, however, and have been raised by Bailey (1983c), Dortch et al. (1984), Godfrey (1989), Lampert (1981), Rowland (1989), Stone (1989), and Vanderwal (in Bird 1992) for shell matrix site distributions in northeastern and southern Australia, Moseley et al. (1992) for coastal Peru, and Bailey (1983c) for northern Spain.

Northeast Australia   Since the nineteenth century, the cultural origin of the shell-bearing sites of the Cape York Peninsula of northern Australia has been contended. Early in the dispute was their attribution to aboriginal activities and a response that they were scrub-fowl mounds (Gilbert in Gould 1865:169) aided by aboriginal assertions that they were bird nesting mounds. Nevertheless, their assumed human origin prevailed through yet another challenge that they were the product of water deposition (Bailey 1993) and a resurgence of the scrub-fowl origin. Instead, Bailey believes that molluscan resources were

Fig. 16 Removal of shell from the Bluffton site, St. John's River, Florida.

scarce in the past 1,000 years and that most of the molluscs collected were discarded in thin scatters on the sandy landscape where shells rapidly dissolved. Dissolution of shell explains the clustering of shell matrix sites on a 60-km stretch of the northern coast of Spain, as well (Bailey 1983c). Abrasive destruction and dissolution were cited to explain the absence of shell-bearing sites in southwestern Australia, too (Dortch et al. 1984). In favored places in all three cases, enough shells were discarded to establish a preservative environment while intermittent thin deposits disappeared.

In another Australian case study, the destructive impact of the winds and water of cyclones on a regional archaeological record has been documented (Bird 1992). Bird compared the sites and site conditions after two cyclones in 1988 and 1989 with the survey information on seventy-eight sites she had compiled in 1987 for the northeast coast. The initial cyclone inundated up to 1,800 hectares of plain and eradicated fourteen sites, 15 percent of those recorded pre-storm. Twenty-three (25 percent) additional sites were modified by wind shearing which reduced the height of deposits, and water erosion which truncated sites. Wave-reworked material was found on the beach and several sites were deflated. In the second cyclone, the beach was breached in eight places, dunes were reshaped, and thousands of hectares were flooded.

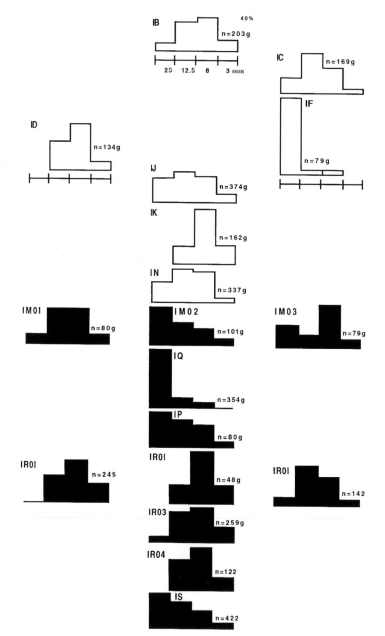

Fig. 17 Grain size distributions, Veneridae clams, Unit 310/300 British Camp site.

Thirty-seven more sites were eradicated including the largest site on record and five sites were reduced in size. In neither storm were new sites exposed or created or old sites buried (Bird 1992:79). In all, 55 percent of the sites recorded in 1987 were eradicated. Rowland (1989:37) estimates that 12,000 cyclones have impacted on this coast in the past 5,500 years. It is no wonder, then, that the coastal sites of this region date to within the past 500 years.

Virgin Islands Lundberg (1985) has brought under suspicion all reputed pre-ceramic era sites on St. Thomas Island in particular and on other Caribbean islands in general. Lundberg untangles a web of natural and cultural formation processes which are responsible for the modern-day juxtaposition of shells and lithic debris at several sites. At one site, the thin and evenly distributed oyster shells, located in the topographically lowest area of site, are an *in situ* natural bed buried during beach progradation. One shell was radiocarbon dated to ca. 1150 BC. Crab holes and tunnels attest to the frantic activity of these faunalturbators in bringing shells to the surface where they have mixed with lithic debris characteristic of the ceramic era culture (although fewer than ten sherds are present in the site). Conch columella "artifacts" identified by an earlier excavation were reinterpreted as naturally fragmented and water worn, rather than shaped by humans. Historic period artifacts span its entire depth, lending credence to the author's claim that some prehistoric items have been transported upward since deposition. On the basis of a pre-ceramic date and the lack of sherds, this and numerous other aceramic sites on St. Thomas and elsewhere in the Caribbean have been interpreted as evidence of a pre-ceramic migration across the Caribbean. Lundberg reminds the reader that humans are not the only movers of shells, nor the only agent of association between shells and artifacts, reminiscent of the Brennan (1977)–Sanger (1981) debate in the northeastern United States.

3.3   Issues in archaeological excavation

The topics previously covered have many implications for archaeological sites and their excavation. Foremost among these implications are that shells should be treated as sedimentary particles and that shell matrix sites and deposits are impacted on by time-averaging processes to some degree which must be determined by the excavator.

Shells as sedimentary particles

Shells have density and roundness, are subject to transport, and offer resistance in air and fluids. In short, they behave in wind, water, and soil like sediments. They are impacted on by a host of physical forces both before and after discard. Classification of shells as sedimentary particles is well established in the geological sciences while rare among archaeologists (e.g. Carter 1990; Dirrigl 1995; P. Ford 1992; Stein 1983; 1992c; Thomas 1985). The chief proponent of this viewpoint is geoarchaeologist Julie Stein and it is most clearly articulated in articles by Stein, Madsen, and Ford in the British Camp report (Stein 1992c). Stein (1983) approached both the 4,000-year-old freshwater SMA Carlston Annis shell mound (Kentucky, US) and the marine shell matrix site of British Camp (Washington, US) as a geologist, asking how the shells, sediments, rocks, and artifacts got into position. In both cases the deposits consisted of over twenty species of molluscs.

> To interpret depositional histories, the size of shells as they are removed from the archaeological context is the variable measured [Figure 17]. Grain size [shell size] distributions reflect the manner in which the shell entered the archaeological record (biological and sedimentological source) and the manner in which the shell has been altered since deposition occurred… The materials that became smaller after they were deposited provide information about changes in the archaeological deposit since deposition, but the materials that entered the record already small provide information about source, transport agents, and environments of deposition. (P. Ford 1992:287)

Stein (1992c various), Stein and Teltser (1989), and P. Ford (1992) point out that humans are a transport agent carrying shells in suspension. In suspension, as whole shells, their size reflects their biological source for there are few processes that can transport whole large shells. In single-species deposits variation in mean sizes between subdeposits probably reflects variation in sedimentological source primarily rather than biological source. In situations where the excavation process contributes significantly to shell size (e.g. *Crassostrea virginica* fractures easily during excavation) this analytical approach must be applied with caution.

Time-averaging

Shell deposits for which more than one discard event is anticipated are time averaged deposits. Time-averaging is furthered most notably by bioturbation but other formation processes contribute to the mixing, addition, and subtraction of classes of remains and stratigraphy. The characteristics of shell deposits that leave them vulnerable to postdepositional mixing "are increased porosity, permeability, and alkalinity, low densities of historically diagnostic artifacts and high densities of shell, and high probabilities of being saturated by the adjacent body of water" (Stein 1992b:1).

Porosity

Porosity of shell deposits should be of major concern to archaeologists. A shell matrix is more porous than a soil matrix and consequently one in which small objects, such as gastropods, flakes, and bones fall downward readily. Being porous it is easy for earthworms, rodents, snails, and tree roots to penetrate the deposit, for charcoal, flakes, seeds, sediments, and fresh water to fill in the interstices. Therefore, it is wrong to assume the contemporaneity of artifacts and ecofacts or the contemporaneity of charcoal and shell pairs at the same level (i.e. Burleigh and Kerney 1982:33), a point argued by others such as Louis Brennan (1977).

To check for downward movement of sea urchin spines through the shell matrix, Pamela Ford (1992:293) calculated the abundance of spines relative to sea urchin jaw elements and test fragments for each facies (deposit) and ranked the percentages for facies from two major zones in the British Camp site. A Mann–Whitney U test indicated no significant difference in the relative abundance of sea urchin spines compared with other sea urchin skeletal elements in the two zones.

The distance between right and left valves of bivalves may indicate the amount of disturbance in a deposit. Koike (1979) mapped and then paired left and right valves of *Meretrix lusoria* excavated from a Jomon (Japan) house. Seventy percent of the pairs were separated by 20 cm or less, with most movement in a horizontal direction and parallel to the slope of the deposit. Little postdepositional disturbance of the deposit was indicated. Given that the results of experiments by Muckle (1985:62) indicate that disarticulated valve pairs usually travel some distance apart upon impact with the ground, their distance apart at the time of excavation may not be indicative of deposit disturbance.

Permeability and alkalinity
Kent (1988:9–11) identifies several taphonomic processes at work on shells in soil which increase the rate of dissolution through the formation of calcium bicarbonate. Plowing increases water percolation and pulls shells to the surface where weathering processes are the most intense. The burrowing activity of worms in particular but also of other creatures facilitates rainwater percolation and exposure to atmospheric oxygen, increasing the rate of chemical decay. Earthworms displace organics downward whose decay releases acids which accelerate the formation of calcium bicarbonate and thus the leaching of calcium carbonate. Plant roots increase the acidity of the immediate environment which increases the rate of chemical alteration. Frost heaving of soil will move large objects – like valves – upward exposing them to more oxygen which accelerates decomposition via chemical weathering.

Whether a shell is situated in an alkaline or acidic environment determines the resistance of $CaCO_3$ to dissolution, determines the type of crystals formed during permineralization, and governs recrystallization. Palmer and Williams (1977) found that the upper levels of shell matrix sites in Florida had pH values which ranged from neutral to moderately acidic but were more alkaline in the lower levels because of less organic matter. All levels measured had a pH in the range of 6.4 to 8.6.

The pH of humic acids is 3.9 and of calcium humate 9.4; iron is mobile at pH 5.5. The reddish-brown color of soil in some situations is due to the transport of ferric humates which are formed in the humus. As the decomposing organics catch in depressions in the site and release humic acids, they "combine with iron leached from the clay to form iron humates. When the leached solution is neutralized by calcium bicarbonate solutions, goethite is precipitated" (Palmer and Williams 1977:24). Goethite occurs in small, hard, reddish-brown nodules up to 9 mm in diameter of hydrous iron oxide.

Joel Gunn's (1995) analysis of the Osprey Marsh site resulted in the discovery that bone, charcoal, and shell will be better preserved in shell clusters containing 2,000 to 6,000 g of oyster shell, than in larger or smaller clusters. Apparently of greatest relevance in preservation is pH. Clusters in this size range appear to have the appropriate pH because bone dissolves in settings both too alkaline and too acidic.

Inundation/saturation
Saturation of a shell deposit from the bottom upward by a high water table was responsible for the creation of two major stratigraphic zones at the British Camp site (Stein 1992a). Greater rates of modifying processes in the lower, saturated zone changed the identifiability of species between the two zones. A Mann–Whitney U test was employed to test the null hypothesis of no difference between the relative abundance of genus-level identifications (*Clinocardium* sp.) and species-level identifications (*Clinocardium nuttallii*), calculated for each facies grouped by zone (P. Ford 1992:291–292). The hypothesis could not be rejected.

The effects of inundation of deposits by tides were demonstrated in experiments conducted by Wing and Quitmyer (1992). In two experimental middens built on two islands in Charlotte Harbor, Florida, 23 percent and 1 percent of the oysters deposited were missing after six months. Ninety-nine percent and 99.6 percent of the uncooked small fish and 75 percent and 87 percent of the uncooked larger fish were missing after six months. Cooked fish survived six months at a much higher rate. Intrusions into these two middens were also noted upon excavation. In Midden I, 554 sprouted seeds were removed, 159 small marine molluscs had been added by agents unknown, and 5 unplanted fish were found. This midden had been inundated for a short period during the experiment and evidenced the greater number of shells lost from and added to the midden. Midden II had hundreds of small land snails but no other obvious intrusions. These two middens indicate that shell loss and midden contents vary with the nature of postdepositional events.

A reading of the paleontological taphonomic literature leads to the conclusion that, for archaeological shell deposits, the working of younger shells into older deposits is a greater problem for stratigraphy than is *in situ* vertical movement of shells of the same age. Mixing will be facilitated by differently sized shells, differently shaped shells, or sediment heterogeneity. Holding sediment constant, shell heaps of multiple species occupied multiple times will suffer from time-averaging processes more than will single species deposits because of the size and shape differences. However, multiple species make it easier to assess visually the extent of mixing. Mixing is fastest and most significant in situations of low net sedimentation while decay should be fastest and most significant in situations of high net sedimentation and water percolation. Time-averaging processes compromise radiocarbon dates, particularly comparisons of "paired" charcoal and shell samples, and shell seasonality studies. Deposits affected to a great extent by time averaging are unsuitable for paleoecological reconstructions.

But there is hope for the archaeologist wishing to investigate the original human behavior responsible for the accumulation with appropriate statistics the arbiter. The Duwamish No. 1 deposit of multiple species in Seattle, Washington, had been assumed to represent a deflated mass of thousands of discard episodes over many years and that all original patterns of species composition had probably been eradicated. The most surprising aspect of the analysis was that the samples from the general heap and from lenses clustered into the same groups as had the samples from features. Far less disturbance of discard events had occurred, apparently, than was assumed at the start of the project. Instead, it was evident that four behavioral chains, anchored by the types of species collected, were visible in the shell lenses and larger deposit (Campbell 1981:242).

3.4   Issues in archaeological laboratory analysis

What processes continue to work once a shell is curated? What is the impact of taphonomic processes on archaeological analytical techniques? These issues are examined in this section.

Curation and conservation of shell

To preserve shells too fragile to excavate individually, Kent recommends removing a chunk of deposit that will fit in a 5 gal bucket and immersing it in a 5 percent gelatin solution (dissolve 50 g gelatin in 950 ml hot tap water) for 24 hours, freshened with another 5 percent bath. After a second 24 hours, drain and cover the mass with a 10 percent formalin bath (commercially available). After 24 hours drain off liquid and air-dry the shell in the bucket for two weeks or more. Clean the shells with a soft brush and infiltrate the shells with polystyrene. (To make polystyrene, dissolve enough styrofoam cups in 900 ml of toluene, *using a fume chamber*, to make a total volume of 1,000 ml. Use gloves and do not inhale [Kent 1988:103].)

After excavation, cleaning of the shell surface is needed. A stiff brush and a dental tool can clean adhering matter off the surface. A cleaner that will not attack the $CaCO_3$ is ethyl acetate. Household chlorine compounds will remove vegetation and sponges but will also bleach the shell if exposure lasts too long. Luster can be restored with a greasy coating such as mineral oil or vaseline (Andrews 1981:xxiii–xxiv). Limy deposit removal requires full-strength muriatic acid and running water (do not touch the shell or acid with skin during treatment) and a paraffin coating over areas to be protected from the acid. Not all species can withstand exposure to this acid.

It is occasionally necessary to stabilize shells for analysis or conservation. Valves that have lost their conchiolin (exposed prisms, deeply incised growth lines) should be cleaned for one to three seconds in 10 percent acetic acid (Kent 1988:13). Valves that have been burned have calcium carbonate crystals adhering to their surface and should be cleaned gently with a soft brush and then hardened with either plastic or gelatin (Kent 1988).

Hardening solutions recommended by Kent for very badly preserved molluscan valves are gelatin and formalin infiltration followed by infiltration of polystyrene in toluene, or simply the latter preparation. For moderately degraded valves a brush application of polystyrene is possible as is infiltration with gelatin and formalin. For completely dry specimens, soaking in a solution of cellulose acetate in acetone is common (Kent 1988). All of these preservative recipes will render the valves unsuitable for ^{14}C and chemical analysis.

Storage of shells in wood-derived containers or formaldehyde resins is to be avoided. Acid-free tissues or inert foam should be used to house shell artifacts and these should be stored in baked enamel steel cabinets, in a dry environment. Wood storage cabinets should be sealed with varnish and thoroughly dried (Davis 1988:14).

Even with new storage arrangements, the old chlorides, formates, and calcium acetates (salts) can continue to damage the shell. Removal of the salts is necessary. Powdery shells often can be found in museum collections. If the shell powder is water soluble, slightly alkaline with chloride levels of 2–4 ppm, then Byne's disease is indicated (Davis 1988). This powder of calcium acetate (or calcium formate or calcium chloride) is formed in the presence of acetic and formic acids found particularly in oak drawers and cardboard. The shells most susceptible are those contaminated with sea salt which hold water molecules from the air in the storage facility. The effects of the deterioration are pitted surfaces and powder. As the pitting of the shell increases, so does the surface area, accelerating the disease. Aragonitic shells are more dense than calcite shells and are less susceptible to Byne's disease.

Kent (1988:16–18) provides a good discussion of techniques for testing for salts, and hardening valves. Briefly, salt testing involves placing a whole powdered shell in distilled or dechlorinated water for one to two hours with occasional agitation and then decanting 1 ml of solution to which are added two drops of 10 percent silver nitrate solution (1 g silver nitrate dissolved in 99 ml of distilled water). Cloudy water is indicative of salts. To remove salts soak the valves in multiple dechlorinated water baths until the salt test is clear. The wet shells should be oven dried at ca. 40°C.

Effects on archaeological analytical techniques

The various taphonomic processes take their toll on shell chemistry. Of concern for archaeologists are chemical composition, isotopes, and amino acids, and the pursuits of paleoenvironmental reconstruction, shell sourcing, dating, and seasonality.

What are the base levels for the important elements in shell? Fresh shell is approximately 40 percent calcium (38–43 percent found Claassen and Sigmann 1993). Shells that lack conchiolin (through degradation or heating) will have less organic matter and, consequently, proportionately more calcium (> 40 percent). In living molluscs, aragonitic skeletons have Sr^{2+} levels of 2,000 to 4,000 ppm. Strontium concentrations are higher in outer shell layers of marine species and lower in inner layers. Iron and manganese levels in shallow marine creatures are in the low 10s ppm. Mg^{2+} is decreased at higher latitudes and in deeper water in high magnesium calcite skeletons. Aragonitic shells have less Mg, ca. 1,000 ppm (Tucker 1991:85–86). Other factors such as the geochemistry of a watershed affect the levels of Mg, Fe, and most other elements. Within the eastern United States, shells living in estuaries of the Gulf of Mexico have higher Mg values than those of the Atlantic. The highest Fe levels are in those shells from rivers draining the mid-Atlantic and Appalachicola, Florida region.

Loss of "marine" or "normal" Mg and Sr is common during shell alteration as is an increase in Fe and Mn if the calcitic shell is in a reducing environment (Pirrie and Marshall 1990:340). It is highly likely that shells have absorbed some iron from their sediment matrix while losing some calcium and strontium. As Whitmer et al. (1989) point out, the question is not whether exchange has taken place, for it surely has, but whether the amount of exchange precludes meaningful elemental assays. Recrystallization, apparent by the absence of drusy (an insoluble residue or encrustation) calcium and preservation of lamellar structure, alters, but preserves to varying degrees, the original chemistry (Tucker 1991:90).

Dissolution of the aragonitic skeleton and the subsequent infilling by calcite (evident as encrustation) result in the complete eradication of the original shell chemistry. While the calcite:aragonite ratio is potentially useful when correlated with oxygen isotope assay for determining local paleotemperature, the dissolution of aragonite has frustrated many such attempts (Dodd and Stanton 1981).

Oxygen isotopes

Isotopes (a species of atom with differing atomic mass and physical properties) are precipitated through the mantle from water inhaled by the mollusc in equilibrium with its water habitat. An increase in water temperature results in a decrease in the ratio of ^{18}O to ^{16}O and ^{17}O (Higham 1996:248) in the new calcium carbonate deposited by the mantle. For tropical water the oxygen isotope range is $+2$ to -4 ppm in molluscs. At this point, I want to discuss the various taphonomic processes that will impact on a shell's suitability for this type of analysis as well as the procedure itself and leave the detailed presentation of the technique until Chapter 6. Isotopes are also discussed in Chapters 5 and 7.

Requirements for an accurate temperature estimate from oxygen isotopic measurements in fresh shells are (quoted from Killingley 1981:153, but see also Higham 1996; Shackleton 1973)

(1) "The animals must deposit $CaCO_3$ in thermodynamic equilibrium with the ambient water."

(2) "The shell must grow throughout the annual temperature range."

(3) "The specimen should live in open water and not in locally confined areas (e.g. rock pools [and estuaries]), where temperature changes would be abnormal."

(4) "A reasonable estimate must be available of the oxygen isotopic composition of the ocean water from which the shell precipitated."

It can prove difficult to know the paleowater ^{18}O value. Even without this value, however, relative temperature reconstructions (e.g. colder water, warmer water), particularly useful for harvest-season estimates, can be offered (e.g. Deith 1986; Higham 1996; Killingley 1981).

There are several points at which taphonomic processes can void a shell's suitability for oxygen isotope analysis. Of concern are abrasion to the surface layer of calcium carbonate, changes in microstructure, and interaction with ground water or fresh water.

Abrasion to the surface layers of calcium carbonate of bivalves is a major impediment to sampling along the growth axis for seasonality work (Killingley 1981) since each horizontally stacked shell layer is a seasonal or annual increment. To sample the same year, only surface calcium carbonate should be taken.

The various microstructures of shell contain different delta (symbolized as ∂) ^{18}O and ∂ ^{13}C percentages (Pirrie and Marshall 1990:340). Again, sampling too deeply into the shell can mix microstructures (see Figure 8). Furthermore, *changes* in microstructure, such as that when aragonite converts to calcite, affect the assay as does recrystallization. Deith (1985:125–126) reports that some molluscan species are more likely to recrystallize than others. Limpet shells are attacked by blue-green algae which leave cavities in the shell. In places where seawater temperature is high, the holes are likely to be filled with secondary carbonate that could be either older or younger than the death of

. the subject specimen. This secondary carbonate disqualifies the specimen for isotopic assay.

Oxygen isotopic values rarely increase during shell dissolution. Of greatest concern to analysts is the possibility of postdepositional exchange of oxygen atoms with those in the ground water or in fresh water. Decreases in oxygen isotopic values are expected where alteration of shell takes place in ground water or fresh water, with their lighter isotopic load derived from the break-down of terrestrial organics, or at elevated temperatures (Pirrie and Marshall 1990:340). Uncharacteristically light isotopic evaluations should indicate freshwater isotopic exchange.

Finally, many investigators like to establish their temperature expectations for the archaeological shells by assaying modern shells, often collected dead from a nearby beach. A better strategy is to collect living animals, recalling that Flessa and Kowalewski (1994:162) found shell assemblages from shallow, near-shore environments to contain shells hundreds of years dead. Clearly, beach shells cannot be assumed to be recently dead.

Dating shells
Two dating techniques are based on changes in shell after death: radiocarbon and protein decay, including amino acid racemization.

Radiocarbon Radiocarbon dating of shell is often a contentious activity as well as a confusing one but there is no good reason to eschew the use of marine shells in dating. Before discussing some of the taphonomic impacts on shells (other than ^{14}C decay), a few definitions are needed.

Fractionation refers to the selection for or discrimination against any of the carbon isotopes, ^{14}C, ^{13}C, or ^{12}C, during processes such as metabolism. $\partial\,^{13}C$, a measure of the ratio $^{13}C/^{12}C$, reflects fractionation in a sample which makes the age appear too *young* (the upper ocean water is about 4 percent to 5 percent deficient in ^{14}C). It is necesary to correct an age for fractionation (Little 1995).

Since the oceans contain old carbon which can be incorporated into newly deposited shell by the living animal, marine shells can also yield dates which are too *old*. A factor is needed to correct for this older carbon which is reservoired in the upper ocean, and it is known as the reservoir factor, symbol R. The reservoir effect today in Antarctica is calculated as $+885 \pm 45$ yrs, in the Mediterranean as 135 ± 85 yrs (Flessa and Kowalewski 1994:159), in the Alaskan Peninsula 814 yrs (Southon et al. 1990), and in the Hudson River valley of New York, 402 yrs (Little 1995). On the east coast of the United States, the fractionation and reservoir effects tend to cancel each other, and "marine shell ^{14}C ages are routinely reported without corrections for [fractionation and reservoir effect]. This is justified, so long as the ocean water ^{14}C deficiency is around 4 to 5%" (Stuiver et al. in Little 1995:122).

After adjusting a date on shell for fractionation and reservoiring, the resulting date needs to be calibrated. Marine samples derive carbon from a marine cycle, not the atmospheric cycle used by trees, so they should not be calibrated with the tree ring calibration curves. Stuiver and Braziunas (1993) have provided marine calibration models. The reservoir factor is part of this calibration.

"If you know an average R (it varies with time), you may subtract it from the shell conventional age to obtain a charcoal-equivalent age for the shell. Recently, Stuiver and Braziunas (1993: Figure 15) have produced charts by which to determine a shell ΔR from a contemporary charcoal conventional age" (Little 1995:122). A means for calculating an average ΔR for a region then is needed for calibration of a conventional shell age. In an effort to create an average ΔR for the Dogan Point site in New York, Little (1995) turned to projectile point and shell date pairs because, unfortunately, calibration by either marine or tree ring model will give results within 100 years for benthic specimens but may show a greater difference with estuarine species (Little 1993b).

The decay rate of radioactive carbon is independent of taphonomic processes. The presence of old carbon is, however, entirely due to diagenetic processes which occurred prior to the life of the subject shell. The quantity of ^{13}C and thus ∂ ^{13}C is reflected in the shell mineralogy. Since aragonitic mineralogy will convert to calcitic, the ^{13}C isotope will be impacted. Recrystallization, erosion, and boring can incorporate younger or older carbon into the sample.

Naiad shells and land snails are particularly maligned as radiocarbon dating samples because of the old carbon problem. Land snails actually ingest calcium carbonate in their grazing and boring. Some live on limestone, many on other molluscs, and many ingest calcium carbonate from loess and sand, calcium which is then deposited in their shells. A maximum of 50 percent of the shell could be old carbon resulting in an age error of one ^{14}C half life theoretically. Some species of snail incorporate at least 10 percent inorganic carbon into their shells giving rise to a ^{14}C assay about 1,000 years excessive (Burleigh and Kerney 1982:32). The actual age excesses have been recorded as high as 3,000 years and as low as 700 years (Goodfriend 1987) although there is no problem with radiocarbon ages in some species and settings (Burleigh and Kerney 1982:32–36; Goodfriend and Mitterer 1993). It is possible to estimate a correction for particular snail species, such as 500 years for *Poteria* in Jamaica (Goodfriend and Mitterer 1993:20) or 1,500 years for several Negev Desert snails (Goodfriend 1991b).

Either younger carbon can be incorporated into the shell during recrystallization, or older carbon through encrustation or boring during life or after death of the creature. Goodfriend (1987:160) has detailed the method by which samples should be cleaned to remove secondary carbon on or in land snails and most radiocarbon labs process bivalves in an appropriate manner. If a shell has a visible rind (analogous to a hydration rim on obsidian) when viewed in cross section in the prismatic zone, the shell should not be radiocarbon dated. Nor should a shell that is riddled with bore holes be submitted for dating. Furthermore, "If a fossil has $\partial\ {}^{13}C$ lying somewhere between the value for its modern day counterpart and the value for its enclosing environment, then this indicates postdepositional exchange of carbon and consequently contamination by younger ${}^{14}C$" (Chappell and Polach 1972).

Protein decay   Schofield (1937) classified Natal South African sites on the basis of the condition, or deterioration, of the shells. Schoute-Vanneck proposed in 1960 that the loss of conchiolin, or proteinaceous matter from shell, could be used as the basis for a relative dating technique and offered examples from South African shell-bearing sites. Assessments of the conchiolin ratio (conchiolin to calcium carbonate) in *Perna perna* shells from four superimposed layers of a site showed decreases in the ratio with depth, as predicted.

Schoute-Vanneck's procedure was refined by Buist (1963) and supplanted by Anderson (1973). Anderson criticized Buist's use of *Chione stutchburyi* and Schoute-Vanneck's site sampling strategy as well as his laboratory procedure. New Zealand species found particularly useful by Anderson were *Perna canaliculus*, *Mytilus edulis*, and *Cellana denticulata*. While progressively older archaeological specimens conformed to expectations about the lessening amount and percentage of conchiolin, fresh shells did not. Apparently in the case of recently dead shells calcium carbonate leaching is initially higher than conchiolin decay (Anderson 1973:557).

A sophisticated version of conchiolin decay dating measures proportions of various proteins bound to free amino acids (Powell et al. 1991). These authors have urged that individual shells not be dated yet.

A more common amino acid dating technique used on molluscs is racemization dating. "Natural proteins are comprised of twenty different amino acids linked by peptide bonds. The strengths of individual peptide bonds vary as a function of the amino acids that comprise them" (Qian et al. 1995:1117). Individual amino acids break away from their protein bonds at different (non-linear) rates during diagenesis and the rate of protein breakdown overall decreases with time. After 200 years through 500 years of diagenesis the accumulation rates of serine, glutamic acid, and glycine slow significantly. Free alanine and free aspartic acid accumulate in a nearly linear manner over at least a 1,700-year period. Most of the protein breakdown does not occur in the same unit of time – some of the free amino acids are lost early on in a shell's history while most of the proteins are still being freed (Powell et al. 1991). Unfortunately, a 1995 assessment of protein decay (Qian et al. 1995:1113) stated that "the mechanisms involved in the diagenesis of proteins remain largely speculative." Problematic are "inadequate techniques for separation of proteinaceous materials into various molecular weight components," the interaction of protein with other organic constituents, variations in the preservation environment, and contaminants.

All of the amino acids in living shells are of the L-amino type. Once the animal dies, these acids begin to convert to the non-proteinaceous D-amino type, a process known as "racemization." Each amino acid has its own racemization rate. Aspartic acid racemizes fastest and can date on a scale as fine as years. Isoleucine and glutamic acid racemize the slowest. In addition, the rate of racemization over time for any one amino acid varies. The initial rate of racemization in tropical land snails of various species was 0.05/100 years but slowed to 0.04/100 years after 100 to 300 years of diagenesis. Racemization rates also differ by shell microstructure with nacre racemizing much more rapidly than prismatic shell (Goodfriend et al. 1995:1128).

Sources of contamination and interference with racemization are (1) the hydrolysis process of sample preparation (Goodfriend et al. 1995; Qian et al. 1995) which results in modern shells which have no D-amino acids showing D-amino acids on the order of 0.03 to 0.08, (2) the temperature of the depositional environment, and (3) the pH of the depositional environment. Inner shell is better buffered from pH changes than is surficial shell which dictates that thin-walled shells, surface $CaCO_3$, and small particle carbonate materials be avoided. Goodfriend (1991b) states that the depth of burial of the sample does not affect the rate of racemization. Best for use are fossil shells from benign environments, such as the deep sea, the tropics, and caves (Hardial and Simpson 1989:58).

Racemization occurs in the presence of water. Goodfriend et al. (1995:1129) speculate that racemization is retarded in empty shells stored in cabinets, where sufficient moisture is absent. However, amino acids can be added to a valve assay through the accidental inclusion of endobionts (clionid sponges, boring clams, gastropods), secondary carbon exchanged with the water in the depositional environment, and inclusion of the periostracum. These contaminants can be eliminated by baths of 30 percent H_2O_2 and 12N HCl (Powell et al. 1991:53).

Seasonality using growth lines
Shells which have been subjected to high heat and then recrystallize lack the original microstructure and surface details and are, therefore, unsuitable for growth line analysis. Fractures in sectioned shells will tend to refract light in such a way as to cause glare when using a microscope. Actual recrystallization of the shell, due to ground water, may cause an encircling band of recrystallized shell (like a hydration rim) to form from the surface inward, which can obscure days' and even years' worth of growth increments.

3.5   Conclusions

It is clear that taphonomic processes modify shell accumulations. Procedures as basic as counting and weighing shells are plagued with numerous, uncontrollable problems such as differential preservation due to depositional conditions, weight loss through dissolution, vulnerability to scavengers, subtraction by humans. More complex operations, such as paleoenvironmental reconstruction, are also afflicted with problems. Most durable in paleoenvironmental reconstructions will be statements about trophic structure, slightly more compromised are statements about taxonomic composition, and least reliable will be numerical abundance statements (Staff et al. 1986:442).

In paleontology, where much sophisticated actualistic work on shell taphonomy has been undertaken, Kidwell and Bosence (1991:118) applaud workers for the creation of classificatory schemes which facilitate assemblage comparisons:

> Classification schemes for fossil assemblages seek taphonomically comparable assemblages. They recognize (a) descriptive categories based on shell diagenesis (Koch and Sohl 1983) and biostratinomic features (Johnson 1960, Brandt 1989) or (b) inferential categories based on likely source of shells, scale of time-averaging, or complexity of post-mortem history.

Archaeologists desperately need comparable classificatory schemes to cope with the variability that nature and humans have created in culturally collected shell deposits. Basic attempts at classificatory schemes were attempted in the 1980s (Chapter 1). More relevant attempts such as that by Dirrigl (1995) have been presented in this chapter.

As for work still needed in paleontology, Kidwell and Bosence (1991:152) call for the development of (a) "diagnostic criteria for specific taphonomic processes at the level of both individual shells and whole assemblages and (b) ranking the relative importance of different processes in a given environment and among environments. Essential to this work will be the development of standardized scales for describing shell condition." Again, no better advice could be offered to archaeologists working with shell deposits.

Hundreds of suggestive statements that reflect experimental work with shells, other classes of material, and shell deposits themselves, can be found in our literature and in conference conversations. By and large, however, much of this material remains anecdotal. We need to undertake experiments with controls and variables, aimed at elucidating formation processes, and to formalize those quasi-experiments already underway. Experiments with land snail assemblages are needed (suggestions in Thomas 1985:148). Experiments utilizing artificial deposits where various classes of artifact and ecofact can be observed, and work in modern deposits should be conducted. Canneries and seafood shops have associated mounds and middens. In the Mississippi River watershed, musselers working for the Japanese pearl industry are creating shell mounds. Herein lie invaluable data on mound collapse, plant colonization and succession, shell attrition, and mound intrusions. We need simultaneously to engage in more ethnoarchaeology and experimentation while excavating shell-bearing sites facies by facies, deposit by deposit, with probabilistic sampling. The knowledge we gain through experimentation will benefit not only those working with shell-bearing sites but also those working in other site types and disciplines.

4

QUANTIFICATION OF
ARCHAEOLOGICAL SHELL

Quantification of shell debris is done typically to reconstruct the environment, to examine site formation processes, or to explore human behavior. Whatever the purpose, the validity of the interpretation depends on the representativeness of the sample of shells examined. The sample of shells available to and manipulated by the analyst must be representative of the site from which it came. With an adequate sample, shell counts and metrics can be generated. Quantification of shells by species, size, and weight is the basis for addressing questions about sample size, fragmentation, abundance, richness, and ubiquity and intensity of exploitation, and, ultimately, questions about site formation, spatial patterning, and habitat reconstruction, presented in subsequent chapters.

4.1   Sampling

Sampling is a difficult issue in archaeology for it must be addressed on many different levels and often must be applied to universes of unknown size. While the excavator must be concerned with the question of adequate subsurface exposure for the research questions under study, the shell analyst must question whether there is an adequate sample of shells for determining habitat, species proportions, the seasonality of harvesting, etc. "Until we can obtain statistically significant samples, our work must to a certain extent remain experimental" (Voigt 1975:88).

Sampling the shell-bearing site

How to sample a shell-bearing site has been discussed by Ambrose (1967), Bowdler (1983), Campbell (1981), Maxwell (1989b), Peacock (1978), Trinkley and Adams (1994), Waselkov (1987), Widmer (1989), and many others. Most archaeologists view the site as the appropriate sampling universe yet give no indication as to total site area or volume. (Higham [1996:2], Sorant and Shenkel [1984] appended by Shenkel [1986], and Stein [1986] present formulae for calculating volumes of shell matrix sites.) An increasing number of excavators, however, believes it is most appropriate to sample at a much smaller level, such as a lens or dump (Ambrose 1967, Willey and McGimsey

1954, Stein 1992a, etc.). Determining what is a representative sample requires knowledge of the volume and variability within the occupational debris (and necessarily access to that debris) and a decision about the confidence level.

A site-wide sampling strategy must be decided case by case, based on the research objective(s), site stratification, variability in contents, distribution of features, origin of deposits, etc. (Shell that has been amassed for architectural purposes need not be sampled in the same fashion as food debris.) With regard to land snail analysis, Thomas (1985: 133) stated:

> the interpretation of the context will influence the sampling strategy (location of samples, size of samples, sampling interval, etc.). Equally, the type of sample required, such as an autochthonous assemblage or one "most contemporary" with the archaeological features, will determine which of the available contexts will be sampled.

There is no specifiable amount of matrix that can be deemed statistically adequate for world-wide application, nor can there be a fixed size of sample useful world-wide, contrary to the aims of Greenwood (1961), Bailey (1975), Bowdler (1983), and others, and the applications of Peacock (1978), Buchanan (1985), and others. An argument has been made, however, that the minimum proportion of the universe that must be investigated in order to gather "*diagnostic artifacts* [my emphasis] from the earliest and the latest occupations of a site" lies somewhere between 38 percent and 50 percent of the site area (O'Neil 1993:527; Trinkley and Adams 1994:113). Perhaps it is this range of site sample that should also be subsampled for biological materials.

Campbell (1981), Peacock (1978), Waselkov (1987), and others have advocated site or component sampling strategies that are flexible and include several different types of exposure, employed probabilistically and non-probabilistically. At Duwamish No. 1, in Seattle, Campbell began investigating with coring. Coring was succeeded by dispersed 2×2-m units that were subsequently enlarged to yield broad horizontal exposures connected by trenches. Since knowledge of component extent and variability is learned as excavation progresses, yet is necessary in planning the sampling strategy, a flexible strategy is essential to the success of the sampling program.

Trinkley and Adams (1994:113), augering shell matrix sites on the coast of South Carolina (US), found a 20-foot interval to be good for identifying separations in shell scatters and for identifying the major components and shell density. Forty-foot augering intervals were inadequate by comparison. Augering at 10-foot intervals did not dramatically improve understanding of the dense large oyster-shell deposits.

The goal of site excavation minimally should be to obtain a probabilistic sample. But a sample of what? A research question gaining great popularity at the end of the twentieth century is the taphonomy of shell matrices. It is highly unlikely that many shell deposits have escaped mixing of some type and thus retain discrete "original" deposits. Instead, we often have time-averaged deposits, or taphofacies. These taphofacies, then, offer a more meaningful sampling universe than the original discard episodes. Excavation by facies is most conducive to isolating the formation processes at work on the deposit. The boundaries of a facies are visually determined and subsampling of larger facies is recommended (Stein 1992c).

Another way to approach the issue of site sampling is to begin at the regional level. At the Marismas Nacionales, in west Mexico, Shenkel (1974) surveyed the area first to determine the types of shell-bearing sites in the park. Once the variation in site types (see Chapter 1) and their distribution was understood, he determined which sites to test and how to sample them.

Sampling for analytical studies

Sampling specific to subsistence studies has been given much attention in the past decade. (Sampling for time of death studies is discussed in Chapter 5.) Appropriate screen sizes have been the focus of most of this attention (e.g., Bowdler 1983:139, Buchanan 1985:40, Shackleton 1988, Wing and Quitmyer 1985, Waselkov 1987) with all authors agreeing that the smaller the mesh used the more accurate the ecofact quantification for it minimizes preservation differences. The failure of most excavators to use $\frac{1}{8}$th-inch mesh or smaller has made regional comparisons of ecofact data difficult (Reitz and Quitmyer 1988).

Column sampling – a vertical series of contiguous same-sized samples – has proponents (e.g., Bernstein 1993, Bowdler 1983, Campbell 1981, Meighan 1969:48, Quitmyer 1985) and critics (e.g., Ham 1982:163, Spiess and Hedden 1983, Trinkley 1981, Waselkov 1987). Steenstrup explored each of fifty Danish shell mounds which were from 3 feet to 10 feet thick, up to 300 yds in length, and 100–200 feet wide using three column samples of 3 ft^2 (Lubbock 1869). Since that time, columns have been a popular way to sample these sites. While column sampling is not designed to recover examples of rare species or isolated deposits, it is useful for sampling the matrix, particularly shell, and is advocated by many faunal analysts for this reason (Figure 18). Because of the highly restricted view of the component's contents, column samples should not be the only source of materials for the faunal analyst. Furthermore, columns should be employed at intervals that match the spatial scale of the activities that created the deposit, a very difficult requirement.

However, column samples both suffer from time-averaging processes and exacerbate them. It is impossible to sample in contiguous, same-sized units, and not mix facies. The archaeologist who recognizes the important role of formation processes in shell aggregates will find non-contiguous equal-volume samples of matrix far more useful.

Several authors have stressed the importance of multiple subsamples from each provenience slated for sampling. At Cnoc Coig on Oronsay (Inner

Fig. 18 Column sample at Dogan Point site, NY.

Hebrides) four subsamples of 4 kg dry weight were removed from the unit walls according to natural strata and water screened though 2-mm and 1-mm mesh to assess the variability within each (Peacock 1978). (These subsamples came from outside the excavation unit but were still within the random sampling units.) Multiple subsamples are a necessary check on variation within a provenience.

   In some subsistence studies sample adequacy has been determined not with size or number of subsamples but with the number of species and the minimum number of individuals (MNI). Wing and Brown (1979:120) assessed sample adequacy at 25 species and an MNI of 200 for sites on the Caribbean coastal plain. Subsistence samples from sites in Kings Bay, Georgia, on the Atlantic coastal plain, were thought adequate when 70 percent of the potential fifty-three vertebrate and invertebrate species were identified. This percentage was achieved with an MNI of 1,500 (Quitmyer 1985:34). Walker (1992) found the point of diminishing returns in the sorting of invertebrate samples from Gulf coastal Florida to be 600 individuals when 70 or more taxa were present. Unfortunately, far fewer taxa are contained in many western Atlantic coastal shell matrix sites. Conversely, that many species and individuals of bivalves alone can be retrieved in a single 3-m-long column from the Archaic shell mounds of the midsouth US. Figures appropriate in these regions have not been offered. Will the potential number of usable species always be an appropriate standard by which to judge adequacy?

Bobrowsky (Bobrowsky and Gadus 1984:106) has generated a formula for North American terrestrial gastropod samples of Quaternary age to calculate the average number of gastropod taxa expected for various sample sizes:

$\#\text{Taxa} = 1.494 \, (\text{NISP})^{0.432}$ generated with 380 snail assemblages r = 0.8497
where NISP = the number of identified specimens

Two sampling examples   At the Duwamish No. 1 site in Seattle, Washington, shells of numerous species appeared in lenses as well as in larger concentrations. Campbell (1981:220–223) collected the lenses as features to offer some analytic control for interpreting the variability in shell samples from larger deposits of shell. In the field, each unit was washed through $\frac{1}{4}$-inch screen and the contents sorted and shell weighed. Shell weights within proveniences ranged from 0 g to 152 kg. Recognizing that it would be impractical to identify all of the shell in the larger samples and the information would be largely redundant anyway, Campbell subsampled the shell. In lenses and strata where shell weight exceeded 200 g the shells were mixed and split in a standard quartering machine to obtain samples of roughly 200 g. The excess shell was discarded. In units with very great quantities of shell, the procedure was modified with random sampling occurring in the field. Bones and artifacts were removed. The remaining shells and rocks were mixed and split and one quarter of the sample by weight was retained. The rest was discarded. The shell in these samples was then quartered to obtain a sample of roughly 200 g and the rest of the shell was discarded. These new samples and those originally weighing less than 200 g were assigned shell sample numbers distinct from their bag numbers. For further processing in the lab, the samples were prioritized. There was no attempt to determine if the differences in shell species composition between proveniences were due to cultural or environmental changes because Campbell could not justify the assumption that the shell data from the four test units were representative of a site-wide temporal trend.

The procedure currently advocated by Stein (various in 1992c) and P. Ford (1992) to sample facies is to collect biological samples (approximately 25 × 25 × 5 cm) from individual facies, pass the samples through nested screens of 25, 12.5, 6, 3, and 1.5 mm hardware mesh cloth, sort all shell larger than 1.5 mm, and classify as matrix all material smaller than 1.5 mm. Shell from each screen size is weighed, condition of valves noted, and relative abundance calculated. Grain size categories, equal to mesh size, are then calculated for every taxon in each screen (P. Ford 1992). It is necessary then to consider the relationship between taxonomic composition and grain size, which Ford pursued using histograms of grain size for each taxon (Figure 17) and the Mann–Whitney U test for significance. The benefits of this and similar analyses (e.g. Claassen and Whyte 1995) are immediately evident for the information they generate about formation processes.

4.2   Quantifying shells

Numerical data retrieved from molluscs often include counts, measurements – height, length, weight, aperture height, umbo height – and completeness. The abundance of shellfish can be recorded as minimum number of individuals (MNI), number of identifiable specimens (NISP), or as weight found within the site. Numerical data collected for deposits include fragmentation, volume, density, and proportion. The diversity, richness of an assemblage, and ubiquity of a species inform on human behavior and the environment. Differences in quantity or abundance of species and size of individuals should be tested for significance with statistical tests. This section begins with a few words about processing shells and coding.

Field processing

Field processing of shells is an attractive option for most excavators given their weight and bulk and the need to use sturdy, and thus expensive, bags when transporting them. When handling shells with sharp edges, rubber "oyster-man" gloves are recommended. Removing shell samples with matrix intact will allow for a ratio of soil to shell and a calculation of shell density. Screening the sample through multiple mesh sizes is recommended to remove the soil, facilitate fragmentation estimates (see below), and generate samples suitable for sorting by workers of different skill levels. The contents of each screen are bagged with unit, level, and screen size indicated on the bag. In the lab, the total weight of the bag contents and the weight of each constituent material are recorded for each bag.

Shells are sorted into taxa, and umbones (bivalves), apices, or umbilici (univalves) separated within each taxon. For symmetrical bivalves it is often possible to discard one half of the valves in a taxon at this point. For asymmetrical bivalves, such as the eastern oyster, different types of information are obtainable from upper and lower valves so it is necessary to retain all whole and some broken valves. Fragments might be discarded at this point. The use of a random sampling of proveniences for the laboratory processing is recommended.

Unit-Level Shell Tally Form 3Mar94-v1

_ _-_ _-_ _ / _ _:_ _ _Date/Time Start
_ _-_ _-_ _ / _ _:_ _ _Date/Time End
____Total Minutes
38BU_____-Site
_____-Unit
Coord m _ _ _._ _West_ _ _._ _South Fea___.___
Level _ _ _ Depth____-____ cm Fea Descrip _____

Garrow & Associates
13 Glenwood Ave
Raleigh NC 27703
919-821-3197

SCDOT Hilton Head Cross
Island Expressway Project

Do List
O **Weight In**
O **Start Time**
O **Finish Form**
O **Save Sample**
O **End Time**
O
O **Coded**

_ _ _ _ ._ _ Weight In

Count   Weight   Cockle Shell (*Clinocardium*)
Tally ---

Count   Weight   Atlantic Ribbed Mussel (*Guekensia demissus*)
Tally ---

Count   Weight   Quahog (*Mercenaria mercenaria*)
Tally ---

Count   Weight   Oyster (*Crassostrea virginica*)
Tally ---

Count   Weight   Channeled Whelk (*Busycon canaliculatum*)
Tally ---

Count   Weight   Moon Snail (*Polinices duplicatus*)
Tally ---

Count   Weight   Razor Clam (*Ensis directus*)
Tally ---

Count   Weight   Impressed odostome (*Odostoma impressa*)
Tally ---

Count   Weight   Other
Tally ---

Save Sample: (3 of each, oddities)

Comments: (condition, color, comparisons)

Excavated By: 1_____2_____3_____4_____Recorded By:_____

Fig. 19 Coding form for molluscan taxa.

Code sheets

Code sheets are best designed for each project. I tend to use two sheets, one which collects data on the group of shells from one provenience, and the other which records the metrical data for individual shells from one provenience. Shell harvest-time data are recorded on yet another form. For coding performed by novice workers, pictures of the species anticipated are useful additions to a coding form (Figure 19).

Counts

One typically derives a count of bivalves present in the sample from the number of umbones of one side or the number of apices/spires/umbilici. This number is reported as the MNI. The most serious problem with this procedure is the assumption that the MNI is best represented by the side of the creature with the highest count of umbones. Not all shells of that side have survived either. There are formulae for predicting the original population in a fossil assemblage (Koike 1979) but they assume that 100 percent of the surviving sample is available to the investigator about to undertake the calculation. It is rare that all the surviving shells are excavated and counted. Shackleton (1988) did not calculate an MNI, preferring to state simply the number of umbones for each species.

Karen Jo Walker (1992:304) prefers MNI to weight or the number of identified specimens (NISP) stating that the primary objective of the zooarchaeologist is to measure relative abundance of species. She asserts that much of the theoretical trouble with MNI is not applicable to seaside cultures "because of the nature of estuarine/marine fauna and the technology used for their exploitation." Maxwell (1989a:10) likewise exempts invertebrate remains from the standard complaints about conversion of MNI to meat weights. (A useful discussion of MNI vs. weight is Bailey [1993].)

A preference for counting the number of bottom valves in the asymmetrical oysters in coastal Texas sites has been expressed by Cox (1994). Cox sorted shells into size classes and then noted that for shells under 6 cm there were equal numbers of upper and lower valves but as the shells got longer, the disparity grew. Lower valves over 12 cm in length outnumbered upper valves over 10 cm by five to one (Karen Cox, personal communication, 1995). Cox suggests deriving an MNI for oysters from the total number of lower umbones plus most, if not all, of the upper umbones from valves over 8 cm in length.

Lower valves of eastern oysters from the 7,000-year-old Dogan Point site in New York easily exfoliated along growth layers into multiple "shells" (Claassen and Whyte 1995). The MNI for the number of oyster tops handled by the Dogan Point excavation project was 9,698, while the number of bottoms was 6,679. Since the top valve is much less likely to exfoliate, a count of them will produce a more meaningful number in a collection of exfoliating specimens.

Weight

Many researchers calculate weight of shelled taxa in grams or kilograms per provenience, an absolute frequency, because of the speed with which this quantification can be conducted. All pieces of shell by taxon are included in the weight. Criticisms of shell weight quantification center primarily on the loss of weight with diagenesis which affects different species at different rates (see Chapter 3). The older the site or the more acidic the soil, the greater the loss of calcium carbonate and conchiolin and the greater the differential loss of calcium carbonate between species. The other concern is that heavier-shelled species are disproportionately represented compared to lighter-shelled species when both are compared to the count of umbones.

There are proponents of volume comparisons and count comparisons rather than weight comparisons. Comparisons using weight samples are urged over comparisons of volume samples by Greenwood (1961). Nor is it possible to say that a count of individuals is a truer picture of dietary use than is the weight of individuals, although it has been customary to calculate meat weights from the number of individuals.

Size

Size measurements are most useful to archaeologists in defining stratigraphy, in studying the growth environment (Chapter 5), and for estimating season of harvest (Chapter 6), and have occasionally been used to explore the mode of harvest, the number of populations sampled, and the identification of accidental species inclusions. Measurements are most frequently taken, however, in hopes of identifying heavy human predation (see Chapter 2), and for estimating meat yield (Chapter 7), uses for which size measurements are the least informative and the most problematic.

Any sample of shell from a site is biased in its biometrics from two vantage points. First, larger specimens have probably been selected over smaller individuals. Second, the human predators have selected specimens from numerous populations and mixed them in the site assemblage. Within one population there is little size variation but, among means of different populations, size variation is often extreme. Consequently, the first bias creates a greater average size than would result from an unbiased sample of the population while the second bias will create an assemblage mean smaller than the mean of any one population with large shells (Gould 1971).

Age is a commonly selected variable for growth studies in molluscs. Size can be used as a substitute for age. Given that mortality is more size dependent than age dependent, it is appropriate to construct size class histograms and survivorship curves. Furthermore, age estimations require a number of assumptions – about the meaning of visible growth rings – that are avoided when size data are used (Cerrato 1980:450).

The size of a shell is determined by the age of the animal, the microenvironment the larva settles in, and ontogenetic growth rate. The mean or modal size of a population is also heavily influenced by recruitment and juvenile survivorship. The relationship between height or length (or any other size parameter) and the age of the shellfish is species-specific and nonlinear (Cerrato 1980:421). When an *age cohort* (individuals who were recruited during the same recruitment episode) is plotted as a size frequency histogram, it will generally appear as a normal or slightly positively skewed distribution. (Positively skewed graphs peak on the left side, negatively skewed graphs peak on the right side.) When a population whose recruitment is seasonal is graphed, it will have a polymodal shape, each peak representing a spawning event. Because of decreasing growth rates with increasing age, three peaks are the most expected of long-lived species when graphed, with fewer peaks quite common. Growth rates and recruitment events can be deduced from these diagrams *if* the assemblage is representative of the population, often not the case with human made collections.

Size frequency histograms are not equivalent to survivorship curves. There are three survivorship curves characteristic of any population of mollusc on a given day. Curve I shows negative skewness (in size or age) and is found in populations with low mortality early in life and high mortality late in life. Curve II is diagonal, indicating constant mortality throughout life. Curve III is positively skewed and characteristic of populations with high mortality in the youngest (smallest) growth classes (Cerrato 1980:443). There are fairly consistent survivorship curves for individual species, with the long-lived ones tending to show Curve I and the short-lived ones Curve III. Shell matrix sites are often composed of dumps from discrete harvest events. If they can be sampled at that scale, then the survivorship curves I, II, or III are to be expected. Viewed over time, rather than on a single day, most molluscan population survivorship curves are sigmoidal in shape (C or S shaped), however (Kurtén in Cerrato 1980:444).

Size measurements of most use to archaeologists are valve height and length (often erroneously called "width") for bivalves and valve height and aperture height for univalves. Measurements are to be made as illustrated in Figures 20 and 21. Instructions for measurement of limpets, chitons, and *Concholepas concholepas* can be found in Jerardino et al. (1992).

Projected mean sizes for fragmented shells in each level of a Chilean coastal site were established using regression equations found in Castilla and Jerez (1986) and Oliva and Castilla (1992) and are presented in Jerardino et al.

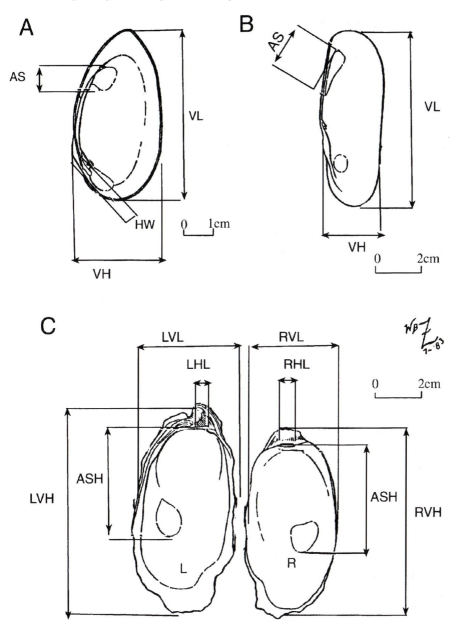

Fig. 20 How to measure the bivalve. HW = hinge width, VL = valve length, VH = valve height, HL = hinge length, ASH = anterior scar height all for left and right valves.

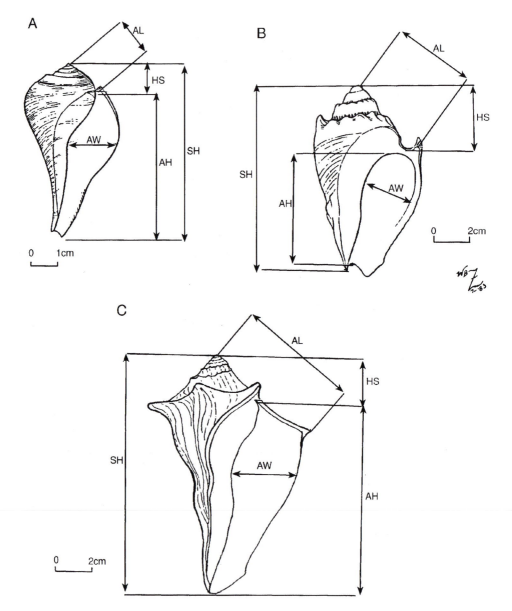

Fig. 21 How to measure the univalve. AW = aperture width, AH = aperture height, SH = shell height, AL = apex length, HS = height of spire.

(1992:48). A regression formula for predicting size of *Perna perna* mussel fragments consisting of the anterior pedal retractor muscle scar can be found in Hall (1980).

Statistical tests are needed to compare size differences between proveniences. Comparison of size differences between levels at the multi-species

Curaumilla-1 site in Chile was performed using the ANOVA statistic (Jerardino et al. 1992). Mean size was the dependent variable and the levels were considered a source of error. When mean percentages were used, the arcsin transformation was used. Lasiak (1992:20) used the Median test and/or the Smirnov test to examine between-site differences in size frequency distribution of numerous species collected from the Transkei coast because neither test is adversely affected by skewness or differences in the form of distributions.

Stratigraphy

At the oyster matrix site of Dogan Point, New York, strata were apparent as differences in shell size (Claassen and Whyte 1995). The strata were labeled as either "giant oyster" or "small oyster" under the presumption that the average size of the shells was changing, rather than that a few individuals were strikingly larger. The act of excavation more frequently broke the longer shells than the shorter shells. With few whole shells to measure and the measurable ones biased in favor of the short shells, total shell length could not be used to investigate the reality of the strata designation. Instead, the umbo height was measured. (Dramatically curved umbones went unmeasured.) An average umbo height was calculated for each provenience, which was then assigned to either giant oyster or small oyster affiliation.

Separating primary from secondary/accidental prey

Primary molluscan prey species would be selected by humans for their large size and thus display very positive skewing, reasoned Wessen (1982), while secondary prey, accidentals, and commensals would show no selectivity, that is, their size graph would approximate symmetry. He calculated the skewness and kurtosis of shell sizes for each species in the Ozette site in Washington (US) (Table 7) and interpreted the presence of various shell species accordingly. Rather than assuming symmetry, however, the investigator should determine whether demographic Curve I, II, or III is the most appropriate for each species under study and expect correspondence in the size class distribution with that curve.

Mode of exploitation

At the Ozette site the mussel species approximated the "normally" distributed natural population (Wessen assumed large numbers of immature animals, a moderate number of adults, and a small number of old animals – Curve I) while three clam species did not, leading to the interpretation that mussels had been harvested as masses of individuals while clams had been hand selected for large size. While longer-lived species of bivalves in temperate climates do tend to evidence the Types I and II curves, the reader is cautioned to define "normal" population distributions on a species by species basis.

Table 7. *Primary and secondary prey bivalves from Ozette Site, Unit V, as separated by skewness and kurtosis values (after Wessen 1982:154)*

Primary prey	Number	Skewness	Kurtosis
Mytilus californianus	32,826	.380	.325
Mytilus edulis	2,593	.298	− .645
Protothaca staminea	16,137	.048	− .460
Saxidomus giganteus	3,763	− .060	− .320
Tresus sp.	396	− .059	1.935
Siliqua patula	15	− 1.217	1.331
Secondary prey			
Macoma nasuta	27	− .560	− .385
Macoma irus	21	− .597	1.001
Macoma secta	15	− .623	− .179
Clinocardium nuttallii	19	− .226	− .679

Number of populations sampled

Spiess and Hedden (1983:103) reasoned that clam (*Mya arenaria*) sizes would not be distributed randomly and homogeneously across the clam flats in live populations, so that digging clams in different areas of the mudflats should yield different clam size distributions. To identify different harvesting episodes (death assemblages) it was necessary to determine differences between samples of clams from either different stratigraphic or horizontal excavation units. This was accomplished using a statistical test for the significance of difference between two means of normal distribution.

Intensity of human predation

Decreasing average shell height in levels from the bottom to the top of a deposit has been used to argue for intensive human predation in dozens of localities around the world, as well as for intensive non-human predation, and for deteriorating habitat (see Chapter 2 and Claassen 1986b:127). These three competing hypotheses have been distinguished by additional observations (also Spennemann 1987). If the average height of shells of the same age changes from earlier to later deposits, then habitat conditions are implicated. If the same age animals have insignificant differences in their average height then the change in height over time suggests the impact of predation (also suggested by Bailey 1983c). Whether that predator is human or not must be determined from observations made about other species whose numbers are correlated with the shelled species under investigation.

There is yet another explanation for the decrease or increase in size of shells over some vertical distance. Shellfish recruit larvae in greater or lesser numbers after each spawning episode (Chapter 2) and each episode impacts on the size frequency histogram for many years to follow. A series of bad recruitment years will create an aged or large-size dominant population profile while a single good year may repress recruitment for several years creating a small-size dominant profile for the first several years (see discussion in Cerrato 1980). Even sporadic good or bad years can skew the population size profile significantly in one direction or the other. With rapid shell harvest and discard, a fairly deep pile of shells can be amassed in one locus at a site, which reflects short-term recruitment success or failure and thus a decreasing or increasing size profile. Chance infrequent human harvest and discard in years of poor recruitment followed by frequent harvest and discard in years of good recruitment will create a declining shell size profile in a vertical sample of shells.

Our attempts to explain declining or increasing shell size in matrix samples have been naive. There is no way for the archaeologist (or malacologist) working with a culturally created shell discard pile to sort out the differential impacts of recruitment, predation-mortality, harvest locales, environmental stimuli, discard behavior, prehistoric sampling, and archaeological sampling to explain a decline in shell size over vertical space. Skewness and kurtosis have been used in several cases but their utility is compromised by cultural behavior, by the inappropriate equating of size frequency histograms with survivorship curves, and by the indiscriminate application of Curve I (high mortality in old age, low in youngest stages). At the least, dozens of samples from one shell-bearing site are needed to establish even the nature of the phenomenon.

Data on size differences in collections of *Perna perna* (brown mussel) from the Transkei coast of South Africa for food are most instructive when making shell size comparisons. Mean and modal sizes differ in collections made only a few months apart and collections from different parts of the coastline are often characterized by different mean and modal sizes particularly when focusing on a single species. Collection from a section of shore long exploited by humans showed positively skewed unimodal distributions of size classes in fifteen out of eighteen months during which collections were monitored. The exceptions were one month with a symmetrical distribution and two months of negatively skewed distributions (Lasiak 1992:21–22). However, when families were allowed to harvest from a closed preserve (no exploitation for the previous nine years) size distributions of monthly collections were just as frequently positively as negatively skewed and only once were symmetrical. Furthermore, while collections made during the first nine months were unimodal in size distribution, bimodal distributions characterized the last nine months of collecting (Lasiak 1992:22). Clearly, there is no simple application of skewness that can be used to identify a newly exploited shellfish population.

It is clear that more work needs to be done with size distributions of commonly exploited molluscan species in frequently and infrequently exploited localities. The work of Theresa Lasiak makes it clear that symmetrical size distributions are rare in collections made by humans and might, when they occur in an archaeological situation other than rarely, be reflecting a size-sorting taphonomic phenomenon. Her observations also indicate that both negatively and positively skewed size distributions can be a regular feature of year-round collecting. Her data make it appear that consistently positively-skewed size distributions are an artifact of consistently exploited habitats.

Actualistic work by paleontologists has resulted in pessimism about the value of molluscan size-frequency data (see Chapter 3). Taphonomic processes are the culprit once again – they result in the under-representation of juveniles in some cases and in the under-representation of larger sized shells in other cases. "Any number of different size distributions can result from a single pattern of mortality owing to taphonomic processes; moreover, any given size distribution can have several possible explanations" (Kidwell and Bosence 1991:142). Archaeologists, too, should be far more wary of shell size data, and far more cautious with the interpretations of size differences between proveniences.

Fragmentation
The completeness of the molluscan specimens and the fragmentation of the deposit provide information on formation processes. Terminology suggested by Kent (1988) for recording the completeness of individual bivalved speci-mens is: intact valve, broken valve (with umbo), and fragment. Similar catego-ries can be applied to univalves, with "individual" referring to a piece with the apical end and columella practically complete, and "fragment" referring to the other pieces. Such a classification scheme will be most useful for species typically made into artifacts or for food species occurring in low numbers.

For sites with hundreds of thousands of shells, a fragmentation ratio is much more efficient and informative than would be observations on individual shells. The search for surfaces and disturbance at the Dogan Point oyster matrix site included an examination of the differing amounts of shell fragmen-tation in 212 column levels. A fragmentation ratio was generated at the time of screening by dividing the weight of shell which caught in the half-inch mesh by the weight of shell which caught in the quarter-inch mesh. The top levels of one column were known to be twenty-year-old backdirt. There the excavation, screening, and weathering process created oyster fragmentation ratios from 0.59 to 1.96 (Claassen and Whyte 1995). Unfortunately, the modern means by which surface- and shallow-lying shells can be fragmented include heavy machinery, yet these ratios were the only source of surface values available. Values for surface levels in all columns ranged from 0.25 to 3.76 (0.25, 0.55, 0.59, 0.60, 0.68, 1.26, 1.48, 1.65, 2.07, 2.82, 3.76).

At the Osprey Marsh site (South Carolina) fragmentation ratios computed in the same manner as at Dogan Point (above) were used to assess feature disturbance (Gunn 1995:197). Feature 4 appeared, from the fragmentation

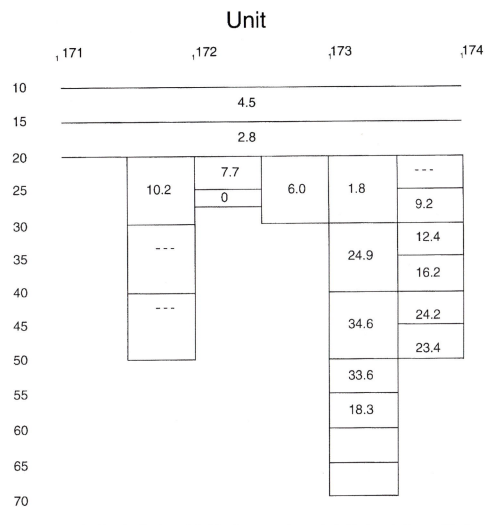

Fig. 22 Distribution of shell by fragmentation ratio in Feature 4, Osprey Marsh, SC.

ratios of arbitrary sublevels, to have received at least three separate dumps of shell (Figure 22). The deepest shell was quite fragmented, the intermediate levels indicated little fragmentation and the surficial levels were very fragmented. The feature was then capped by 20 cm of sediments containing very fragmented shell.

Fragmentation values are potentially useful for identifying buried surfaces and for distinguishing different biological and sedimentological sources. A more sophisticated fragmentation study was conducted by P. Ford (1992) who utilized fragmentation to address the issue of differences between stratigraphic zones in the British Camp site of Washington.

Abundance

The abundance – often labeled "density" – of a species of mollusc can be stated in either relative or absolute terms. It refers to the number of individuals or elements of a species – MNI, NISP, or weight. Although each of these measures has already been addressed their use in comparisons between excavation units and species is considered here.

Relative or percentage frequencies are probably the most commonly encountered statistic generated for shells in sites with more than one molluscan species and the one which bears most of the interpretative weight in those reports. It is very common practice to take the weight (or MNI) of every shell species in a single excavation unit and divide by the total shell weight (or MNI) in a single excavation unit to derive a percentage. (Since all of the shell is totaled to make 100 percent of the shell, the percentage of one species is relative to all of the others, constituting a *relative* frequency.) Percentages are then compared across excavation units. A greater or lesser percentage of one species or one ecological group either from a single unit or compared across units is thought to reveal information about the habitat, human behavior, or formation processes. These percentages are not comparable, however, because each is calculated using a subsample, and subsamples are of varying sizes. Begler and Keatinge (1979) point out that in order to compare weights or counts among different levels one must compute "the total weight recovered from the excavated block for each species separately and then calculate the proportion of the remains of each species represented in each level." It also allows for the comparison of one shell species with another within the level. When abundance is calculated in this manner for individual species, horizontal distribution will be obvious, and can be compared interspecifically.

Grayson (1984) and Thomas (1985) among others have criticized the use and interpretation of relative frequencies. Grayson points out that relative percentages are predicated upon the assumption that all individuals captured of each species have been recovered in the excavation and tallied in the laboratory analyses. Short of this situation, the relative abundances are biased in numerous ways that do not apply uniformly to every species being tallied in the frequencies. Sample size is one such bias that impacts relative frequencies and is discussed in detail in Grayson (1984, Chapter 4). The following quote summarizes his objections:

> changing relative abundances that have been detected by these studies may often not be reflecting the different values of the parameters of interest, but may instead be reflecting the differing sizes of the samples from which the relative abundances have been derived.

The sample size problem is fairly easy to detect. Grayson recommends rank ordering the faunal assemblages being examined in terms of NISP or MNI (sample size), next "rank order them in terms of the relative abundances of the taxon of interest," and then "test to see if a significant rank order correlation coefficient emerges" (Grayson 1984:130).

Sample size is not the only potential or actual problem with relative frequencies. A superabundant species will greatly distort the frequencies (Thomas 1985). Thomas (1985:139), working with the South Street long-barrow assemblage, showed that an apparent decline in the broken earth specialist *Pomatias elegans* was due to the choice of relative percentages – large numbers of open-country species increased but while *P. elegans* stayed abundant, its percentage decreased.

Furthermore, Thomas argues that the fundamental assumptions upon which relative proportions of species rely cannot be met. For instance, molluscan communities do not "saturate their environments" so, consequently, "individual species of molluscs may fluctuate in abundance independently of other species" (1985:134) and one species may decline in numbers because of predation but the other species do not then necessarily increase in numbers.

Absolute abundance of shell, an alternative measure to relative abundance, is the MNI, NISP, or weight of shell in any provenience, untransformed. In some cases the raw numbers are compared to (divided by) some non-shell entity that each shell sample has in common, e.g. soil weight or volume, flake count or weight, charcoal weight. The resulting value, i.e. twenty gastropods per 10 g of charcoal or 45 valves per kilogram of soil, allows molluscan species to vary independently of one another as in the example of predation given above. Thomas points out that absolute abundance values can be statistically manipulated as well. Unfortunately, weight, volume, and count ratios are only comparable with other studies that have used the same divisor. Both relative and absolute values for comparing abundance are dependent on the rapidity with which the deposits were sealed and the decay that has occurred since deposition.

Absolute frequencies have other noteworthy problems. Frequencies themselves cannot inform on the cause of changes. Jerardino (1995) offers a valuable discussion of both the uses of and problems with density (abundance) values in a presentation of research at the Tortoise Cave shell-bearing site in South Africa. She suggests supplemental values be generated such as depositional rate, aerial extent of settlement, and quantities of artifacts. Thomas (1985:135) specifies that "absolute snail frequencies ... can only be meaningful when assemblages can be assigned to discrete units of time," and sees the only solution to be the simultaneous use of both relative and absolute frequencies. Each has its utility and each will present the researcher with very different pictures of variation in space and time (see Figure 23).

Taxonomic richness and diversity
Taxonomic richness is the number of taxa in an assemblage, a number often compared with other site assemblages and interpreted. Diversity is the number

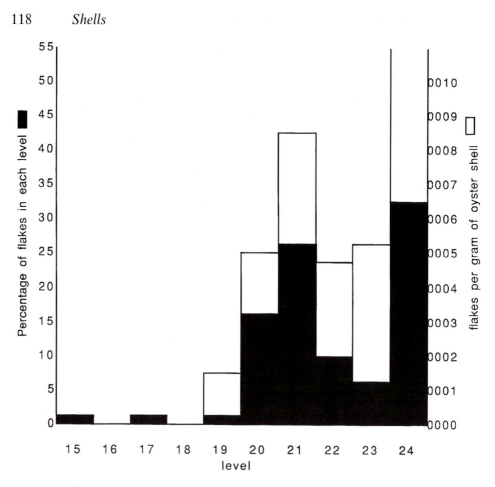

Fig. 23 Comparison of absolute and relative frequency calculations for lithics at Dogan Point, NY.

of individuals (MNI or NISP) distributed across all the identified species or taxa. Indices (Grayson 1984, Kenward 1978), curves generated by the rarefaction method (Grayson 1984, Styles 1981), and the two-sided Smirnov test (Grayson 1984:152–158) are used to measure diversity and richness.

Popular formulae used to measure species diversity are the Shannon–Wiener and the Simpson's. The Simpson's index (D) is easy to calculate:

$$D = 1 - \sum_{i=1}^{s} (P_i)^2$$

where P_i is the proportion of individuals of species i in the assemblage, and s is the total number of species.

As in any index or formula which relies on MNI or NISP, diversity indices are affected by sample size. Grayson (1984: Chapter 5) gives several examples of interpretations of diversity or richness indices and formulae offered by archaeologists which are marred by sample size. He also warns that their meaning is unclear when applied to assemblages whose formation processes are unknown but that diversity indices will "define the precise kinds of information that are needed to resolve their meaning" (Grayson 1984:167).

Thomas (1985:144, 148) acknowledges some potential value for use of diversity indices with land snail assemblages (see Baur 1987 for a more positive assessment) but states that the interpretation of indices is difficult. Locally derived assemblages with low diversity might be interpreted as reflecting habitats of low stability unsuitable for molluscs, or habitats of great stability favoring a few competitively superior species. Low diversity even raises the question of whether the assemblage was composed of native species.

Many studies have demonstrated that the larger the sample the greater the number of taxa recognized although the rate of adding new species slows considerably after some determinable point. Comparison of taxonomic richness and diversity between proveniences is complicated if there are different sample sizes of components, lenses, features, or levels employed. The same can be said for comparison between sites. While the investigator may think that column samples provide uniform sample size, the quantity of shell or any other constituent of the matrix changes from provenience to provenience, even though volume of sample stays constant. Differences in sample size of shell remains must be dealt with analytically. One can examine the relationship between sample size and diversity for each sample from the site by plotting the logarithm of sample weight and the number of taxa identified per sample.

Bobrowsky has asserted that curvilinear regression equations can describe the increase in species richness as a function of increasing sample size for unique geographical areas and time periods. He proposes that the relationship between sample size and richness of North American terrestrial gastropod samples of Quaternary age is

$$\text{richness} = 1.494 \, (\text{NISP})^{0.432}$$

based on 380 assemblages. The resulting solution "represents the average number of gastropod taxa expected for varying sized samples" (Bobrowsky and Gadus 1984:106). The observed number of taxa divided by the expected number quantifies the residuals.

Rarefaction is another measure used to compare samples of widely varying size when investigating community diversity. It is appropriately applied to invertebrates for it requires the counting of true individuals. The "rarefaction curve is a graph of the estimated species richness of sub-samples drawn from a collection, plotted against the size of sub-sample: it is a deterministic transform of the collection's species-abundance distribution" (Tipper 1979:423).

The generation of rarefaction curves (see Grayson 1984:151–158, Tipper 1979) requires several conditions. The collections to be compared should (1) be taxonomically similar (e.g. bivalves, molluscs), (2) have been obtained using standardized sampling and analytical procedures, (3) be from similar habitats, even intrahabitat, and (4) be restricted to interpolation of values not greater than the number of individuals in the parent collection. Eight formulae for rarefaction are presented in Tipper (1979). These curves can be compared statistically but Tipper suggests that it might be more efficient to compare the species abundance distributions directly using a test such as a two-sided Smirnov.

Ubiquity

The number of proveniences in which a taxon is recovered represents species ubiquity. Schneider (in Styles 1981:41) constructed a ubiquity index preferably applied to episodes of feature fill, rather than excavation units. This graphic index is a plot of the number of units containing species x on one axis and the median number of shells per unit for that species on the other. Multiple species indices are plotted on one graph for comparison of ubiquity. It may be possible to identify differential diets, discard areas, or activity areas within a site, formation processes such as erosion, or other topics of interest, using ubiquity.

4.3   Summary

The quantification of shell remains as MNI, NISP, or weight, from a site is rather straightforward. Complications arise in using the results of quantification and measurement, however, linked as they are to issues of sampling and preservation (Chapter 3; Waselkov 1987:153–157). Thomas (1985:149) calls for "improvements in the basic quantification of [land snail] species abundance to avoid ecological and logical pitfalls and to allow greater use of mathematical approaches to data analysis." Even when sites are sampled in such a way as to generate representative samples, the time and expense involved in the laboratory processing often result in non-representative samples of the site being analyzed or reported. We must at least couch the results in language that makes clear the preliminary status of the findings and suggest how larger sample sizes might be expected to alter the results.

The analytical protocol of the late 1990s was not the protocol of malacologists and even archaeologists prior to the mid-1960s rendering comparison between assemblages gathered in different decades extremely difficult and rudimentary. For instance, Gilbertson (1985:171) specifies the troubles with quantitative comparisons – studies which offer only species lists cannot be compared with studies producing frequency data. Richness, ubiquity, and abundance are impossible to reconstruct without visiting the earlier collection. Species occurring in very low abundance may be a taphonomic product but are invisible in lists. Nor are volume-based quantifications comparable to weight-based assessments. For these reasons, projects wishing to address a paleoenvironment on a scale larger than a single site need to review the available data base to plan analysis for comparability or to budget for collection visits and reanalysis.

The point of shell measurements, weights, and counts for many investigators is, occasionally, to reconstruct the carrying capacity of the aqueous habitat, and, frequently, to reconstruct human diet. The challenges and problems in such applications of shell metrics are numerous and are explored in Chapters 5 and 7.

5

PALEOENVIRONMENTAL
RECONSTRUCTION

Species ecology, shell shape, and shell chemistry are the three main aspects of molluscs which are used to retrodict paleoenvironments. Many archaeological investigations of the paleoenvironment around a site begin with simple observations about proportions of species and their habitat requirements. Shell shape is also frequently recognized as having encoded information about habitat. Chemical assays are becoming increasingly common. It is unfortunate that while much is known about the ecology of aquatic invertebrates of commercial interest, little is known about most other species.

5.1 Species ecology

Presence/absence, and abundance of individuals in each species are often sufficient to establish the environmental parameters of an ancient human activity locale. Whether the molluscan fauna are primarily terrestrial or aquatic, the interpretation proceeds from the same base – knowledge of the ecological requirements and constraints for individual taxa.

Terrestrial habitat reconstruction

Land snails were recognized several hundred years ago as a source of paleoenvironmental information. The earliest applications were recorded in the US, where the observations on paleoassemblages were common until the 1940s. Quantification of gastropods, however, was rare in the US until the late 1960s (Bobrowsky 1984:78–79). An early British worker, Mrs. Maud Cunnington, offered a Bronze Age date for Stonehenge based on its gastropod assemblage (Cunnington 1933). B. W. Sparks made popular the use of histograms for presenting relative frequencies (Evans 1972:12). Sampling experiments allowed John Evans (1972:83) to establish the requisite sample size of 200 individuals to capture the broad taxonomic composition of an assemblage.

Factors controlling the distribution and abundance of land snails are examined in Evans (1972). Among these factors are soil pH, calcium availability, water availability and retention, and temperature. Little is known about food requirements for most species and little is known about what other factors impact on adaptation, such as species cohabitation, colonization, or adaptation to changing environmental conditions (Thomas 1985). Evans (1972) did, however, summarize what is known for several dozen species common in British archaeological sites, exemplified in Figure 24.

It is assumed by many that "if we knew enough about key limiting factors determining the distribution and abundance of a particular species, these could be extrapolated into the past" (Thomas 1985:135) constituting a substantive uniformitarianism. But are the environmental conditions of today replicated in the past era under study? Has gastropod social behavior remained invariant? Have genetic changes not occurred? Nor will laboratory observations fill the gaps in our knowledge about species ecology and gastropod communities since the "distribution and abundance of a species is determined by the complex interaction of a large number of physical and biotic variables which are not readily predictable" (Thomas 1985:136). Our inability to verify that all factors in the present equal the past situation is further compounded by the facts that we know little about the ecology of most species and know even less about adaptive responses – abundance, distribution – to environmental change (explored in Thomas 1985:144), or interaction between species.

In addition to information about the environment gleaned from individual species, information can be derived from molluscan communities, or associations of species, within knowledge limitations. O'Connor (1988) stresses the need for continued field observations of species associations. Complicating the application of community data to archaeological assemblages is our inability to distinguish time-averaged associations and real communities. Furthermore, the real communities could have been in transition with uncommon species associations and thus appear to be time-averaged postdepositional assemblages. This issue is further explored in Thomas (1985). Relevant to community analysis is that fact that most species in England are catholic in their requirements and excluded from analysis, a practice that clearly skews the environmental information.

In light of the catholic species problem, Thomas (1985:142) recommends the following sorting procedure (reproduced verbatim):

(1) Assign the various species to their "exclusive" ecological groups in the usual way.
(2) Assess the ecological balance which is suggested by the resulting frequencies.
(3) Reassign "catholic" elements according to their known ecological tolerances (i.e. if the overall balance of an assemblage is toward "open-country," those "catholic" elements which are quite compatible with this interpretation should be assigned to the open-country group).

This approach could be further refined by weighting the habitats, using, for instance, species abundance.

Land snail ecological requirements tell us the most about the range of microhabitats around a site (Evans 1972:112), or within a "few tens of metres of the sampling site" (Paul 1987:91). To broaden their geographical scope, one should procure samples from as many contemporaneous contexts as possible

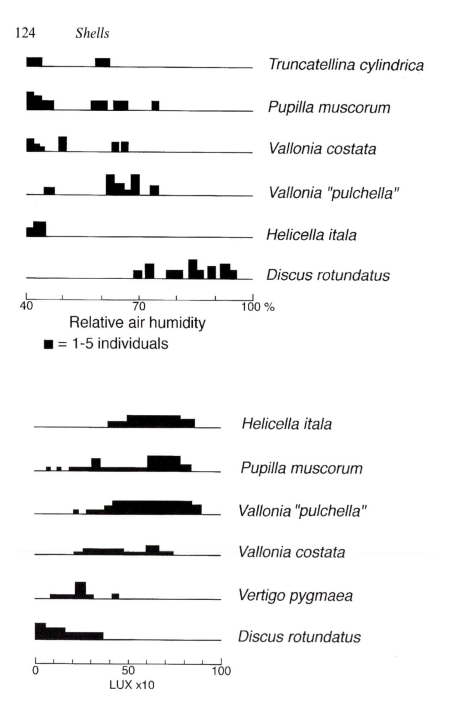

Truncatellina cylindrica

Pupilla muscorum

Vallonia costata

Vallonia "pulchella"

Helicella itala

Discus rotundatus

Relative air humidity

■ = 1-5 individuals

Helicella itala

Pupilla muscorum

Vallonia "pulchella"

Vallonia costata

Vertigo pygmaea

Discus rotundatus

LUX x10

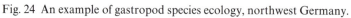

Fig. 24 An example of gastropod species ecology, northwest Germany.

within a restricted area (Thomas 1985:148). The following examples of paleoecological reconstruction employing land snail assemblages are offered as a sampling of the types of ecological reconstructions possible.

Evolving landscape
The shell matrix site of Cnoc Coig on Oronsay Island (Scotland) was founded upon a sand dune. There are three clear horizons of molluscan fauna. Fourteen samples of unspecified size and variable weight were collected in 10-cm increments from the profile of one pit at the edge of the marine shell deposit (Paul 1987). Land snails from sample 1, the deepest, were of moderate diversity (nine species) and abundant and indicated that several different habitats surrounded the sampling pit 5,000 years ago, including woodland or scrub. The paucity of snails in samples 2 and 3 suggested a rapid accumulation of sand followed by several short-lived soils. Overall, the gastropods in the first molluscan horizon indicated increasing stability of the dune through vegetation and a variety of habitats surrounding it.

Molluscan horizon B began with a "massive" increase in abundance of land snails, but not in diversity, coinciding with the first deposits of limpets and, obviously, human use of the dune. Several open-ground species and four catholic species reach peak abundance in the lower half of this horizon, reflecting conditions around the periphery of the marine shell deposit. Succeeding this indication is the peak abundance of all the shade-demanding and woodland species probably reflecting not a change in conditions surrounding the marine shell deposit but conditions upon the shell deposit. The sand dune habitat had receded from the sampling point.

Molluscan horizon C brackets an apparently abandoned site, allowing for the growth of acidic vegetation. No marine shells are present in the upper 30 cm of the profile and terrestrial molluscs are greatly reduced in abundance, eventually disappearing (Paul 1987).

Land clearance/open land
The gastropod fauna from the 3,000-year-old archaeological site of Smyth Crossing on the Nueces River of Texas indicated that the site was initially situated on a bare gravel bar (absence of *Helicina orbiculata*), followed by an open riparian woodland (*H. orbiculata* present; large populations of *Gastrocopta pellucida, Helicodiscus singleyanus*), then a dense woodland (presence of slug *Deroceras laeve*) evolving into a savanna (increased *Rabdotus mooreanus*) with loss of downwood (a decrease in number of *H. orbiculata* and others) (Neck 1987).

Evans used both the gastropod species and shell condition from many Neolithic sites to investigate the Neolithic environment. At a chambered long barrow in England, Evans (1972:264) found two soil zones. In the deeper soil he encountered a mixture of shade and open-country fauna. In the upper soil open country species prevailed such as *Vallonia costata* and *Helicella itala* implying a succession from woodland to open grassland. The dominant shade species was more eroded and pitted on the apices than the other species indicating a greater degree of time averaging in the lower zone than in the superficial zone.

Molluscan species ecology has also been used to differentiate pasture from hay meadow (Robinson 1988) with the conclusion that few hay meadows existed on flood plains of the upper Thames River prior to the Saxon period. The pasturage gastropod assemblage was, surprisingly, just three *aquatic* species.

Increased/decreased moisture

A large assemblage of terrestrial snails at Ancn, Peru signaled to Lanning (1967:48, 51) the prior occurrence of lomas in an area too dry to support lomas today. In a re-evaluation by Craig, the absence of the lomas was attributed to grazing, and the assemblage of snails to wind transport and drop in depressions. Ossa and Moseley (1972) took a deposit of land snails at Quirihuac to indicate their dietary use but Craig (1992) presents evidence that they signal an ancient El Niño event. Its rains stimulate dormant snails to hatch, reproduce, and grow rapidly, flourishing in a two- to three-year period of vegetation growth and high soil moisture. Catastrophic death occurs at the end of this anomalous period.

Aquatic habitat reconstruction

The simplest technique for reconstructing aquatic habitat and the one most frequently used in archaeology is species ecology. Often glossed over by those who employ ecological profiles is the fact that molluscs have tolerance *ranges* for many ecological factors. Furthermore, there are differing environmental parameters for maintaining life, for reproducing, and for recruitment. For instance, the more stream habitat studies consulted, the greater the recorded diversity in naiad species' response to water depth, substrate, and current speed.

As with terrestrial molluscs, it is useful to divide aquatic molluscs into categories that reflect ecological conditions (Table 8). There are marine epifaunal species habituated to rocky beaches, and marine infaunal species adapted for burrowing into a soft substrate (e.g. mud), two logical sorting categories. There are marine species which live in cold water and those which live in warm water. Among freshwater naiads there are those species which are habituated to deep or shallow water, to slow or fast water, to riffles or mud, and there are generalists. The result of sorting shells in this manner is proportions of molluscs in relevant habitat groupings.

Freshwater puddles, ditches
O'Connor asks the question if human-made "freshwater habitats have developed characteristic malacofaunas" (1988:61)? If so, could archaeomalacologists hope to answer questions like "was this ditch permanently wet or only seasonally so; was the water clear or stagnant; was it vegetated or clear?" His conclusion was affirmative to the first question but that extensive field observation of species associations was needed before the latter questions could be addressed. Emil Haury (1937:57) reasoned that the presence of two aquatic snail species – *Helisoma trivolvis* and *Succinea avara* – in Hohokam (US) irrigation canals signaled that some water must have remained in the ditches most of the time.

Tidal position/shoreline characteristics
Voigt (1982) investigated the environment surrounding the 125,000-year-old Klasies River Mouth cave sites on the coast of South Africa by assigning the shells recovered to the littoral zones from which they derived (Table 8, Figure 25). Based on the species recovered, Voigt found evidence for a lower sea level during periods one and four of the Middle Stone Age, evident as greater numbers of individuals which would have lived in the splash zone. Numerous papers in the volume *Paleoshorelines and Prehistory: An Investigation of Method* (Johnson 1992) address sea-level changes while demonstrating various methods and hypotheses in use.

The rarity of the upper intertidal rock-dwelling mussel *Perumytilus purpuratus* in the site of Lo Demás suggested an "absence of rocks large enough to extend into the upper intertidal zone" during the Andean Late Horizon. This information led to conclusions about the type of watercraft that could have been launched from the water front, and the types of habitats accessible to shore fisherfolk. A subsequent increase in the abundance of *Semimytilus algosus* at the expense of *Donax obesulus* was interpreted as evidence for the creation of a rock pier or jetty at the town's waterfront (Sandweiss 1996; Sandweiss and Rodríguez 1991).

Salinity determination
Several approaches to determining water salinity are available: species salinity tolerance range, present and absent species, species density, parasites, and shell chemistry (discussed in shell chemistry section).

All marine molluscs have a range of salinity they can tolerate as adults (typically given in parts per thousand – ppt) and a narrower range that is required for successful recruitment of juveniles. Non molluscan species such as the encrusting bryozoa *Conopeum* sp. are also valuable in establishing these parameters. All species found at the Dogan Point oyster deposit can be accommodated with a salinity range of 18–22 ppt, a range that would have permitted oyster recruitment. In examining the paleosalinity of Charlotte

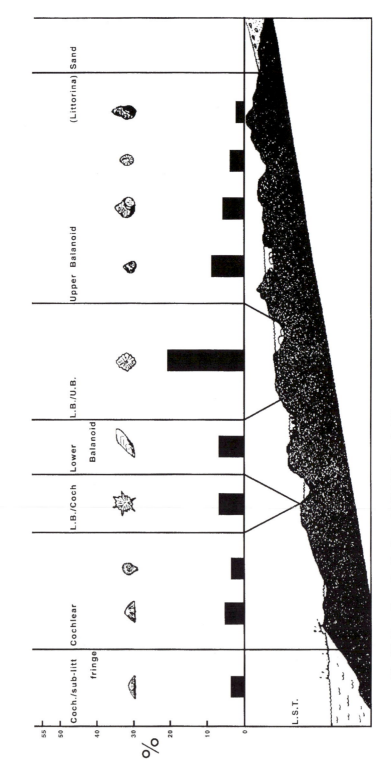

Fig. 25 Zonation of collecting at MSA IV, South Africa.

Harbor, Florida, Walker (1992:281) used a ratio of crested oyster (*Ostreola equestris*) whose lower salinity tolerance is ca. 28 ppt to the eastern oyster (*C. virginica*) based on MNI.

Molluscan predators and associates increase with increasing salinity and can help define the salinity regime in greater detail. Parker and Carriker (1960) found that *C. virginica* will be invaded more frequently by boring organisms such as sponges, barnacles, bryozoans, and algae as water salinity surpasses 15 ppt.

Cliona sponges bore holes into subtidal oysters and other subtidal species. The damage is characterized by a large number of interconnected holes, not single or double holes. Larger bore holes are made by larger sponges that are associated with higher salinity. Kent (1988:41) reports that *Cliona* species often differ on the upper and lower valves of eastern oysters since the lower valves are colonized by *Cliona* species from adjacent shells but the upper shell is colonized by *Cliona* species newly settled from the water. Consequently, the *number* of *Cliona* holes is usually larger on the bottom valve. The differences between *Cliona* species on the upper and lower valves may record rapid salinity changes. Kent has constructed a frequency table of large and small boreholes correlated with salinity regime for *C. virginica* populations of the northwestern Atlantic. Cox and Cox (1993, abbreviated in Cox 1994) modified Kent's categories to accommodate better the ecology of central Texas oysters. Table 8 presents both the Maryland and the central Texas correlations of *Cliona* sponge borehole sizes and salinity. Kent specifies that sets of shells, not individual shells, are to be assigned a salinity regime and comparisons are to be made between samples of similar shell size (1988:41).

The polychaete worm of the genus *Polydora* attacks oysters in Texas in water with less than 15 ppt salinity. It leaves chemically etched V-shaped tunnels both ends of which are open to the exterior. On the inside surface of the valve the oyster protects itself from the worm's hole by laying down more shell material with a blister appearance. Interior "mud blisters" are the result. Cox and Cox (1993:89–90) observed that those shells that had both *Cliona* bore holes and *Polydora* tunnels frequently had only one type or the other in the space of the last growth increment, indicating that the water salinity had shifted from one regime to another during the animal's lifetime. In situations of highly fluctuating salinity the valves tend to show the salinity regime in which the most time is spent. Cox and Cox (1993:90–91) discuss other molluscan indicators of salinity for the central Texas coast such as the encrusting hooked mussel (*Ischadium recurvum*) and scorched mussel (*Brachidontes exustus*).

The amount of clustering in eastern oysters also increases with increasing salinity. Oyster reefs typically form in waters of 25 ppt salinity and higher. Bottom valves of clustered oysters will evidence flattened places or attachment scars "at the umbones over one-half the valve height" (Kent 1988:33).

Table 8. Cliona *sponge borehole–salinity correlations for oyster (*C. virginica*)* *(after Kent [1988] and Cox and Cox [1993])*

Borehole percentages	Salinity regime
None to very few small holes	TX: 5–10 ppt for large part of year, rarely > 15 ppt MD: < 10 ppt for about half year, rarely > 20 ppt
Small holes, no large holes	TX: 10–15 ppt majority of year, rarely > 20 ppt MD: < 10 ppt quarter of year, < 15 ppt half of year, occasionally > 20 ppt
Small holes more common than large	TX: 15–20 ppt majority of year, short fluctuations on both sides of range MD: < 15 ppt occasionally, > 20 ppt for quarter to half year
Large holes more common than small	TX: 20–25 ppt majority of year, some fluctuations on both sides of range MD: < 15 ppt rarely, > 20 ppt most of year
Large holes only	TX: 20–25 ppt with little time below 20 ppt

Global climate change

Molluscan species ecology is also powerful enough to suggest and support hypotheses of global climate/weather changes. Several examples are given below of changes in currents and water temperature, El Niño expression, and air temperature.

 Two aspects of the terrestrial gastropods recovered in several archaeological sites in Kent, England are suggestive of the known warmer air temperature in the mid-Holocene (Burleigh and Kerney 1982:31). The first of these is a larger shell size in *P. elegans* and the other is the greater percentage of shells of *Cepaea nemoralis* (28 percent) with color banding when compared to the present (4.3 percent). Many early British post-glacial sites contain a large frequency of unbanded *C. nemoralis*, characteristic of warmer summers than at present. The co-occurrence of these two species morphs is so strong in early Holocene sites as to pose a potential relative dating strategy. Coinciding with this evidence of warmer air temperature from terrestrial molluscs is the presence of the freshwater *Corbicula fluminalis* bivalve which is indicative of annual air temperatures 1–2°C higher than the present (Gilbertson 1985:169).

 Several studies have used molluscan species ratios to argue for a change in water temperature. Changes in ocean water temperatures are usually related to major climatic changes. Kidder (1959) identified a change from warm- to cold-water species in Jomon sites. Voigt (1982) interpreted the shift in numerical superiority from *Perna perna* to *Perna granatina* (in combination with *Patella oculus*) to a change in water temperature from warm to cold water off the coast of South Africa. Braun (1974) identified a change in current flow in ancient times off the northwestern Atlantic coast based on the proportions of known cold-water and warm-water bivalved species. From the 4500–3000 BC Ostra site in Peru came a warm-water molluscan assemblage where today the cold Humboldt current flows. Sites just to the north and postdating 3000 BC have the accustomed cold-water species (Sandweiss 1996:135; Sandweiss et al. 1996).

This mid-Holocene difference in molluscan assemblages from today's communities in Peru is also found on the Atlantic coast of Argentina, the Siberian coast of the Sea of Japan, and in Greenland. Warmer water would eliminate the effects of El Niño ("global climate perturbation that occurs at irregular intervals and varying intensities" [Sandweiss 1996:129]) and pollen data elsewhere in South America support the interpretation that El Niño did not occur in the Terminal Pleistocene through middle Holocene eras, starting up only after 3000 BC (Sandweiss 1996:135; Sandweiss et al. 1996).

Two probable El Niño events are evident in the molluscan data from the site of El Paraso, Peru. Abundance of the wedge clam (*Mesodesma donacium*), which has been observed to take up to ten or more years to recover its numbers after an El Niño, while local mussels take less than seven months, "shows marked variation between and among levels," twice dominating, then trailing the other abundant species (Sandweiss 1996:138). The detection of El Niño events is important because these episodes have dramatic effects on the spatial, temporal, and taxonomic character of a littoral community, and on the abundance of individuals. As a consequence, human communities exploiting coastal resources are also stressed.

Assemblage-community fidelity

Three questions commonly asked by archaeologists are (1) what was the paleoenvironment of this site, (2) which habitats were exploited for molluscs, and (3) to what extent did these people practice selectivity? All questions require knowledge of the living marine community at the time of harvesting, often a poorly defined period of time. This reconstruction is complicated further by possible seasonal visitation, and possible use by sequential generations of a human community. Typically the archaeologist assumes that the modern habitats and marine communities near the site have been stable throughout the period of time since occupation and thus relies on contemporary taxonomic composition and numerical ranking in contemporary habitats and communities to establish those past parameters. Unfortunately for archaeologists, not only are the sites time averaged but also the living aquatic community sampled by the prehistoric humans and archaeologists are viewed by some ecologists as time averaged. The modeling of an aquatic community "as a cumulative series of temporally contiguous interactions over long time intervals is poorly developed" (Staff et al. 1986:442).

Neither the habitat configuration nor the aquatic communities are necessarily stable. Aquatic communities are characterized by short-term and long-term fluctuations in taxonomic composition and in numbers of individuals. The research of Staff et al. (1986) demonstrates that not even bivalved species are stable in number of individuals month to month (Figure 10).

Pollution, predators, unstable substrates, changes in water temperature and salinity due to changes in currents and shorelines, ice damage, wave transport of larvae into unsuitable environments, individually or in combination, produce short-lived bed locations, alter community composition, and modify population numbers (Little and Andrews 1986). Rollins et al. (1990:471) cite an example of the differential impact of El Niño on the population size of large shelled species and small shelled intertidal species off Peru. Meehan (1982) documents the impact of storms on shellfish beds in northern Australia. Longer term changes in sedimentation, water temperature, currents, salinity, elevation, and substrate bring about dramatic differences in faunal assemblages that have been far easier for archaeologists to identify.

In order to answer the three questions specified above, it is necessary to compare data sets from live and dead populations. Taphonomists proceed to assess species richness and taxonomic composition by asking (1) the number of species found alive only, (2) the number of species found dead only, and (3) the number of species found dead and alive (Kidwell and Bosence 1991:129). When the archaeologist asks "What percentage of the shelly species found alive are also found dead?" the fidelity of past and present number and composition is much higher than when the question is reversed: "What percentage of *species* found dead are also found alive?" In the latter case, studies have found between 33 percent and 54 percent of the species overlap for entire study areas, and 42 percent to 57 percent overlap in individual facies (Kidwell and Bosence 1991:129). Another question revealing fidelity of samples is, "What percent of the dead *individuals* are from *species* found alive?" The range of research results is 6 percent to 100 percent with a mean of 70 to 90 percent. Perhaps of greatest interest to archaeologists attempting to demonstrate selectivity is that few of the top dead taxa occur in the same rank order of abundance as in the live community. For paleontologists, the differences in ranking between live and dead animal data sets are more likely to be due to taphonomy than to biology or culture. For archaeologists, however, the explanation is more likely to be cultural, while the preserved set will be further modified by taphonomy.

In numerous examples of actualistic studies, researchers have found that the longer the collecting period for a study in a live community, the greater will be the fidelity found in the fossil assemblage. This observation also means that archaeological assemblages which were harvested continuously over hundreds or thousands of years should have a high fidelity with their original communities. To conduct a survey of the modern community, the longest lived species should dictate the duration of the survey. In lagoons that period of time should span several years while an adequate study of the live community on the continental shelf would require many decades of enumeration.

Because of taphonomic impacts on molluscan deposits, Staff et al. (1986) found biomass figures to be far better estimates of taxonomic ranking than was number of individuals. Keeping in mind that "taphonomy works at the level of the individual taxon ... numerical abundance and those community attributes derived from it, such as diversity, are the most gravely compromised" by taphonomy (Staff et al. 1986:44). Archaeological deposits can be either subsets of the live community or richer than the community at any one time due to time averaging of repeated inputs of shells collected from multiple habitats. Size frequency distributions will be time averaged as well (Kidwell and Bosence 1991:128).

A unique situation found on the north coast of Peru made it possible to inspect a natural bed of molluscs and a nearby equally aged cultural assemblage for fidelity (Sandweiss 1996:136). It was found that the cultural deposit contained a greater percentage of the larger species than did the natural bed "reflecting human selection for economically more important (that is, larger) species" (Sandweiss et al. 1983:282).

The warnings of natural and cultural assemblage infidelity appear less ominous when the findings of several other projects are highlighted. David Yesner (1977, 1981:154) demonstrated evidence of "proportional hunting," as he called it, for prehistoric occupants of Umnak Island in the Aleutian archipelago by using biomass for comparison. Sea urchins constitute the overwhelming bulk of strandflat biomass on Umnak Island today and in its Chaluka site of 4,000 years ago. Furthermore, mussels, limpets, and chitons were harvested in rank order equivalent to their modern biomass rank. While not all edible species were chosen for predation, the vast majority of those chosen were killed proportional to their natural occurrence. Lobdell (1980:220) also found that the littoral zone adjacent to a site on Yukon Island (Alaska) was identical in species proportions to that in the midden. Wessen (1982) provides a detailed example of proportional gathering by the shellfishers at Ozette, Washington. A comparison of Littler's (1980) biomass figures for the Channel Islands of southern California with midden species proportions (e.g. Meighan 1959, Reinman 1964) from those islands is yet another confirmation of proportional gathering. Voigt's study (1982:165) of the shoreline contiguous to the Klasies River Mouth sites in South Africa indicates that proportional gathering applies to the oldest known human shellfishing in the world.

In the parlance of archaeologists, "proportional" means that the dead taxa occur in quantities of individuals in the same rank order as they do in the living community. Violated in this view of proportionality is the notion of biological community (the proportion of epifauna to infauna, of grazers to suspension feeders to filter feeders, of gastropods to bivalves), all measures of interest to biologists in reconstructing the community and trophic levels. Such a violation is standard practice among paleontologists, however, working with shell deposits. They, too, have concluded that "the temporally persistent core of the community can be captured by the shelly death assemblage" but that "certain trophic groups and life habits will inevitably be underrepresented" (Kidwell and Bosence 1991:128). Rather than retrodicting a shelly community at a particular point in time, however, paleontologists recognize that they are generating pictures of the long-term average composition of the local community (Kidwell and Bosence 1991:123).

Archaeologists have frequently attempted to explain the cause of changes in species proportions. Changes in proportions of shell species in a site, like changes in shell size (Chapter 4), usually are hypothesized to result from a change in gastronomical whim, dietary shifts required by human exploitation, technological advances that permit the exploitation of new habitats or species, or environmental changes that extirpate some species and favor others. The reader is referred to Chapter 2 for a discussion of these and other competing hypotheses.

5.2   Shell shape/size

Shell shape is most often used to retrodict aquatic environment and less often used to interpret terrestrial conditions. It is infrequently employed in climate studies.

Aquatic habitat reconstruction

Naiad shell shape and/or size is often indicative of environmental particulars such as size of river, water temperature, or current speed (Figure 26). Form–habitat relationships were noted early in this century although many were contradictory.

As early as 1879 Morse had attributed decreased shell size and shape changes to changes in saltwater temperature in Japan. Matteson (1960) identified dwarfing in Early Archaic collections of naiads from the Illinois River valley (US) and attributed the cause either to persistently colder water temperatures or to a sustained lack of sufficient food in the Early Holocene. In an earlier article (1955) he had attributed dwarfing to slow-moving water. Klippel et al. (1978) found dwarfing in *Amblema plicata* and related the cause to slow moving water. Chatters (1986) found that growth rates in *Margaritifera margaritifera* from the Columbia River (Washington/Oregon) were greater between 6,000 and 8,000 years ago, attributing that phenomenon to variation in water temperature.

Roscoe (1967:6) summarized shell shape implications for the naiad *M. margaritifera* indicating that controversy rather than agreement surrounds the

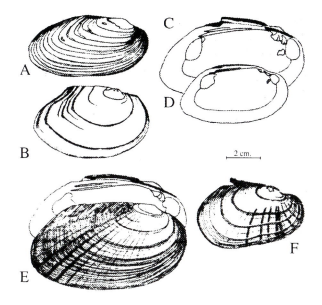

Fig. 26 Morphological differences in select naiads with water depth differences. A, B *Anodonta grandis* in 7 m and 1 m depth of water; C, D *Elliptio complanata* in 10 m and 17 m depth of water; E, F *Lampsilis radiata* in 0.5 m and 3.5 m depth of water, Seneca Lake, New York.

correlation of shell shape with environmental factors. Tevesz and Carter's (1980) review of the literature on naiads is far more positive about the potential of shape characteristics to correlate significantly with paleoecology. These authors identified two groups of publications, those correlating shell form and habitat (e.g., lake, small stream, etc.) and those correlating specific features of shell morphology, such as thickness or arc, to particular aspects of the environment such as water alkalinity and current rate. They were able to reaffirm several regularities:

(1) Within one stream, many naiad species will increase in obesity downstream.
(2) Shell obesity (thickness [of paired valves] divided by length) is positively correlated with stream size and negatively so with water velocity.
(3) Within one species, lake dwellers tend to be more obese than river dwellers.
(4) Small stream or creek species are smaller than those characteristic of large rivers.
(5) There tends to be an increased height in individuals and species living in lakes or slow-moving water.
(6) Curved or well-rounded ventral borders, and an expanded posterior end seem to be more typical of individuals and species living in large lakes, rivers, or slow-flowing water. The opposite can be said of individuals and species living in fast-moving water or small streams.

However, Tevesz and Carter were quick to point out that sexual dimorphism, ontogeny, and growth compensation confuse the correlations. Not until sexual maturity is achieved do many environmental effects on shell growth appear. Furthermore, changes in one shell dimension are often accompanied by changes in others. Such morphological covariance increases the difficulty of identifying causal relationships between form and environment (Tevesz and Carter 1980:304).

Building on shell shape and environmental correlations for 133 naiad species, Warren (1991) has proposed a quantified environmental gradient analysis to reconstruct environment in the Mississippi River watershed. Naiad species are scored 0, 0.5, or 1.0 based on the frequency of observation in several (1) types of water bodies, (2) water depths, (3) current velocities, and (4) substrate compositions, and the scores converted to a habitat profile. Warren sees the benefits of quantifying habitats in this way to be comparability between sites, and use of adaptational variations.

Tidal position

Saltwater shells also evidence shape and habitat correlations. Limpet (*Patella* sp.) (Jones 1985), dogwhelk (*Nucella lapillus*) (Andrews et al. 1985), and barnacle shapes (Bourget 1980) inform on the intertidal position occupied during life and the degree of exposure of the coast. Rollins et al. (1990:472) reference similar applications for *Venerupis rhomboides*, *Littorina irrorata*, and several other species.

Exposure to waves creates squat dogwhelks while sheltered areas allow for elongated shells. Andrews et al. (1985:72) examined shape of dogwhelks from the Oronsay heaps using the ratio of shell height to aperture height and offered three caveats to the interpretation of the ratio. (1) Not only shelter from wave stress but also intense crab predation create elongated shells. (2) The relationship between island gene pools and shell biometry is poorly known. These shapes may reflect genetics more than wave exposure. (3) The biological exposure scales developed for *Nucella* in South Wales, Norway, and Oronsay, Scotland are good only for about a 100-mile radius of the sample sites. Andrews et al. concluded that the Mesolithic inhabitants on Oronsay benefited from calmer seas and identified the collection locales exploited by them from each shell heap.

Oysters are excellent marine molluscs for predicting growth environment from shell shape. Thickness of *C. virginica* valves tends to increase with increasing average water temperature, salinity, and turbidity. Individuals living in deep, swift water are typically elongated with a height/length ratio (HLR) greater than 2.0. Oysters harvested from a hard substrate of packed sand in the intertidal zone or in shallow water generally have strong radial ribs and tinted valves. Reef oysters are also found in the intertidal zone frequently and like the sand oysters have ribs and color tinting on the shells, due to sunlight (Kent 1988:30).

Substrate

The environment in which an oyster grows affects its shell shape and is reflected in the HLR. Two sets of ratios with which to interpret substrate of growth habitat are available for North American archaeologists working with eastern oysters. The HLR figures offered by Kent (1988), generated with oyster populations in Maryland, distinguish four habitats: beaches of firmly packed sand (< 1.3), mixed mud with sand (1.3–2.0), soft mud bottoms, generally in channels (> 2.0) and reefs, characterized by a HLR greater than 2.0. Crook (1992), utilizing oysters from Georgia, similarly distinguished four habitats: soft mud along small tidal creeks (1.73), firm bottoms along larger tidal streams or softer muddy bottoms within tidal flats (1.67), bank communities in large tidal streams on either firm or dead oyster substrates (1.74, 1.80), and reef communities living on oyster substrate (3.14).

The different interpretations of the same HLR value are both striking and significant. At the late prehistoric site of Osprey Marsh, South Carolina, the HLR ranged from 2.79 to 1.25 (Gunn 1995). Using the Georgia figures, proveniences with average values below 1.67 cannot be interpreted, and the rest could have come from any but the reef habitat. Using the Maryland values there were nineteen proveniences composed of bed oysters, fourteen composed of reef oysters, two composed of channel oysters, and two composed of sand oysters. The lack of specificity of the Crook figures probably represents differences in a wide range of ecological parameters between Maryland and Georgia and a need for studies in both areas to include larger sample sizes in an effort to refine HLR–habitat correlations.

Kent (1988) specifies that sets of oysters, not individual oysters, be assigned a HLR and substrate. Techniques for making measurements of crooked shells are suggested there (Kent 1988:33–37). The HLR of sets of shells can be compared if the shells are roughly of similar size or if the values are regressed (Kent 1988:34).

Climate reconstruction

Baerreis (1980) retrodicted summer rainfall, annual rainfall, January mean temperatures, and length of growing season in early to mid-Holocene Iowa (US) using terrestrial gastropod length measurements. Correlation coefficients indicated that mean length correlated best with length of growing season in modern samples of *Carychium exiguum*, with mean summer rainfall amount in *Gastrocopta holzingeri*, with annual rainfall in *G. contracta*, and with mean January temperature in *Cionella lubrica*. Regression formulae then allowed for the computation of each of these climatic variables using samples of twenty-five or more snails from the ten horizons at the Cherokee site.

Gould (1971) demonstrated that the height of *Cerion uva*, a land snail, was greatest on sections of coast where it was buffeted from trade winds. The mean height of archaeological specimens from four sites on Curaçao is taller than that of sixty-nine modern populations. Gould suggests that the ancient shells came from relic populations genetically programmed for large size when rainfall was greater over the Venezuelan islands.

5.3   Shell chemistry

The chemical constituents of shell have been used primarily to reconstruct the paleoenvironment in the vicinity of archaeological sites (e.g., Hill 1975, Lee and Wilson 1969). They also have been used to suggest the origin point or harvest area for artifactual specimens (Claassen and Sigmann 1993, Shackleton and Renfrew 1970). Chemical constituents are increasingly being used to address issues of global climate change. The foci of elemental studies have been calcium, magnesium, and strontium. A growing number of studies are also employing oxygen and carbon isotopes to derive environmental information.

There are at least eight sources of variation in quantities of elements within shell: species, calcite-to-aragonite ratio, geological environment, temperature, salinity, body part, diagenesis, and time. Genetic character or species was found by Turekian and Armstrong (1960:133) to be the most critical variable determining chemical concentrations in shell. For example, aluminum in the northern quahog clam *Mercenaria mercenaria* ranges from 11–120 ppm while in *Busycon* the range is 146–471 ppm.

The calcite to aragonite ratio is strongly related to, first, the species and, second, the water temperature of the animal's environment. All of the groups of gastropods analyzed by Chave (1954) showed a positive correlation between the magnesium content of the hard parts and the temperature of the water in which they grew. This ratio, then, varies from animal to animal within species and does influence the amount of Mg and, to a lesser degree, Sr, deposited in the shell. Miller (1980:9) however, concluded that temperature and salinity cause small variations in elemental composition in *Mercenaria* with salinity being of less importance.

Shells have been transported to land-locked regions for over 40,000 years during which time the geological environment has changed. Erosion could have eliminated some geological sources and exposed others changing the chemistry of the watershed, creating time as a variable for a sourcing study. Projects that rely on chemical signatures (see Chapter 8) using fundamental elements in shell growth, rather than relying on one or two trace elements, will minimize the effects of time on watershed chemistry.

Reservoiring of elements has been reported across the shell and through layers of shell (e.g. Chave 1954). In three samples from a single *Busycon sinistrum* specimen, two from different parts of the lip and one from the columella, the variation in strontium was from 881 to 1,368 mg/g, in magnesium from 44.5 to 73.4 mg/g, in iron from 5.4 to 37.8 mg/g, and in Ca from 40.8 to 42.5 percent (Claassen and Sigmann 1993).

Perhaps the two most popular elements to assay in shell are calcium and strontium. Calcium content in shell is approximately 40 percent and is often used in ratios for comparisons. Greater percentages of calcium may indicate burned shell. (Decreased levels of organics in shell due to heating lead to percents of calcium exceeding the expected.) Deviations from 40 percent could also be indicating diagenesis. Additional sources of errors in measuring calcium are discussed in Hill (1975). Strontium concentrations increase in outer shell layers and decrease in inner layers, requiring whole-shell samples.

Oxygen and carbon isotopes are increasingly popular for both modern ecological and paleoenvironmental work. The first assay of oxygen isotopes in archaeological shells was by Emiliani who calculated temperatures at the Arene Candide cave in Italy in the 1950s (Higham 1996).

Isotopes are used to reconstruct long term climatic regimes as revealed in rainfall patterns and upwelling histories (discussed in this chapter), to identify shell source areas (Chapter 8), to investigate mammalian diets (Chapter 7), and to determine time of shell harvest (Chapter 6). Taphonomic factors affecting isotopes are discussed in Chapter 3.

Goodfriend is the leading researcher in land molluscan isotopes for the purpose of retrodicting environments. He commonly collects gastropod assemblages from rodent burrows and occasionally from archaeological sites. Age uniformity (the extent of time averaging) of the assemblages is checked using amino acid epimer ratios; experience has shown that rodent burrow assemblages "nearly always show uniform D-aile/L-ile ratios" or, are not time averaged (Goodfriend 1991a:418).

Several examples of paleoenvironmental reconstructions based on elements or isotopes can be found below. These questions concern the terrestrial environment, the aquatic environment, and global climate.

Aquatic habitat reconstructions

Freshwater stream flow

Many of the studies relating shell chemistry and habitat have attempted to retrodict stream flows at the time of site occupation. Assumptions necessary for this work are that (1) the concentration of the various elements decreases with increasing stream discharge, and (2) naiads deposit the alkaline earth metals in their shell in proportion to their prevalence in the water. Durum and Haffty (1961) observed that in some streams the Sr:Ca ratio increases with a decrease in discharge, while in others the opposite is true. Consequently, then, specific stream reactions must be discerned before the paleohydrology of a specific stream can be adduced. Hill (1975), citing assumption 1, concluded that the higher Sr level and greater Sr range in Horizon VIII shells from the Koster site (Illinois) indicated a low water stage of the Illinois River and a significant increase in discharge by Horizon IV times. Hill's assumption of decreasing Sr with decreasing water flow was in fact contradicted by his own assay of seasonal strontium levels in the Illinois River, which indicated that its levels remained constant regardless of flow (1975:122). Further work with this ratio indicates that rather than stream flow, water level may be captured by this ratio.

Salinity

Salinity information can be gleaned from $\partial^{13}C$ values as the oxygen isotopic composition of less saline water is lighter "as a result of dilution by isotopically light fresh water" (Deith 1986:69). Since there is a 0.2 ppt isotopic discrimination from the water temperature, it is necessary to sample the shell throughout the entire seasonal range to isolate the effects of salinity before comparing one shell's record with another shell's record (Deith 1986:69). The shells from a more saline environment should have a more positive range of ∂ values than would shells from a less saline environment.

Associated with six of the oysters radiocarbon dated from the oyster matrix site of Dogan Point on the Hudson River are $\partial^{13}C$ figures ranging from -5.1 to -3.7. These figures decrease in negativity as time approaches the present indicating that the Hudson River became increasingly saline after 200 BC (Little 1995). Little remarks that "the river at the time of the most substantial use of the site (4400–5500 ^{14}C yrs B.P.) was slightly more than 50% marine. For a low $\partial^{13}C$, humus or plant debris is a likely input" (Little 1995). Salinity can also be deduced from the Sr:Na ratio and $\partial^{18}O$ modeling.

Water body/origin point

The geographical origin of shells has been investigated using isotopes and chemical signatures. Derivation from one of several estuaries (Mook 1971), or shores (Deith 1986), and bays (Claassen and Sigmann 1993 and Chapter 8) have been the research goals.

Oxygen isotopes should have a more negative ratio in estuaries with rich detrital and phytoplankton levels. Could the size differences in cockle shells in a Scottish site reflect collection from different (more and less rich) sections of shore, wondered Deith (1986:72)? When the archaeological specimens did not demonstrate the same variation in range of oxygen isotope as did modern control samples, the hypothesis was rejected.

Sea level

Sea level changes have been investigated with strontium:calcium ratios (Guilderson et al. 1994) in corals. Strontium concentration in sea water increases with lower sea level. The first use of Ca:Sr with archaeological shells to determine sea level may have been by Gunn (1995:214–225) who found evidence that sulfur, chlorine, and copper increase with high sea level and decrease with low sea level.

The $\partial^{13}C$ values for shell samples radiocarbon dated from Brazilian sambaquis were used to reconstruct sea level for the São Paulo coast of Brazil (Suguio et al. 1992). Some sambaquis are as much as 54 km from the modern shoreline indicating period(s) of higher water. Shells collected from lagoons have more carbon derived from land organisms and consequently will have more negative $\partial^{13}C$ values than will shells harvested in areas flushed regularly with marine water. Sites of the same age but sequentially greater distance from the ocean should have shells with more and more negative $\partial^{13}C$ values. With the initial and final layers of dozens of sambaquis dated, the authors confirmed that the sambaquis were located at contemporary shorelines, and thus they were able to work out the rate of sea level advancement and retreat.

Water temperature

Working from the established relationship that oxygen isotope composition of shell is a function of both ambient water isotope composition (∂w) and the sea temperature during shell deposition, Cohen et al. (1992) reasoned that significant deviations from the present value of ∂w would occur during periods of glacial expansion. The growth of glaciers extracted and trapped isotopically light water. To investigate local South African seawater temperature fluctuations, they used an aragonite:calcite ratio applied to fresh specimens of the limpet *Patella granularis*, whose aragonite and calcite layers were discrete and easily measured. The width of each layer was used for the ratio. The aragonite layer was seen to increase by 45 percent with each 10 °C increase in water temperature.

For their investigation of past local sea temperatures, they turned to *Patella granatina* and oxygen isotopes. Decreasing isotope values over the past 12,500 years were interpreted as a period of ocean ∂w recovery from the glacial maximum. However, isotopic enrichment periods punctuated this pattern: at 11,000–10,000 ya, 4,000 to 2,000 ya, and 750 to 400 ya. The first of these punctuations was identified as the Younger Dryas era, formerly only identified in the northern hemisphere (Cohen et al. 1992).

Global climate

In his study of air mass circulation changes and rainfall patterns during the Holocene for the Negev Desert (Israel), Goodfriend (1990) powdered individual *Trochoidea seetzeni* snails, processed the powder for carbon dioxide measurement, measured each sample twice at least, and averaged the values. Modern specimens from the northern Negev Desert have a mean shell carbonate $\partial^{18}O$ value of + 0.83 ppt while the Holocene snail values began at that

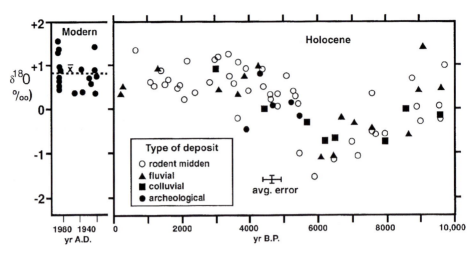

Fig. 27 $\partial^{18}O$ values of shell carbonate of the land snail *Trochoidea seetzeni* from the northern Negev Desert.

level and decreased until 6,500–5,950 ya (Figure 27). These figures indicated that prior to 3,500 ya, frequency of storm systems from northeast Africa was greater, with rainfall almost double the current annual levels. By 3,500 ya $\partial^{18}O$ values equal modern ones indicating that the contemporary air circulation pattern was established then.

Goodfriend (1990) found further support for increased rainfall during the middle Holocene in a study of carbon isotope ratios ($^{13}C:^{12}C$) in the same snail species, derived from forage on plant species of the Chenopodiaceae. C_4 chenopods are found today in areas receiving less than 230 mm of rainfall. The analysis indicated that twice the modern rainfall amount fell during the period 6,500 to 3,000 ya, with a transition zone located 20 km south of its present position.

5.4   Summary

Molluscan shell has proven to be a powerful tool in paleoenvironmental reconstructions of both local habitats and climate. Both simple and sophisticated techniques are available and employed. Shell shape, species ecology, and shell chemistry can all inform on local terrestrial and aquatic conditions, and on regional, hemispheric, or global climate. There are some caveats, however, almost all of which could be diminished in importance or deleted with extensive and intensive field observations of individuals, individual species, and species assemblages.

In Carter's (1990) estimation, the potential for paleoenvironmental reconstruction utilizing snails from *buried* soils is rather poor, affording, at best, limited interpretations of broad habitat groupings. Impeding more useful applications are problems of taphonomy, several of which are covered in Chapter 3. Land snails in shell matrix sites and in karst topography are not likely to be age stratified. When I introduced a seasoned land snail taxonomist to the assemblage from the Dogan Point oyster site, I was told there was no point in any analysis – no temporal specificity possible – since snails overwinter by traveling deep into a deposit, frequently dying there. Nevertheless, Evans has shown that for soil matrix sites significant environmental changes can be detected in assemblages of snails found in only 10 cm or less of calcareous soil. Portending later criticisms of paleoecological reconstructions based on land snail ecology, Thomas (1985) specified that future investigations needed to generate a better idea of time–depth relations of assemblages obtained in modern soil situations with known land-use histories. He also suggested that subtle environmental changes might be found in annual growth records. Ironically, since Evans wrote his important summation of British land snail studies from archaeological sites (Evans 1972) and specified their micro-local relevance, these creatures have assumed an important role in global climate studies based on their isotopic and amino acid components. Land snail assemblages may be more compromised by taphonomy than are marine shell deposits and thus may be less useful in species ecological studies but Evans and others have clearly demonstrated their potential for reconstructing some past land uses.

We are lacking much vital information about species ecology. New chemical techniques and morphological–habitat relationships are being uncovered yearly that are improving the resolution of species, shape, and chemistry with particular environments and thus human behaviors. Some of these new techniques and observations are also making the species ecological data less crucial, as long as money is not a problem.

Shell shape is perhaps the best method for reconstructing habitat with freshwater molluscs although the relationships between shape and habitat are tendencies, rather than certainties. A significant complicating factor is immaturity of the naiad animal. A number of marine species, including rock-dwelling species and the eastern oyster, have strong shape correlations with shoreline position.

There have been numerous studies of the factors that influence the relationship between shell chemical composition and water chemical composition (see particularly Rosenberg 1980 for marine molluscs). Many authors report correlations between strontium, magnesium (the two most thoroughly studied), and calcium, with salinity, water temperature, age of animal, etc., which often contradict one another (e.g., Harriss and Pilkey 1966, Rosenberg 1990, Swann et al. 1984, Turekian and Armstrong 1960). The reader should be wary of an uncritical adoption of any chemical–environmental relationships.

About the confusion Rosenberg (1980:133–135) said:

The environmental and evolutionary significance of the chemical composition of bivalve shells is poorly understood; not one single bivalve species has been completely or adequately described chemically. There is evidence that the Ca, Sr, Mg, and organic matter concentrations within the shell change throughout ontogeny. The shell may be composed of trace amounts of sulfates and hydroxides, as well as metal carbonates other than $CaCO_3$, complicating predictions of elemental distribution based on stoichiometric considerations alone. The amino acid concentration varies from layer to layer. Our knowledge, however, is fragmentary, and detailed maps of these various shell components is lacking. Distributions along dorsal–ventral and anterior–posterior shell axes are poorly defined. Variations from specimen to specimen, from population to population, and from species to species have not been adequately quantified.

Nor has the confusion abated significantly since 1980. A decade later, Rosenberg (1990:1) observed that no chemical distribution maps had yet appeared for any shell species, and that actual concentration levels of trace elements often differed from predictions producing "large error bias, or uncertainties, in correlations between environmental parameters and skeletal composition."

Archaeomalacological studies of environmental change should proceed cautiously in generating or weighing data about these relationships. There is little doubt that long-term and even short-term environmental changes in variables important to shell growth and human collection affect species and species ratios in detectable ways but these relationships are still being explored in the 1990s.

A few examples of statistical tests have appeared in this chapter and elsewhere in this manual. As the statistician Nick Fieller has pointed out (1997), statistics are changing constantly as are statistical programs. SPSS packets, for instance, when they are issued are five to fifteen years behind statistical developments. The statistics that archaeologists learned in graduate school are already out of date. In the 1970s archaeologists learned to use chi square, Mann–Whitney U, and factor analysis. Today we should be using log percents, principal component analysis and co-rotations, or ordinal logistic discriminant analysis, and correspondence analysis with MINITAB.

Long-term curation of well-provenienced and dated molluscan assemblages is important to the future of archaeological interpretation. Several authors have called for increased publication of archaeological land molluscan assemblages as well as increased field observations. Curation of collections will mean that they are available in the future when skilled researchers are more numerous, when the questions are better defined, when a technique popular in one country diffuses to another not currently favoring these skills, and when paleoenvironmental reconstruction is a more common research objective. Every shell assemblage offers information on the depositional environment of the site as well. Many of these techniques are readily learned and applied.

Curation of old molluscan assemblages is also important to researchers in other disciplines, particularly the biological sciences. Therein reside irreplaceable baseline data for studies of modern climate and pollution. These topics can be addressed with species ecology and fidelity studies or with shell chemistry. The smallest land snail and bivalve usually contain enough isotopes, calcium, and amino acids to satisfy the sampling requirements of most of the techniques currently employed.

It is rare in the western hemisphere for excavation projects to plan for the collection of land snails and even rarer for the collections to be analyzed and published. While land snail assemblages collected from shell matrix deposits are of questionable temporal use, the situations in which non-time-averaged assemblages are to be expected need to be identified.

The skeleton made of calcium carbonate is a treasure chest of environmental evidence. Archaeologists have not made systematic use of this potential and the applications that can be found are greatly influenced by the sociology of archaeology; the various techniques discussed here are concentrated in pockets of popularity and regional investigative custom. Greater depth and distribution of knowledge in the requisite areas of species ecology, chemistry, and results will no doubt help break down regional boundaries to investigative practice.

6

SEASON OF DEATH

Beginning in the late 1960s a number of articles appeared in the malacological literature which demonstrated that shell is deposited whenever the mantle of the animal is extended, and this deposition is affected by a host of variables including some that are periodic in expression (e.g. tidal regimes). As a consequence, molluscs contain records of the passage of parts of days, days, clusters of days and years (Pannella and MacClintock 1968) and offer the potential for revealing annual fluctuation in many phenomena. Herein lay the potential for addressing an archaeological question of great significance – when had the shells at a site been harvested? Knowing when during the calendar year shellfish were harvested, known as shell seasonality, is a crucial element of understanding subsistence scheduling, site function, and settlement pattern.

The first attempt by archaeologists to determine when shells had been harvested relied on growth lines of *Tivela stultorum* from southern California (Chace 1969, Weide 1969). A study based on the height of scallop shells was conducted by Perlman in 1973 and Shackleton (1973) addressed seasonal collecting in a South African site that same year using isotopes. By 1974, then, all three methods in use in the 1990s of determining harvest time for shell-bearing creatures – growth line, oxygen isotope, and demography – had been introduced. Given that biologists, malacologists, and fisheries bureau workers recognized annuli (annual growth lines) on the surface of many species prior to the close of the nineteenth century and in shell cross-sections as early as 1914 (Isely 1914) it is somewhat surprising that the growth line technique did not appear earlier in archaeology.

In this chapter I will discuss each of the three techniques. Growth-line analysis is the most widely used technique and, consequently, is the most apt to be misused. I give it the greatest attention. Demographic characteristics are the easiest to employ, the least prone to misuse, and accommodate the largest sample sizes.

6.1   Demography

Populations of shelled animals go through annual phases of reproduction and recruitment. For many species there is but one reproductive period before death. The young recruits of these short-lived species are considerably smaller in size in the first months of growth than are the adults. The mean or modal

146

size of a population, or the distribution of individuals within size classes, could be used to identify segments of the year when these species were harvested.

Fluctuation in the mean and the standard deviation of height and length measurements typifies many populations of shellfish of all species and life duration. In months during and just past the typical period of recruitment, the mean shell height is reduced and the standard deviation increases. In the months just prior to the recruitment period, the mean height will be high and the standard deviation low since most individuals will have achieved adult height. Moreau (1980) calculated the mean and standard deviation of the height of long-lived bivalved shells *Chione* sp., *Anadara multicostata*, *Mactra isthmica*, *Mactra velata*, *Arca pacifica*, *Glycymeris* sp., and those of the gastropods *Strombus granulatus*, *Strombus gracilior*, and *Hexaplex regius* from each provenience at a Costa Rican site and proposed that the molluscs had been harvested over two rainy seasons and one dry season.

Some species are very short-lived. If the recruitment period is known and a death assemblage isolated, size can be used to indicate the month of life at the time of death. This technique has been used on at least two short lived bivalve taxa, *Donax variabilis* and *Pecten irradians*. Both species have life expectancies around two years. It possibly could be useful for dozens of other bivalved species.

Donax variabilis, a mid-tidal bivalve, has a seventeen-month life span beginning with spawning in March or April. In April the modal size peaks in the 3-mm length class with 17 mm in July, and 20 mm in October. By January the population evidences a peak in the 23-mm size class. Growth graphs are reproduced in Claassen (1986a) and Sigler-Eisenberg and Russo (1986).

Bay scallop (*Argopecten irradians concentricus*), which lives approximately sixteen months, was used by Perlman (1973) to infer season of harvest for New England (US) sites. Recently, size class changes through its one-year life cycle have been adopted for Florida sites (Russo and Quitmyer 1996:Figure 1). Growth begins in the winter and mass mortalities follow spawning.

From Florida's Gulf coast come statistics that indicate that the mean shell height in January is ca. 15 mm, in March ca. 21 mm, in May ca. 45 mm, and August through November ca. 60 mm, or in winter has an average of less than 20 mm, by June average 50 mm, and September 60 mm (Russo and Quitmyer 1996:218). Mean size of a death assemblage is the better statistic for scallops and other short-lived large molluscs that were targeted by humans for collection.

Kent (1988: 60) reported on his attempt to determine the time of death in *C. virginica* by measuring the size of first-year oysters (spat) attached to adult oysters. The exercise was abandoned because spat evidence highly variable growth rates and dead spat could not be consistently identified and sorted out from spat which were alive at the time the adult was collected.

Gastropods are also candidates for seasonality based on demographics.

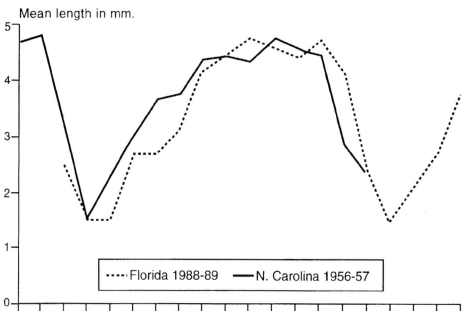

Fig. 28 Growth control for *Boonea impressa*.

Spiess and Hedden (1983) have applied this technique to univalves *Littorina littorea, Nucella lapillus,* and *Buccinum undatum.* Barber (1982) interpreted archaeological specimens of the marine gastropod *Littorina saxatilis* from Maine (US) using published studies of age–length–month correlations from Brittany populations, a questionable practice given the environmental differences between the two areas.

The parasitic gastropod *Boonea impressa* lives approximately one year, beginning in late spring and dying the next spring, based on growth-rate data from the southern end of its range – Texas, northeast Florida, and North Carolina. Therefore, an April harvest has both short (1 mm) and tall (7 mm) odostomes while the shortest population is present in June (Figure 28). In spite of the fact that *B. impressa* spawns throughout the year (and therefore a small individual could be collected in any month), the spring cohort is the largest and dominates the growth graph. The biological studies cited by Russo (1991) calculated the *mean* growth of each monthly death assemblage while Russo used *modal* size classes, partly to offset the possibility of mixed deposits. It is meaningless and an error to attempt to assign individual shells to a month or period in the year.

Another possibility for seasonality information lies in the population size and seasonal parameters for some species. For examples, juveniles of the tiny bivalve *Mulinia lateralis* come to shore in huge numbers in the winter where humans or other predators could intentionally or unintentionally gather them. Large quantities of the bryozoan *Conopeum* sp. found on economically useful bivalves are also a winter phenomenon.

The requirements for correlating demographic characteristics with time of collection are a growth control of several years' duration that demonstrates the temporal specificity of at least a few size classes, or a median or mean size of shell. Since size class distributions and means are the target statistics, sample sizes must be large. The projects utilizing *Donax variabilis* have been characterized by samples of 1,000 valves from each provenience. Necessary sample size is not discussed in Russo's study but those controls consist of up to 1,600 individuals. The fact that no equipment or cost beyond a caliper is required facilitates the use of every individual collected.

It is crucial in interpreting the results that single death assemblages are isolated. It is this requirement that makes the use of the commensal species *Mulinia lateralis* or *Boonea impressa* most treacherous. Both are so small that they should be expected to have fallen downward in a porous shell matrix. Retrieving specimens of commensal species from sealed pits that appear to have been filled in a very brief period will give the greatest confidence. Using species that are target prey for humans, such as scallops and coquina clams, raises the issue of size selection by the predators. The bryozoa abundance does hold some potential for archaeologists since the taxa colonize oyster shells and are therefore relatively inert in the site and since they are not selected by humans.

Because of the ease of processing these samples, the lack of equipment, low to nonexistent costs, and the potential for very large sample sizes, I believe that the demographic techniques used on commensal species are to be preferred over the other two techniques. I strongly encourage researchers to turn their attention in the coming decades to developing controls focused on shell height or length for short-lived species and to addressing site formation processes to isolate single death assemblages.

6.2   Oxygen isotopes

The use of oxygen isotopes to determine the death time of a shell relies on the ratio of the oxygen isotopes ^{16}O to ^{18}O or $\partial\ ^{18}O$. The isotopic ratio is determined by that in the water from which the carbonate was precipitated and by the temperature of the water at the time of precipitation. Where water temperature is the only significant variable, ^{18}O will fall ca. 0.2 ppt for each one degree Celsius rise in water temperature (Shackleton 1973). If the ratio in the water does not change during the life of the animal then the ratio in the shell will vary only with water temperature which presumably varies only seasonally. Death during warmer water (negative delta value) or death during cooler water (positive delta value) will be indicated by the isotope ratio.

Impacts of taphonomy on shells used in this technique have been explored in Chapter 3, and its use in paleoenvironmental reconstructions is discussed in Chapter 5. The method and its theoretical underpinnings are explained in detail in Rye and Sommer (1980).

Assay technique

Samples of shell from young adult animals (emphasized in Bailey et al. 1983, Deith 1986, Higham 1996) are removed in frequent intervals from the exterior side of the shell, umbo, or apex to margin, using a small dental drill. Samples as small as 0.3 mg are then put into solution with phosphoric acid and their carbon dioxide analyzed via mass spectrometry.

Usable species

Shells to be employed in oxygen isotopic analysis for seasonality determinations need (1) sufficient annual variation in the water temperature of their habitat, (2) a constant ∂ value or ratio of the water, and (3) no isotopic exchange with ground water in archaeological context (Higham 1996, Killingley 1981, Shackleton 1973). The animal's age has a major impact on both ^{18}O and ^{13}C isotopic levels in a shell. Samples from different annuli will differ in values (Barrera et al. 1990, Godfrey 1988) but, within any one annual increment, there is no difference in isotope value contributed by sample location (Barrera et al. 1990). Different species also vary in their sensitivity to oxygen isotopes and their utility (Deith 1988b, Godfrey 1988). For instance the isotopic profiles of the limpet genera *Patella* and *Tapes decussatus* have proven unreliable and earlier studies which employed them should be reassessed (Deith 1988b:135). Since the last days of life at the margin must be sampled, old adults in long lived species prove difficult to sample because months, even years, are compacted at the margin. Young and short lived individuals are needed. Successful work has been conducted with individuals of the species *Cardium edule, Cerastoderma glaucum, Cerithium vulgatum, Donax deltoides, Haliotis cracherodii, Macoma balthica, Monodonta turbinata, Mya arenaria, Mytilus edulis, Mytilus californianus, Perna perna, Thais emarginata,* and others.

The controls

Control shells have indicated that two shells might not produce exactly the same quantity of isotope, even when from the same population and killed on the same day. Godfrey (1988) found alarming variation in results from shells which had died at the same time. The differences in isotopic values suggested they had died at different times of the year. However, when a life series of samples was taken from two shells, both indicated death during the coolest season.

Several investigators assert that monthly resolution is not possible (Bailey et al. 1983, Godfrey 1988) nor may precise isotopic readings be assigned to groups of months or to seasons (Deith 1988b:143). When interpreting the profiles of various Mediterranean species, Deith found that it was impossible to distinguish late autumn from winter given the variation in isotopic range from year to year. Furthermore, "in the summer, when shell growth is fast and sea temperatures fluctuate considerably, the isotopic curve is not smooth. An edge value which registers a downward turn on the graph may thus be part of the summer fluctuations or may be the beginning of the autumn change to more positive values" (Deith 1988b:143). (The same problem is encountered with growth-line analysis, see below.) Instead of identifying isotopic values with specific months, Deith advocates considering the sequence of values prior to that at the margin and what the majority of the curves from other samples are showing to assign harvest time to the individual specimen.

Deith (1988b) attributed the variation in the modern shells' readings to age variation, where younger animals record environmental changes faster than do older animals. (The same situation has been uncovered for annulus formation.) Bailey et al. (1983) suspected different readings from different animals harvested the same day were due to the drill sampling, or differential growth rates. Godfrey (1988) cited "isotope offset" or expected variation within every population in shell isotope values for different values in samples of known death date. To accommodate these expected variations in isotopic readings within a single population, Godfrey, Deith, and Bailey et al. found it is necessary to take a life series of samples from each shell.

By plotting the isotope value of each sample against distance from umbo a visual picture of water temperatures, and thus years and seasons, is created. It is the direction of the values preceding the margin's assay that determines the "season" of harvest, during warming water, during cooling water, during warm- or cold-water periods. Increasingly positive ∂ values are interpreted to mean decreasing water temperature, and vice versa.

Control collections of animals killed monthly over several years are rare in this technique, since actual temperatures and specific months are not the research goals. Most investigators assume that they know when during the year cold and warm water occurs. Godfrey (1988) made monthly collections of *Donax deltoides* in southwest Victoria, Australia, and selected ten specimens from each month to assay at their margins. He found variation within a month that spanned the average values of half a year and that older individuals' growth slowed significantly. Killingley (1983) used surface water temperature records to create a fifty-year average of monthly mean temperature off the coast of Baja Norte, Mexico, to provide him guidance. Where control shells are routinely employed is to explore the suitability of a species. It does not appear that blind tests have been conducted. Can a known harvest period be interpreted correctly and at what frequency?

Sampling the site

Higham (1996) began his research on blue mussel (*Mytilus edulis aoteanus*) with fourteen shells, a sample size constrained by the "cost of the analysis, the availability of suitable shells, and the nature of the project." Only seven shells proved usable which he considered to be an inadequate sample size although a discussion of seasonality was proffered for the Shag River Mouth site in New Zealand. Killingley (1981:156) presented the results of fourteen *Mytilus californianus* shells from the Punta Minitas site in Mexico, in order to demonstrate the utility of the technique, but retracted their usefulness for seasonality interpretation by saying that he could not support the required assumption that these shells were a random sample of a homogeneous shell population.

Deith (1986:69) specifies that the shells to be run should come from a single deposit. If one believes that the deposit to be sampled is a homogeneous shell population harvested in a single month or season then one need only be concerned about the number of shells necessary. Apparently Killingley thought fourteen shells from such a deposit would be sufficient. However, if one wants to sample a shell matrix *site* then both the origin of the shells and the number of shells are at issue. If one believes that shell matrix sites accumulate through dozens and even hundreds of discard events, representing dozens and hundreds of harvests, then the goals should be to sample as many of these harvest events as possible and to estimate the number of harvests sampled. It does not appear that three shells or seven shells are adequate for assessing seasonality of anything grander than the harvest episode preserved in small sealed pits with small quantities of shells.

Isotopic determination of harvest time is recommended when rocky coast species are contained in a deposit. Although this is the most expensive technique of the three, sample sizes must not be ignored. It is ultimately a much cheaper technique than is growth line analysis given the two years or more of control collections that must be assembled and analyzed. The success that other disciplines are enjoying with oxygen isotopes (see particularly studies reviewed in Chapter 5) indicates that once archaeologists can overcome the monetary problems of sample sizes (in the numbers of shells analyzed) this technique will prove quite powerful.

6.3   Incremental growth technique

Numerous geologists, biologists, and malacologists have experimentally demonstrated the annual occurrence of growth breaks (also called rings, annuli) in a large number of shallow-water species (Barker 1964; Caddy and Billard 1976; Clark 1968, 1979; Craig and Hallam 1963; Davenport 1938; Gordon and Carriker 1978; House and Farrow 1968; Jones et al. 1978; Koike 1980; Mason 1957; Pannella and MacClintock 1968; Wilbur 1972; etc.). Annual patterns have been identified rarely in deep sea molluscan species.

Annual growth consists of a set of days when shell rich in calcium carbonate and conchiolin is deposited and a set of days when shell poor in calcium carbonate but rich in conchiolin is deposited. To the naked eye the former increment is tinted brown or white from the high $CaCO_3$ content and the latter set is gray. (The color scheme is reversed in transmitted microscope light.) A labeled cross-section of *M. mercenaria* is presented in Figure 7a.

Any disturbance which lasts long enough, such as some hurricanes or spawning, will cause a band of gray or transparent shell to form. When the animal is closed for a day or more, the extrapallial fluid dissolves away the calcium to liberate the oxygen necessary for anaerobic breathing. Long periods of closure cause the formation of a band of gray-tinted shell (rich in organic matter). For those species which can osmoregulate for many weeks at a time, the slow daily accretion of gray shell can become wide enough to tempt the analyst to interpret it as the annual period of slow growth.

Clark (1979) provides a detailed look at shell microstructure that the analyst should be familiar with when "reading" a shell, particularly quahog (*Mercenaria mercenaria*). (A petrographic microscope is not necessary.) In quahog, the annulus is marked on the surface by a notch. Internally, the annulus is recognizable as a dark line in the homogeneous layer forming the boundary between a transparent band (slow growth) and an opaque band (fast growth) of shell. Crossed-lamellar structure also corresponds to the slow-growth region and is bounded by the break in the senile region.

When viewed in cross-section, the slow-growth period in naiads is often marked by repeated starts and stops of growth with periostracum, prismatic, and nacreous layers emerging from underneath an older nacreous layer (Tevesz and Carter 1980). False annuli do occur and will be discussed in a later section.

The biological literature clearly indicates that individual shells do not grow at a uniform rate throughout the year or even throughout the "growing season," and frequently do not grow similar amounts during the same calendar period in different years. In the Bideford River of Prince Edward Island, Canada, June 1–July 13, 1939, the average increase in *M. mercenaria* shell length was 2.45 mm or 56.5 microns per day. In 1940, in the same locale and same period, the average length increase was 45.3 microns per day. At Glouchester Pt., Virginia, mid-March to mid-May 1955, the average increase was 30.8 microns per day but in 1956 it was 19.3 microns per day (Ansell 1968:394–395). On the North Shore of Cape Cod four studies of annual growth for shells 4 cm long at the time of measurement, collected in four different years, indicated increments of 24 mm, 20 mm, 10 mm, and 6 mm.

Ansell also compiled seasonal growth information from numerous latitudes. Seasonal growth (meaning increase in shell length) of quahogs living in mud from Narragansett Bay in 1951 proceeded in the following manner:

mid-April–June 18	3.09 mm	48.3 microns/day
June 18–July 16	5.36 mm	191.4 microns/day
July 16–Sept. 14	2.90 mm	103.6 microns/day
Sept. 14–mid-Nov.	0.20 mm	3.2 microns/day

Nor is there a uniform rate of seasonal growth in *any other record* presented by Ansell. Although I have utilized different measures of growth, data I compiled further illustrate that shell growth rates are unpredictable (Claassen 1990).

Growth controls

The key to the application of the incremental growth technique to archaeological shell assemblages lies in the growth control. What most archaeologists and many malacologists have failed to realize is that growth is neither uniform across years nor regular throughout the year (seasons). It is impossible to assay the conformity of an individual's growth or to interpret that growth pattern in a vacuum, without reference to a set of shells. Growth controls should consist, at a minimum, of dozens of specimens killed at least monthly over at least two full years. Control shells should then be either thin sectioned or peeled for archiving.

Sadly, growth controls have been poorly developed in many archaeological applications. The existing controls for projects conducted in the United States are contained in Table 9. In the southeastern US there has been much greater concern with growth variation and patterning. Northeastern controls are often incomplete in monthly coverage, small in sample size, and represent no more than the growth situation for one year. Even when controls are made, the variation in individual responses to growth stimuli is often ignored. Several archaeologists have assumed that all shells start growing on a set day, a zero point, to which counts of daily lines could be added to determine time of death, even though the controls do not support this contention (Claassen 1990). The lack of controls and the length of time required to set up proper controls are a serious impediment to the application of this technique.

Preparing a specimen

One valve of a bivalve should be chosen for examination. Early projects examined the surficial lines on shells, but most recent projects have utilized cross-sectioning techniques.

External observation
Annual indications of growth can be seen on the surface of most shells.

Unfortunately, for most bivalves, annual lines, spawning lines, and trauma lines are similarly registered on the surface of the shells and are difficult, if not impossible, to distinguish. Lutz (1976) warned against the use of surficial lines when he found that the number of surface rings varied from three to six on two-year-old *Mytilus edulis* from Maine. Jones et al. (1978) experimentally determined that for the surf clam, *Spisula solidissima*, the identification of annual external growth lines led to the overestimation of the age of young clams and underestimation of the age of old clams. Surficial examination of growth lines in the bottom hinge of eastern oyster, *Crassostrea virginica*, is advocated by Custer and Doms (1990) and others. Russo evaluated the attempts to use the external lines but concluded that "no method for determining [oyster] seasonality has ever been forwarded in any detail to be replicable by independent researchers" (1991). Examination of internal growth lines in oyster is underway (Herbert and Steponaitis 1993).

During senility the growth rate slows considerably with a very high number of annual bands compressed together. This phenomenon renders surficial counting of annuli nearly impossible on long-lived animals.

Cross-section preparation

There are three ways to view internal growth, all of which require sectioning of the shell: thick section, thin section, and acetate peel. Cutting a valve into two halves is all that is required for thick sections. Specimens that are poorly preserved may require embedding in a matrix prior to sectioning although their readability may not warrant the effort. Researchers working with an extremely thin-shelled species or with a small section of a shell such as a chondrophore will find embedded specimens easier to manipulate. Impregnating poorly preserved specimens with an epoxy may also be done but is rarely needed for degraded specimens can rarely be read.

Thin sections and acetate peels are useful when measurements are wanted, when photographic enlargements are wanted, and when archival (control) specimens are prepared for long-term storage. Clark (1979) preferred thin sections over peels to study mineralogy and crystallography. Color variations were visible on polished sections but not on acetate peels, while lines could be observed on peels but were difficult to see on polished sections (Clark 1979, Lutz 1976.) O'Brien and Peter (1983:3) found their accuracy in assigning the correct time of death to specimens with known death dates to be higher with thin sections (78 percent) than with either thick sections or peels (both < 50 percent). Ham and Irvine (1975) reported thin sections to be more reliable than thick sections. I have found that thin-section readings are markedly different from readings of thick sections. Consistency in type of section is necessary.

Typical geological sectioning blades and saws are unsuitable for cutting many species because of the damage they do to the prismatic layer. Specialized equipment, particularly a low-speed saw, is preferable. Beyond the expense of

Table 9. Shell seasonality controls in North America
(Indicated are the months and years of collecting, and the number of animals collected.)

	Species	J	F	M	A	M	J	J	A	S	O	N	D	N=	Year	Ref.
Penobscot Bay MA	M.a.	6	–	–	8	7	9	12	4	4	4	–	–	54	82-83	1
Damariscotta ME	M.a.	–	10	10	10	10	10	10	10	10	10	10	10	110	1980	2
Eastham MA	M.m.	–	12	10	12	11	13	13	10	–	10	6	12	109	81-82	3
? MA	A.i.	–	–	–	–	–	x	x	x	–	–	–	–	53	71-72	4
Narragansett RI	M.m.	–	10	10	12	10	10	10	10	10	9	10	11	112	82-83	5
Shark Inlet NJ	M.m.	–	6	–	6	–	6	–	6	–	6	–	6	36	1981	6
L.Egg Harbor NJ	M.m.	41	45	40	36	39	36	35	37	37	37	35	44	462	1986	6
		46	41	34	37	37	37	31	40	39	38	36	34	450	1987	6
		37	36	30	27	35	33	29	38	–	–	–	41	306	1988	6
St. Mary's R. VA	C.v.	–	–	–	–	–	9	–	–	8	–	–	11	28	<88	7
Bird Shoals NC	M.m.	–	13	–	19	–	11	–	11	24	8	–	8	94	1981	6
		34	34	23	40	36	39	–	–	–	–	–	–	206	1984	6
		–	–	–	–	–	–	–	–	–	–	–	–	184	1985	6
		43	33	37	33	50	48	50	52	50	52	47	35	497	1986	6
		35	30	29	35	42	45	45	48	52	30	38	31	466	1987	6
		37	33	38	34	42	47	53	41	47	44	35	31	372	1988	6
Kings Bay GA	M.m.	x	x	x	x	x	–	x	x	x	x	x	x	69	81-82	8
various, Texas	R.c.	–	–	–	–	–	–	–	25	–	–	–	–	25	1969	9
		–	–	–	–	–	–	32	27	–	–	–	–	59	1971	9
		–	–	–	–	45	–	–	50	84	22	–	–	201	1972	9
		–	–	–	–	–	–	–	14	14	–	34	–	48	1973	9
		–	–	–	–	–	–	50	50	45	50	–	34	229	1974	9
		–	100	200	100	195	75	–	–	–	–	100	–	770	1975	9
Palmetto Bend TX	R.c.	–	50	50	50	50	50	50	50	50	50	50	–	500	74-75	10
Escambia Bay FL	R.c.	–	–	11	–	60	96	33	–	40	–	51	–	291	1984	6
Alaqua FL	R.c.	–	–	10	–	14	–	12	–	–	–	10	–	46	1983	6
		–	13	–	–	–	–	–	12	–	12	15	–	52	1984	6
		–	–	–	–	–	–	–	–	33	35	39	32	139	1985	6

														n	Year	Ref
Tampa Bay FL		36	41	38	33	35	35	30	20	28	30	32	31	389	1986	6
		33	24	31	31	31	31	31	32	32	32	29	31	368	1987	6
		32	32	29	30	—	—	—	—	—	—	—	—	123	1988	6
Alligator Harbor	M.c.	18	14	22	14	16	17	21	20	—	24	31	55	252	83–84	6
	D.v.	x	—	x	x	—	x	x	—	—	x	—	—	?<	1968	11
Ozette, WA	P.s.	—	—	5	5	5	5	—	5	—	5	—	10	35	78–79	12
Boundary Bay BC	many	—	—	8	10	—	—	—	—	—	—	—	—	18	80–81	13

Key:
A.i. = *Argopecten irradians*
C.v. = *Crassostrea virginica*
D.v. = *Donax variabilis*
M.a. = *Mya arenaria*
M.c. = *Mercenaria campechiensis*
M.m. = *Mercenaria mercenaria*
P.s. = *Protothaca staminea*
R.c. = *Rangia cuneata*

1, Spiess and Hedden 1983; 2, Hancock 1982; 3, Hancock 1984; 4, Perlman 1973; 5, Bernstein 1993; 6, Claassen 1991b; 7, Kent 1988; 8, Quitmyer et al. 1985; 9, Aten 1981; 10, Skelton 1978; 11, Tiffany 1968; 12, Wessen 1982; 13, Ham 1982.

the low-speed saw, thin sections and peels require additional supplies and labor time. Generally, acetate peels require a higher magnification for viewing than do thin sections.

To thin section a bivalve for a control collection (subject shells are only cross-sectioned), I select one valve, mount it in a chuck for the Buehler Company's Isomet low-speed saw, and cut it perpendicular to the direction of growth, the cut passing through the umbo. Once cut, the new surface is ground on sandpaper by an electric grinder using any one of several grit sizes. The prepared edge is first pushed into a shallow pool of epoxy and then pushed firmly onto a glass slide. (It is often possible to mount more than one shell on one slide.) The date of death or the provenience is incised into the slide. The slide-mounted half valve is then mounted onto a hot waffle chuck with melted wax on its surface. Once dry, the chuck with slide is put on the Isomet low-speed saw, and a cut one-tenth of a millimeter wide is made. The slide and chuck are put back onto the hot plate to melt the bond. The thin section is ground carefully using a slide holder and polished to ensure transparency using the electric grinder.

The glass-mounted thin section or peel can be inserted directly into a photographic enlarger and used in place of a negative. Both section and peel can be inserted into a slide duplicator to produce a color transparency of the image, even inserted into microfiche readers or slide projectors for class viewing and measuring.

Problems in reading incremental growth structures

Cross-sectioning shells does not eliminate all problems in identifying annuli. Interpreting or reading the sectioned shell occasionally is impossible and frequently is problematic. Most bivalve species are best read at the margin but for some species the hinge is the preferred target area (e.g. *C. virginica*). Subsequent problems center around visualizing the target area and distinguishing the boundaries of annual growth increments.

Any investigation which involves aging or measuring of annual growth in shell must avoid incorrect identification of annuli – either ending the increment prematurely or extending it too far. There are several tricks useful for identifying false, missing, and extra annuli. One is to rely on the pattern of internal growth lines in a shell in making decisions about which bands represent the annual periods of fast and slow growth. If the previous increments are approximately the same size as the suspect increment, or if the pattern is one of decreasing growth, then the year designation may be valid. Many times a storm disturbance will result in sand grains lodging in a deep chasm between daily increments. Another clue is the occurrence of two sets of slow-growth lines "too close" together. A very thin band of gray lines and/or an occasionally very precisely bounded gray set may be clues to an origin in an irregular event. There are shells where all annuli are very thin and precisely delineated (Figure 7a). I have usually found that a final growth increment whose measurement exceeds that of the previous year, upon second inspection, has been incorrectly delineated. In many naiads a bump or pustule of shell corresponds to the place where the annuli exits the shell.

Lighting has a great deal to do with the image and consequently should be toyed with for almost every shell examined. I frequently change the angle of the mirror reflecting the light source into the microscope and even change the reflecting surface, seesawing from a glossy finish to a glassy finish. The adjustment I make most often is to change from one face of the slide to the other. Upon occasion I even change from transmitted light to reflected light. Some color patterns are best viewed with natural light. Without standardizing the section thickness, thin sections will vary in thickness (neither the saw chucks nor the glass slides are as uniform in thickness as we might imagine) which will bend light differently. One should add to this variability the differences in epoxy viscosity between batches, which also interferes with the passage of light.

It is most frequently senile animals that cannot be read (Figure 29) . Since it is difficult to judge what growth phase they are in, often the senile growth animals cannot and should not be included in seasonality work. Therefore, I have produced growth control data tables with and without these troublesome shells (Table 10).

Determining expected growth

Many researchers have divided annual shell growth into quarters or thirds of the calendar year and then estimated which quarter or third is represented by the observed amount of growth since the last annuli. Monks (1977:381) defined a spring death as a shell with less than 25 percent of the previous year's growth accomplished, summer death as 25–50 percent, fall death 50–75 percent and winter death 75–100 percent accomplished. Ferguson (1975:9) described spring death as 7–33 percent of the previous year's shell, summer as 33 to 75 percent, fall as 75–100 percent, and winter as 0–6 percent of the growth. "The annual growth measurement was then divided by three, resulting in an approximation of growth for a given season," said Drover (1974:227). In each case, the underlying assumption is that of a uniform growth rate across three or four divisions of the calendar year. A second assumption is that this growth rate is duplicated in all other years. It is clear from the control data previously presented in this chapter that the first assumption is not valid.

That growth rates are not consistent among shellfish (demonstrated by Ansell's 1968 data presented above) is aptly shown with a curve-fitting exercise. The author fit numerous annual growth sequences to seven types of curves. In a sample of eleven *M. mercenaria* shells from one North Carolina site five

Fig. 29 Incremental growth in a senile animal (growing edge to left). Black shell is fast growth while white shell is slow growth. What constitutes a growth increment? Are all slow growth increments at the left end annual periods of slow growth?

different curves were chosen as the best fit. For a subsample of 117 shells where the correlation coefficient of curve fit was r = .80 or better and the sequence of growth was four years or longer, the hyperbolic curve was chosen as the best descriptor (for 41 percent of the shells) and the exponential curve a distant second (21 percent). The frequency with which the other curves were the best fit is the geometric curve (12 percent), log curve (11 percent), quadratic (8 percent), inverse linear (4 percent), and linear (3 percent). Clearly the assumption of uniform growth among individuals is false.

Do the various methods for predicting the expected growth provide significantly different solutions? I examined several shells killed on the same day. Selecting one animal I averaged the annual growth of the previous four years of life, to find that the achieved growth was only 17 percent of that predicted. Using a mean of the previous two years yielded an achievement of 25 percent of the predicted growth, while comparing the 33 mm of actual growth to that achieved in the previous year of life indicated 31 percent of the growth had transpired at the time of death. The results then were growth predictions that indicated 17 percent, 25 percent, and 31 percent of the growth had been

Table 10a. *Growth variation at Bird Shoals, NC: percent of all quahogs* (Mercenaria mercenaria) *dying in fast growth*

Year	Jan	Feb	Mar	Apr	May	Jun	Jul	Aug	Sep	Oct	Nov	Dec
1980	–	–	–	–	–	–	5	–	–	–	–	–
1981	–	93	–	95	–	19	–	0	–	0	–	88
1984	100	100	100	98	86	8	–	–	–	–	–	–
1985	–	–	–	–	–	–	–	–	10	56	77	86
1986	100	97	97	100	54	6	0	4	31	33	92	97
1987	94	97	90	100	60	4	0	0	6	48	77	58
1988	100	91	100	94	90	34	0	0	28	–	–	–
Range in fast growth percent												
Max	100	100	100	100	90	34	5	4	31	56	92	97
Min	94	91	90	94	54	4	0	0	5	0	77	58
N	149	144	127	161	170	190	172	151	196	134	120	105

Table 10b. *Percent of measurable quahogs dying in fast growth* (*without seniles*)

Year	Jan	Feb	Mar	Apr	May	Jun	Jul	Aug	Sep	Oct	Nov	Dec
1980	–	–	–	–	–	–	0	–	–	–	–	–
1981	–	90	–	93	–	22	–	0	–	0	–	80
1982	–	86	–	–	–	–	–	–	–	–	–	–
1984	100	100	100	97	91	9	–	–	–	–	–	–
1985	–	–	–	–	–	–	–	–	13	58	82	86
1986	100	97	100	100	54	6	0	6	31	32	92	96
1987	94	96	95	100	53	0	0	0	8	46	76	52
1988	100	93	100	97	89	36	0	0	20	–	–	–
Range												
Max	100	100	100	100	91	36	0	6	31	58	92	96
Min	94	86	95	93	53	0	0	0	8	0	76	52
N	145	126	108	147	145	171	144	130	169	119	115	139

achieved, to some investigators indicative of death during either the first quarter or second quarter of the year. These values demonstrate an alarming *lack* of agreement between methods. Clearly, the method by which an investigator generates the expected value greatly influences the perception of when the animal died. Which method is more accurate?

The accuracy of the prediction method was tested in two ways with the data from North Carolina quahog shells. First, the various methods were used to predict the amount of growth in the final *full* year of life, the penultimate year, a known quantity in every case. Second, blind samples were run against monthly growth profiles which had been constructed with the various averaging methods. After the month of death was predicted, the true death time was revealed offering some discriminating data on those prediction methods. The results of each test are given below and in Claassen (1990, 1993).

The fewer the number of years used in generating the expected value the more accurate the calculation of growth achieved for North Carolina quahog shells. When only the previous full year of life (penultimate year) was used as the basis for the expected growth, 19 percent of the predicted values fell within 90–110 percent of the actual value (N = 242 shells). When the previous two years were averaged, 7 percent of the predicted values came similarly close to the actual value, and when three years were averaged, the figure was also 7 percent.

Predicted growth values were calculated for a set of eight quahogs using five-year, four-year, three-year, and two-year means, and the prior year, and using curve fitting. Again, the growth to be predicted was that of the final *full* year of life, a known quantity. In 50 percent of the cases, curve fitting yielded a prediction of shell growth that was 90–110 percent of what actually accumulated. For four specimens curve fitting gave the best prediction, for three specimens using only the last year gave the best prediction. The four-year mean and the two-year mean each gave the most accurate prediction in one case.

For New Jersey quahogs an average of the growth in the prior two years more often correctly predicted the actual growth (17 percent of 319 cases). When only the previous year was used as the expected value, growth for 15 percent of 384 shells came within 10 percent of the actual growth. When three years' growth was averaged the prediction was accurate in only 8 percent of the 219 cases.

Measuring annual growth increments is not only a time-consuming process that requires multiple years of life to be visible in each shell selected but the manner by which one predicts the ultimate growth increment varies with species and even within populations. Most troublesome is the failure for growth percentages to equate to specific months or even seasons (see below). There is, in fact, no merit in measuring or predicting expected growth.

Interpretive procedures

Four growth line procedures are commonly employed to derive an estimate of shellfishing seasonality and will be compared here. These are (1) percentage of animals in fast and slow growth, (2) percentage of animals in three opaque and three translucent growth phases, (3) daily line counts, and (4) comparison of growth in the death year to that of previous years. A review of the various aspects of each of these techniques and then the accuracy of the results generated in these different ways are assessed. I will ultimately conclude that those techniques which require measurements of annuli and counting of daily lines are of the least value in this work while the strongest interpretation comes from the joint use of both the fast/slow and opaque/translucent techniques.

Fast/slow

The simplest technique of those to be discussed here is the calculation of the percentage of animals dying in fast growth. Thin sections are not required (but recall that thin sections can be read more reliably that thick sections), no measuring is required, and no decisions need be made about growth in previous years. Animals as young as one year can be used. No other growth-line technique can be executed as quickly as this one. It takes approximately twenty minutes to examine a set of forty-five shells for color at the margin. Measuring annuli for forty-five shells takes approximately two and a half hours. The F/S technique can be applied to a greater percentage of prepared shells.

Unfortunately, only a few percentages are monthly specific and most interpretations are no finer than four to eight months. Given that the interpretations derived from measurements are no more accurate than those derived from this far simpler method, the use of the F/S technique is preferable to that of measuring. Since the largest sample sizes can be obtained with this technique it should be used in every study in tandem with other techniques. The F/S technique is not robust enough to be relied upon as the sole source of data for shell seasonality.

Interpretation is still troublesome with this technique, in spite of the elimination of measurements. The assignment of an individual shell to either fast or slow growth at the time of its death, based as it is on color, seems rather straightforward, but it is not. When viewing a thin section illuminated from the bottom, brown shell equals opaque or fast growth and white shell signifies translucent or slow growth. Subsequent examinations of the same shell should agree with the growth phase assignment, i.e., changes in interpretation should be rare. But far more often than expected, subsequent examinations and interpretations contradicted earlier determinations. Table 11 indicates how often I changed my mind about what growth phase a shell was in at death and even the number of shells that were readable. In general, the longer I viewed shells, the more confidence I had in my ability to interpret the coloration, thus the readable sample sizes usually increase with each reading.

Two different determinations are being made when using the fast/slow technique for each shell and a change in either can result in a contradictory interpretation of death time. First, the reader must determine the shell color at the margin. A color change only a few days thick can often be overlooked as can an epoxy edge effect or a lighting problem. Second, the shell color must be *interpreted* – does it indicate a seasonal period of fast growth (or slow growth) or an unseasonable growth spurt (or slow down)? An animal which died in slow growth may actually have been experiencing temporary trouble in what was its annual phase of fast growth. Unseasonable temperatures could account for small increments of either fast or slow growth in the "wrong" season. Determining what season of growth the animal was in is far less straightfor-

Table 11. *Variation in reading marginal color for F/S technique on New Jersey* M. mercenaria (*number of animals in fast growth at time of death*)

	Reading 1	Reading 2	Reading 3
December 1985	23 of 29[1]	32 of 40	35 of 41
January 1986	17 of 37	19 of 41	28 of 41
February 1986	16 of 28	28 of 43	27 of 45
March 1986	21 of 29	18 of 39	18 of 39
April 1986	33 of 37	32 of 34	32 of 36
May 1986	25 of 26	36 of 40	
June 1986	14 of 32	6 of 36	
July 1986	5 of 32	0 of 36	
August 1986	5 of 31	1 of 37	
September 1986	10 of 31	16 of 36	11 of 37
October 1986	10 of 29	16 of 36	14 of 37
November 1986	17 of 32	21 of 35	17 of 35

[1] Variation in this second number reflects reading success. In the December 1985 example each subsequent attempt to read the prepared shells resulted in a greater number of specimens being interpretable. Fifty shells were prepared in each month.

ward than determining what color marks the margin. Most contradictions evident in Table 11 are due to a change in interpretation of the *meaning* of the color. Contradictions are more prevalent in some months when weather is typically quite variable such as May and October.

Opaque/translucent

The O/T technique as described in Quitmyer et al. (1985) divides the molluscan year into fast (opaque) and slow (translucent) growth and each of these categories into three subdivisions, O1, O2, O3 or T1, T2, T3. If the animal died in fast growth, for instance, the actual phase is determined by comparing the amount of fast growth in that last year to that achieved in the penultimate year's fast-growth period. If the new fast-growth is less than 50 percent of the old fast growth, the phase assigned is O1, if 50–99 percent O2, and if 100 percent or more, O3. Application of the technique requires only rudimentary measurements but does require specimens with at least the full record of the previous year of life. This requirement reduces the usable sample size of prepared sections below that obtainable with the F/S procedure. However, the finer subdivisions of the molluscan year allow for finer subdivisions of the human calendar than is possible with any other procedure examined.

This procedure shares the same interpretive problems as described for the F/S procedure. When is slow growth actually seasonal slow growth or an interruption of fast growth (and vice versa)? I had greater success in assigning translucent phases when I required white shell to occur in the prismatic zone of *M. mercenaria*. Contradictions in multiple readings of the shells are comparatively rare, however, and errors are generally clerical in nature, e.g. recording O1 instead of T1.

Daily line counts

Early paleontological work with fossil and modern shells addressed the length of the solar year several epochs ago by counting the number of daily lines between annuli. Several archaeologists have continued this practice apparently with the idea that this technique is more accurate than any of the others. Instead, it is the most difficult technique to apply and gives unreliable results.

To count daily lines a high magnification is needed particularly in the senile region. Keeping track of one's place in the dozens of daily lines in view is difficult and moving the shell across the view is confusing. Many researchers count lines from microphotographs, adding to the cost of the process. Clark (1968:800) demonstrated that daily growth lines are not an infallible record of a day's passage. He also argued for the use of maximum counts, not average counts, as most representative of a population.

Counting daily lines is motivated by the idea that there is a zero date or a short period of days during which all shellfish in a community begin to grow, starting a new molluscan year. Bernstein (1993), Deith (1983), Hancock (1984), and Kioke (1980) made small monthly growth control collections and counted, for each individual, the number of daily lines added since the last annulus. By counting back with a calendar, one finds that in Bernstein's collection of shells from Narragansett Bay, RI, new growth began as early as January 27 and as late as May 14, a 109-day window. Hancock's control from Cape Cod (for which I have arbitrarily had to assign the day of the month the collection was made) indicates growth was initiated anywhere from November 3 to January 7, a two-month, 65-day period (Claassen 1990). Deith's (1988b) control consisted of shells collected in only May and September over a three-year period, and resulted in a beginning date of April 22 plus or minus ten days and an ending date of September 25 plus or minus twenty-one days. She found that in Scottish specimens of *Cerastoderma edule* growth-line counts were only good for distinguishing five months, April through September, and that the other seven months were indistinguishable with this technique and this species from this latitude. Koike (1980) specified the zero point in *Meretrix lusoria* to be February 14 with a standard deviation of $\pm$ 17.6 days. Her control spanned twelve months from June 22 to May 11, 1971–72 (Koike 1980:29–30). Adding other years to these various growth controls will broaden the ranges even more.

The assumption of an essentially uniform date for growth initiation has been the basis of much of the work in the Northeastern US (e.g. Bernstein 1993,

Hancock 1984), in Scotland (Deith 1986, 1988b), and in Japan (e.g. Koike 1980, Koike and Okamura 1994, Toizumi 1994) but it cannot be sustained. Bernstein's assignment of April 1 as the arbitrary start-up or zero date to which daily line counts are added, even though the actual window is January 27 to May 14, means that his estimates could be 2.5 months too late or 1.5 months too early, an error range which spans a third of the year and one full season. Toizumi (1994) thought one could simply count lines as one counts days on the calendar and derive a harvest time, apparently unaware that on a single day shellfish with many different daily line counts could be harvested. Toizumi extrapolated the harvest times derived from daily line counts on shells retrieved from a single column sample to the stratigraphic unit and thence the seasonality of the fish found within that unit and finally the site at large.

Measurements of annual growth
One of the earliest applications of growth-line data to the question of shellfishing seasonality was to measure the amount of growth achieved in the final year of life, compare that to some estimate of the expected amount of growth the creature would have achieved if it had lived the full year, and then correlate the amount of growth to the anticipated amount of time it would take to grow that much in a year. Serious problems with this method have been largely unrecognized. Trouble arises in estimating the expected growth, and in growth-rate variation due to aging and environmental fluctuations (see above, Determining Expected Growth).

Table 12 (Amount of Growth) depicts the variation in the amount of growth achieved in different months and years in quahogs living in Little Egg Harbor, New Jersey. Dividing the growth in the final full year of life into the subsequent growth achieved at the time of death results in a range of percentages in January 1986 of 7 percent to 89 percent of the previous year's growth. It should be apparent in Tables 10 and 12 that there is tremendous similarity in growth values from month to month and tremendous variation in growth timing from year to year. As discussed in the earlier section, Determining Expected Growth, using measurements to *predict when a prehistoric shellfish died* is unreliable.

Accuracy of growth-line seasonality studies
Beyond these individual procedures, the archaeological shell, fish, and tooth seasonality studies available fall into one of two camps reflecting attitudes about what type of sample is to be interpreted. The normative assumptions that all shells respond to growth stimuli identically, and that the timing of these stimuli is predictable each year, have resulted in the practice of assigning harvest time to individual shells. With large growth controls it is clear that neither assumption is true but that there is marked growth variation in any population on any day of the year. But the range and mean of that variation, as well as the element varying, all vary in a patterned way throughout the year.

Table 12. *Growth statistics for a New Jersey control collection of* M. mercenaria *(1,281 shells are included in the first and second methods, 887 in third)*

	Year	Opaque, translucent %						Fast%	Amount of growth
		O1	O2	O3	T1	T2	T3		
Jan	86	76	5	10	5	5	0	66	7%–89%
	87	50	20	0	10	15	5	44	2%–146%
	88	62	7	0	3	10	7	75	2%–66%
	Total	54	12	2	5	9	4		2%–146%
Feb	86	73	0	0	20	7	0	61	5%–93%
	87	70	4	4	4	13	4	56	3%–97%
	88	63	19	11	4	0	4	82	5%–69%
	Total	68	9	6	8	6	3		3%–97%
Mar	86	46	8	8	23	15	0	49	5%–147%
	87	60	16	0	12	4	8	70	13%–100%
	88	43	26	9	4	0	17	56	3%–66%
	Total	51	18	5	11	5	10		3%–147%
Apr	86	74	16	5	0	0	5	92	7%–89%
	87	54	0	4	29	13	0	55	8%–89%
	88	62	24	14	0	0	0	96	6%–65%
	Total	61	14	8	9	5	0		6%–89%
May	86	31	38	31	0	0	0	90	15%–120%
	87	74	11	9	0	0	6	81	8%–89%
	88	15	46	38	0	0	0	89	8%–90%
	Total	40	28	22	0	0	2		8%–120%
June	86	5	8	3	65	0	0	17	9%–123%
	87	47	16	0	34	0	3	62	8%–57%
	88	22	39	22	17	0	0	79	14%–100%
	Total	26	18	6	49	0	1		8%–123%
July	86	0	0	0	100	0	0	0	26%–110%
	87	17	0	0	21	17	34	26	13%–126%
	88	0	0	0	82	9	9	11	9%–154%
	Total	12	0	0	64	9	16		9%–154%
Aug	86	4	0	0	59	30	7	3	22%–115%
	87	15	0	0	46	15	23	15	12%–133%
	88	0	0	0	68	16	16	6	40%–135%
	Total	9	0	0	55	20	15		12%–135%
Sep	86	40	0	0	20	30	10	38	8%–86%
	87	17	0	0	21	24	38	16	14%–139%
	Total	29	0	0	20	27	24		8%–139%
Oct	86	55	0	0	30	10	5	38	2%–85%
	87	27	3	13	7	20	30	37	3%–97%
	Total	38	2	8	16	16	20		2%–97%
Nov	86	56	12	0	16	12	4	51	9%–117%
	87	60	0	0	7	0	33	65	6%–86%
	Total	58	8	0	13	8	15		6%–117%
Dec	85	82	4	0	11	4	0	79	4%–93%
	86	48	7	0	15	11	19	38	9%–92%
	87	74	8	0	4	0	13	81	3%–93%
	Total	68	6	0	10	5	10		3%–93%

Because variation in growth is expected and accounted for in those studies where the researcher recognizes growth variation, only sets of archaeological shells are interpreted and only one harvest time is predicted for any one set. Because variation is present in growth records in a population, researchers who assign death times to individual shells always conclude at least two seasons of shellfishing.

Blind samples can indicate differences in accuracy of the growth-line procedures discussed herein. Two blind samples were generated for the author during a three-year collecting program in Bird Shoals, NC. Each blind sample was compared to the controls for F/S, O/T, and measurements (Claassen 1993). The data from these blind samples were not part of those used to construct the controls.

Sample 99 consisted of eleven thin-sectioned shells, none of which died in fast growth. Ninety-one percent of those shells were in phase T1 at death and 9 percent were in phase T2. The mean growth percent was 55.03 percent and the range of measurements was 29–84 percent of previous year's growth. Referring to Table 10, the percent of shells in fast growth at the time of death quickly targets a harvest time of August, September, or October. The O/T characteristics indicate collection during July or August. When considering growth measurements using the last year of life to generate the expected value, the mean was similar to that for June but the minimum value resembled that for July. Since both July and August are implicated twice by these various estimators, the collection date was predicted to have been during one of those months. In fact, this collection was made on two different days, one in June and one in July, 1986 (Table 13).

Sample 88 contained only nine shells. Forty-four percent of these shells died during fast growth. Growth phase O1 was dominant, T3 was secondary, and O2, O3, and T1 were absent. The mean growth percentage was 58.38 percent and the range in percents was from 5 percent to 137 percent. The percentage of shells in fast growth at the time of death is typical of October. The O/T profile is indicative of the period September through November (Table 12). The mean growth percent is similar to June, July, and September, and the range is indistinct. September and October are implicated twice and were assumed to indicate the period of collection. The collection was actually made September 12, 1987 (Table 13).

Two additional blind samples were procured from collecting activities in southern New Jersey (Claassen 1993:74). Sample 1 had seventeen shells, sample 2, twenty shells. In each of these cases predictions based on mean growth and range of growth percents were off by one month or completely failed to bracket the actual collection time (Table 13). Estimates of harvest time using the O/T procedure and the F/S procedure were consistently within one month or indicated the correct month of harvest. It appears that even greater calendrical specificity is possible when data sets from both procedures are combined and

Table 13. *Accuracy of seasonality methods in predicting death time using blind tests*

Technique	NC 99 n = 11	NC 88 n = 9	NJ 1 n = 17	NJ 2 n = 20
F/S	Aug, Sep, Oct	Oct	Jul, Aug	Dec, Jan, Mar, Apr, Jun
O/T	Jul, Aug	Sep, Oct, Nov	Jul, Aug	Sep, Oct, Nov, Dec, Jan
Mean	Jun	Jun, Jul, Sep	Jun, Jul, Aug	May, Jun, Sep
Range	Jul	??	Aug	Oct, Dec–Apr
Conclusion	Jul–Aug	Sep–Oct	Aug	Dec–Jan
Actual date	Jul 15, Aug 16	Sep 12	Jul 15	Jan 17

compared to the combined data sets from the control collection. Even then, an error range of four weeks should be expected. To restate these findings, the two color based techniques are superior in accuracy to daily line counts or increment measurements.

Sampling for growth-line studies

Sampling requirements for growth line seasonality work have been greatly neglected. How many shells are needed in a control? How many readable shells are needed in the archaeological set to be interpreted with a particular control? How many shells are needed from a shell matrix site to determine harvesting seasonality? Each of these questions will now be explored.

Sampling for the growth control

The growth control used by most researchers is usually inadequate for the archaeological task, being comprised of too few animals killed too infrequently in too few years. Even more alarming is the failure, in many of the premier studies in various regions, to refer to any growth control (Jensen 1982, Pallant 1990). Many North American shell seasonality controls lack animals killed at regular intervals throughout a calendar year (Table 9). While acknowledging that water temperature is a major stimulus to growth initiation and slow-down, researchers typically sampled only one calendar year. In order to employ these controls in archaeological work, a normative view of annual growth is demanded. One has to assume that conditions in the year of collecting for the control were "normal" and that the growth response throughout the year was "normal." (Fish and tooth growth-line controls suffer from the same assumptions.)

Collecting *M. mercenaria* in North Carolina from 1980 to 1988 has resulted in live animals killed every calendar month throughout the year, each month represented in at least four years, some months in six years. A similar collecting regime was conducted in New Jersey over four calendar years (Table 9).

Analysis of over 3,000 cross-sections clearly indicates that a model of annual shell growth based on only one or even two years of control specimens would be erroneous. With three to six years of data to examine, no calendar month has a unique range of growth measures and a Scheffe test for differences between means for different measures of growth each month could identify no more than two gross "seasons" in either locale. Season 1 is September through June and season 2, July through August.

Another problematic feature of most researchers' growth controls is the small number of individuals collected in a year (Table 9, e.g. Maine, Massachusetts, Virginia). Several workers had monthly sample sizes of as few as ten shells. It is assumed that the reaction of a population of shellfish (or fish or deer) to environmental stimuli is adequately reflected in the behavior (growth) of an extremely small subsample of animals.

The larger the sample size, the greater the variability seen in growth response. That variability then must be captured in the growth measures, not ignored, averaged, or standardized. Larger sample sizes and more inquisitive sampling programs can correct the errors associated with these controls.

Sample sizes needed to use the controls

How many shells are needed to duplicate the growth patterns generated by the control collections presented in Tables 10 and 12? In other words, how many readable shells must subsequent researchers have in their sets of shells in order to use these controls? The answer will be dependent on the control in use. Furthermore, the different procedures for interpreting shell growth in a set of shells have different sample size requirements.

The F/S method utilizes percents. The more shells there are, the smaller the subdivisions of 100 and the greater the replicability of the results when an equally large or larger second sample is compared. In setting up the F/S controls for New Jersey and North Carolina large numbers of shells (1,000 +) were used; it is now possible to identify some percentage points that appear to be quite temporally specific. Percentages of New Jersey animals in fast growth that are temporally specific (Table 12) are 91–96 April only; 88–90 April–May; 83–87 May only; 3–15 July–August. Many other percents are specific to three months out of twelve. What sample size is necessary to allow for the realization of these and other temporally specific percentages?

If only four shells were used the possible percentages would be 25, 50, 75, and 100. Twenty-five percent of shells dying in fast growth could represent harvest during June, July, or September, according to Table 12. Fifty percent of shells dying in fast growth could represent harvest in January, March, June, or December and 75 percent January, February, April, June, and December. If a sample size of ten archaeological shells from one provenience was used, the resulting percentages of animals dying in fast growth would be multiples of ten. If one shell, 10 percent, died in fast growth the assemblage could be assigned to July or August or if nine shells, 90 percent, died in fast growth, April–May would be indicated, but it would not be possible to derive other specific percentages, such as 83–87 percent. In fact, a sample size of at least twenty shells is necessary to get percentage values of 5, 10, 15, 85, 90, and 95 which would allow for the identification of all of the temporally specific intervals. Therefore, in order to use the temporal specificity that is in the New Jersey fast/slow control chart (Table 12), one must employ a minimum of twenty shells from each archaeological provenience. The use of fewer shells dictates broad temporal interpretations.

The percentages in the 40th percentile may be unique to October in the Bird Shoal, North Carolina control (Table 10). In order to derive at least three percents in that percentile mathematically, one would have to have at least twenty-five shells, which I propose as the minimum number of shells for use of the Bird Shoals F/S control with archaeological data.

For the O/T technique there are three sampling criteria. It is necessary to duplicate (1) the presence/absence of categories, (2) the ranking of the six categories and (3) the shape of the curve or the magnitude of the differences between categories. The best situation is to use archaeological sample sizes that match or exceed those employed in the controls. However, there are minimum numbers of shells that are necessary to meet the three criteria given above when smaller samples are necessary.

The New Jersey control sample for April 18, 1988 had thirty-one shells for which an assignment of death in O/T terms could be made. The distribution was

	O1	O2	O3	T1	T2	T3	T?
N =	18	7	4				2

The criteria for duplication are (1) Categories O1, O2, O3, and a T phase must be represented, (2) the descending rank order of O1, O2, O3, and T3 must be duplicated, and (3) the number of cases in O1 must be twice the number of cases in O2 and four times the number of case in O3. What size subsample is necessary to meet these three criteria?

To address this problem I wrote all thirty-one observations on separate slips of paper and drew first a 10 percent sample at random and then drew successively larger samples until the three criteria were met. The slips were returned to the box before drawing the next sample.

Sample	Slips Drawn	Criteria met
10% of 31 = 3	O1,O1,O1	none
20% of 31 = 6	O2,O1,O2,O1,O3,O1	none
50% of 31 = 15	O1,O2,T?, O1,O1,O1,O3,O1,T?,O3,O2,O1, O2,O2,O3	#1
70% of 31 = 22	O1,O2,T?, O3,O3,O1,O1,O1,O1,O1,O2,O1,O1, O1,O1,O2,O2,O1,O1,O2,O2,T?	#1,#3
70% of 31 = 22	O2,O2,O1,T?, O3,O1,O1,O1,O3,O3,O1,O1,O1, O1,O2,O2,O2,O2,O1,O1,O1,O2,O1	#1, #2, #3

In this example, a draw of twenty-two shells was necessary to meet the three criteria, or a 70-percent subsample. Additional drawings would result in a slightly different figure. Again a sample size of 20+ shells is implicated for using this control.

When all samples from the same month are combined as is the case in the creation of these multi-year controls, even larger samples are needed to meet the three criteria. For the O/T technique, let us consider the composite ("total") New Jersey January with eighty-six observations (Table 12). The compilation has all six categories present, a rank order of O1, O2, T2, and more than four times more O1 specimens than O2. None of the individual years satisfies criterion #1, January 87 satisfies criterion #2, and January 86 and January 88 satisfy the third. In a sampling exercise similar to the one illustrated above, fifty-four shells or 63 percent of those in the control for January were required to match the composite on all three criteria. It seems then that to best use these control histograms, subsequent researchers must have a shell sample size that is at least 63 percent of the shells used in the largest month included. The largest month is July with one hundred-one shells; 63 percent of that number is a minimum sample of sixty-three shells.

Archaeological sample size
Understanding of sample sizes of archaeological shells for seasonality study is equally underdeveloped. Some researchers have offered *site* seasonality interpretations on *one* shell and most *site* seasonality studies involve fewer than fifty shells (Claassen 1990, 1991b). Analysts appear to believe that growth is so uniform among shells, and human behavior so uniform in all dump episodes, that the seasonality of a component and even a site can be proffered on only a handful of shells. "The sample size was small (N = 21) [from 5 sites], because from microgrowth analysis highly accurate ontogenetic data can be obtained" (Pallant 1990). Such accuracy is simply not supported by growth controls.

Even when sample sizes are large, e.g., 1,162 naiad shells from the Deweese mound of Kentucky (Claassen 1990), the shells came from a single column. Unless one can demonstrate that a site is the product of a single occupation with shellfishing in only one season, then seasonality studies based on incremental growth structures must embrace a site-sampling strategy of large numbers of samples from large numbers of archaeological units spread across each component.

Maxwell (1989a, 1989b) has given attention to sampling for archaeological shell seasonality work. He advocates cluster samples from natural strata combined with stratified random samples. The sampling provenience chosen should closely approximate a deposit of shells harvested at one time. (I have satisfied this requirement, in as much as it can be in an archaeological situation, by requiring the shells analyzed as a set to come from very small areas, such as 30 cm × 30 cm × 5 cm proveniences, or from sealed pits.) A minimum of two sets of shells collected from each sampling provenience and analyzed separately would add confidence to the results.

Based on requirements for obtaining a normal distribution of sampling errors, Maxwell states that *forty or more usable shells* should be derived from each sample (Maxwell 1989a:8; 1989b). Depending on the fragmentation and ground-water chemistry of the site, a considerably larger initial sample size may be required to obtain forty usable (i.e. readable) shells. I have found anywhere from 13 percent to 94 percent of the valves I prepare to be unreadable.

To sample a site adequately for harvest-time studies of shellfishing:

(1) use a large sample from any one provenience
(2) interpret groups of shells, not individuals
(3) draw samples from multiple locations in the site
(4) examine different species of shellfish

Seasonality studies based on incremental growth structures must embrace a site-sampling strategy of large numbers of observations from large numbers of archaeological units spread across the component. Fortunately, sampling problems are easily corrected by better sampling regimes and by using more efficient sectioning techniques.

6.4 Summary

Basic assumptions about shell growth influence the prediction of harvest season. The normative assumptions that all shells respond to growth stimuli identically or essentially so, and that the timing of these stimuli is predictable each year have resulted in the practice of assigning harvest time to individual shells and small samples. With large growth controls it is clear that neither assumption is true but that there is marked growth variation in any population on any day in the year. But the range and mean of that variation, as well as the element varying, all vary in a patterned way throughout the year. Because variation in growth is expected and accounted for in those studies where the researcher recognizes growth variation, only sets of archaeological shells are interpreted and only one harvest time is predicted for any one set.

It is an unfortunate fact that the techniques detailed here are far more powerful than their application to archaeological samples can support. Three problems plague season-of-death studies. (1) We must be able to isolate death assemblages. Certain types of deposits can support such an assumption – the sealed pit, species-specific facies, extremely small collection units such as the column sample of $35 \times 35 \times 5$ cm. (2) We must collect adequate numbers of shells both for the controls and from the archaeological site. For growth-line studies archaeological samples greater than twenty readable individuals per death assemblage and even as many as forty readable shells are required. For demographic studies hundreds of specimens per archaeological sample is best but will diminish confidence in having sampled a single death assemblage. (3) Unseasonable water temperatures for prolonged periods of time will create false annuli, missing annuli, and misleading oxygen isotopic results.

All three classes of technique suffer from problems 1 and 2. If the sampled deposit can be demonstrated to have temporal integrity (rather than being time-averaged), the greatest potential for season of death studies rests with the demographic technique. Demographic characteristics are not particularly plagued by unseasonable water temperature. The demographic technique is the easiest to apply, the quickest, and the cheapest to conduct, the least affected by taphonomy, and thus offers the greatest comparability and replicability. Yet another advantage to the demographic technique is that absolutely any-one who can find the growth controls or create them and procure a caliper can conduct the analysis. But even with this potential we must be disciplined in collecting our own control samples of several years' duration and be careful to sample deposits with temporal integrity, not components, sites, or regions.

7

DIETARY RECONSTRUCTION

Dietary reconstruction – who ate how much of what at this site during which part of the year – is the aspect of shell analysis that has generated the most work and the most critical thinking over the past one hundred years. Scientific precision through quantification of bone and shell remains has been a concern of researchers throughout this period. The California school of quantification dominated the enterprise in the first half of the twentieth century with attempts to calculate number of years, number of people, and volume of heaps. This body of work was preceded by the efforts of Dall in the Aleutians (1877) and Statham (1892) in Australia and was soundly criticized by Walker (1883). Almost two decades after radiocarbon dating silenced the Californians, Shawcross (1967) revived their endeavors. Immediately, Ambrose (1967) published an extremely critical evaluation of it. Nevertheless, quantification for dietary interpretation was extremely popular in the next twenty years.

Today reconstructing diet is less popular. Several sources of information about historic societies have served as cautionary tales and more voices have urged a move away from the types of assumptions evident in the California school. In this chapter I will discuss some ethnographies bearing on gathering and consumer behavior (including optimal foraging theory), the quantitative methods applied to mollusc shells to estimate diet indirectly (including allometric formulae and nutritional values of molluscs), and human bone chemistry, a direct method of assaying the diet of people utilizing molluscs.

7.1   Ethnographies and molluscan flesh use

Ethnographies are often the primary source for understanding the role of shellfish in the diet of a society. These sources of information are not without their biases and omissions, several of which apply specifically to shellfish consumption (see Claassen 1991b and Meehan 1982 for lengthier discussions).

Women almost universally act as primary collectors of shellfish. It is at least in part the identification of women with shellfishing that is responsible for the common reputation of shellfish and molluscs as a low-priority foodstuff in ethnohistoric and ethnographic accounts. It is not surprising that male explorers and priests heard male whale-hunters, chiefs, warriors, and trading partners describe shellfish as inessential, a low-ranking food, and untasty. Related to the low ranking that is accorded a molluscan diet is its inappro-

175

priateness for banquets and ceremonial feasts. In at least one Polynesian culture, molluscs collected by women are deemed unsuitable for guests (Kirch and Dye 1979). Instead, a male host will dive for a particular deep-dwelling bivalve species, whose meat is presented to the guest.

While Aleuts (Alaska) have verbalized their own low opinions of shellfish, Laughlin (1974/75) has argued that the availability of intertidal resources, particularly shellfish, has provided food, autonomy, and a social contribution for elderly, young, and infirm Aleuts. Moreover, Laughlin argues that the reliance on shellfish was responsible for the extreme longevity of both prehistoric and historic Aleuts.

Some ethnographers recorded their own ideas about the suitability of molluscs as food drawing from both Old Testament teachings and the association of this food with lower-class scavengers and prisoners. In fifteenth- and sixteenth-century England, apprentices and those living in poorhouses were fed mussels, thus imparting a social stigma to mussel consumption (Meehan 1982:8). I suspect that the nomen "mussel" for freshwater bivalves in the United States and England resulted from the analogous sociological context of their use – by the poor and the uncouth – since there is no resemblance to the marine mussels.

Even in the best of culture contact situations and ethnographic observation, there may be little relationship between the observed society's attitude about molluscs and the role molluscs played in the diet of extinct societies. For example, Larsen et al. (1992:210) found that on the Georgia coast the pre-agriculturist's diet was "highly focused on marine resources," the early maize period saw an increase in maize intake at the expense of marine species, but the late agricultural period showed much less maize consumption and increased marine foods. During the historic mission period, however, terrestrial foods greatly outweighed marine foods. Consequently, in that region, it is a mistake to interpret archaic shellfish use by reference to historic-period evaluations and descriptions of shellfish flesh use.

Bait

Ethnographies make it clear that molluscan flesh also was gathered for bait. Historic accounts of *Rangia cuneata* used for shrimp bait prompted Riser (1987) to propose that shell deposits of *R. cuneata* along the Gulf Coast of Louisiana and Mississippi represented shrimp bait and shrimp drying platforms. The association of clams with shrimp has also been made in Mexico. Thin scatters of the brackish clam *Neocyrena ordinaria* on the Pacific coast of Chiapas have been interpreted as drying platforms for shrimp (Voorhies et al. 1991).

Roy Salls (1988) believes that many of the abalone heaps on the California coast may be the debris of fish bait processing. Northwest Coast groups were

Table 14. *Fish and bait used*

	Bait			
Fish prey	Conch	Welk	Crab	Other
Triggerfish	x	x	x	sandfish
Tallie	x	x		
Grunt	x		x	
Yellow jacks			x	feathers, sprots
Schoolmater	x		x	coney
Chubs	x		x	
Muttonfish	x			
Snapper	x			
Nassau grouper	x			grouper, triggerfish
Rock hind	x			coney
Wrasses	x			
Boxfish	x		x	
Bonefish			x	
Parrotfish	x		x	
Coney	x			coney
Rockfish	x			

known to use mussels (*Mytilus californianus*) for fish bait, cockle for salmon trolling, urchins for kelp greenling bait, and octopus as halibut bait (Ellis and Swan 1981). Rock lobsters were used to attract fish in the Caribbean (Goode 1884). Many species of naiads have been used to fish in fresh water (Goode 1884) and a large pearl gleaned from a mussel used for fish bait launched the Black River pearl rush of 1897 in the Ozarks (US) (Claassen 1994). The mid-Holocene-aged heaps of aquatic snails on the St. John's River in Florida are comprised of the same gastropod species that modern fishermen use on their trot lines for catfish (Mark Brooks, personal communication, 1989).

I recorded women and men on San Salvador Island in 1988 using gastropods, chitons, and land crabs for bait on hooks, in fish pots, and to bait an area (chumming). Fourteen species of fish reportedly would take conch (*Strombus gigas*) bait and one fisherman insisted that no fish would pass conch. Welks (*Cittarium pica*) were used for triggerfish and tallie, and dead terrestrial and hermit crabs used in chum and on hooks attracted eight species (Table 14). On San Salvador, men and a few women collected shellfish with some frequency for their fishing activities.

This use for shellfish, fish, crab, lobster, and octopus flesh seriously challenges models of optimal foraging. Assuming that shellfish collecting is solely for food and done by women, this activity is usually paired with other gathering activities such as plant collecting in time and effort estimates. (This is indeed occasionally the case among the Anbarra. But then we know little about fishing from Meehan's study.) On San Salvador, shellfishing was more often observed and reported by men in conjunction with fishing activities. Never has shellfishing been counted in the costs of fishing. Assuming that shellfish are collected solely for human consumption, hundreds of archaeological reports have quantified nutritional yields for shell debris versus vertebrates and others have argued ranking issues and original diets. Today when conch meat can be sold on the island within twelve hours for $1.20 an animal or $12 a dozen, I saw thirty-three conch feet and twelve shells spent in baiting four fish pots for an expected return of four to eight Nassau groupers, small grouper bringing $6 each when skinned and cleaned. On another day twelve conch were used to bait four pots with the same catch expectations. I leave it to someone else to make the data fit an optimal foraging argument. Assuming that shellfish are collected by women solely for food, shell deposits are interpreted as either base camps or women's special activity areas, depending on the artifactual debris associated.

The modern use of shellfish as bait also calls into question the assumption by archaeologists that shell debris in association with prehistoric pottery is contemporaneous with that pottery. Informants related frequently swimming to a key to gather scurb (chiton), welk, and bleeding teeth. At the south end of the island (where today there is visible shell and pottery in a blowout), they removed the meats, discarded the shells, fished, and returned to the mainland.

In addition to this non-food use for molluscan flesh, there are other molluscs in sites that may not have been consumed. While commensals and accidentals are obvious candidates, gastropods are not so obvious. Bobrowsky (1984) summarizes a century of debate about the food relevance of gastropods.

Gathering and consumer behavior

Some authors have attributed the different dietary import of shellfish in archaeological situations to the biases inherent in the various forms of data and different methods of analyses (e.g. Bailey 1975:2). While methodological practices are certainly suspect in some cases, there is a growing recognition among prehistorians that gathering behavior varies, as does adaptation to aquatic resources (e.g. Bailey 1983b, Meighan 1989, Rowley-Conwy 1983). There are also many unexamined assumptions about food consumption.

Gathering

Little research has been conducted into the nature of gathering in horticultural, agricultural, or industrial societies. Archaeologists tend to assume food gathering is insignificant in food-producing societies and differs from that by hunter-gatherers only in percent of dietary contribution. The dietary role of shellfish in prehistoric societies has been interpreted as supplemental based on ethnographic information from modern hunter-gatherers. For prehistoric food producers, however, shellfish may have served as a seasonal staple (Claassen 1986a).

The horticultural Gwembe of Tonga gather wild foods intensively during one season each year collecting a much broader range of taxa than do their classic hunter-gatherer neighbors, the San (Scudder 1971). The role of gathering in agricultural systems in Mexico (Wilken 1970) and Greece (Forbes 1976) has been said to differ from that of the San in the role the food plays in the diet and in energy input/output terms. Deith (1988a:116) summarized these differences in gathering by agriculturists in Greece as follows: (1) gathered wild foods are relishes, not staples, (2) a different suite of plants are gathered, primarily garden weeds, (3) the people do not go out deliberately to collect wild foods, and (4) the division of labor characteristic of hunter-gatherers is absent.

The dense shell matrix sites of Tierra del Fuego, Australia, Tasmania, Oronsay, northern Spain, and the interior mid-South of the United States were probably created by hunter-gatherers, while most of those of the coastal southeastern United States, Mesoamerica, Brazil, Pacific Islands, and Japan were probably created by horticulturists. Large shell-bearing sites of the eastern Pacific Coast (Aleutian Islands, Northwest Coast, California's Channel Islands), and the Maritimes of eastern Canada were left by maritime-focused societies. Even if the ecofacts in all of these sites are human food debris, there is the great possibility that the gathering activities differed in important ways, and that the food played different roles.

Consumption

Collecting and eating shellfish and other intertidal resources are usually viewed as catholic behaviors within a community (but see Bowdler 1976, Waselkov 1987). An assumption that all people eat shellfish is particularly evident in the "California school" where the number of band members was divided into the available calories to derive length of occupation. While these mathematical puzzles are no longer as popular as they once were (but see Akazawa 1988), the assumption that all members of a community consume molluscs still appears. McManamon (1984:392) has proposed that a change in women's time allocation in the summer months to accommodate the time required by corn agriculture precluded summer shellfishing. Yet this would be relevant as an explanation for the lack of summer-harvested shellfish only if we assume that all adult women shellfished and all adult women subsequently hoed and that only prime-of-life women would collect. Bowdler's (1976) and Meehan's (1982) reviews of Australian ethnographic situations clearly indicate that all the members of a community do not participate equally in shellfishing or fishing or in consuming these foods. In Anbarra families (Australia) where adult women do not care to collect, shellfish are rarely consumed. Meehan provided our first example of women being honored with status and title in a hunting-gathering society for their gathering activities.

Among the Fish Creek Aborigines in Arnhem Land, male hunters ate a greater proportion of animal foods than did non-hunters and each individual man ate all the fish he caught. Women consumed the fish they caught while out or took it back to camp for other family members while men brought back large game to be shared with other men (Bowdler 1976:251–252). In Kuna (Panama) dietary practices of old, women alone consumed lady fish, needlefish, and barracuda (Hale et al. 1996). Among the Bantu speakers of coastal South Africa, men never consume shellfish (Bigalke 1973). In the pre-contact and contact era of Tlingit culture, proportionately more women than men consumed shellfish, and more women and men of lower rank consumed shellfish (Moss 1993:643) and a greater variety of species (Wessen 1982).

It is highly likely that, in most societies, the habitual gatherer of plants, gatherer of intertidal resources, fisher, or hunter will consume greater amounts of the prey over a lifetime, than will those not involved in that food-procurement activity. It is highly likely that there are gender-specific diets among many hunter-gatherers (references in Bowdler 1976:251) and to a lesser degree among horticulturists. Furthermore, one of the consequences of gender-specific diets is that the foodstuffs of women, gathered or caught and often consumed away from camp, may well be significantly under-represented in a site's record which may be dominated by bones, the product of men's hunt and men's diet (Bowdler 1976:252).

The assumption that food procured will always be returned to a larger group of people for uniform consumption (e.g. California school authors, Yengoyan 1968:187) is simply not tenable in light of ethnographic information. Feeding often probably did not follow the democratic practice of our society, and involved taboos, allergies, and taste preferences. Neither is the assumption that all women did all female tasks nor that all men did all male tasks tenable. Long before there were craft, religious, or political specialists, and since their development, there has been accommodation of aptitudes in tasks for individuals.

Isotopic assays support this challenge to uniform feeding in several cases as do other visible aspects of skeletons such as dental health and growth stress indicators. Isotopic differences have been noted by van der Merwe and Vogel (1978) suggesting that maize farming women of the midwestern US consumed more wild plants than did men. Larsen et al. (1992) found that while marine foods were a dietary staple for most individuals on Georgia's (US) coast, a few individuals in the early Deptford period had diets dominated by terrestrial products. Other types of skeletal data indicate that Early Period (5,500 to 3,200 ya) men in the Central Valley of California had greater access to protein and that Late Period (850 to 200 ya) women were nutritionally compromised (Hollimon 1991). Among Jomon hunter-gatherers of Japan, men and women had different diets (Chisholm et al. 1992). The one child in a large sample of skeletons from sites in British Columbia (Canada) had a significantly different

$\partial^{13}C$ from the adults (Chisholm et al. 1983), as have other skeletal children in the province (Lovell cited in Chisholm et al. 1983:397).

That molluscs frequently are reported to be a low-priority foodstuff and of little nutritional value has undoubtedly biased models of prehistoric subsistence, and, in particular, has frustrated and challenged modeling attempts based on optimal foraging theory (OFT) (e.g. Lewis 1979, Perlman 1973, Yesner 1981). Based on principles of evolutionary ecology, OFT assumes that individuals will engage in behaviors that lead to an increase in their reproductive fitness. It assumes that foragers will seek to maximize their foraging efficiency in terms of such variables as search time, pursuit time, and kilocalorie yields per kilocalorie expended. Moreover, it employs only one concept of "work": laborious, onerous work that is to be minimized in duration and frequency. The work of foraging and gathering is to be undertaken with efficiency such that there is a cost minimization of calories and of time spent.

There are several reasons for the poor fit between shellfishing and OFT; specifically we can turn to Betty Meehan's (1982) portrayal of shellfishing by Anbarra women and children. It should be of interest to optimal foraging modelers that the Anbarra women intentionally collected from beds where the shellfish were smaller and less plentiful than at neighboring beds (which they also harvested), that on 91 of 194 days (47 percent) shellfish were gathered, only a single species was collected although dozens of other edible species were in the same beds, and that one species which is exposed twice daily nearly every day of the lunar cycle represented only 7 percent of all shellfish collected in the year of observation, being ignored in preference to better-tasting species exposed on only some days of the lunar cycle. Thus, we see that among the Anbarra the activity of shellfishing is far from the OFT concept of "efficient" if energy is the currency; some women even walked the round trip and collected although their companions gathered for several hours.

Among other things, OFT was designed to measure the fitness of an individual's foraging behavior over a brief interval of time (Keene 1983, McCay 1981). As Keene and others point out, however, this emphasis on the individual forager may not be appropriate when studying humans. Social reproduction requires more than the reproduction of individuals and more than the feeding of animals. Again turning to the Anbarra, we see that shellfishing is a social event involving a dozen or more women and sometimes including as many as four generations. Children play nearby or collect their own shellfish supply; adult conversation is almost constant. The actual collecting permits a woman to be absolutely alone for short periods of time, "alone" with other adult women, or "alone" with her children.

I made similar observations while watching and participating in shellfishing on San Salvador Island, Bahamas. In this mixed subsistence system, which includes agriculture and purchased foodstuffs, shellfishing represents for women and their children recreation and family time. As play, it was pursued as we might describe work: there was a goal of filling a container, collecting was continuous, the necessary tools were transported to the rocks, all persons present participated in the activity, and there was task specialization by age. If enough molluscs were collected, rewards were the temporary thwarting of the cash economy and a dietary substance which was not available for purchase.

I do not deny that some optimizing behavior may be going on among the Anbarra but it is not optimal foraging behavior if *energy* is the currency, as in most OFT applications. Not only would optimal foraging modelers have us consider all food getting activities to be work rather than play or pleasure, but they would also have us consider all activities that result in edibles to be subsistence activities. Perhaps we need to think in terms of subsistence, socio-subsistence, and ideo-subsistence activities, to paraphrase Binford (1962).

Abandoning shellfishing
Before concluding this subsection, I wish to make some comments on why at least Bahamian women have stopped collecting shellfish for food in the twenti-eth century. The reasons are multiple but fairly simple. (1) Young adults have left most of the Bahamian Islands, to relocate in Nassau for jobs and many (most?) able-bodied older men work off-island at least part of the year. Most do not consider Nassau to be an appropriate environment for their children, however, and many children are sent back to grandmothers to be raised. Older women, who may have shellfished as girls, simply do not have time once they are adults to shellfish as they raise two generations of children. (2) Aged women on the islands do not believe that they are still capable of negotiating the rocky intertidal coastline where the target species live. (3) The better collecting locales are harder to get to now. In the past donkeys provided transportation but today donkeys are gone and cars are scarce. Many locales along the island shore are consequently inaccessible. (4) Several fundamentalist religious groups have gained members on the islands in the past two decades. Both the Jehovah's Witnesses and the Seventh Day Adventists take literally the Biblical injunction not to consume creatures that crawl on their bellies which in this setting means specifically shellfish and crabs. Nor should they handle them. Other less literal congregations, such as the Church of God, meet four evenings a week which impedes evening fishing and crabbing for those who have jobs. These same reasons occur around the world among peoples who once har-vested ample quantities of a "free" foodstuff and could benefit from doing so today. Swadling (1980) specifically mentions that in New Guinea the popular-ity of Seventh Day Adventist membership precludes molluscs as a food source.

Ethnographic observations make it clear that many faunal analysts have been too cavalier about dietary reconstructions. Numerous caveats should be appended to most dietary reconstructions in our literature.

7.2   Indirect methods of estimating the role of molluscs in human diet

In this section I will summarize some of the discussion and methods in use for reconstructing indirectly the dietary role of shellfish in human diets. These types of analyses usually proceed through a research process which follows a series of steps. After the shells are quantified, either as MNI or as weight, that value is converted into a representative meat weight which is then compared to the meat weight estimate of vertebrate species. Meat weights are often converted into protein, carbohydrate, and mineral derivatives to predict the specific role in the diet held by shellfish or to talk about the nutritional adequacy of the diet, although this type of investigation is less common now than it was a decade ago.

Nutritional value of shellfish

Which feature of shellfish flesh is the most relevant one for nutritional assessment? Arguments have been made for the central role of three competing components of the meat: protein, calories, and minerals.

Inter-specific variation in molluscan nutritional values is great. Once published nutritional information on shellfish species is gathered in one place (Table 15), it is evident that caloric values range from 54 to 234 kilocalories per 100 g of wet flesh and the carbohydrates range from 0 g to 8.9 g. Pacific molluscs are generally higher in calories than those of the Atlantic. But even the range of kilocalories in the Atlantic species encompasses that of rabbit, croaker, shark, and crab (Table 15). The most common bivalves in eastern US deposits – *C. virginica*, *M. mercenaria*, and *Mya arenária* – exceed in grams of carbohydrates turkey, quail, rabbit, and shark and can rival drum, catfish, and deer. Collecting 100 g of molluscan flesh does not represent much human time or energy if the prey lives in the intertidal zone and only slightly more energy if it lives in a river bottom.

Protein content varies seasonally. Erlandson (1988) believes that the primary dietary role of shellfish was as a source of protein. Turning again to Table 15, protein ranges from 8 percent to 77 percent of the tissue or 5.5 g to 22 g. If one takes 40 g of protein as a daily requirement, as Erlandson did (1988:105), then 100 g of shellfish flesh can provide anywhere from 14 percent to 55 percent of that need. Nearly all western Atlantic shellfish species listed in Table 15 can rival the protein value of most fishes. Protein, however, cannot be ingested in large quantities over even a few days without leading to illness and, if over several days, death (Noli and Avery 1988). The notion that shellfish could have been the sole or even main source of food for long periods of time is incompatible with human nutrition.

Since the caloric, mineral, protein, carbohydrate, and fat proportions vary in molluscs seasonally, by sex, and in differing environmental situations, it is

Table 15. Nutritional variation across species ((100g unit, or * = unknown)[a]

	Kcal	Protein	Fat	Carbo	Pmg	Camg	Kmg	Ref.[b]
Marine molluscs								
Western Atlantic								
Argopecten gibbus (20)*		15.9–18.5%	.1–.3%		160–270	20–60		3
Argopecten gibbus (4)		15.6–16.4g	.5–.7g					4
Argopecten irradians (24)		13.4–17.0g	.3–.9g	1.4–1.9g				4
*Chiton marmoratus**		47.7%	6.2%					7
*Cittarium pica**		65.15%	1.4g					7
Crassostrea virginica	4.5–10.3%	.56–2.4%		1.9–4.7%				Table 16
Donax variabilis	54							1
Geukensia demissa	95	14.4g			236	88		14
Littorina littorea	74	15.30–18.0g	1.4g					1
Mercenaria mercenaria	54–95	9.73–16.8%	.79–1.86%	1.9–3.3%	110–206	17–73		Table 16
Mya arenaria (20)	89	5.5–11.7g	.4–2.6g	1.7%				3
Mya arenaria (10)	87	9.7–15.6g	1.4–2.5g	2.9g				4
Mytilus edulis	95	8.9–17.2g	1.7–2.0g	3.3g				1
Mytilus sp.		14.40g	2.20g					8
*Nerita peloronta**		42.68%	6.20					7
Neocyrena ordinaria		6.2–10.4g	1.5–3.4g	.1–.9g				6
Ostrea edulis	59	8.6–13.1g	0.9–1.9g	5.9g				1
*Placopecten magellanicus**		17.1–19.0%	.02–.3%		150–320	20–30	3	7
*Purpura patula**		67.95%	1.1					7
octopus	70	12.7	1.9	158	45			15
Eastern Atlantic								
Buccinum undatum	91	18.5–68.0g	1.4–1.9g					1
Cardium edule	48	11.0–13.2g	0.3g	3.4g				1
Western Pacific								
*Batissa violacea**	105	48.9%				180	505	9
Pecten maximus		17.5g	0.10			163		9
*Tapes hiantina**		77.0%					746	9
Telescopium telescopium						144	500	9
Eastern Pacific								
Clinocardium nuttallii	79	13.50g	0.70g	4.7g				8
Haliotis sp.	98	18.70g	0.50g	3.4g				8
Haliotis kamtschatkana (4)		10.4–18.2g	.3–.7g					4
Mopalia muscosa	234	22.00g	16.30g	0				8
Ostrea lurida	82	9.60g	2.50g	5.4g				8

	Kcal			Carbo	Camg	Pmg	Kmg	Ref
Protothaca staminea	77	13.50g	1.00g	3.5g				8
Saxidomus nuttalli	79	13.00g	1.20g	4.1g				8
Tivela stultorum	74	11.20g	1.40g	4.0g	607			8
US fresh water molluscs								
Actinonaias ligamentina	58	7.80g	0.70g	4.5g	520	320	26	10
*Megalonaias nervosa**		8–9%			604			13
Pleurocera canaliculata	58	10.40g	1.20g	1.5g	108	1182	46	11
Proptera alata	77	9.50g	0.80g	7.8g	812	370	41	11
Viviparus georgianus	72	11.10g						12
Miscellaneous molluscs								
Pecten spp. (7)		12.9–14.8g	.09–.43g		180–250	20–80		4
Venerupis semi decusata		12.2–13.6g	.70–.90g					4
Volegalea wardiana		0.1g			158	680		4
Other food								
Juglans nigra (walnut)	525	10.6g	51.5g	5.0g				1
Phaseolus vulgaris (bean)	272	22.1g	1.7g	45.0g				8
Pinus monophylla (pine)	481	7.8g	24.0g	58.4g				8
Quercus agrifolia (acorns)	254	4.6g	9.8g	36.8g			175	8
Salvia columbariae (chia)	447	21.6g	20.2g		1154			8
Zea mays (corn)	348	8.9g	3.9g	72.2g				1
Colinus virginianus (quail)	168	25.0g	6.8g	0g				10
Meleagris gallopavo (turkey)	218	20.1g	14.7g	0g				10
M. gallopavo	171	28.0g	6.5g	0g				1
Odocoileus virginianus (deer)	198	35.0g	6.4g	0g				1
O. virgincanus	126	21.0g	4.0g	0g	249	10		10
Sylvilagus sp. (rabbit)	73	21.0g	5.0g	0g			385	8
Sylvilagus floridanus	135	21.0g	5.0g	0g				10
S. floridanus	179	27.3g	7.7g	0g				1
G. lineatus (croaker)	79	18.0g	0.80g	0g				8
A. grunniens (drum)	121	17.3g	5.2g	0g			286	10
Ictalurus sp. (catfish)	103	17.6g	3.1g	0g			330	10
M. vulgaris (shark)	91	19.70g	0.90g	1.1g				8
N. maculatus (shark)	189	15.30g	13.1g	2.5g				8
Phoca vitulina (seal)	143	26.00g						8
C. sapidus (crab)	82	11.9–19.2g	0.4–1.5g	0.5–2.0g				4

[a] I have specified grams or percent according to the referenced analysis but the information necessary to standardize these figures is lacking.

[b] References:

1, Waselkov 1987:120; 3, Sidwell et al. 1973:19; 4, Sidwell et al. 1974:various; 5, Claassen 1991b; 6, Voorhies 1976:142; 7, Goodwin 1979:407; 8, Erlandson 1988:104; 9, Meehan 1982:143; 10, Parmalee and Klippel 1974; 11, Klippel and Morey 1986; 12, Cumbaa 1976:52; 13, Post 1982:71; 14, Trinkley and Adams 1994:103; 15, Pennington 1994.

Abbreviations: Camg = calcium; Carbo = carbohydrates; Kcal = Kilocalories; Kmg = phosphorus; Pmg = potassium.

Table 16. *Variation in nutritional value within a species (100 g unit, or * = unknown)*[a]

	Kcal	Protein	Fat	Carbohydrates	Ref.
Crassostrea virginica	66	8.4–12.0g	1.8–2.50	3.4–6.5	1
Crassostrea virginica (20)*	6.7–10.3%	0.75–1.9%			3
Crassostrea virginica (21)*	4.5–7.9%	0.56–2.0%			3
Crassostrea virginica (24)	5.6–10.0%	0.70–2.4%		1.9–4.7%	4
Mercenaria mercenaria					5
(collected in February)[1]	54	9.73%	.79%	1.95%	
	83	15.30%	1.09%	3.03%	
	90	16.30%	1.37%	3.04%	
(collected in October)	87	14.90%	1.59%	3.31%	
	74	14.60%	1.78%	3.18%	
	95	16.80%	1.86%	2.65%	
*Mercenaria mercenaria**	3.2–6.2%	.10–.42%			3
	92	12.8g			14
Neocyrena ordinaria					6
		10.4g	2.7g	0.9g	
		8.2g	1.7g	0.2g	
		7.2g	1.5g	0.1g	
		7.7g	2.2g	0.2g	
		6.2g	3.4g	0.5g	
Megalonaias gigantea		•			13
Oct, Athens AL[2]		5.9%	.35%		
		5.2%	.19%		
		6.0%	.50%		
Nov, Rome TN		8.3%	1.7%		
		8.1%	0.7%		
		8.5%	1.2%		
Jan, New Johnsonville TN		5.2%	.33%		
		5.6%	.31%		
		6.1%	.26%		

[a] Key see Table 15 for explanation and for abbreviations.
[1] Each entry is an average of three animals.
[2] Each entry is an average of eight animals.

necessary to try to specify the season of collection (Chapter 6). Six assays of the bivalve *M. mercenaria* from the same collection point, taken six months apart, indicated a range in calories of 54 to 95, in protein of 9.7 percent to 16.8 percent, in fat from 0.79 percent to 1.86 percent and in carbohydrates of 1.95 g to 3.31 g (Table 16).

An additional problem with reconstructing the nutritional value of molluscs is determining which of the species and individuals were indeed used for human food. A number of uses for shells and for shellfish flesh do not involve them in human nutrition. Furthermore edible species may be present from fish or bird stomach contents, some species will be accidentals, some individuals will be dead when collected.

Walker (1992) uses species, size, quantity of individuals, and archaeological context to determine commensals or accidental species. The smaller the screen mesh used, the greater the number of commensals or accidentals there will be in the collection. Jones and Richman (1995:46–49) offer species proportions of epibionts, or accidentals, collected during mussel (*Mytilus californianus*) harvesting experiments. *M. californianus* made up 89 percent of the collection, barnacle (*Balanus glandula*) 7 percent, *Lepus pacifica* 2 percent and all others less than 0.2 percent (*Katharina tunicata, Collisella scabra, Collisella pelta, Collisella limatula, Pisaster ochraceus, Cancer antennaris, Tellina modesta, Tegula funebralis*). They predict that the presence of the same accidentals in the same proportions can be used to identify a species as an accidental and the collection technique of stripping.

Procedures have been described in Chapter 3 to facilitate the identification of specimens collected dead. Generally speaking, the smaller the species the more likely it is to be from the stomachs of birds or fish which were cleaned on location in prehistory.

Nor may the food species represent immediate consumption by the collectors or consumption by the collectors at all. Drying shellfish for delayed consumption and for trade in dried meat were common activities as was the use of flesh for fish, crustacean, and bird bait.

Given the tremendous inter- and intra-taxonomic variation in all nutrients in a mollusc, one can argue either that shellfish are poor sources of nutrition or that they are adequate sources merely by choosing an appropriate species and time of year to illustrate the point. Specific figures for species found in specific sites, rather than average figures, will greatly enhance discussions of molluscan nutritional value.

Meat weight

Several methods of estimating the weight of the flesh that once was contained in a shell have been used – average meat weight to shell weight ratio, meat volume to shell count, and allometric correlations. Allometric formulae have emerged as the preferred method for predicting meat weight when large samples of living animals are used to derive the values (Quitmyer 1985, Reitz et al. 1987).

Linear allometric formulae for univalves and bivalves based on a measurement can be found in Reitz et al. (1987). They utilized the formula

$$\log y = \log a + b(\log x) \text{ or } y = ax^b$$

where y is total body weight in grams and x is any other measured dimension.

Rollins et al. (1990:473) reported that linear regression of meat weight with either shell length, height, or weight in a live population was the most efficient and accurate method of obtaining an estimate of meat weight for archaeological shells. For the El Paraiso site in Peru, they report weighing all of the identified shell pieces of each species from each excavation unit to derive a total weight, then counting the MNI for each species in each unit, and, finally, calculating meat weight for each species from each unit as [a(weight) + b(MNI)]. a and b are coefficients of regression calculated from the experimental data on live specimens. Deriving a total weight of a species for each excavation unit represents a tremendous saving in time over measuring some dimension on every whole shell. Importantly, Maxwell (1989a) warns that the geographical specificity of these formulae has yet to be explored.

Meat weight and shell weight correlations in the bivalve *Rangia cuneata* proved unsuccessful. Statistician Gary Pritchard, who used 406 *R. cuneata* collected monthly during 1986 from Choctawhatchee Bay, Florida, with known meat weights, could find no useful meat weight correlation with shell length. This failure suggests that with a large enough control sample, variation in any chosen parameter could be so great that there is little correlation between meat and shell.

> In *R. cuneata*, the meat weight cannot be estimated from the length measurement using simple linear regression methods which have historically been the tools of the shell researcher. In the case of *R. cuneata* the variability inherent in shell lengths and meat weights for the species is so great that there is no strong relationship between the two ... The shape of the data ... shows that no model would be more appropriate than the linear model because the data do not show any significant trend other than towards linearity but with a variance so large that linear analysis will not produce meaningful results. (Gary Pritchard in Claassen 1988)

It is unfortunate that none of the studies reporting success with allometry has engaged a blind sample – taken a live sample of known meat weight – and predicted the meat weight for the sample using the correlations derived from the control set of shells. In short, we do not know the accuracy of these formulae when used on live samples not a part of the control group. Nor is the impact of dissolution of archaeological shells on measures of shell weight considered in any of these studies.

It is possible to offer a test at this time using the species *Mercenaria mercenaria* (quahog) and the formula provided by Quitmyer (1985):

$$\log a = -0.50 \quad \text{slope } b = 0.94 \quad x = \text{shell weight}$$

Over an eight-year period I commissioned the collection of fifty quahogs monthly from Bird Shoals, North Carolina (US). Each animal's shell and meat were weighed. From this data base I selected the September 15, 1985 (N = 49) and December 12, 1985 (N = 35) collections and subjected their shell weight data to Quitmyer's formula. Table 17 presents a comparison of the known meat weight with the predicted meat weight. The estimated meat weights for

Table 17. *Actual and predicted meat weights of North Carolina* Mercenaria mercenaria *calculated using formula from Quitmyer 1985*

| | September 15, 1985 | | | December 12, 1985 | |
| | meat weight g | | | meat weight g | |
Shell g	Predicted	Actual	Shell g	Predicted	Actual
68.10	16.717	14.43	82.05	19.917	11.54
126.44	29.907	24.47	52.00	12.973	11.00
99.04	23.772	14.60	47.36	11.882	5.45
78.61	19.132	14.42	112.52	26.801	14.35
193.93	44.708	31.60	57.71	14.308	11.72
77.65	18.912	8.52	62.94	15.524	9.25
64.80	15.954	8.05	57.04	14.152	7.16
66.80	16.417	13.05	30.50	7.857	4.48
51.32	12.814	8.64	73.93	18.059	10.30
47.61	11.941	14.30	27.95	7.238	4.02
70.13	17.185	10.54	58.92	14.590	7.41
178.05	41.258	28.60	13.53	3.659	3.33
71.70	17.546	9.95	23.73	6.206	4.87
74.85	18.270	13.43	25.76	6.703	6.21
48.43	12.134	9.01	21.75	5.718	5.82
56.91	14.121	8.93	51.30	12.809	5.23
55.60	13.816	7.80	60.61	14.983	8.21
65.15	16.035	11.40	19.78	5.229	4.32
75.92	18.515	15.30	32.75	8.400	5.08
59.66	14.762	7.88	14.55	3.918	1.97
41.81	10.568	5.88	34.06	8.716	5.44
26.12	6.791	3.62	18.33	4.868	5.44
52.85	13.172	11.52	14.53	3.913	1.79
58.30	14.445	10.41	84.76	20.535	10.54
58.58	14.511	9.79	52.41	13.069	5.95
38.93	9.883	5.82	28.57	7.388	3.14
37.01	9.424	4.80	43.96	11.078	6.13
39.84	10.100	8.28	12.88	3.494	1.87
33.03	8.468	5.56	66.47	16.341	9.01
23.95	6.260	4.91	14.68	3.951	2.19
23.25	6.087	3.84	14.45	3.893	2.23
36.54	9.311	5.09	44.48	11.201	4.70
27.20	7.055	6.23	35.17	8.983	6.06
22.25	5.841	4.40	80.44	19.550	9.44
24.56	6.409	2.93	36.26	9.244	5.05
23.01	6.028	3.55			
39.91	10.116	6.24			
29.11	7.520	3.81			
14.23	3.837	1.28			
22.56	5.918	3.31			
41.14	10.409	6.52			
17.72	4.716	2.44			
10.59	2.907	1.99			
15.31	4.110	2.66			
16.16	4.324	2.86			
19.89	5.257	2.57			
21.32	5.611	3.78			
16.14	4.319	2.12			
17.71	4.713	2.69			

September always exceeded the actual meat weight (as they do using the Bernstein [1993] formula). For the set killed in September, the actual sum was 413.82 g of meat while the predicted amount was 612.03 g (greater by 148 percent). For the smaller set killed in December the actual meat weight was 220.7 g and the predicted meat weight was 377.15 g (greater by 171 percent). The smaller the number of individuals the larger the error in the estimate, at least in this situation. Statistically the two sets of values, the actual and predicted meat weights, are so different that they indicate two different populations of shellfish (paired t = − 12.6621, .0001 probability) as is the case with the Bernstein formula where the predicted meat weight was 2,432 g and the actual was 634 g (greater by 400 percent). I had similar results when attempting to use the formulae for predicting meat weights of *Rangia cuneata*.

Nor was the use of measurements any better. Again, using the Quitmyer (1985) solutions:

$$\log a = -1.28 \quad \text{slope } b = 2.5 \quad x = \text{shell length}$$

I drew data from a January (1988) collection of *M. mercenaria* (N = 22) from Great Bay, New Jersey. While the original work specified measurements in millimeters (Quitmyer 1985:41) the order of magnitude in the error was twice the expected figure which was corrected when the length measurements were adjusted to centimeter increments. Every predicted value was less than the actual weight of meat, and the two sets of weights differed by 194 g, 56 percent less than actual.

A recent paper by Robert Warren (1997) found that volumetric capacity regressions were stronger than those using shell weight or measurements. To calculate volumetric capacity for naiads, he took eight measurements, and substituted for height, the distance from hinge to pallial line. He found the use of raw data to be the weakest and transformed non-linear data the strongest. Warren concluded that pan-species formulae are more powerful than regional formulae for individual species.

My conclusion from this examination of allometric formulae using *Rangia cuneata* and *M. mercenaria* is that formulae tailored to individual species at least, fail the archaeological challenge, in the way they have been proposed for use (raw data, no geographical constraints). I urge every worker who wants to employ allometric formulae first to compare the predicted meat weights with known meat weights of a sample of shells.

Given (1) shell taphonomy, (2) the woefully inadequate sizes of *analyzed samples* from shell deposits (inadequate for reconstructing prehistoric diet), (3) our frequent inability to estimate the statistical universe of shell deposits, (4) numerous uses for shell independent of the fleshly food it covers and the flesh, (5) the possibility of discarding shell at places other than the "main" or conspicuous garbage dump, (6) the complexity of human nutrition and diet, (7) unknown cooking practices and their impact on nutritional derivatives, (8) the practice of drying shellfish flesh for delayed consumption or trade, and (9) the frequent seasonal use of shellfish meat, the value of meat weight estimates of shellfish flesh is little. When these estimates are combined with similarly derived estimates for vertebrate flesh and plants to talk about nutrition and dietary makeup, the enterprise is hopeless.

7.3   Assaying shellfish contribution to the diet using bone chemistry

The problems outlined above for the many indirect methods of determining diet largely disappear when one attempts to reconstruct diet more directly using human bone. Several aspects of bone chemistry can inform on the presence and dietary proportions of marine foods in the diet. Since adult bone remodels approximately every decade, bone chemistry results potentially are indicative of habitual diets in the last ten years of life (Price et al. 1994).

Stable isotopes

The stable isotopes of carbon 13 and 12 and nitrogen 15 and 14 in ratio (abbreviated as ∂ ["delta"] ^{13}C and ∂ ^{15}N), contained in bone apatite provide information on the customary or time-averaged diet. Bone collagen has been found to reflect disproportionately the carbon isotope composition of dietary protein while apatite reflects the carbon isotope values of the whole diet and is preferred for this work. Earlier samples of bone collagen cannot simply be reinterpreted because the protein percentage in the diet must be calculated before calculating the isotope values (deFrance et al. 1996); consequently studies relying on collagen need to be redone (e.g. Chisholm et al. 1983).

Plants trap carbon through several different pathways, two of which are labeled C_3 and C_4. C_3 plants fix carbon into three-carbon acids. C_4 plants fix carbon into four-carbon acids. These pathways can be differentiated with ∂ ^{13}C calculation. Marine fish, molluscs, and marine mammals have ∂ ^{13}C values between C_3 and C_4 carbon chains. Where no C_4 plant was consumed the ∂ ^{13}C value informs on marine food consumption but where both C_4 plants and marine foods were consumed, it is necessary to compare the ∂ ^{13}C value to a ∂ ^{15}N value. Animals concentrate nitrogen in their tissue while most plants do not. If ∂ ^{13}C values are less negative (in the range of -17 to -14) and ∂ ^{15}N values more positive (12 to 16) then marine foods or molluscan foods are implicated (Larsen et al. 1992:201, Schoeninger and Peebles 1981).

A study of twelve skeletons from four coastal sites on three Caribbean islands, while suffering from sample size, offers intriguing results (deFrance et al. 1996). The isotopic work indicated that C_4 plants were important in the diet but the botanical remains did not. Furthermore, the osteochemical results indicated less use of marine resources than terrestrial ones while the faunal

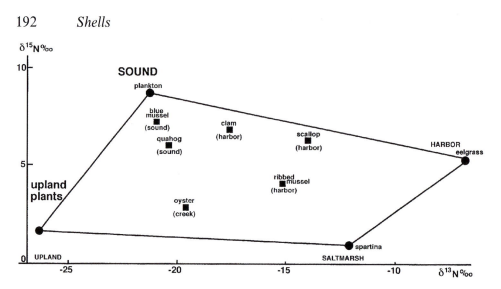

Fig. 30 Isotopic values of bases of food webs at Nantucket Sound, eelgrass near shore, *Spartina* in saltmarshes and upland detritus in creeks. Isotope values of filter feeding bivalves reflect the mixture of foods in different locations X-axis should read "$\partial^{13}C$."

remains – shells, fishbone – strongly contradicted that interpretation. The same contradiction between abundant shell remains but little or no chemical confirmation of shellfish consumption has been reported in several sites in southern California as well (Jones 1996:254). These results reinforce my point that all the faunal remains may not directly contribute to human diet. If the shells discarded in the sites were harvested largely for fish bait, then the apparent consumption of marine resources would be reduced to just the fish.

Isotope studies of skeletal material from two sites in Panama revealed yet another paradox. Apparently the occupants of the older Cerro Mangote site consumed fewer marine foods than did the later occupants of Sitio Sierra, even though the latter site is twice as far from the shore (Cooke et al. 1996). One possible resolution to the surprising results is that Cerro Mangote was occupied for brief episodes when marine foods were consumed but that the greater proportion of diet was maize consumed during the rest of the year. Sitio Sierra's would have been a more sedentary population.

Greater refinement of isotopic values for marine-based diets recently has been offered by Little (1993a, Little and Schoeninger 1995). Isotopic assays of Nantucket Island (Massachusetts, US) flora and fauna show that *Spartina* grass (C_4) and phytoplankton have a high $\partial^{13}C$ value, but that the plants along the shore (C_3) have low $\partial^{13}C$ values as does eelgrass. Both the saltmarsh *Spartina* and shore plants have a low $\partial^{15}N$ value reflecting the terrestrially derived nitrogen, while the phytoplankton and eelgrass of the harbor have a higher $\partial^{15}N$ value.

The filter feeders reflect the nitrogen and carbon isotopic values of the

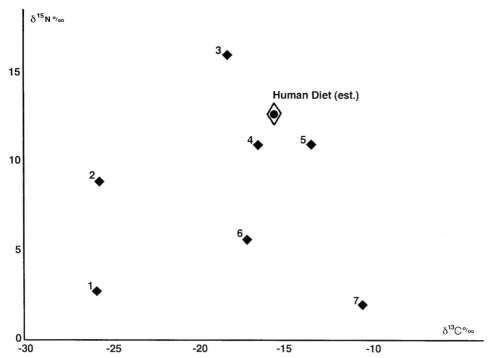

Fig. 31 Schematic display of average $\partial^{13}C$ and $\partial^{13}N$ for estimated Late Woodland Nantucket diet and seven food groups. (1) Elderberry, shadberry, orache, sea rocket and deer; (2) calamus roots, cattail roots and white perch; (3) bluefish, striped bass, halibut; (4) whelk, moonshell, snail, scup, flounder, crab; (5) lobster, cunner, eel; (6) quahog, clam, scallop, oyster, ribbed mussel and blue mussel; (7) maize.

detritus in their creek, harbor, saltmarsh, or eelgrass habitats (Figure 30). "Oysters in creeks and ribbed mussels in saltmarshes show lower $\partial^{15}N$ values than scallops living in eelgrass beds, or blue mussels or quahogs at the north shore outside the harbor. Scallops, with an eelgrass habitat, show a high $\partial^{13}C$ value" (Little 1993a:196).

These plants form the basis of several food chains. With each trophic level change, $\partial^{13}C$ increases by approximately 1.7 ppt while $\partial^{15}N$ values increase about 3.6 ppt (Little 1993a:197). Little estimates that the average bivalve diet for prehistoric New Englanders created a $\partial^{15}N$ value of 1.8 ppt. The isotopic positions of seven food groups found on Nantucket Island are plotted in Figure 31 and their contribution to human diet can be distinguished in human bone. Sophisticated analyses such as this one will do much to transfer our attention away from the weak inferences about human diet provided by the counts, weights, and biomass of site ecofacts, onto the much stronger inferences provided by bone and ecofact chemistry.

Barium and strontium

Strontium (Sr) is concentrated in many plants and in the flesh and shells of molluscs. Therefore, a habitual diet rich in plant foods or molluscs will be higher in strontium than would be one rich in terrestrial meat and lacking molluscs. Ophel found that ^{90}Sr "was concentrated 730-fold in the meat of fresh water [lake] molluscs" (cited in Schoeninger and Peebles 1981:393). Two other strontium isotopes in ratio, $^{87}Sr:^{86}Sr$, have been utilized in a preliminary way by Sealy et al. (1991) to distinguish between interior, terrestrial coast, and marine coast dietary zones.

Salt water has a much lower barium (Ba) to strontium ratio than is found in terrestrial environments so that marine taxa also have a lower ratio than terrestrial fauna and flora. "The Ba/Sr ratio, applied to archaeological [human] bone, readily distinguishes large differences in the consumption of marine resources, and, in some cases, it is possible to distinguish relatively small differences" (Burton and Price 1990:552). Burton and Price found that barium, by itself, distinguished trophic level better than did strontium, giving differences of several orders of magnitude between terrestrial and marine barium values. These differences carry over into human bone where ratios of Ba:Sr can be used to distinguish predominantly marine from terrestrial diets (Burton and Price 1991). The differences between fresh water, shell, and fish fell within one standard deviation of terrestrial animals so that those dietary elements cannot be separated with the Ba:Sr ratio (Burton and Price 1990:548).

7.4   Summary

Critical reviews of dietary reconstruction have appeared in every phase of its popularity: in 1883, in 1967, in 1979, and increasingly so since. Today far fewer archaeologists are comfortable with the requisite assumptions underlying every facet of the calculations. Biases against shellfish have been uncovered in old ethnographies and new ones challenge assumptions of uniform diets and the exclusive role of shells and molluscan flesh in human food chains. They also illuminate greater variation in gathering behavior than recognized previously, some of which renders optimal foraging theory inappropriate.

Aside from these ethnographic based challenges to the enterprise, trouble has appeared in the typical methods used to estimate nutrition and meat weights. As our sophistication with ecology has improved, we have learned that variation is the rule – variation in the nutritional content of individual molluscs with season, age, and health, variation in human nutritional requirements, variation in individual and population sizes of prey. Older meat-weight estimation methods have been judged inadequate, and allometric formulae fail to inspire confidence when applied to samples of known meat weight.

Inadequate samples also mar putative dietary reconstructions. Assumptions of uniform diets, invariable molluscan physiques, shells as food debris, and predictable human behavior have resulted in naive site-sampling schemes and nutritional assignments.

The tiers of assumptions that have to be made to achieve the goal of dietary reconstruction when one starts with shells are so many that the effort is futile. Today, many archaeologists are no longer willing to make those assumptions and forego the indirect means of estimating dietary components and value (e.g. Begler and Keatinge 1979:221, Bowdler 1976, Claassen 1991b).

A far more direct avenue to understanding habitual diet is afforded by bone chemistry. Although bringing a new set of problems, diet as reconstructed through bone chemistry eliminates most of the problems associated with the more indirect methods of investigation. Rapid progress is being made in refining the techniques, in specifying the contributions of different food groups and the harvesting activities in different zones of the coast. Sampling issues remain, however. It is necessary that differences in at least gender, age, and class be investigated in any skeletal population. Several studies have resulted in unexpected dietary variation and practices which are forcing archaeologists to consider more seriously the social lives of their skeletal population.

8

THE SHELL ARTIFACT

Shell, the raw material, has had cultural importance great and small in many of the world's societies. A tremendous variety of shell artifacts is evident in the archaeological record – containers, boat bailers, decorative elements for live-stock, people, houses, and graves, money, games, medicine, etc. In spite of this variety, only a few ways of producing and analyzing shell objects are known. Modified and unmodified shells were important also in political and social systems as symbols of various ideas. They were so important, in fact, that many species of shell were moved great distances. Sourcing shells to a water body offers important information for unraveling contacts between groups. The movement of shell across the landscape indicates a conduit for the movement of ideas, flora, and fauna, even pathogens. The integration of shell into past social systems as an artifact that has often traveled great distances and symbol-izes great concepts is explored below.

8.1   Shell artifact production and analysis

There are various ways of modifying whole shells which are found repeatedly around the globe. Groove and snap are the principal ways of breaking shell, while grinding is the easiest way of producing a hole. The giant clam (*Tridacna gigas*) was first broken into smaller pieces that were put into a vice and sawn into plates by only a handful of New Guinea shell-working specialists (Safer and Gill 1982:33). Bead production typically involved fracturing the shell or grooving and snapping the shell (see Francis 1982). For instance, beads of the Mediterranean bivalve *Cerastoderma glaucum* started with blanks cut or chip-ped from valve sections, then roughly shaped by grinding. The convex side of the blank was smoothed first, then drilling commenced from the concave side. A second round of smoothing was followed by rounding of the circumference (Shackleton 1988:99–103). To manufacture a tool in ancient Texas cultures from the lip of a gastropod shell, the body and penultimate whorl sections were broken away from the columella and spire by percussion both with and without prior scoring (Hall 1981:215). The blank was battered around the edges into a rough preform of the finished artifact. A limestone or sandstone abrader was used to grind the edges and faces of the blank into the final form. Perforations using a chert drill completed the artifact.

Techniques for shell working in the southwestern US included incising,

196

carving, abrading, mosaic, inlay, drilling, and etching. Etching was performed with a brew made from fruit of the sahuaro cactus. The shell was covered with pitch to preserve a final shape then acid was applied to the exposed portions of the shell. Etched shell was often painted.

Drilling could be accomplished using a hard drill (stone) on a softer shell or by using a soft drill (bone, reed) on harder shell. The stone drill could be handheld and rotated with a twist of the wrist while applying pressure or spun between the palms of the hands. Faster drilling was generated by the bow drill or pump drill, the latter introduced to native Americans by the Spanish. Drilling with a soft drill was accomplished when an abrasive such as sand was added and the drill was twirled between the palms (Janota 1980:35–36).

Both women and men have been identified as shell workers. A complete shell-working kit was found in the ancient grave of a woman in Texas (Hall 1981:215) and women were said to be the native wampum producers in New York. In New Guinea men modified the giant clam shell and prepared the kula ring arm bands and disk beads.

Analysis of shell artifacts

The most consistently obvious artifacts are beads when a stringing hole has been prepared. Much more problematic in sites are the unmodified whole aquatic gastropods and the nicked and broken bivalves. In this section I will present examples of analyses that have explored the patterning in possible artifacts and analyses of identified artifacts.

Bead analysis

Finished beads   Cut shell beads have had far more quantification of their attributes than has any other type of shell artifact. Several measurements are useful for deriving typologies, comparing specimens, and exploring production.

Useful data categories for cut shell beads are (1) maximum diameter, (2) minimum diameter, (3) maximum thickness, (4) maximum bore-hole diameter at one surface, and (5) internal bore-hole diameter, usually a minimum diameter. Measurement (5) can be accomplished using a set of graduated Allan wrenches or nails and recording the smallest one that will pass through the bead. All five measurements inform on production techniques such as group or individual bead grinding (or bead sets versus accumulated beads), size of drill, skill in drilling. The ratio of maximum diameter to maximum thickness is the basis of a bead typology with bore-hole diameters suggestive of subdivisions in that typology.

For whole-shell beads the measurements of (1) shell height, (2) maximum shell diameter, (3) location of stringing hole, and (4) mode of producing

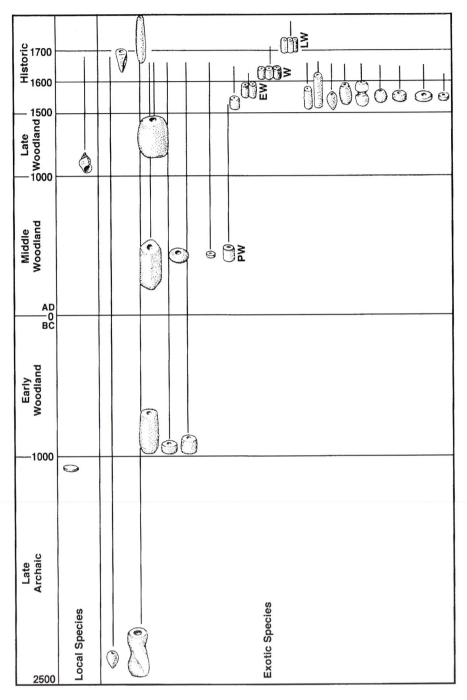

Fig. 32 Graphic of shell bead style sequence, western New York.

stringing hole are informative. To locate the position of a stringing hole made in the body of the gastropod, the shell can be gridded (mentally or with a template). Holding the apex up and the siphon down, the x- and y-axes create a grid. The hole will fall within one numbered cell of the grid.

For beads found in graves, observations on the age and sex of the person and the position of the beads with respect to the body are important for understanding costume or other bead use. Using such data regionally specific bead styles were identified for the eastern US 5,000 to 3,000 ya (Claassen 1996a). One graphic display style for a bead assemblage is demonstrated in Figure 32.

Bead production debris   The Chumash chiefdom of southern California was the origin point for several types of *Olivella* beads circulating in the region. Santa Cruz Island sites frequently yield the debris resulting from bead manufacture. Arnold and Munns (1994) reasoned that analysis of detritus would allow inferences about the types of beads made at various localities over time, as well as the intensity and organization of production. Four assemblages of detritus representing the full chronological range were sampled by removing multiple levels 1 m square and 5 cm thick. Density of detritus was quantified as number of pieces per cubic meter. The samples were then screened through $\frac{1}{8}$-inch mesh and sorted into the categories detritus, bead blanks, production stages (chipped, drilled, ground), and finished beads. Each category of material was rescreened through quarter-inch and eighth-inch mesh and classified into thirty-six categories according to shell part. Preferred in the Early Period were beads manufactured from wall pieces and beads manufactured from callus pieces in the later period. Six of the thirty-six fragment categories (wall, base and wall, callus spoon, callus and wall, base, wall-callus-spire) showed temporal patterning in the quarter-inch fraction and were subjected, as row percent data, to Ward's minimum variance clustering which verified the earlier–later temporal division. Densities of blanks, beads in production, and completed beads from sites on the mainland and the island verified that bead production was the focus of island communities and that bead consumption occurred on the mainland.

Gastropod tools
There is, from over fifty years of research, consensus that broken whelk (*Busycon* and *Busycotypus*, Figure 8), tulip (*Fasciolaria*), and conch (*Strombus, Melongena, Pleuroploca*) shells found in Florida sites are tools. Marquardt's (1992) typology of these tools is based on hafting style, lip treatment, and columella length or absence. Hafting styles found were unhafted (or lack of hafting indication), natural aperture combined with hole, and two full holes on opposite walls. In some tools the lip was broken completely away so that only the spire and columella remained, in some the most recent lip was broken off,

Type A

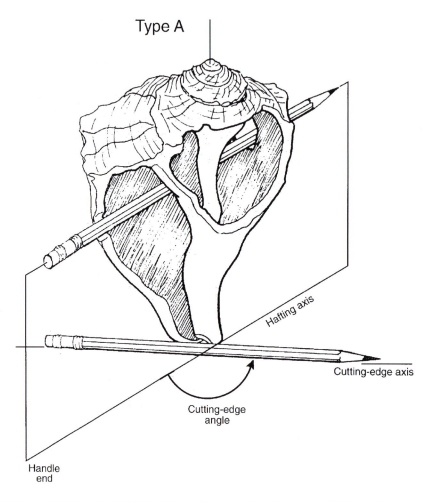

Fig. 33 Measuring columella edge angles. Steps: (1) Rest tool on table, align columella vertically; (2) insert pencil through hafting holes to determine hafting axis; (3) lay another pencil on the table, tucked up against the cutting-edge surface, to determine cutting-edge axis; (4) cutting-edge angle is the angle between cutting-edge axis and handle-end of hafting axis (around the open side of the shell tool).

and in some the full lip was present. The columella may have been shortened, removed, or angled. Columella edge angles were measured as in Figure 33. The resulting tool typology identified gastropod tool blanks, anvils, dippers/ vessels, net mesh gauges (Figure 34a), pounders, grinder/pulverizers, handles (Figure 34b), sinkers/plummets, planes, adzes, adz/celts (Figure 34c), spindle whorls, gorgets, and beads, and hammers (90-degree edge angle, Figure 34d), cutting edged tools (oblique angles).

A

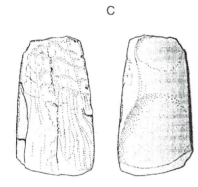

Shell Net Mesh Gauges

B

Notched gastropod shell handles

C

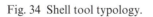

Adzes and Adze/Celts

D

Gastropod hammers, Type G

Fig. 34 Shell tool typology.

Bivalve tools

The earliest bivalve tools may have been retouched African naiads *Etheria elliptica* and *Mutela nilotica*. Williamson (in Toth and Woods [1989]) suggested that retouched edges of these shells served as butchering knives for Plio-Pleistocene hominids. Experimentation by Toth and Woods indicated that the unretouched edges of oyster (*C. virginica*) and the mussel (*Mytilus edulis*) were inadequate for butchery. Toth and Woods battered the margins of oysters with other oyster shells to produce a denticulated edge that was then useful in butchering. Retouching did not, however, result in "flakes," scars, or bulbs of percussion. They observed that the striations produced by shell knives on green bone were "similar to those produced by stone cutting edges" (Toth and Woods 1989:254).

Flaked marine shell tool industries have been recognized in several prehistoric settings including Sonora, Mexico (Rosenthal cited in de Williams 1975), the Italian Mousterian (Stiner 1993), North Queensland, Australia (Beaton 1985), Florida (Marquardt 1992), and the Great Plains of the US (Picha 1995) as well as other places. Expedient (little expenditure of effort or time in manufacture or curation) shell technology among the northern Great Plains tribes involved flaking and grinding of naiad shell. Picha reports fracture difficult to control in naiads but grooving and snapping easier. Stiner (1993:118) reported a telltale visual difference between shell tools, with their entire margins flaked, and non-tools with unbattered edges. Stephenson (1971:79) observed that use damage on shell was marked by smoothing, polish, or striations on the margin.

Lima et al. (1986) present a typology of fractured bivalves. Their analysis began by gridding the valve to locate the placement and extent of fractures, seen in Figure 35. Most of the fractured bivalves were venerids (equally distributed between right and left valves) offering thick working edges. Examples of types are (1) arciform break on margin, (2) transverse break in medial region, (3) transverse and diagonal breaks on margin forming sharp projections, (4) triangular marginal fragment, etc. Most of these types were thought to be created by or for perforating and scraping wood and bone. Most numerous were those valves with denticulated margins, possible fish scalers. On most fractured valves the hinge was present and the edge of the dorsal face was the preferred working edge.

Bivalve tools recovered from the Charlotte Harbor sites of Florida's west coast were anvils, choppers, knives/scrapers, net mesh gauges, and unidentified notched, perforated, and hourglass-shaped valves (Marquardt 1992). Valves with severe blunting and chipping of the posterior edge of the ventral margin were labeled choppers. Adz/celts are triangular venerid shell fragments with serrated working edges on the ventral margin. Shells with perforations in the superior portion of their valves may have been net weights.

Many studies warn the investigator not to confuse marginal chipping and

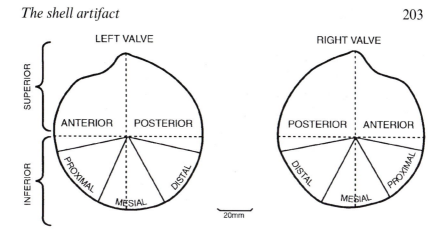

Fig. 35 Grid for modified bivalves.

very round holes drilled by predators with use damage caused by humans (e.g. Shackleton 1988, Spanier 1986). Experimentation with shell tools is rare and edge wear studies for shell are even rarer. Birds fracture shells as do crabs. Wave and storm damage can also result in fractured valves (see Chapter 3). Toth and Woods warn that distinguishing the intentionally retouched edge from taphonomic processes might be impossible.

8.2   Shell symbolism

Various aspects of shell have been accorded symbolic, iconographic, and indexical meaning (O'Sullivan et al. 1983). Of importance are color, particularly whiteness; shape, particularly for aquatic gastropods; size; and the calcium carbonate powder rendered by grinding or burning. General categories for shell symbolism are the births of important religious personages or whole groups, celestial likeness, well-being, and currency.

Perhaps the most widespread symbolic role for shell is as the womb from which emerged an important mythical figure. The sea and shell gave birth to Aphrodite in Greek mythology (Stix et al. 1984). From Chilean graves of ca. 3000 BC come vases painted with a goddess emerging from a shell (Stix et al. 1984). The birth of the Mexican figure Quetzalcoatl (in one version) is as a full-grown man emerging from a gastropod after which he lived in a palace built of shells. He is often shown seated on a pedestal carved in the form of a shell (Stix et al. 1984).

Even when no specific individual is implicated, shell often carries a metaphorical role in fertility. "Any object which resembled the sexual organs of men or woman [sic] was, in antiquity, considered to be a potent amulet in putting to flight evil spirits, which are easily shocked" (Ritchie 1974:193). Hence came the association of shells with Venus, goddess of love, and also the belief that these shells were good luck charms. This genital imagery has been brought into the twentieth century and spread world-wide in the species names of hundreds of molluscs such as *fornicata*, *labiosum*, *semen*, *seminalis*, *virginea*, *vagina*, and even more graphically in common names.

The aperture side of the cowrie shell was supposed to resemble the vulva. Cowries were worn by women of Pompeii and other places, to prevent sterility. Women are the wearers of cowries among Bedouins (girdles), in the Volga River region (head and breast ornaments), the unmarried Maasi and Akamba girls of Africa, in Tibet (girdles), and by the Chettis of India. The expectant mother among the African Ewe wears cowries (Jackson 1916b). The Bimi (Africa) plant a small tree by the side of the road and locate chalk marks and a mound of earth with cowries, yams, and plantains nearby as a memorial to a birth at that place (Figure 36).

On the New Hebrides island of Aurora, the first woman came from a cowrie. The Samoans believed that gods are present in some of the molluscs and that humans formed from a species of mussel.

Among the Haida and Kaigani of the northeastern Pacific coast, the first people sprang from a cockle shell (Jackson 1916b:54–55). Haida people originated from molluscs, evident in the belief that "creator/trickster Raven is shown standing on a giant clamshell, with tiny humans emerging from within the valves... After the flood, Raven dug a clam ... and released the Haida [men] from within the shell" (MacDonald cited in Moss 1993:644). In order to get females, some of the men were induced by Raven to have sex with chitons. The Manhousat women's feast of the chitons further demonstrates their association with chitons. To ensure hunting luck, both the Northwest coast male hunter and his wife had to refrain from sex and shellfish (Moss 1993:644). The Tlingit word for "container" can mean box, coffin, womb, the opposite moiety, as well as bivalve shell (Moss 1993:647). This association of molluscs with sexuality has been blamed in part for the paucity of ethnographic information on molluscs in these native societies (Moss 1993:643).

It is not uncommon to encounter imitation molluscs produced by artisans in stone, metal, shell, bone, clay, and whale tooth (e.g. Aztecs; Chinese [Namio 1974]; Africans [Jackson 1916b:54]). These endeavors are further illustration of the spiritual and secular importance of molluscs in many societies.

Information on shell symbolism is particularly rich for several American cultures yet overlooked by archaeologists when analyzing shells. Several of the examples to be given below focus on the color of shells: white, bright, yellow. I wonder if assemblages of non-food debris shells could profitably be analyzed by sorting them into color categories? I offer several examples of shell symbolism in American and European cultures to illustrate the significance of shell use and, consequently, the significance of archaeologists' omission of ideological concerns.

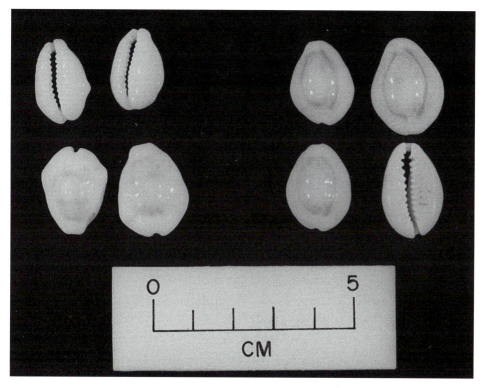

Fig. 36 Cowrie shells.

Northeastern US

Symbolic colors for the pre-Contact Northeastern Algonquians, Siouans, and Iroquoians were white, sky blue-greenness for life and social states of being, red for fire and antisocial states of being such as vengeance, and black for lack of life and asocial states of being such as death and mourning. Items appropriately colored were used in rituals to effect change from one state of being to another. Particularly meaningful were white shells. The Grandfathers of the Underwater World were the keepers of white shell, crystal, and native copper, and of the game animals. These items were appropriately given back when the abodes of the Grandfathers (caves, deep springs, waterfalls, others) were encountered (Hamell 1983). In the possession of real human man-beings, the precious white (shell, crystal, some stone) and red (ochre, some stones, red cedar) items represented "long life (immortality through resuscitation), well-being ... and success, particularly in the conceptually related activities of hunting and fishing, warfare, and courtship" (Hamell 1983:25). A hunter would gaze upon a decorated object to bring on good thought, or concentrate upon a desire in order to bring it to pass. The more precious items one possessed the more well-being accrued. Wealth was much well-being. One could accumulate well-being or display it through gifts to the living or dead (Hamell 1987:76).

The barrel or round shape of shell beads was ritually linked to berries, also of round or barrel shape. Berries had restorative powers imbued by their shape and, if red, by their color. They symbolize the soul's liminal state of being and the substance by which one resolved liminality. "Since the early sixteenth century, berries (and fruits) have been described as conspicuous attributes of the spirit world, afterworld, or other world" (Hamell 1983:9). Metaphorically, shell beads are berries. Shell beads (wampum) resolved the liminality at death and of a visitor who reached the village's edge (where berries grew), or the World's Rim, and "wealth, medicine, or charms were the tokens of successful encounters and ritualized reciprocal exchanges with" those at the World's Rim (Hamell 1987:77).

Hamell (1983) explains that the native attraction to European bangles and beads was due to the immediately evident use of the white, black, and red glass beads, other glass items in general, trade cloth, and light-colored metals in this native symbol system. The influx of precious items energized and led to an historic native elaboration of this system and soon included white and purple (black) shell wampum.

"White, red, and black shells have contrasting and complementary functions, values, and meanings in ritual" (Hamell 1983:7). Shell beads were medicine (and thus appropriately included in medicine bundles) and a wealth of them meant a wealth of well-being. In the mortuary setting they had a restorative role in ritual from both their berry form and their color that effected transformation in the state of being of the deceased. Hamell contends that white shell beads had this symbolism in the Northeast for some 6,000 years.

Many US-trained archaeologists assume that shell beads in graves constituted wealth. Instead, it seems reasonable that the preponderance of shell beads in child burials represent well-being extended to the sick child by parents and kin. Once the child died, white beads effected passage from this world. The observation that women are accorded shell beads less often than children and men may be signaling a difference in the amount of well-being or liminality of women.

Mesoamerican shell symbolism

Among Mesoamerican cultures shell was associated with death. Both God N (god sign for 5) and the conch shell he carries upon his back are associated with the underworld, death, and the five unlucky days at the end of year. The Long Nose God K is also occasionally shown with a conch shell. The shell became associated with the moon goddess Ixchel, who was the goddess of fertility and childbirth, and a water deity (Andrews 1969:48). A gastropod was the glyphic zero and south, and when compounded in glyphs it meant completion.

Thompson has the following to say about the shell in Maya hieroglyphic writing:

> [S]hells, particularly the conch and other univalves, symbolize the earth, the underworld, and the realm of the dead situated therein. Shells added as a prefix to the glyph of the sun convert that deity to his nocturnal form, as lord of the night, because during the night the sun was believed to travel through the underworld from west to east to reach again his point of rising in the east. Similarly, a conventionalized univalve shell, inverted and flanked with additional elements is the glyph for south on the monuments (but not in the codices), because that direction is under the guardianship of the death god, the lord of the underworld. Again, the glyph for day commonly used in lunar calculations and in distance numbers is a conventionalized shell because the count appears to have been by nights or sunrises. (1960:49)

The Aztecs held a special respect for the gastropod as the following poem clearly indicates (unattributed excerpt in Templo Mayor Museum):

> En su infinite belleza,
> el caracol nos recuerda
> el aqua, el mar, la lluvia, la fertilidad
> en fin, todo aquello que forma parte
> de la Vida y de la Muerte...
> el caracol is símbolo de la vida
> El artista que lo creó
> no sólo hizo vida através de la forma
> sino que unió volumen y ritmo
> y logró con líneas que se desparraman
> suavemente, el movimiento constante y
> eterno del símbolo Vital

South America

Away from the Ecuadorian coast where both the red bivalve *Spondylus pictorum* and the white gastropod *Strombus gigas* can be fished, these two species are nearly always found paired in archaeological context. *S. pictorum* is found significantly modified into "small ornaments or jewelry or in context suggesting elite or ritual associations. *Strombus* was not carved or otherwise modified, but it was sometimes incised with ritual themes" (Paulsen 1974:603). The two are also found paired as icons on sculpture and ceramics. Paulsen concludes that the importance of *Strombus* was functional and probably secondary to the raw material of *Spondylus*. Until 2500 BC these two shells are found only at trade centers on major routes. By 800 BC the two appear along with other icons on the central obelisk at Chavin de Huantar. By 600 BC, a second deity on an obelisk is portrayed with only these two shells, *Strombus* in the right hand and *Spondylus* in the left. If the obelisks at Chavin de Huantar and elsewhere represent oracles then *Spondylus* was the visual symbol and *Strombus* the voice (Paulsen 1974:605).

But the role of shells in cosmic symbolism in the Andes was more profound than just presented. Also important among Ecuadorian shell imports and appearing as early (2000 BC) as the conch and *Spondylus* were the nacreous pearl oysters *Pteria sterna* and *Pinctada mazatlantica*. Their principal physical characteristic was their refraction of light which made them glimmer and shine (Mester 1989:158). The oyster shells were cut into flat rectangular pendants and sewn onto cloth or suspended from building members, along with other shimmering objects, objects of gold, rock crystal, silver. In Andean cosmology shimmering and gleaming objects represented or were beauty and moral excellence. Shininess was connected with the Sun; shiny objects symbolized the celestial sphere and signified the Inca ruler. Pearls and rock crystals were called "quispe" and both were metaphors for sparkling water such as rain and hail, water thought to be morally pure. Mester found numerous examples of pearls and pearl shell being worn on important occasions "to legitimize an event," in fact pearls pertained to the royal dynasty (Mester 1989:161).

Red *Spondylus* shell, on the other hand, pertained to a terrestrial symbolic complex. Red was the color of war and the targets of warfare, non-Incas. (As an antisocial state of being, war was also marked by red in the northeastern US.) It was also the color of Andean soil, the water in the irrigation ditches, and the potting clay and, consequently, red symbolized agricultural fertility as well as the class of vanquished farmers.

To summarize Andean color symbolism and cosmology, there "is a metaphorical connection between light, bright colors, celestial elements, and the upper moiety of Inca society. These are contrasted with a similar group of symbols relating dark colors, terrestrial elements, and the lower moiety" (Mester 1989:162). Enlarging the red/white color dualism was a color vocabulary that "measured social distance from the King." Light and bright colors symbolized nobility and the solar deity.

Similar shell bead symbolism is found among the Kogi Indians of Columbia who also have a dual color system. The Cosmic Mother, symbolized by female items – water, crystals, caves – is opposed to Death, symbolized by male items – snakes, arrows, crabs, and blue color. In the struggle against Death, the Cosmic Mother and the Kogi use shell beads and rock crystals, classified as living and powerful because they are white and gleaming. Dark beads are dead (Mester 1989:164).

European shell symbolism of the Christian era

The apostle James or Santiago, a fisherman, was associated early in the history of Christianity with a scallop shell (*Pecten jacobaeus*) and depicted frequently in the Middle Ages. Scallops were transported to the pilgrimage site of Compostela, Spain, to be sold outside the cathedral. Individuals reported cures simply from touching them (Stix et al. 1984). Heraldry made repeated and frequent use of shells, particularly the scallop, possibly as early as the twelfth century to indicate that a male figure had made a pilgrimage to Palestine (Goode 1884:709). Architects of the Renaissance saw in shells architectural perfection and moved the scallop motif into buildings – in fountains, niches, adornos, tombs, and pedestals. The spiral apex of the miraculous thatcheria (*Thatcheria mirabilis*) is said to have given da Vinci the idea for the spiral staircase (Conklin 1985:230).

Collector mania spread throughout Europe during the Era of Exploration, becoming particularly strong among the Dutch who not only collected shells but made them the subject of paintings. It was the Rococo era that took shells to their decorative height. *Rocaille*, a French contraction of the phrase "travail de coquille" or "shell work," gave rise to the term Rococo. Elaborately carved shells and shell buttons were fine crafts of the era, as were items inlaid with shell. Many everyday items, such as boxes and tableware, were shaped like shells. "In Christian symbolism the shell signified purity, resurrection, redemption on the Day of Judgment, and forgiveness through pilgrimage. The Rococo laughingly discarded any touch of such religious sentiment, and treated the shell as a joyous design element" (Stix et al. 1984:27). During the Victorian era, the respectability of the shell declined, although its popularity did not. A newer symbolism was that of distant and exciting places. It was also used in the manner of a Valentine, particularly by sailors (Stix et al. 1984:28). Today that romantic function seems to have disappeared, with only the "shell as memoir" and shell as something-pretty-to-see-and-feel remaining of those earlier associations.

Well-being

Bound up in these symbol systems are the uses of shell to monitor well-being: as money which symbolizes well-being, as offerings which ensure well-being, as games which examine well-being, and as medicine which restores well-being.

Money

The characteristics of money most commonly cited make it clear that shells are perfectly suited to monetary use and may have even determined the characteristics of metal money. These characteristics are homogeneity, divisibility, portability, and durability. Both unmodified shells and modified shells have constituted money, a medium of exchange which condensed value. Those shells which have served as money in an unmodified state (with the exception of stringing holes) are limpets (*Fissurella aculeata*) used by some coastal California people (Goode 1884:701), *Dentalium* shells among the Pomo and Yurok of California, and cowries in China, Thailand, India, and many Pacific Islands, prior to European influence, and in the eastern US, west Africa, and India after European influence. In addition, *Olivella* shells in west Africa,

Marginella shells in Timbuctu, and *Turbinella pyrum* shells in India have been currency.

A currency based on modified shells was one in California based on Pismo clams and *Olivella* callus disk beads (Arnold and Munns 1994). Wampum (cut beads of *Mercenaria mercenaria* and *Busycon* spp.) was a European currency in New York and New England. Arguably used as money are the cut and ornamented green turban snail shells (*Turbo marmoratus*) prepared by the Chambri of New Guinea or the yards of *Nassarius* sp. shells strung on vines and used by the Tolai of Melanesia (Safer and Gill 1982:63, 66).

Offerings/votive caches
Over forty species are commonly recovered from contexts in Mayan sites that indicate their use as offerings in tombs (rare except at Tikal), in caches, and in cenotes (Andrews 1969:49–52). Included in tombs were unmodified specimens of the genera *Spondylus*, *Oliva*, *Strombus*, *Ficus*, *Arca*, *Chione*, and the naiad *Nephronaias*. Caches contained unmodified *Melongena corona*, *M. melongena*, *Anomia simplex*, *Neritina meleagris*, *Spondylus princeps*, and *Prunum a. virgineum*, to name those with more than twelve representatives. Recovered from cenotes were *Dinocardium r. vanhyningi*, *Pleuroploca gigantea*, *Strombus costatus*, *Atrina seminuda*, *Trachycardium isocardia*, *Chione cancellata*, and some fifteen others (Andrews 1969:52–53).

Votive shells in Greek sanctuaries are frequently encountered, and typically consist of the taxa *Tridacna*, *Conus*, *Phalium*. A dedicatory cache containing shells and beads was found under the Assur ziggurat (Reese 1989). At Tikal, the contents of structure and monument caches were most often paired bivalves (Moholy-Nagy 1963:73).

Among Puebloans of the southwestern US whole shells, beads, and shell fragments had important roles in rituals. A mixture of shell fragments and turquoise with or without corn meal was used to summon a shaman (Santa Domingo), was used for Rain Chief prayer-sticks (Zuni), to deposit under a new house (Zuni), or as an offering for deer, eagle, or rabbit (Laguna). White shell beads were hung on prayer sticks when offspring or a specific cure were requested. *Olivella* and abalone shells were used in war cults. *Olivella* and scallop shells were attached to the Hopi Snake Society bandoleer (Parsons 1974). *Olivella* shells were found alone on wrist guards and dance bandoleers.

Many an ordinary home in the Tamil country of India had a sacred chank shell positioned under the initial stones of the structure (Hornell 1915). "When a new Hindu temple is built, a new shrine established, or a god added to the set worshipped in a temple, the dedicatory ceremonies include a libation from the mouths of 108 chank shells, or, still more auspicious, from 1,008. These shells are filled with water and flowers" (Hornell 1915).

Fortune telling/games/communication
Games originated as fortunetelling with shells often serving as die. In this

century cowries have been used to determine one's fortunes in Liberia, to determine guilt of murder in Togo, or the outcome of a proposed war (cowries landing aperture up portend peace, aperture down, success in war) among the Egbas, and the cause of death among forest tribes of east Africa (Jackson 1916b:33). Cowries are central to the games of jagay in Sierra Leone, kawadi kelia and the Hindu pachisi, dhola of the Maldive Islands, edris a jin in Syria, and pasit in Burma (Jackson 1916b).

Messages have also been communicated between societies via shells. The role of wampum in treaty negotiations is well documented. The Yoruba use the number of cowries and the way they are strung to convey emotions such as defiance or failure, relationship and meeting, separation and enmity, etc.; the Jebu use odd numbers of cowries to signal evil and even numbers to signal good will. Petrie dismissed strung cowries found in Egypt as amulets (Jackson 1916b:41).

Medicine

Shells are often part of medicine bundles and rituals. Such is the case among the northeastern US Indians (e.g. Hamell 1983, Jackson 1916a), among peoples in Sierra Leone (Jackson 1916b), the Puebloans of the southwestern US, and many other groups. As representatives of life (northeastern US), the Sun (Inca), fertility (many African groups), food (Puebloans, US), and well-being (Hindus; northeastern US), in that they repel evil eye (e.g. India, Hungary, Norway, Egypt) and move one out of liminal states, and a multitude of them means much well-being, shells and shell beads are inherently medicine.

In many societies, shells symbolize the breath, sputum, heart, or soul. For this reason, shells are placed in the mouth (e.g. Basket Makers, southwestern US), and in the hand of corpses (e.g. China), and cowrie shells were associated with head hunting in tribes of east central Africa.

Sorcerers of central and southern Africa employ the giant African land snail (*Archachatina marginata*) for evil (Lunda in Zambi), or for good (Lulua of Zaire) (Safer and Gill 1982:122–123). Shells, specifically the black-lipped pearl oyster, are also used by sorcerers in Australia for benevolent and malevolent purposes. Pointers of oyster shoot illness or death into a victim, and drive away bad spirits, and disks of oyster cure sickness by passing through the body (Safer and Gill 1982:125). The pearl oyster shell (*Pinctada margaritifera*) is associated with rain and thus fertility in the southwestern US.

Shells and the creatures inside also are ingredients in medicines. The fluids, meat, and shell of the giant African land snail are used for food, medicine, and amulets in the high forest zone and the savanna area. The shell is used in medicine for treating dysentery and stomach ache (Agbelusi and Ejidike 1992). Powdered shell from cowries and chanks is used against smallpox and in Ayurvedic medicines in India, Tibet, and China, and is offered to smallpox fetishes by the Bassair of Togo. Finger rings of *Turbinella pyrum* (sacred chank) ward off skin troubles (Hornell 1915). Calcined *Murex* shells were used to clean teeth among ancient Mediterranean-area dwellers while the operculum, once boiled in oil, was used to retain hair (Reese 1979–80:85). Sea urchin shells were used as an astringent in Dalmatia (Harvey 1956:24).

8.3   Movement of shell

Hundreds of articles and books have presented evidence for the movement of shells overland, far from their sources. Unfortunately, it is not the purpose of this manual to review this literature, but instead to indicate methods of conducting the inquiry.

Chemical sourcing of shell

Central Mexico is surrounded by four marine water bodies, each with some distinctive molluscan taxa. In this setting it is unusually easy to trace the origin and movement of shells between coastline and site (Andrews 1969). Other similarly fortuitous settings can be found in the cultures of the North American Southwest, where shells from the Pacific, the Gulf of California, and the Gulf of Mexico commingle; and in the Near East where many molluscan taxa are easily assigned Indo-Pacific or Mediterranean provenience. In China, very old texts play a similar role to geography in telling us that cowrie shells were first seized from southern coastal tribes and later entered from the Indian Ocean via the western border of Chinese culture (Namio 1974).

In most other culture areas, however, and even in the Chinese example, taxa have no geographically specific provenience and thus frustrate the wishes of archaeologists to know more precisely the origin of exotic raw materials and the human groups having contact. Discussions of the origin of marine shells found in the interior eastern United States rarely move beyond a citation of a species range. Lynn Ceci (1989) found that shell beads recovered from Archaic-period burials in New York State represent south Atlantic coast species. Unfortunately the range of habitats for most of the species involved encompasses all, or at best half, of the coastline of the eastern United States. The most extensive study of shell distribution in the eastern United States to date, that by Ann Ottesen (1979), did not even attempt to speculate on shell sources, citing the lack of species identification in reports, possible errors in classification, and large natural ranges as problematic.

Fortunately, chemical means of sourcing shells have been applied in at least two settings, Europe (Shackleton and Renfrew 1970) and the eastern US (Claassen and Sigmann 1993). The first chemical testing of shell for sourcing purposes, that by Shackleton and Renfrew (1970), examined both ornamental artifacts and unmodified shells from Neolithic sites 4000 to 2500 BC in the

Balkans and eastern Europe. Distinctive oxygen-isotopic profiles (see Chapters 3, 6 for details on this technique) for the Black and Aegean seas, checked with modern samples of *Nassa reticulata* and *Chamelia gallina*, allowed the sourcing of *Spondylus gaederopus* shell artifacts to the Aegean Sea. In continuous water bodies such as the Atlantic or Gulf of Mexico, however, there is little hope of distinguishing oxygen-isotopic profiles.

Katherine Miller (1980) examined 163 shells of *M. mercenaria* from late prehistoric sites in Maine (seven sites), Massachusetts (five sites), Long Island, (eighteen sites), and Georgia (nine sites) using neutron activation (NAA) and atomic absorption spectroscopy (AAS) in an effort to see if geographical distinctions were evident in the shell chemistry. If geochemical signatures could be identified then sourcing of marine shells traded inland as artifacts would be possible. Data were gathered on ten elements (Na, Ba, Sc, La, Mn, Sm, Sr, Mg, Al, and Br) in shell and were sought but not found for sixteen others (K, Rb, Cs, Ce, Eu, Lu, Hf, Th, Ta, Cr, Co, Ni, Zr, As, Yb, and Sb). Discriminate-function analysis of the sixty-two shells from Long Island, NY and St. Catherine's Island, Georgia correctly sourced 83 percent of these shells using only six elements – Br, Mg, Sm, Sr, Ba, and Al in order of their discriminatory power. Omitting Mg and Al from the analysis, 85 percent of the samples were correctly located (Miller 1980:84–85).

Q-mode factor analysis indicated that shells from the north shore of Long Island tend to have low Sm and Sc but ranged from high to low in Ba, Br, and Sr. Shells from the south shore of Long Island are low in Sr, Sm, and Sc but high in Br and Ba. Again, the four elements Br, Ba, Sr, and Sm are particularly useful in distinguishing between locales; Mg and Al are probably useful.

The conclusions drawn by Miller (1980:95) were:

(1) Variation within a shell results more from yearly differences among growth bands than from physiological differences among parts of shells. Twenty samples from four areas of five shells did not subdivide statistically into any groupings.

(2) Variation within a locale results more from yearly differences among growth bands than from differences in individual genetics.

(3) Shells from animals alive in the 1970s and 1980s should not be used to establish a data base for sourcing prehistoric marine shell found inland. Archaeological and modern shells from St. Catherine's Island were quite distinct.

(4) Temporal variation among pre-Contact shells is insignificant relative to variation among locations.

(5) Distinctions among geographical groups of shells can be made on a regional level. Shells from Long Island and St. Catherine's Island were distinctive chemically as were shells from the north and south shore of Long Island.

Miller's project remains the most sophisticated study of archaeological shell chemistry to date. She is to be commended for the selection of samples, sample size, elements chosen, and questions addressed – within-shell variation, within-county variation, interregional variation, and temporal variation in chemistry within the same watershed.

Water in different river systems, at the mouths of rivers, and in different bays has been shown to vary in chemical signature, according to the geochemistry of a watershed. While sourcing to a specific bay or river may prove improbable, there is much geological evidence for geochemical regions in the eastern United States that can facilitate a subdivision of coastline.

Support for such an approach to the sourcing of a general, non-point specific, substance such as shell can be found in a study by Clarke in 1906 of water chemistry in the eastern United States. Clarke (1924) found through chemical assay that the rivers of the Middle Atlantic slope, from the Hudson to the Potomac, formed a class distinct from the rivers of New England and those south of the Potomac. Thus, we have the geochemical basis for Miller's (1980) finding of a distinct shell chemistry between Massachusetts and Georgia quahog. The south Atlantic slope rivers are also distinctive because they are all low in salinity and relatively high in percentages of silica and alkalies. Calcium is low in all of them as well (Clarke 1924:48). Table 18 summarizes some of the chemical data for rivers Clarke studied.

The chemical differences between these areas are often obvious. As Table 18 shows, the rivers of Texas, draining land west of the Mississippi, are much higher in magnesium and calcium than any of the Atlantic slope rivers. Calcium is noticeably lowest in the rivers of the Carolinas. Many researchers have identified the geological environment as one of the sources of elemental variation in shell.

The watershed occupied by molluscs may have a distinctive geochemical signature created by erosion of rock and sediments. Shellfish are susceptible to this geochemistry through feeding. For example, a primary food of the whelks (*Busycon* spp., *Busycotypus* spp.) is the eastern oyster, which typically lives in the mouths of tidal rivers. Feeding in this location ensures that the whelks take up the geochemistry of the watershed directly through the water as well as indirectly by ingesting food that has that same geochemical makeup. This chemical relationship was explored by the author and chemist Samuella Sigmann (Claassen and Sigmann 1993, chemical basis presented in Chapter 5) in an effort to source a common marine shell found throughout the eastern US, the left-handed whelk (*Busycon sinistrum*).

It was necessary to establish a provenience postulate, that is, that there is greater between-region difference in shell chemistry than within-region difference, before attempting to source shells of unknown provenience. It was also necessary to examine the influence of diagenesis, body part, species, and age on the values derived.

Data from whelk shells collected from throughout the Atlantic and Gulf (Claassen and Sigmann 1993) compared well visually (Table 19) with the water assay data of Clarke (Table 18). With regard to iron, the eastern Gulf and eastern tropics are similar to one another with their low range. They are very different from the central Gulf.

Table 18. *Levels of some chemicals (ppm) in select eastern United States rivers as of 1906–1907*[1]

River	Mg	Fe	Ca
Hudson, NY	3.8	.15	21.0
Broadkill Estuary, DE[a]	3.4		17.3
Neuse, NC	1.8	1.40	5.9
Cape Fear, NC	1.5	.78	5.0
Pee Dee, SC	1.3	.31	6.9
Saluda, SC	1.3	.38	8.4
Wateree, SC	1.8	.28	6.3
Goose Creek SC	1.4		5.6
Savannah, SC/GA	0.8	.44	5.7
Appalachicola, FL	1.4	.86	8.8
Mobile Basin, AL	2.9	.53	13.0
Tombigbee, AL	1.8	.63	18.0
Mississippi, at New Orleans	8.4	.13	32.0
Mississippi location unspecified	6.8		29.6
Brazos (Waco), TX	19.0	.26	121.0
Colorado (Glidden), TX	19.1		56.8
Rio Grande (Laredo), TX	23.0		104.0

[1] Data from Clarke 1924 except for Broadkill Estuary, which is from Swann et al. 1984.

The strongest regionalism was expressed in the magnesium assays. For magnesium, the north Atlantic range does not overlap that of the south Atlantic, and the Atlantic specimens are distinct from the Gulf specimens. The highest values were obtained from western Gulf coast specimens, which is no doubt responsible for the highest Mg:Ca ratios in this same area. With regard to this ratio, at this time it appears that the north and middle Atlantic ratio can be expected to be less than 2.00 while the temperate Gulf coast ratios will be greater than 2.00. For strontium, the values and ratios obtained in Gulf waters generally exceed those from Atlantic waters. The highest Sr:Ca ratios come from the central and western Gulf.

Shell assay values do indicate regional differences in elements and signatures when compared within this experimental set and with elemental values from waters of the eastern United States, differences that are useful in sourcing artifacts of marine shell to coastal section. Magnesium appears to be the single most useful element for distinguishing regions.

Shell sourcing has some theoretical problems not relevant to the same degree to other substances commonly sourced. Foremost among these problems is the vulnerability of shell to taphonomic processes (see Chapter 3). Embedded checks and cluster analysis do much to assay the impacts of

Table 19. *Regional differences in shell chemistry of* Busycon *sp. specimens (from Claassen and Sigmann 1993) (mg/g for Fe, Mg, Sr, mg/pph for Ca)*

Name	Fe	Mg	Sr	Ca	Sr/Ca	Mg/Ca	Fe/Ca	Mg/Sr
North Atlantic								
Minimum	10.5	54.5	849	38.8	21.88	1.38	.27	.05
Maximum	21.7	95.3	1,278	43.8	29.18	2.46	.55	.11
Hudson River	43.1	90.0	1,209	39.1	30.92	2.30	1.10	.07
Mid-Atlantic								
Minimum	5.4	44.5	881	39.7	21.59	1.09	.13	.05
Maximum	39.4	73.4	1,368	43.1	32.19	1.73	.93	.06
South Atlantic								
Minimum	12.6	72.4	874	39.4	22.18	1.69	.32	.07
Maximum	25.2	155.0	1,160	43.5	28.60	3.56	.58	.13
Tropical water, Atlantic								
	22.5	124.0	846	40.1	21.10	3.09	.56	.15
Tropical water, Gulf								
Minimum	7.6	75.8	886	40.6	21.80	1.78	.18	.06
Maximum	18.4	122.8	1,557	43.6	35.71	3.02	.45	.14
Tampa Bay								
Minimum	27.8	48.1	1,113	40.2	27.62	1.19	.69	.04
Maximum	119.9	96.2	1,674	42.7	41.13	2.36	2.95	.06
Eastern Gulf Coast								
Minimum	0.0	96.9	1,392	41.5	33.54	2.38	.00	.07
Maximum	18.0	109.5	1,489	41.6	35.67	2.64	.43	.08
Central Gulf Coast								
Minimum	12.0	93.2	1,147	39.5	27.77	2.18	.29	.07
Maximum	35.9	198.5	1,768	42.7	44.76	4.81	.84	.17
Western Gulf Coast								
Minimum	5.8	94.3	1,130	38.2	26.22	2.45	.15	.06
Maximum	66.2	371.7	2,012	43.1	52.67	8.62	1.73	.33

diagenesis, however. Both the cost of the work (AAS about $35/sample) and the difficulty in procuring artifactual samples for destructive analysis make respectable sample sizes and the necessary multiple samples from the same locales difficult to amass. Nevertheless, shell sourcing is possible and can be accomplished with a number of different analytical techniques. It is not possible, however, with any chemical technique, to determine the mechanism of shell movement, whether trading, gifting, or fetching. Only the archaeologist can offer that assessment, often assisted in making a determination by the quantity of shells of one species involved.

Table 20. *Immigrant marine molluscs established in North America (after Carlton 1992)*

Species	Native to	Introduced to	Year
Gastropoda			
Clanculus ater	NW Pacific	NE Pacific – Canada	1964
Cecina manchurica	NW Pacific	NE Pacific – Canada	1963
Littorina littorea	NE Atlantic	NW Atlantic	< 1840
Batillaria attramentaria	NW Pacific	NE Pacific – Canada	1920s
		California	1941
Sabia conica	NW Pacific	NE Pacific – Canada	1940
Crepidula convexa	NW Atlantic	NE Pacific	
		San Francisco Bay	1898
Crepidula fornicata	NW Atlantic	NE Pacific	1905?
		San Francisco Bay	1898
Crepidula plana	NW Atlantic	NE Pacific	
		San Francisco Bay	1901
Ceratostoma inornatum	NW Pacific	NE Pacific – Canada	1931
Urosalpinx cinerea	NW Atlantic	NE Pacific – Canada	1890
Busycotypus canaliculatus	NW Atlantic	NE Pacific – California	1938
Ilyanassa obsoleta	NW Atlantic	NE Pacific – Canada	1952
		San Francisco Bay	1907
Nassarius fraterculus	NW Pacific	NE Pacific – Canada	1959
Ovatella myosotis	NE Atlantic	NW Atlantic – Canada	
	NW Atlantic	NE Pacific – Canada	1965
		Mexico	1972
Siphonaria pectinata	Mediterranean	NW Atlantic	< 1900
Bivalvia			
Mytilus galloprovincialis	Mediterranean	NE Pacific – California	< 1880s
Musculista senhousia	NW Pacific	NE Pacific – Canada	1959
Geukensia demissa	NW Atlantic	NE Pacific – California	1894
Perna perna	SW Atlantic	Gulf of Mexico	1990
Anomia chinensis	NW Pacific	NE Pacific – Washington	1924
Crassostrea gigas	NW Pacific	NE Pacific	1930s
Crassostrea virginica	NW Atlantic	NE Pacific – Washington	1917
Ostrea edulis	NE Atlantic	NW Atlantic – Maine	1949
Rangia cuneata	Gulf Mexico	NW Atlantic – Virginia	1955
Macoma balthica	NW Atlantic	NE Pacific – California	< 1900
Theora lubrica	NW Pacific	NE Pacific – California	1968
Dreissena polymorpha	NE Atlantic	NW Atlantic – NY	1992
		Great Lakes	1988
Mytilopsis leucophaeata	Gulf Mexico	NW Atlantic – NY	1937
Trapezium liratum	NW Pacific	NE Pacific – Canada	1947
Corbicula fluminea	NW Pacific	NE Pacific	1920s
	NE Pacific	NW Atlantic	1920s
Venerupis philippinarum	NW Pacific	NE Pacific – Canada	1936
Gemma gemma	NW Atlantic	NE Pacific – California	1974
Mercenaria mercenaria	NW Atlantic	NE Pacific – California	1967
Petricola pholadiformis	NW Atlantic	NE Pacific – Washington	1943
		San Francisco Bay	1927
Mya arenaria	NW Atlantic	NE Pacific – Alaska	1946
		California	< 1911
Potamocorbula amurensis	NW Pacific	NE Pacific – California	1986
Lyrodus pedicellatus	Indo-Pacific	NE Pacific – California	1871
Lyrodus takanoshimensis	NW Pacific	NE Pacific – Canada	1981
Teredo bartschi	NW Atlantic	Gulf California	< 1971
Teredo navalis	NE Atlantic	NE Pacific – Canada	1963
		San Francisco Bay	1913
	NE Atlantic	NW Atlantic	< 1839
Teredo furcifera	Caribbean	NW Atlantic – NJ	1974

Table 21. *Indo-Pacific species established in the Mediterranean since 1869 (Barash and Danin 1986)*

Gastropods	First report	Bivalves	First report
Diodora rueppelli	1948	*Brachidontes variabilis*	1931
Minolia nedyma	1966	*Malleus regula*	1931
Cerithium scabridum	1912	*Pinctada radiata*	1899
Rhinoclavis kochi	1963	*Paphia textile*	1948
Strombus decorus	1983	*Gastrochaena cymbium*	1972
Thais carinifera	1972		
Bursatella leachi savigniana	1976		
Hypselodoris infucata	1974		
Melibe fimbriata	1966		

Modern dispersal of species

The international trade in shell is extensive in the late twentieth century and has been so since the beginning of the nineteenth century. Not only are shell-based industries the impetus for this trade but it is also fueled by aquaculture. Both univalve and bivalve populations have been moved from the Old World to the New World to provide continuity in food and medical practices. Accidental movements have also occurred between countries when transplanting food species and when discharging ballast water in foreign ports. Table 20 lists the known importations of living animals to the coasts of North America which subsequently resulted in the establishment of viable populations (Carlton 1992). Table 21 gives the fourteen Indo-Pacific species to have become permanent residents in the Mediterranean.

There are several aspects of the modern trade in shell and movement of live populations which should interest archaeologists. It will become increasingly important for the archaeologist to know of the historic movements of molluscan species and the industrial uses of molluscs in order to distinguish prehistoric from historic activities and early historic from later historic activities. Both at the origin point of these trade activities and at the manufacturing point there are opportunities for ethnoarchaeological observations of greatest relevance to shell deposit formation processes and sampling strategies.

8.4   Summary

Shell, the material, has offered humans tools and symbols for hundreds of thousands of years. Artifact typologies for bivalve and univalve tools are rudimentary and microwear traces poorly researched. The physical properties of "shell" are well known and applied occasionally in ceramic study, but the property differences between nacreous and non-nacreous shells of relevance to artifact manufacture are not understood well.

Sourcing shell, a non-point-specific resource, once seemed unlikely but is well within the range of the possible in the 1990s. In some settings sample sizes of control shells can be small while in other settings (like a long coastline) the needed large sample sizes may hinder sourcing work.

The overwhelming impression given by world-wide use of shell is that white, light, bright shell represents life – as breath, other body liquid, eyes, fertility. As life symbol it can turn the evil eye, make fertile, make sickness disappear, heal wounds. In quantity it is well-being amassed, it is wealth; it is also well-being given away when gifted. Nearly all of the uses of whole or modified shell – decoration, powder, offering, oracle, container, amulet, dice, money, message – in the past and the present, are medicinal. Shells are meant to bring or ensure well-being. In the final chapter, the social realms within which shell circulated are further explored.

9

SHELLS AND SOCIAL ORGANIZATION

Shells are tools by which we may investigate not only paleoenvironments and human diets but also human interactions. As demonstrated in Chapter 8, shell has often been made into objects which function in the sociological and ideological spheres of a culture. Unmodified shells have served similarly. The manipulation of shell within a community can signify behaviors as transient as activity areas or beliefs as embedded as gender and class. The procurement of shells has implications for geographical knowledge, and, if trade can be demonstrated, for the interaction of cultures. Shell matrix sites may attest to essential subsistence activities (and to gender) in the form of villages and processing camps, to commercial activity as processing and manufacturing loci, or even to world-view as mounds. In this chapter I will explore how humans may have manipulated shells within their social group and how shellfish and shells may figure into settlement patterns, in intergroup interactions, and in world-view. The material will be organized into two broad subdivisions, "Organization of Work" encompassing activity areas, scheduling, and settlement patterns, and "Political Institutions," including gender, class/status, trade, and religion.

9.1 Organization of work

Within communities shellfish flesh and shells may be processed, shared, discarded, curated, gifted, modified, etc. according to ideas about associations of activities, feeding, cleanliness, and health, and social organizing principles such as gender, lineage, class, etc. These ideas are possible to investigate only if the researcher allows that there might be differential distribution of shelled taxa across a site, either in molluscan demographic variables (size, numbers) or in species occurrence. Few archaeologists have identified shell heaps as arenas for investigating social organization although shell artifacts are frequently attributed to the social or ideological realms of cultural behavior. There are a few examples of investigation at shell matrix sites into activity areas, lineage affiliation, class, and gender by archaeologists (Bowdler 1976; Claassen 1991a, 1991b; 1996a, 1996b; Hofman 1985; Wessen 1982; Williams and Bendremer 1997) and numerous examples of studies of commercial activities which investigate social variables by non-archaeologists and archaeologists (e.g. Claassen 1994; Coker 1919; Gangaly and Bandyopadhyay 1963; Hogendorn and

Johnson 1986). Because the social dimensions of shell use, rather than shell procurement and marketing, are so under-appreciated by archaeologists, I have chosen to focus this section of this chapter there.

Scheduling space

Scheduling work is both an individual and a family matter. In many instances it is also a community's concern. Scheduling can involve where an activity will occur as well as when and who will do it. Decisions are played out at both the community and the regional levels.

Site catchment analysis was frequently applied to shell-bearing sites in the 1970s and early 1980s. Clark and Lerner (1980) found very little difference in habitat zone proportions of catchment circles or distances to zones among twenty-eight Asturian (Cantabria) shell heaps. From this uniformity they concluded that these sites were the only base camps in the seasonal round of this social group.

Rowley-Conwy (1983:123–124) found that small shell-bearing coastal sites in Denmark had greater water in the catchment area while larger sites had less, further defining the differences in sites based on the artifact recovered. Tartaglia (1980) found that catchments were larger for inland Chumash villages than for coastal villages. McGovern (1980), however, argues that 10-km catchments are much too restrictive for coastal dwellers who had boats.

The decline in use of site catchment analyses reflects the profession-wide decline in this and similar ecological-based models for understanding social organization. There are other ways, however, that space and time scheduling have been investigated. The Ozette site on the coast of Washington state (US) was a village of the Makah people until 1920 AD. The preservation of a 350-year-old portion of this village by mudslide makes for excellent delineation of roofed and unroofed areas, and multiple family units within long houses. Gary Wessen (1982) eschewed the typical dietary information squeezed from shell debris in favor of an investigation of the social dynamics of flesh consumption and shell use within this community. (All topical areas in this section of this chapter rely heavily on this investigation.)

Several lines of evidence indicate that Ozette house floors were periodically cleaned yet primary and de facto refuse deposits of shellfish remains are still detectable in these abandoned houses. Secondary deposits of shells (removed from the activity areas of processing and consumption) were expected to be composed principally of primary food prey species in greater quantities and greater densities than found inside houses. Secondary prey and inadvertently collected species were also expected to occur outside in higher proportions than inside. Species assigned to the use categories decorative/symbolic/ceremonial, and ground shell artifacts as indicated by ethnographies, were expected to show a higher incidence in quantity and density indoors.

Most of the species apportioned according to expectations. The exceptions indicated probable errors in use category assignment. For example, *Siliqua patula* (razor clam) was categorized as a primary prey species but only 29 percent of the individuals were found in exterior contexts. All *Macoma* species had an extremely strong interior bias but had been classed as secondary food prey. Exotic species typically had very strongly biased interior distributions, and three species found in the site but not in the literature (so were uncategorized) also had a strong interior bias suggesting decorative or artifactual uses (Wessen 1982:157–162).

Where blue mussels were processed was also investigated at Ozette. A lack of skewness in mussel size (Table 7) suggested mass harvesting. If correct, the inadvertent gastropod *Thais emarginata* would have been returned to the house as would tiny young mussels in the tangle of mussel byssal threads. The small size of both should exempt them from complete removal during house cleaning, if mussels were processed indoors. Group areas suitable for multi-family processing would be the center of houses and should be distinct from the discard piles created after the meals, which would have been consumed in more private spaces. The snails and tiny mussels did cluster in the center of the houses. Each house had a large area of high density shell in the north central portion of the floor as well. Furthermore, in House 1 some family units had shell debris while others did not, possibly indicating dietary preferences.

Ground shell tools were found in three dense clusters in House 1 associated with families 1, 3, and 10 but only units 3 and 10 also yielded large unmodified shells. The highest ranking family (family 1) had access to tools it did not make, concluded Wessen (1982:187).

Scheduling time

The shell-bearing Morton site in southeastern Scotland is intriguing for its unusual density of flint debris which suggests that this camp was established primarily to gather flint from area beaches and hills. Deith (1986) queried how the two most obvious gathering activities were scheduled, proposing that shellfishing was embedded in flint-gathering trips.

Various stone sources were located to the north, south, and southeast of the camp each with a distinctive coastal configuration and associated molluscan fauna. It was possible, using cockle shells (*Cerastoderma edule*), their modal sizes, and oxygen isotopes, to distinguish shells collected from the three sections of coast and from tidal position in one of these sections. Deith had reasoned that if the shellfishing was embedded in flint-collecting forays, (1) the section of shoreline exploited most frequently would be the one nearest to the camp (the southern coastline), and would indicate collection during many different times in the tide cycle, (2) the coastline north of the camp would be used occasionally, and (3) the far southeastern shoreline would rarely be collected since the flint gatherers would have a chance to gather at the closer southern shoreline on their way home. Furthermore, shellfishing should not be confined to a specific season since she thought that flint resources would be sought year-round. While the published investigation suffers from inadequate sample sizes of archaeological shells, it demonstrates an unusual sophistication in expectations and test implications for examining work organization in a shell matrix site.

In most of the world's societies women harvest the bulk of shellfish used for food. Consequently, they most likely ingest the bulk of shellfish food. The exploration of symbolism in Chapter 8 makes it clear that molluscs are associated particularly with women. As a result of these associations between women and shellfish, assumptions are usually made about the gender of the shellfishers which have implications for dietary reconstruction, optimal foraging theory, and interpretations of site function. Given these assumptions changes in cultural behavior related to shellfishing have specific implications for the activities, diet, and time management of women (and to a lesser extent children). It is this awareness that has begun to stimulate studies of gender and shellfishing in the archaeological record.

Archaeologists struggling to explain the advent or demise of shellfishing in a region's prehistory often have failed to ask what their data imply about changes in the activities of women or about the possible reorganization of the social units that collect and consume shellfish. The initial collecting of shellfish during the Pleistocene is telling us something about changes in labor allocation. How were activities that were previously engaged in modified by this new activity? The intensification of shellfishing in the Early Holocene is telling us something about women's activities and diets as well as men's. The cessation of intensive shellfishing in many parts of the world in the mid- and late Holocene is equally suggestive of changing exploitative strategies, changing relationships between men and women, changing community goals, changing lore and symbolism, changing site types, site size, and settlement patterns. In each of the customary explanations for changes in molluscan species, numbers, and sizes (environmental change, overexploitation) and the less common ecological explanations (competitive exclusion, poor recruitment) the social implications are the same: the activities and diets of women (and to lesser extents those of children and men) will change. In late prehistoric examples from southeastern Australia and the coast of New England (US), we are introduced to the notion that rather than the species record and the activities changing because of some external process, they may have changed because women decided to allocate their time differently (see also Claassen 1991a).

The archaeological record of the Bass Point site in New South Wales, Australia has a stratified dense shell deposit the upper layer of which contains all of the shell fish-hooks and blanks. With the introduction of fish hooks, the turban shell (*Ninella torquata*), the triton (*Cabestana spengleri*), and the cart-

224   *Shells*

rut shell (*Dicathais orbita*), all caught during low tides, declined in importance, while mussels (*M. edulis*), which can be caught any time of day or night, increased. No convincing environmental argument could explain the change in mollusc species. More bone and bone points were found in the older layers. Ethnographies indicate that native men spear fish and women utilize hook and line to fish (Bowdler 1976:254–255) sitting for hours in their boats.

Bowdler believes that the adoption of line fishing signals the advent of women as fishers about 600 years ago. Spending hours in the boats would mean that on many days they either missed their opportunity to gather molluscs during low tide or had not the energy both to fish and to gather. Instead, they switched to gathering mussels which were not affected significantly by tides as a labor saving maneuver and harvested the larger, more succulent molluscs on the rare occasions when time and tides coincided. As a result, coastal sites older than 600 years and lacking hooks contain fish speared and animals hunted by men, and large shellfish harvested by women, whereas more recent sites contain fish and mussels caught by women and fish speared by men (Bowdler 1976:256). In this case the modifications in shell and fish sizes and shell and fish species are attributed not to environmental change, not to overexploitation, not to competitive exclusion, not to poor recruitment, but to changes in technology and work.

The increase in the number of shell matrix sites and their size in late prehistoric New England has been interpreted by Williams and Bendremer (1997) as a reflection of the choice by women to intensify shellfishing and the derivative production activities of dried flesh and beads. The impetus for greater dried shellfish meat production was to trade with interior groups for maize and for other commodities and to trade or use shell beads, particularly wampum, for amassing well-being (see Chapter 8). This decision significantly changed the cultural interactions between coastal and interior groups, changed coastal settlement patterns, changed the mobility of women, changed the relative proportions of molluscan species in the sites, and changed the contributions of men's and women's productive activities.

Settlement patterns

Settlement, camp, and special activity area site selection is based ultimately upon issues of work and activity organization, issues of social organization. Will the needed resources be close enough, dense enough, accessible, suitable? These concerns will also govern the reuse of a locality and, over time, the formation of a settlement pattern. In this section I will explore the implications for social organization reflected in the creation of visible shell deposits and in the disappearance of massed shell from regional records.

Why shell matrix sites are reused

Many shell matrix sites are thought to be comprised of many discontinuous occupations. Why would specific sites be reused in areas with essentially a continuous distribution of molluscs, such as sea coasts, lakes, and rivers? This question is often answered for shell matrix sites by citing improved drainage on floodplains with each season of discard (e.g. Bailey 1983c:568). In many cases the camp or village was initially located for some particular resource which would stimulate reuse for the same reason.

The majority of the twenty-eight concheros of Cantabria, Spain are found clustered on a 60-km stretch of coastal plain (Figure 37). Located as they often are in cave mouths at the inland edge of the coastal plain, they had optimal access to animal resources of the plain and the hills. Bailey (1983c:571–572) argues that these sites were initially founded during the Pleistocene and reused because of the terrestrial resources in their vicinity, particularly the animals. He points out that the quantity of shell in these sites decreases with increasing distance from the shore line, with a sharp fall off after 5 km. For people who lived farther than 5 km away, it is more likely that they discarded shells at seaside processing camps or casually as they opened them. These thin deposits have either been inundated or have disintegrated in the past 10,000 years. As sea level rose during the late Pleistocene it moved closer to these cave-dwelling hunters, increasing the discard of shells there and accounting for the apparent intensification of shellfishing which was, rather, an intensification of discard activities. The "major shell-midden deposits would only occur where unusual topographic conditions happened to favour repeated and intensive occupation very close to the contemporaneous shoreline" (Bailey 1983c:576).

Sandweiss et al. (1989) envision a similar scenario for the Ring site on the coast of Peru. The lowest levels of this shell ring have fewer shells than do the upper levels, correlating with first greater then lesser distance from an advancing sea shore. They, too, think the site was originally selected 10,000 years ago for access to terrestrial resources and later developed into a maritime focal village. They are at a loss, however, to explain the favor accorded this particular location prior to its becoming a permanent settlement.

These cases suggest that in many situations a site was reused for reasons related to circumstances that arise after the initial use of the locality, making it increasingly attractive with the passage of time. In addition to improved drainage or an advancing shoreline, shell matrix sites may also have become increasingly attractive because of the evolving plant communities growing on them. The concentration of calcium is attractive to many species of plant and creates a unique environment. In the coastal southeastern US plants which often signal the presence of subsurface shell deposits are cedars, live oaks, "the shell midden plant," and no doubt others. Studies done early in the twentieth century indicated that "mound vegetation is unique, presenting a striking contrast to the vegetation of the surrounding marsh," "they support a more or

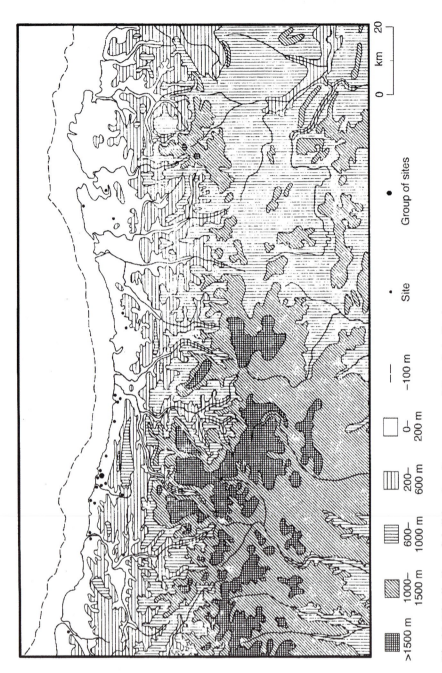

Group of sites ●

Site •

– – – –100 m

□ 0–200 m

▤ 200–600 m

▥ 600–1000 m

▨ 1000–1500 m

▦ >1500 m

Fig. 37 Distribution of shell-bearing sites on coast of Cantabria, Spain.

less specialized vegetation," "plants found [on coastal shell mounds] are found nowhere else in the area" (Dorroh 1971:3). Specifically, coastal shell mounds are "dominated by several species of grasses, rushes, succulent dicots, and several woody species" (Dorroh 1971:4).

Bruce Smith has argued that the repeatedly disturbed mid-Holocene-aged naiad shell mounds on rivers in Kentucky, Tennessee, and Alabama created anthropogenic habitats ideal for the coevolution of native floodplain plants undergoing domestication, and terms these shell mounds "domestilocalities" (Smith 1992:52). These localities offered sunlight, soil fertility, soil disturbance, and the continual introduction of seeds. These anthropogenic habitats were created around the world in interior as well as coastal locations and no doubt supported distinctive plant communities that complimented the access to aquatic resources. In forested environments, leaves soon cover the white shells, so it may well have been the plants, rather than the shells, that drew people back to the same exact location season after season. Systematic plant inventories on and off shell-bearing sites would do much to advance this argument.

In 1968 Binford published an extremely influential article purporting to explain the advent of agriculture as an effort to turn marginal subsistence areas (non-coastal locations) into suitable places to live. Coastal areas were clearly optimal because of the rich marine resources at hand, evident in the large size and frequency of shell deposits, and their proximity to terrestrial resources. In problematizing the occurrence of shell matrix sites during the 1970s, in response to Binford's theory, it was mistakenly assumed that these are common sites world-wide. With some distance from the influence of that article, archaeologists began to notice that Mesolithic and Archaic shell matrix sites were, in fact, rare and began to problematize their distribution at the regional scale. Much more such work needs to occur. I will highlight such a case for Mesolithic Europe in this section and another situated in the southern US in the section on religion, below.

The tiny, isolated Scottish island of Oronsay is home to six shell mounds of substantial size, five of which have been tested and indicate utilization during different seasons. Shell-bearing sites elsewhere in the British Isles are small and infrequent or absent altogether, such as on the neighboring island of Colonsay, in southwestern Scotland, and the southern, western and northern coasts of Britain. In fact, within Europe, only Jutland, Brittany, Cantabria, and central Portugal have shell matrix sites of comparable size and density, while most of the rest of the European coastline lacks any shell matrix sites at all, even in those areas where uplift has preserved the entire Holocene record. Why are these sites so rare? Why was Oronsay selected? Could Oronsay support a year-round population? Why is the artifact assemblage so depauperate (questions of Mellars 1978)?

Several authors believe the explanation for the paucity of similar sites lies in time management (Bailey 1978, Mellars 1978). The calories gained from the energy expended in the collection and transport of molluscs do not warrant the activity (Bailey 1978) except in situations where large quantities of shellfish were available requiring limited amounts of human movement and where other food resources of higher yield were in short supply. Oronsay, and small islands in general would seem to fit both circumstances and the latter prerequisite would explain the diminished tool kits, concluded Mellars (1978:394). However, a concentration of small shell sites elsewhere in Scotland occurs in contradiction to both of these expectations. A more encompassing explanation offered by Mellars is that population pressure on optimal resources necessitated the collection of molluscs. If the pressure on resources happened in only six or so places in all of Europe's aquatic zones, then there was very little resource pressure at all in the mid-Holocene. While I think that both explanations fail the task, this type of questioning is essential. Whether it be why shell sites are so often multicomponent, why they formed, or why they ceased to exist, these questions bring shell matrix sites back into the realm of anthropology.

9.2   Political institutions

Political institutions can be investigated with data from shell matrix sites and their regional distributions. Lineage, class affiliations, and status are commonly explored in archaeology through shell artifacts. These social axes can also be revealed in some class-stratified societies through the mere quantities of shell debris and the distribution of that debris throughout multifamily houses.

Lineage/family

Ethnographies about US Northwest Pacific coast groups indicate that resource zones were owned. Wessen (1982:172–174) investigated the possible ownership of primary food shellfish by households at Ozette. House 5 had little blue mussel which is found today in the immediate vicinity of the site while the other three houses in the data set had plentiful mussel. House 5 had twice the quantity of *Saxidomus giganteus* and half that of *Protothaca staminea* compared to the other three houses. The same was true of two chiton species. The systematic separation of House 5 indicated something other than taste preferences. Wessen believed it to be separate collecting rights. House 5 collected at a greater distance from the village than did the other three households who collected in the immediate surroundings suggesting that the members of House 5 were unrelated to those in the other three houses.

Class/status

Commoners consumed more shellfish flesh than did the nobility in Andean societies (Sandweiss 1996). The same was true of people on the Northwest coast of the US (Moss 1993, Wessen 1982:165). Among the Manhousat, while a chief would consume shellfish, he was not expected to gather and dry them (Ellis and Swan 1981:52). Young Northwest coast men were taught to avoid shellfish (excepting *Dentalium*) for molluscs would bring poverty through laziness. Instead men were to distinguish themselves by more arduous activities such as fishing and whaling. Dreaming of clams portended poverty. Outcasts are "people of the beach" (Moss 1993:641).

Wessen reasoned that the shells of primary and secondary food species at Ozette should be less frequent around high status households and that shells of those species classed as decorative/symbolic/ceremonial (DSC) should be more prevalent yet unevenly distributed in high status houses. Four contemporaneous households at Ozette were examined. House 1 had the least shell on its exterior and the lowest species diversity, House 2 had six times more shell than the others. When considering the DSC species, all major species were found only in House 1 with exotics amounting to more than 90 percent of those shells. All whale barnacles, *Coronula diadema* (so named because they live on whales), also were recovered only from House 1. These observations seem to indicate that the people residing in House 1 were higher ranked than the others and may have included a whaler.

The highest status families typically occupied one end of the house. At Ozette, the distribution of the DSC species indicated that the highest ranking family in House 1 lived in the north end of the house. The minor DSC species found in Houses 2 and 5 were also confined to the family units in the northern corners of the house.

Religion

The symbolism for shells in the Americas clearly indicate a religious role for shells in general and for some specific shells (Chapter 8). Nevertheless, archaeologists assume that shells deposited in a site represent food debris and that burials, if present, are placed in garbage.

In eastern North America shell was often used as a burial covering. The mid-Holocene O'Neal site in Alabama had layers of clean shell alternating with layers of other material. Several burials had been surrounded with clean shell and the pits sealed with a layer of clean shell (Webb and DeJarnette 1942:134). The oldest shell matrix site in South Carolina has shell in mortuary context. Many other mid-Holocene sites have burials in shell deposits suggestive of tumuli (e.g. Maritime Archaic of eastern Canada).

Much later in time in eastern Tennessee, sites had initial burials placed in tombs with capping naiad shell layers on the upper surface (Hamilton culture). As burials accumulated shell was used periodically to cap the accretion mounds with the next burials placed directly on the shells (Lewis and Kneberg

1946:137). In one burial a missing skull was indicated by a mass of *Olivella* beads. The Calusa site of Pineland (Florida) also had burials in the plaza area with alternating layers of white sand, black sand and shell above the body. Many of the prehistoric dog burials in the northeastern United States have been encountered within and below shell deposits, often composed of un-opened shells (Kerber 1997).

It is possible that in these cultures the unmodified shells had much the same symbolism as is found among the Maya and Aztec: death, south, completion, the underworld. In most of these sites, neither the shell nor the burial is conspicuous.

There are also data to support the contention that unmodified shells were heaped up into mortuary *facilities*. A possible religious or sacred special use has been suggested for Neolithic shell-bearing sites on lakes in Denmark. At three sites the association of shells, fire, stone, charcoal layers, and, at one site, a trunk boat, was interpreted by Troels-Smith as marking sacrificial settings (Noe-Nygaard 1983:137).

Curiously, the oldest mounds in North America are comprised of shells. From the interior rivers of the eastern US (e.g. Green, Tennessee, Savannah, St. John's) come dates of 7,320, 7,180, 6,645, 6,010, 5,870, and 5,730 rcy at the shell heaps of Kirkland, Anderson, Ervin, Vaughn, Hayes, and Carlston Annis, respectively, members of the Shell Mound Archaic culture (SMA). (See Figure 16 for one site example.) The Vaughn mound is a mid-Holocene site located in Mississippi where 6,500 years ago low earthen and shell mounds were erected over flexed or semiflexed corpses. The mound seems to have grown by ac-cretion until the entire basal half consisted solely of smaller, contiguous burial mounds (Atkinson 1974).

A few observers have noted a high incidence of paired valves in these mounds. At the Deweese shell mound a single column sample (35 × 35 cm) taken from the center of the mound by the author had 15+ layers, each of which contained a minimum of 30 percent paired valves and several had 100 percent of the valves paired. Village or camp activities – walking, digging, running, scuffing, tossing, dumping – are not conducive to maintaining bivalve pairs. While the quantification of this phenomenon is poorly developed, pair-ing this extensive suggests that this mound, and others with pairing, were not villages or camps.

There is also the indirect evidence that these were sacred mounds provided by the later use of the mounds for burials and for loci of earthen and sand burial mounds. For instance, the center of the McKelvey Mound was directly positioned over a considerable shell heap which itself contained sherds, bones, burials, and occasional artifacts. Copena burial mounds were often erected atop Archaic mounds (Claassen 1996a). That Woodland and Mississippian peoples continued to utilize these mounds as burial loci further suggests the places had accumulated considerable "power" and were part of a symbolic landscape. The shell rings of coastal South Carolina (Figure 3) and Georgia (also containing burials) may also have been ceremonial structures (Sassaman 1993).

The location on the landscape of these mid-Holocene shell and dirt burial mounds raises an interesting question. They are restricted to only a few rivers yet over 100 rivers in the eastern US have been commercially exploited for molluscs for a century (Claassen 1994). Malacologists have retrodicted the abundance of shellfish in the Mississippi River watershed into the Pleistocene. The richest shell sources gleaned in the past one hundred years are rarely the places where prehistoric shell matrix sites are found. The modern exploitation, which is measured in tons per sheller per season, far outpaces the assumed prehistoric harvesting efforts and these beds and rivers are still producing shells.

The implication of this incongruity between the locations of prehistoric shell-bearing sites and historic musseling endeavors is that social considerations of 8,000 to 4,000 years ago overrode environmental considerations to determine where these sites were founded and where they persisted. The environmental determinism argument cites changes that impacted on the entire eastern United States. It is because mid-Holocene shell-dirt mounds occur in so few places that optimal foraging theory, environmental change, or overexploitation cannot explain either their advent or their demise 3,700 years ago. Instead, sites attributable to the SMA constituted a landscape shaped by social concerns. These heaps were probably power points, places were spirits were concentrated, and where death or liminality was symbolized by piles of naiad shells and ornaments of marine shell. They may well have been seasonal aggregation points. It may be quite important that the Green River flows out of Mammoth Cave, the world's largest cave system. As such these shell matrix sites constituted a sacred landscape which archaeologists have been slow to recognize (Figure 38).

There are dozens of other regional records with unusual concentrations of shell which deserve re-examination for possible religious import. From the coasts of Florida are the Horr's Island mounds dated to 6,330, 5,670, 4,470 rcy etc. and the nine shell mounds at Tomoka (Russo 1996:263). From Nayarit, Mexico, the Matanchén complex site of SB-4 has a shell mound with dates of 4,100, 4,000, and 3,810 rcy (Mountjoy et al. 1972). It is quite possibly the oldest mound in western Mexico.

At Horr's Island, Russo found that nearly 2,000 years of shell accumulation had been under way before the three shell and sand mounds were constructed 5,000 years ago. Intrusive burials appeared 1,000 years later. Mound A is over 6 m tall and composed of alternating layers of sand and shell. He argues that most of the mound accumulated gradually through the primary deposition of shell debris generated by on-mound ritual activities rather than by permanent occupation. The numerous mounds at the site were constructed/renewed

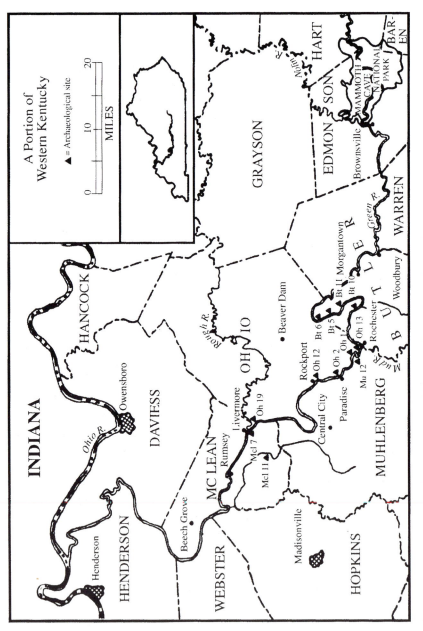

Fig. 38 Distribution of shell matrix sites (SMA) on the Green River, Kentucky.

gradually so that no permanently supported leadership was necessary (Russo 1996).

The concept of sacred landscapes is far more common among European archaeologists than American ones yet even in Europe shell matrix sites are automatically attributed to secular activities. With an increasing awareness of the symbolism of shells and the religious lives of ancient peoples and a renewed determination by archaeologists of the English-speaking world to examine social organization more examples of sacred landscapes and activities will come to light.

9.3   Trade

In the nineteenth century it was not uncommon to see shell vendors in the streets of London or to see marine shells among the items offered by the country peddler. Although vendors also worked the cities of the US, it was more common for dealers to rent a store for several weeks or months and sell shells by auction. Many of these shells were derived from Florida and were bought by individuals who produced jewelry and shell flowers using shells and opercula (Goode 1884:710).

Landlocked native peoples had no less desire for marine shell. Marine shell has been found far inland in archaeological sites in all regions of the world. The most famous of these marine shell circulation systems is the Kula of the south Pacific (Malinowski 1922). White *Conus millepunctatus* was made into arm bands and red *Spondylus* cut into beads strung as necklaces 2 m to 5 m in length. Necklaces were fashioned in two styles, one with finer disk beads and a big shell pendant, the other made of bigger disk beads with a central cowrie shell. The arm bands circulate counterclockwise, the necklaces clockwise within and between islands and between male trading partners. Kula partners trade not only arm bands or necklaces but also smaller gifts and obligations. More important men have more partners. The kula shell exchange circulates "not only objects of material culture, but also customs, songs, art motives and general cultural influences travel along the kula route" (Malinowski 1922:92).

The mere presence of non-local goods has suggested to many archaeologists the very cause for increasingly complex forms of social aggregation. Meso-american data have been the subject of numerous theories attributing the growth of a pre-Columbian community and even a region to a "desire ... to take advantage of the growing long-distance demand for ornamental shell" (Zeitlen 1978:204) as well as other products. Spencer (1982) likewise sees the transition from chiefdom to state in the Valley of Oaxaca, Mexico, as intimately involved with the forcible extraction of luxury goods like shells from neighboring regions. Flannery (1968:107–108) has suggested that the underlying function of the highly visible movement of luxury items such as shell, obsidian, and jade was, more importantly, to facilitate the movement of foodstuffs around the Mexican–Mayan region.

How shells circulated, whether by fetching, down the line trading, trade fairs, or taxation, is a question that continues to plague most archaeological regions. The name "Shell Mound Archaic" lumps together deep shell deposits on several rivers in the southern United States yet the raw materials used in beads clearly separate them into distinct molluscan zones. Sites on the Alabama portion of the Tennessee River contain truly exotic genera such as *Tridacna* from the Pacific, *Dentalium* from the Florida Keys, and cowrie shells. Similar Atlantic *Dentalium* beads occur in only two sites on the Green River in Kentucky where coal and *Busycon* columella beads are commonly strung together, as are the freshwater snails of genus *Leptoxis* (= *Anculosa*). Shell beads are quite rare on the two Atlantic drainage rivers, the St. John's River in Florida, and the Savannah River on the South Carolina–Georgia border, and they are rare on the section of the Tennessee River between Alabama and Kentucky, where copper beads are common. Such distinctive shell species and bead styles would seem to indicate that these otherwise culturally similar groups (having burials of dogs and flexed people in mounded shell or nearby) did not meet at trade fairs, rarely intermarried, and rarely gifted beads.

If by trade is meant a steady, predictable, and standardized exchange between villages and cultures, trade in shell is not easily demonstrated in eastern North America. In many cases the quantities of marine shell are so small as to negate notions of commerce or organization in the movement of shell (e.g. Claassen 1996a). The sourcing study of Claassen and Sigmann (1993) found that during the late prehistoric period at the major ceremonial center of Cahokia three *Busycon sinistrum* specimens found in a cache came from the eastern Gulf of Mexico, the tropics, and the southern Atlantic. That three shells from three different locations were cached together suggests a central collection point in peninsular Florida and a common arrival time at Cahokia. Furthermore, that three shells could have come from one collecting locale but did not, suggests that a quantity of shells larger than that easily procured from one bay was being gathered in this central location and packed out together. Regardless, pilgrims could have made the trip to Cahokia with shells in tow, as frequently as could traders.

Trade is one of many social aspects of shell use that needs to be more carefully scrutinized. Not only is the mechanism behind the movement of shell infrequently investigated (but see Mitchell 1996 for an African case), but also the need for exotic shell is rarely problematized. For instance, each of the rivers hosting SMA heaps contained dozens of naiad species which are today made into jewelry and used to culture pearls and could have provided the shell used in manufacturing beads, gorgets, atlatl weights, hairpins, and other (unrecognizable) objects for which only marine shell was employed. Why did these groups need to secure marine shell for these items? What symbolism did freshwater naiads carry, did marine shells carry? What symbolism did beads carry? Was the crucial aspect of marine shell preference its point of origin, at the edge of this world?

9.4 Conclusion

The use of artifacts and shell matrix sites to explore social organization is the research arena least well developed by archaeologists who work with shell. In this chapter I have explored how humans have thought about shell and shellfish and how their thoughts about the seasons, each other, and other worlds are embedded in shell artifacts and shell matrix sites. The organization of work, that is the scheduling of space and time, has been investigated, as have political institutions and trade.

Writers around the world have queried which coastal area marine shells come from, but often leave unproblematized which mechanism(s) of human interaction is suggested by the quantities of exotic shell and why people needed to import marine shells for ornaments when local freshwater shells could have been used. In China, Japan, Europe, and the Americas, naiad populations were available and underexploited for ornaments. Why did people make a distinction between marine and riverine shells and how was that distinction defined? Shell items have been associated with the dead, in dozens of prehistoric cultures, yet few have asked why this would be so (e.g. Bar-Yosef Mayer 1997:109). What symbolic role did shell play, did beads play, did pendants play, in individual cultures of the past?

Gary Wessen (1982:194) believes that "with adequate analytical techniques, virtually all shellfish-related behaviors may be examined utilizing archaeologically recovered shellfish materials." For a discipline that is becoming increasingly less satisfied with environment-centered explanations for change in the archaeological record, investigating social organization may be attractive to the very people who might otherwise turn away from shell analysis and shell matrix sites, steeped as they are in the environmental archaeology of the past three decades. After more than 150 years of archaeological interest in shell, there are still many frontiers in shell research, such as shell as mediator of social organization. Shell has served our ancestors equally as a food item and as a symbol for beliefs held dear, and shellfish have been equally important for their flesh and their shell.

The future of shell-based archaeological analyses looks quite bright. In fact, it is time for these types of site and this material to be accorded the status of a research specialty, for both educational programs and individuals. The growing wealth of knowledge specific to molluscs which can reveal information as elementary as the salinity of the water or as fundamental as regional interactions, requires individuals who are familiar with all these possibilities when shell matrix sites and shell deposits are to be excavated.

REFERENCES

Abbott, Tucker 1972. *Kingdom of the Seashell* (New York, Crown Publishers).

　　1977. Clam, *Encyclopedia Americana* (New York, Americana Corp.).

Agbelusi, E. and Ejidike, B. 1992. Utilization of the African Giant Land Snail *Archachatina marginata* in the Humid Area of Nigeria, *Tropical Agriculture* (Trinidad) 69:88–92.

Ahlstedt, Steven and Jenkinson, John 1986. A Mussel Die-Off in the Powell River, Virginia and Tennessee. Ms. on file Department of Fisheries and Wildlife Sciences, Virginia Polytechnic Institute, Blacksburg.

Akazawa, Takeru 1988. Variability in the Types of Fishing Adaptation of the Later Jomon Hunter-Gatherers c. 2500 to 300 B.C., in Bailey, G. and Parkington, J. (eds.), *The Archaeology of Prehistoric Coastlines* (Cambridge University Press) 78–92.

Albertzart, Linda and Wilkinson, Bruce 1990. Barrier Backbeach Shell Assemblages from the Central Texas Gulf Coast, *Palaios* 5:346–355.

Alexandersson, E. 1979. Marine Maceration, *Sedimentology* 26:845–852.

Allen, D. C. and Cheatum, E. P. 1961. Ecological Implications of Fresh-Water and Land Gastropods in Texas Archeological Studies, *Bulletin of the Texas Archeological Society* 31:291–316.

Ambrose, William 1967. Archaeology and Shell Middens, *Archaeology and Physical Anthropology in Oceania* 2:169–187.

American Malacological Union 1988. *Common and Scientific Names of Aquatic Invertebrates from the United States and Canada: Mollusks.* American Fisheries Society Special Publication 16 (Bethesda, Maryland, American Fisheries Society).

Anderson, Atholl 1973. The Conchiolin Dating Method, *New Zealand Journal of Science* 16:553–558.

　　1981. A Model of Prehistoric Collecting on the Rocky Shore, *Journal of Archaeological Science* 8:109–120.

Anderson, Donald 1989. Toxic Algal Blooms and Red Tides: A Global Perspective, in Okaichi, T., Anderson, D., and Nemoto, T. (eds.), *Red Tides: Biology, Environmental Science, and Toxicology* (New York, Elsevier) 11–16.

Andrews, Jean 1971. *Sea Shells of the Texas Coast* (Austin, University of Texas Press).

　　1981. *Texas Shells: A Field Guide* (Austin, University of Texas Press).

Andrews, M., Gilbertson, D., Kent, M., and Mellars, P. 1985. Biometric Studies of Morphological Variation in the Intertidal Gastropod *Nucella lapillus* (L): Environmental and Palaeoeconomic Significance, *Journal of Biogeography* 12:71–87.

Andrews, Wyllys IV 1969. *The Archaeological Use and Distribution of Mollusca in the Maya Lowlands.* New Orleans, Middle American Research Institute Publication 34 (Tulane, Tulane University Press).

Ansell, A. 1968. The Rate of Growth of the Hard Clam *Mercenaria mercenaria* Throughout the Geographical Range, *Journal, Conseil International Pour L'Exploration de La Mer* 31:364–409.

236

Arnold, Jeanne and Munns, Ann 1994. Independent or Attached Specialization: The Organization of Shell Bead Production in California, *Journal of Field Archaeology* 21:473–489.

Aten, Lawrence 1981. Determining Seasonality of *Rangia cuneata* from Gulf Coast Shell Middens, *Texas Archaeological Society Bulletin* 52:179–200.

Atkinson, James 1974. Appendix A: Test Excavations at the Vaughn Mound Site, in Archeological Survey and Test Excavations in the Upper-Central Tombigbee River Valley, compiled by Marc Rucker. National Park Service Contract no. CX500031589.

Attenbrow, Val 1992. Shell Bed or Shell Midden, *Australian Archaeology* 34:3–21.

Baerreis, David 1980. Habitat and Climatic Interpretation from Terrestrial Gastropods at the Cherokee Site, in Anderson, D. and Semken, H. (eds.), *The Cherokee Excavations: Mid-Holocene Ecology and Human Adaptation in Northwestern Iowa* (New York, Academic Press) 101–122.

Bailey, Geoff 1975. The Role of Molluscs in Coastal Economies: The Results of Midden Analysis in Australia, *Journal of Archaeological Science* 2:45–62.

1978. Shell Middens as Indicators of Postglacial Economies: A Territorial Perspective, in Mellars, P. (ed.), *The Early Postglacial Settlement of Northern Europe* (University of Pittsburgh Press) 37–63.

1983a (ed.). *Hunter-Gatherer Economy in Prehistory: A European Example* (Cambridge University Press).

1983b. Introduction, in Bailey, G. (ed.) *Hunter-Gatherer Economy in Prehistory: A European Example* (Cambridge University Press) 1–6.

1983c. Problems of Site Formation and the Interpretation of Spatial and Temporal Discontinuities in the Distribution of Coastal Middens, in Masters, Pam and Fleming, N. (eds.), *Quaternary Coastlines* (Orlando, Academic Press) 559–582.

1993. Shell Mounds in 1972 and 1992: Reflections on Recent Controversies at Ballina and Weipa, *Australian Archaeology* 37:2–18.

Bailey, Geoff, Deith, Margaret, and Shackleton, Nicholas 1983. Oxygen Isotope Analysis and Seasonality Determinations: Limits and Potential of a New Technique, *American Antiquity* 48:390–398.

Bar-Yosef Mayer, Daniella 1997. Neolithic Shell Bead Production in Sinai, *Journal of Archaeological Science* 24:97–111.

Barash, A. and Danin, Z. 1986. Further Additions to the Knowledge of Indo-Pacific Mollusca in the Mediterranean Sea, *Spixiana* 9(2):117–141.

Barber, Russell 1982. The Wheeler's Site: A Specialized Shellfish Processing Station on the Merrimack River, *Peabody Museum Monographs* 7 (Cambridge, Massachusetts, Peabody Museum).

Barker, R. 1964. Microtextural Variations in Pelecypod Shells, *Malacologia* 2:69–86.

Barrera, Enriqueta, Tevesz, Michael, and Carter, Joseph 1990. Variations in Oxygen and Carbon Isotopic Compositions and Microstructure of the Shell of *Adamussium colbecki* (Bivalvia), *Palaios* 5:149–159.

Bates, John 1986. Mussel Kills: A Thirty Year Perspective. Ms. on file Department of Fisheries and Wildlife Sciences, Virginia Polytechnic Institute, Blacksburg.

Baur, M. 1987. Richness of Land Snail Species, *Basteria* 51:129–133.

Beaton, John 1985. Evidence for a Coastal Occupation Time-Lag at Princess Charlotte Bay (North Queensland) and Implications for Coastal Colonization and Population Growth Theories for Aboriginal Australia, *Archaeology in Oceania* 20:1–20.

Begler, Elsie and Keatinge, Richard 1979. Theoretical Goals and Methodological Realities: Problems in the Reconstruction of Prehistoric Subsistence Economies, *World Archaeology* 11:208–226.

Bernstein, David 1993. *Prehistoric Subsistence on the Southern New England Coast: The Record from Narragansett Bay* (San Diego, Academic Press).

Bigalke, E. 1973. The Exploitation of Shellfish by Coastal Tribesmen of the Transkei, *Annals Cape Province Museum* (Natural History) 9:159–175.

Binford, Lewis 1962. Archaeology as Anthropology, *American Antiquity* 28:217–225.

  1968. Post Pleistocene Adaptations, in Binford, S. and Binford, L. (eds.), *New Perspectives in Archaeology* (Chicago, Aldine Publishing) 313–341.

  1978. *Nunamiut Ethnoarchaeology* (New York, Academic Press).

  1980. Willow Smoke and Dogs' Tails: Hunter-Gatherer Settlement and Archaeological Site Formation, *American Antiquity* 45:4–20.

Bird, Michele 1992. The Impact of Tropical Cyclones on the Archaeological Record: an Australian Example, *Archaeology in Oceania* 27:75–86.

Bobrowsky, Peter 1984. The History and Science of Gastropods in Archaeology, *American Antiquity* 49:77–93.

Bobrowsky, Peter and Gadus, Tom 1984. Archaeomalacological Significance of the Hall Shelter, Perry County, Kentucky, USA, *North American Archaeologist* 5(2):89–110.

Bocek, Barbara 1986. Rodent Ecology and Burrowing Behavior: Predicted Effects on Archaeological Site Formation, *American Antiquity* 51:589–602.

Bourget, Edwin 1980. Barnacle Shell Growth and its Relationship to Environmental Factors, in Rhoads, D. and Lutz, R. (eds.), *Skeletal Growth of Aquatic Organisms: Biological Records of Environmental Changes* (New York, Plenum Press) 466–492.

Bowdler, Sandra 1976. Hook, Line, and Dilly Bag: An Interpretation of an Australian Coastal Shell Midden, *Mankind* 10:248–258.

  1983. Sieving Seashells: Midden Analysis in Australian Archaeology, in Connah, G. (ed.), *Australian Field Archaeology: A Guide to Techniques* (Canberra, Australian Institute of Aboriginal Studies) 135–143.

Brandt, D. 1989. Taphonomic Grades as a Classification for Fossiliferous Assemblages and Implications for Paleoecology, *Palaios* 4:303–309.

Braun, David 1974. Explanatory Models for the Evolution of Coastal Adaptation in Prehistoric Eastern New England, *American Antiquity* 39:582–596.

Brennan, Louis 1977. The Midden is the Message, *Archaeology of Eastern North America* 5:122–137.

Brinton, D. G. 1867. Artificial Shell Deposits of the United States, *Annual Report of the Smithsonian Institution for 1866*, 356–358.

Brown, David S. 1978. Pulmonate Molluscs as Intermediate Hosts for Digenetic Trematodes, in Fretter, V. and Peake, J. (eds.), *Pulmonates* Vol. II (London, Academic Press) 287–333.

  1994. *Freshwater Snails of Africa and Their Medical Importance* 2nd edn (London, Taylor and Francis).

Buchanan, W. 1985. Sea Shells Ashore. M.A. Thesis, Archaeology, University of Cape Town South Africa.

Buist, A. 1963. Note on Conchiolin Dating, *New Zealand Archaeological Association Newsletter* 6(2):114.

Burleigh, R. and Kerney, M. 1982. Some Chronological Implications of a Fossil Molluscan Assemblage from a Neolithic Site at Brook, Kent, England, *Journal of Archaeological Science* 9:29–38.

Burton, James and Price, Douglas 1990. The Ratio of Barium to Strontium as a Paleodietary Indicator of Consumption of Marine Resources, *Journal of Archaeological Science* 17:547–557.

  1991. Paleodietary Applications of Barium Values in Bone, in Pernicka, E. and Wagner, G. (eds.), *Proceedings of the 27th International Symposium on Archaeometry, Heidelberg 1990* (Basel, Berkhauser Verlag) 787–795.

Caddy, J. and Billard, A. 1976. A First Estimate of Production from an Unexploited Population of the Bar Clam *Spisula solidissima*. Technical Report Marine Environmental Data Service, Canada 648:1–13.

Callender, Russell, Staff, George, Powell, Eric, and MacDonald, Ian 1990. Gulf of Mexico Hydrocarbon Seep Communities V. Biofacies and Shell Orientation of Autochthonous Shell Beds Below Storm Wave Base, *Palaios* 5:2–14.

Campbell, Sarah 1981. *The Duwamish No. 1 Site, A Lower Puget Sound Shell Midden*. Office of Public Archaeology, Research Report 1 (Seattle, University of Washington).

Carlton, James 1992. Introduced Marine and Estuarine Mollusks of North America: An End-of-the-20th-Century Perspective, *Journal of Shellfish Research* 11:489–505.

Carstens, K. and Watson, P. (eds.) 1996. *Of Caves and Shell Mounds* (Tuscaloosa University of Alabama Press).

Carter, Joseph 1980. Environmental and Biological Controls of Bivalve Shell Mineralogy and Microstructure, in Rhoads, D. and Lutz, R. (eds.), *Skeletal Growth of Aquatic Organisms* (New York, Plenum Press) 69–114.

Carter, S. 1990. Stratigraphy and Taphonomy of Shells in Calcareous Soils, *Journal of Archaeological Science* 17:195–207.

Carucci, James 1992. Cultural and Natural Patterning in Prehistoric Marine Foodshell from Palau, Micronesia, Ph.D. dissertation, Anthropology, Southern Illinois University.

Castilla, Juan and Jerez, G. 1986. Artisanal Fishery and Development of Data Base for Managing Loco (*Concholepas concholepas*) Resource in Chile, *Canadian Special Publications Fishery Aquatic Science* 92:133–139.

Catterall, C. and Poiner, I. 1987. The Potential Impact of Human Gathering on Shellfish Populations, with Reference to Some NE Australian Intertidal Flats, *Oikos* 50:114–122.

Ceci, Lynn 1984. Shell Midden Deposits as Coastal Resources, *World Archaeology* 16:62–74.
  1989. Tracing Wampum's Origins: Shell Bead Evidence from Archaeological Sites in Western and Coastal New York, in Hayes, C. (ed.), *Proceedings of the 1986 Shell Bead Conference: Selected Papers*, Rochester Museum and Science Center Research Records No. 20, 63–80.

Cerrato, Robert 1980. Demographic Analysis of Bivalve Populations, in Rhoads, D. and Lutz, R. (eds.), *Skeletal Growth of Aquatic Organisms: Biological Records of Environmental Changes* (New York, Plenum Press) 417–468.

Chace, Paul 1969. Biological Archaeology of Some Coastal Middens, Orange County, CA, *Pacific Coast Archaeological Society Quarterly* 5(2):65–77.

Chadbourne, P. A. 1859. Oyster Shell Deposit in Damariscotta, *Collections of the Maine Historical Society* 6:347–351.

Chang, Kwang-chih 1986. *The Archaeology of Ancient China*, 4th edn (Yale University Press).

Chappell, John 1982. Sea Levels and Sediments: Some Features of the Context of Coastal Archaeological Sites in the Tropics, *Archaeology in Oceania* 17:69–78.

Chappell, John and Polach, Henry 1972. Some Effects of Partial Recrystallization on [14]C Dating Late Pleistocene Corals and Molluscs, *Quaternary Research* 2:244–252.

Chatters, James 1986. Shell of *Margaritifera margaritifera falcata* as a Source of Paleoenvironmental and Cultural Data. Pit 3, 4, 5 Project Shasta County, California, Archaeological Report 86–5, Central Washington Archaeological Survey, Central Washington University (Ellensburg, WA).

Chave, Keith 1954. Aspects of the Biogeochemistry of Magnesium (1) Calcareous Marine Organisms, *Journal of Geology* 62:266–283.
  1964. Skeletal Durability and Preservation, in Imbrie, J. and Newell, N. (eds.), *Approaches to Paleoecology* (New York, Wiley and Sons Inc.) 377–387.

Chisholm, Brian, Koike, Hiroko, and Nakai, Nobuyuki 1992. Carbon Isotopic Determination of Paleodiet in Japan: Marine versus Terrestrial Resources, in Aikens, M. and

Rhee, S. (eds.), *Pacific Northeast Asia in Prehistory* (Pullman, Washington State University Press) 69–74.

Chisholm, Brian, Nelson, Erle, and Schwarcz, Henry 1983. Marine and Terrestrial Protein in Prehistoric Diets on the British Columbia Coast, *Current Anthropology* 24:396–398.

Christenson, Andrew 1985. The Identification and Study of Indian Shell Middens in Eastern North America: 1643–1861, *North American Archaeologist* 6(3):227–243.

Claassen, Cheryl 1986a. Shellfishing Seasons in the Prehistoric Southeastern United States, *American Antiquity* 51:21–37.

1986b. Temporal Patterns in Marine Shellfish Species Use Along the Atlantic Coast in the Southeastern United States, *Southeastern Archaeology* 5:120–137.

1988. Shell Seasonality Using Incremental Growth Lines. Final Report to the National Science Foundation, grant #BSN-8507714, Washington, D.C.

1990. The Role of Technique in Shell Seasonality Studies: A Reply to Lightfoot and Cerrato, *Archaeology of Eastern North America* 18:75–87.

1991a. Gender, Shellfishing, and the Shell Mound Archaic, in Gero, J. and Conkey, M. (eds.), *Engendering Archaeology: Women and Production in Prehistory*, (Cambridge, Blackwells) 276–300.

1991b. Normative Thinking and Shell-Bearing Sites, in Schiffer, M. (ed.), *Archaeological Method and Theory*, Vol. III (Tucson, University of Arizona Press) 249–298.

1993. Problems and Choices in Shell Seasonality Studies and Their Impact on Results, *Archaeozoologia* 5(2):55–76.

1994. Washboards, Pigtoes, and Muckets: Historic Musseling Industries in the Mississippi Watershed, *Historic Archaeology* 28(2):1–145.

1995a. Dogan Point and its Social Context, in Claassen, C. (ed.), *Dogan Point: A Shell Matrix Site in the Lower Hudson Valley*, Occasional Papers in Northeastern Anthropology, 14 (Bethlehem, Conn., Archaeological Services) 65–78.

1995b. Lithics and Lithic Areas, in Claassen, C. (ed.), *Dogan Point: A Shell Matrix Site in the Lower Hudson Valley*, Occasional Papers in Northeastern Anthropology, 14 (Bethlehem, Conn., Archaeological Services) 65–78.

1996a. A Consideration of the Social Organization of the Shell Mound Archaic, in Sassaman, K. and Anderson, D. (eds.), *Archaeology of the Mid-Holocene Southeast* (Gainesville, University of Florida Press) 235–258.

1996b. Research Problems with Shells from Green River Shell Matrix Sites, in Carstens, K. and Watson, P. (eds.), *Of Caves and Shell Mounds*, (Tuscaloosa University of Alabama Press) 132–139.

Claassen, Cheryl (ed.), 1995c. *Dogan Point: A Shell Matrix Site in the Lower Hudson Valley*, Occasional Papers in Northeastern Anthropology, 14 (Bethlehem, Conn., Archaeological Services).

Claassen, Cheryl and Sigmann, Samuella 1993. Sourcing *Busycon* Artifacts of the Eastern United States, *American Antiquity* 58:333–347.

Claassen, Cheryl and Whyte, Thomas 1995. Biological Remains, in Claassen, C. (ed.), *Dogan Point: A Shell Matrix Site in the Lower Hudson Valley*, Occasional Papers in Northeastern Anthropology, 14 (Bethlehem, Conn., Archaeological Services) 65–78.

Clark, Geoffrey and Lerner, Shereen 1980. Prehistoric Resource Utilization in Early Holocene Cantabrian Spain, *Anthropology UCLA* 10(1/2):53–96.

Clark, George 1968. Mollusk Shell: Daily Growth Lines, *Science* 161:800–802.

1979. Seasonal Growth Variations in the Shells of Recent and Prehistoric Specimens of *Mercenaria mercenaria* from St. Catherine's Island, in Thomas, D. and Larsen, C. (eds.), *The Anthropology of St. Catherine's Island 2. The Refuge-Deptford Mortuary Complex*, Anthropological Papers of the American Museum of Natural History 56, Part 1 (New York,

American Museum of Natural History) 161–172.

Clarke, F. 1924. *The Composition of the River and Lake Waters of the United States.* United States Geological Survey Professional Paper No. 135 (Washington, D.C., Government Printing Office).

Clarke, Louise and Clarke, Arthur 1980. Zooarchaeological Analyses of Mollusc Remains from Yuquot, British Columbia, *History and Archaeology* 43:37–57.

Cohen, Anne, Parkington, John, Brundrit, Geoff, and van der Merwe, Nikolaas 1992. A Holocene Marine Climate Record in Mollusc Shells from the Southwest African Coast, *Quaternary Research* 38:379–383.

Coker, Robert 1919. *Fresh-Water Mussels and Mussel Industries of the United States.* Bulletin of the U.S. Bureau of Fisheries for 1917–1918 (Washington, D.C., Government Printing Office).

Conklin, William 1985. *Nature's Art: The Inner and Outer Dimensions of the Shell* (Columbia, University of South Carolina Press).

Cooke, Richard, Norr, Lynette, and Piperno, Dolores 1996. Native Americans and the Panamanian Landscape, in Reitz, E., Newsom, L., and Scudder, S. (eds.), *Case Studies in Environmental Archaeology* (New York, Plenum) 103–126.

Coutts, Peter 1969. The State of Preservation of Shell Material in Midden Sites, *Transactions of the Royal Society of New Zealand* 2(9):135–137.

Cox, Kim 1994. Oysters as Ecofacts, *Bulletin of the Texas Archeological Society* 62:219–247.

Cox, Kim and Cox, Susan 1993. Appendix: Oyster Analysis at White's Point, in *A Model of Holocene Environmental and Human Adaptive Change on the Central Texas Coast: Geoarchaeological Investigations at White's Point, Nueces Bay, and Surrounding Area,* by Ricklis, R. pp. 81–122, Coastal Archaeological Studies, Inc., Corpus Christi, TX.

Craig, Alan 1992. Archaeological Occurrences of Andean Land Snails, *Andean Past* 3:127–135.

Craig, G. and Hallam, A. 1963. Size Frequency and Growth Ring Analysis of *Mytilus edulis* and *Cardium edule* and their Paleoecological Significance, *Paleontology* 6:731–750.

Crook, Morgan 1992. Oyster Sources and Their Prehistoric Use on the Georgia Coast, *Journal of Archaeological Science* 19:483–496.

Cumbaa, Stephen 1976. A Reconsideration of Freshwater Shellfish Exploitation in the Florida Archaic, *Florida Anthropologist* 29:49–59.

Cunnington, Maud 1933. Evidence of Climate Derived from Snail Shells and Its Bearing on the Date of Stonehenge, *Wiltshire Archaeology Natural History Magazine* 46:350–355.

Currey, J. 1980. Mechanical Properties of Mollusc Shell, in *The Mechanical Properties of Biological Materials,* Symposia of the Society for Experimental Biology 34 (Cambridge University Press) 75–98.

Custer, Jay and Doms, Keith 1990. Analysis of Microgrowth Patterns of the American Oyster (*Crassostrea virginica*) in the Middle Atlantic Region of Eastern North America: Archaeological Applications, *Journal of Archaeological Science* 17:151–160.

Cutler, Alan and Flessa, Karl 1990. Fossils Out of Sequence: Computer Simulations and Strategies for Dealing with Stratigraphic Disorder, *Palaios* 5:227–235.

Dall, William 1877. On Succession in the Shell-heaps of the Aleutian Islands, *United States Geological and Geographic Survey, Contributions to North American Ethnology* 1:41–91.

Darwin, Charles 1839. Journal of Researches into the Geology and Natural History of the Various Countries Visited by H. M. S. Beagle from 1832–1836 (London, Henry Colburn).

Davenport, C. 1938. Growth Lines in Fossil Pectens as Indicators of Past Climates, *Journal of Paleontology* 12:514–515.

Davis, Betty 1981. Indian, Sea Otter, and Shellfish Interrelationships, *Society for California Archaeology Occasional Papers* 3:33–42.

Davis, Nancy 1988. Conservation of Archaeological Shell Artifacts, in Hayes, C. (ed.), *Proceed-*

ings of the 1986 Shell Bead Conference: Selected Papers, Rochester Museum and Science Center, Research Records No. 20 (New York) 13–16.

deFrance, Susan, Keegan, William, and Newsom, Lee 1996. The Archaeobotanical, Bone, Isotope, and Zooarchaeological Records from Caribbean Sites in Comparative Perspective, in Reitz, E., Newsom, L., and Scudder, S. (eds.), *Case Studies in Environmental Archaeology* (New York, Plenum) 289–304.

de Williams, Anita 1975. Sea Shell Usage in Baja California, *Pacific Coast Archaeological Society Quarterly* 11(1):1–22.

Deith, Margaret 1983. Seasonality of Shell Collecting, Determined by Oxygen Isotope Analysis of Marine Shells from Asturian Sites in Cantabria, in Grigson, C. and Clutton-Brock, J. (eds.), *Animals in Archaeology vol. 2: Shell Middens, Fishes and Birds*, British Archaeological Reports, International Series 183 (Oxford, BAR), 67–76.

    1985. Seasonality from Shells: An Evaluation of Two Techniques for Seasonal Dating of Marine Molluscs, in Fieller, N., Gilbertson, D., and Ralph, N. (eds.), *Palaeobiological Investigations*, British Archaeological Reports, International Series 266 (Oxford, BAR), 119–136.

    1986. Subsistence Strategies at a Mesolithic Camp Site: Evidence from Stable Isotope Analyses of Shells, *Journal of Archaeological Science* 13:61–78.

    1988a. A Molluscan Perspective on the Role of Foraging in Neolithic Farming Economies, in Bailey, G. and Parkington, J. (eds.), *The Archaeology of Prehistoric Coastlines* (Cambridge University Press) 116–124.

    1988b. Oxygen Isotope Analyses of Marine Molluscs from Franchthi Cave, in Shackleton, J. (compiler),*Marine Molluscan Remains from Franchthi Cave* (Indiana University Press), 133–155.

Dirrigl, Frank 1995. Prehistoric Mahican Subsistence: Insights from the Zooarchaeological Analysis of the Goldkrest Site. Report submitted to Archaeological Research Specialists.

Dodd, J. and Stanton, R. 1981. *Paleoecology, Concepts and Applications* (New York, Wiley).

Dorroh, Rita, 1971. The Vegetation of Indian Shell Mounds and Rings of the South Carolina Coast. MA Thesis, Biology, University of South Carolina, Columbia.

Dortch, Charles, Kendrick, George, and Morse, Kate 1984. Aboriginal Mollusc Exploitation in Southwestern Australia, *Archaeology in Oceania* 19:81–104.

Drinnan, R. 1957. The Winter Feeding of the Oystercatcher (*Haematopus ostralegus*) on the Edible Cockle (*Cardium edule*), *Journal of Animal Ecology* 26:441–469.

Driscoll, Egbert 1970. Selective Bivalve Shell Destruction in Marine Environments, A Field Study, *Journal of Sedimentary Petrology* 40:898–905.

Drover, Christopher 1974. Seasonal Exploitation of Chione Clams on the Southern California Coast, *Journal of California Anthropology* 1:224–231.

Durán, René, Castilla, Juan, and Oliva, Doris 1987. Intensity of Human Predation on Rocky Shores at Las Cruces in Central Chile, *Environmental Conservation* 14:143–149.

Durum, W. and Haffty, J. 1961. Occurrence of Minor Elements in Water, *Geological Survey Circular* 445 (Washington, D.C., U.S. Department of the Interior).

Eldredge, P., Eversole, A., and Whetstone, J. 1976. Comparative Survival and Growth Rates of Hard Clams *Mercenaria mercenaria* from a South Carolina Estuary, *Proceedings of the National Shellfisheries Association* 69:30–39.

Ellis, David and Swan, Luke 1981. *Teachings of the Tides – Uses of Marine Invertebrates by the Manhousat People* (Namino, B.C., Theytus Books).

Emerson, William and Jacobson, Morris 1976. *The American Museum of Natural History Guide to Shells: Land, Freshwater, and Marine, from Nova Scotia to Florida* (New York, Knopf).

Emery, K. 1968. Positions of Empty Pelecypod Valves on the Continental Shelf, *Journal of Sedimentary Petrology* 38:1264–1269.

Erlandson, Jon 1988. The Role of Shellfish in Prehistoric Economies: A Protein Perspective, *American Antiquity* 53:102–109.

Evans, John 1972. *Land Snails in Archaeology* (London, Academic Press).

Ferguson, Robert 1975. Seasonality Study of Prehistoric Bivalves from the Boardwalk Site (GbTo-31), Prince Rupert, British Columbia. Manuscript on file at the National Museum of Man, Ottawa, Ontario.

Fieller, Nick 1997. Statistical Methods for Analysing Archaeomalacological Assemblages, Paper delivered at the Annual Meeting of the Society for American Archaeology, Nashville.

Flannery, Kent 1968. The Olmec and the Valley of Oaxaca: A Model for Inter-regional Interaction in Formative Times, in Benson, E. (ed.), *Dumbarton Oaks Conference on the Olmec* (Washington, D.C., Dumbarton Oaks Research Library and Collection) 79–110.

Flessa, Karl and Kowalewski, Michal 1994. Shell Survival and Time-Averaging in Nearshore and Shelf Environments: Estimates from the Radiocarbon Literature, *Lethaia* 27:153–165.

Forbes, M. 1976. Gathering in the Argolid: A Subsistence Subsystem in a Greek Agricultural Community, *Annals of the New York Academy of Science* 268:251–264.

Forchhammer, G., Steenstrup, Japetus, and Worsaae, J. 1851–1857. *Untersogelser i geologisk-antiquarisk Retning* (Copenhagen, Danish National Museum).

Ford, Pamela 1992. Interpreting the Grain Size Distributions of Archaeological Shell, in Stein, J. (ed.), *Deciphering a Shell Midden* (San Diego, Academic Press) 283–325.

Ford, Susan 1992. Avoiding the Transmission of Disease in Commercial Culture of Molluscs, with Special Reference to *Perkinsus Marinus* (Dermo) and *Haplosporidium Nelsoni* (MSX), *Journal of Shellfish Research* 11(2):539–546.

Francis, Peter 1982. Experiments with Early Techniques for Making Whole Shells into Beads, *Current Anthropology* 23:713–714.

Frey, Robert and Dorjes, Jurgen 1988. Fair- and Foul-Weather Shell Accumulations on a Georgia Beach, *Palaios* 3:561–576.

Fursich, Franz and Aberhan, Martin 1990. Significance of Time-Averaging for Palaeocommunity Analysis, *Lethaia* 23:143–152.

Gangaly, N. and Bandyopadhyay, K. 1963. Conch-Shell Industry – A Type Study. Government of West Bengal State Statistical Bureau, West Bengal Government Press, Alipore.

Gautier, A. 1976. Appendix G: Freshwater Mollusks and Mammals from Upper Paleolithic Sites Near Idfu and Isna, in Wendorf, F. and Schild, R. (eds.), *Prehistory of the Nile Valley* (New York, Academic Press) 349–364.

Gilbertson, D. 1985. Past and Present Distributions of *Hydrobia ulvae* (Pennant), Gastropoda, and *Macoma balthica* (L.), Bivalvia, Along the Southern Shores of the Severn Estuary in Relation to Water Pollution, Field Survey and Laboratory Methods, in Fieller, N., Gilbertson, D., and Ralph, N. (eds.), *Palaeobiological Investigations*, British Archaeological Reports, International Series 266 (Oxford, BAR), 167–179.

Gill, Edmund 1954. Aboriginal Kitchen Middens and Marine Shell Beds, *Mankind* 4(6):249–254.

Godfrey, Michael 1988. Oxygen Isotope Analysis: A Means for Determining the Seasonal Gathering of the Pipi (*Donax deltoides*) by Aborigines in Prehistoric Australia, *Archaeology in Oceania* 23:17–21.

1989. Shell Midden Chronology in Southwestern Victoria: Reflections of Change in Prehistoric Population and Subsistence?, *Archaeology in Oceania* 24:65–69.

Gonzales, C., Ordonez, J., and Maala, A. 1989. Red Tide: The Philippine Experience, in Okaichi, T., Anderson, D., and Nemoto, T. (eds.), *Red Tides: Biology, Environmental Science, and Toxicology* (New York, Elsevier) 45–48.

Goode, George 1884. *The Fisheries and Fisheries Industry of the United States* (Washington, D.C., U.S. Government Printing Office).

Goodfriend, Glenn 1987. Radiocarbon Age Anomalies in Shell Carbonate of Land Snails from

Semi-Arid Areas, *Radiocarbon* 29:159–167.

1990. Rainfall in the Negev Desert During the Middle Holocene, Based on ^{13}C of Organic Matter in Land Snail Shell, *Quaternary Research* 34:186–197.

1991a. Holocene Trends in ^{18}O in Land Snail Shells from the Negev Desert and their Implications for Changes in Rainfall Source Areas, *Quaternary Research* 35:417–426.

1991b. Patterns of Racemization and Epimerization of Amino Acids in Land Snail Shells over the Course of the Holocene, *Geochimica et Cosmochimica Acta* 55:293–302.

Goodfriend, Glenn, Kashgarian, Michaele, and Harasewych, M. 1995. Use of Aspartic Acid Racemization and Post-Bomb ^{14}C to Reconstruct Growth Rate and Longevity of the Deep-Water Slit Shell *Entemnotrochus adansonianus*, *Geochimica et Cosmochimica Acta* 59:1125–1129.

Goodfriend, Glenn and Mitterer, Richard 1993. A 45,000-yr Record of a Tropical Lowland Biota: The Land Snail Fauna From Cave Sediments at Coco Reef, Jamaica, *Geological Society of America Bulletin* 105:18–29.

Goodwin, Christopher 1979. The Prehistoric Cultural Ecology of St. Kitts, West Indies: A Case Study in Island Archeology, Ph.D. dissertation, Anthropology, Arizona State University.

Gordon, J. and Carriker, Melbourne 1978. Growth Lines in a Bivalve Mollusk: Sub-Daily Patterns and Dissolution of Shell, *Science* 202:519–521.

Gould, J. 1865. *Handbook to the Birds of Australia* (London, Landsdowne Press).

Gould, Stephen 1971. The Paleontology and Evolution of Cerion II: Age and Fauna of Indian Shell Middens on Curaçao and Aruba, *Breviora* 372.

Grayson, Donald 1984. *Quantitative Zooarchaeology: Topics in the Analysis of Archaeological Faunas* (New York, Academic Press).

Greenwood, Roberta 1961. Quantitative Analysis of Shells From a Site in Goleta, California, *American Antiquity* 26:416–420.

Griffin, John 1952. Early Hunters of Florida, *Florida Wildlife* March: no pagination.

Guilderson, Thomas, Fairbanks, Richard, and Rubenstone, James 1994. Tropical Temperature Variations Since 20,000 Years Ago: Modulation Interhemispheric Climate Change, *Science* 263:663–665.

Gunn, Joel 1995. Osprey Marsh: Archaeological Data Recovery Investigations at Sites 38Bu905 and 38Bu921 along the Hilton Head Cross Island Expressway, Beaufort County, South Carolina, Report submitted to South Carolina Department of Transportation, by Garrow and Associates, Inc.

Gunn, R. 1846. On the Heaps of Recent Shells Which Exist Along the Shores of Tasmania, *Tasmania Journal* 2.

Hale, Stephen, Diaz, Domingo, and Mendéz, Marucio 1996. Mammals to Land, Fish to the Sea and Garbage for New Land: The Taphonomy of Midden Formation Among the Maritime Kuna of Panama and Implications for Midden Interpretation, Paper presented at the Annual Meeting of the Southeastern Archaeological Conference, Birmingham, Alabama.

Hall, Grant 1981. *Allens Creek*. Texas Archaeological Survey Research Report 61 (Austin, University of Texas).

Hall, Martin 1980. A Method for Obtaining Metrical Data from Fragmentary Molluscan Material Found at Archaeological Sites, *South African Journal of Science* 76:280–281.

Ham, Leonard 1982. Seasonality, Shell Midden Layers and Coast Salish Subsistence Activities at the Crescent Beach site, DgRr1, Ph.D. dissertation, Archaeology, University British Columbia.

Ham, Leonard and Irvine, Moira 1975. Techniques for Determining Seasonality of Shell Middens from Marine Mollusc Remains, *Syesis* 8:363–373.

Hamell, George 1983. Trading in Metaphors: The Magic of Beads, in Hayes, C. (ed.), *Proceedings of the 1982 Glass Trade Bead Conference*, Rochester Museum and Science Center

Research Records No. 16 (New York) 5–28.

1987. Strawberries, Floating Islands, and Rabbit Captains: Mythical Realities and European Contact in the Northeast During the Sixteenth and Seventeenth Centuries, *Journal of Canadian Studies* 21(4):72–94.

Hancock, D. and Simpson, A. 1962. Parameters of Marine Invertebrate Populations, in Le Cren, E. and Holgate M. (eds.), *The Exploitation of Natural Animal Populations* (Oxford, Blackwell) 29–50.

Hancock, Mary 1982. The Determination of Archaeological Site Seasonality Using the Remains of *Mya arenaria*: Examples from the Central Maine Coast, M.A. Thesis, Institute for Quaternary Studies, University of Maine.

1984. Analysis of Shellfish Remains: Seasonality Information, in McManamon, F. (ed.), *Chapters in the Archaeology of Cape Cod*, I. Vol. II (Washington D.C., U.S. Department of Interior) 121–156.

Hardial, R. and Simpson, C. 1989. Dating of Archaeological Material by Amino Acid Racemisation Reaction Using HPLC, *Analytical Proceedings* 26:57–58.

Harman, Willard 1970. New Distribution Records and Ecological Notes on Central New York Unioı acea, *American Midland Naturalist* 84:46–58.

Harriss, R. and Pilkey, O. 1966. Temperature and Salinity Control of the Concentration of Skin Na, Mn, and Fe in *Dendraster excentricus*, *Biological Science* 20:235–238.

Haury, Emil 1937. The Snaketown Canal, in Gladwin, H., Haury, E., Sayles, E., and Gladwin, N. (eds.), *Excavations at Snaketown: Material Culture* (Gila Pueblo, Medallion Papers) 50–58.

Harvey, Ethel 1956. *The American Arbacia and Other Sea Urchins* (Princeton, Princeton University Press).

Herbert, Joseph and Steponaitis, Laurie 1993. Estimating Seasonality from Oyster Shell Growth Segments, Paper presented at the Southeastern Archaeological Conference, Raleigh, N.C.

Higham, Tom 1996. Shellfish and Seasonality, in Anderson, A., Smith, I., and Allingham, B. (eds.), *Shag Mouth: The Archaeology of an Early Southern Maori Village* New Zealand Archaeological Association Monograph 20:245–253.

Hill, Fred 1975. Effects of the Environment on Animal Exploitation by Archaic Inhabitants of the Koster Site, Illinois, Ph.D. dissertation, Biology, University of Louisville.

Hockey, P. and Bosman, A. 1986. Man as an Intertidal Predator in Transkei: Disturbance, Community Convergence and Management of a Natural Food Supply, *Oikos* 46:3–14.

Hockey, P., Bosman, A., and Siegfried, W. 1988. Patterns and Correlates of Shellfish Exploitation by Coastal People in Transkei: An Enigma of Protein Production, *Journal of Applied Ecology* 25:353–363.

Hofman, Jack 1985. Middle Archaic Ritual and Shell Midden Archaeology: Considering the Significance of Cremations, in Whyte, T., Boyd, C., and Riggs, B., (eds.), *Exploring Tennessee Prehistory* (Knoxville, Report of Investigations No. 42, Anthropology, University of Tennessee) 1–22.

Hogendorn, Jan and Johnson, Marion 1986. *The Shell Money of the Slave Trade* (Cambridge University Press).

Hollimon, Sandra 1991. Health Consequences of Divisions of Labor Among the Chumash Indians of Southern California, in Walde, D. and Willows, N. (eds.), *The Archaeology of Gender*, Proceedings of the 22nd Annual Chacmool Conference (University of Calgary) 462–469.

Hollingworth, Neville and Barker, Michael 1991. Colour Pattern Preservation in the Fossil Record: Taphonomy and Diagenetic Significance, in Donovan, S. (ed.), *The Process of Fossilization* (Columbia University Press) 105–119.

Hornell, James 1915. *The Indian Conch and its Relation to Hindu Life and Religion* (London, Williams and Norgate).

House, M. and Farrow, G. 1968. Daily Growth Banding in the Shell of the Cockle, *Cardium edule, Nature* 219:1384–1386.

Hughes, Philip and Sullivan, Marjorie 1974. The Re-Deposition of Midden Material by Storm Waves, *Journal and Proceedings, Royal Society of New South Wales* 107:6–10.

Hughes, Roger 1986. *A Functional Biology of Marine Gastropods* (Baltimore, MD, Johns Hopkins University Press).

Isely, F. 1914. *Experimental Study of the Growth and Migration of Freshwater Mussels.* Bureau of Fisheries Document 792 (Washington, D.C.).

Jablonski, David 1985. Molluscan Development, in Bottjer, D., Hickman, C., and Ward, P. (eds.), *Mollusks, Notes for a Short Course* (Knoxville, Paleontological Society) 33–49

Jackson, Wilfrid 1916a. The Money Cowry (*Cypraea moneta*, L.) as a Sacred Object among North American Indians, *Manchester Memoirs* 60(4):1–10.

1916b. The Use of Cowry-shells for the Purposes of Currency, Amulets, and Charms, *Manchester Memoirs* 60(13):1–72.

Janota, Beverly 1980. A Preliminary Study of the Shell Ornaments of the Texas Coast Between Galveston Bay and the Nueces River, in Highley, L. and Hester, T. (eds.), *Papers on the Archaeology of the Texas Coast.* Center of Archaeological Research, University of Texas, San Antonio Special Report #11:29–49.

Jenkinson, John 1986. Mussel Die-Offs Below Pickwick Landing Dam, Tennessee River, 1985 and 1986. Ms. on file Department of Fisheries and Wildlife Sciences, Virginia Polytechnic Institute, Blacksburg.

Jensen, Hanne 1982. Skaldyrssaeson, *Skalk* 3:9–10.

Jerardino, Antonieta 1995. The Problem With Density Values in Archaeological Analysis: A Case Study from Tortoise Cave, Western Cape, South Africa, *South African Archaeological Bulletin* 50:21–27.

Jerardino, Antonieta, Castilla, Juan, Ramrez, José, and Hermosilla, Nuriluz 1992. Early Coastal Subsistence Patterns in Central Chile: A Systematic Study of the Marine-Invertebrate Fauna from the Site of Curaumilla-1, *Latin American Antiquity* 3:43–62.

Johnson, Lucille (ed.), 1992. *Paleoshorelines and Prehistory: An Investigation of Method,* (Boca Raton, CRC Press).

Johnson, Ralph 1960. Models and Methods for Analysis of the Mode of Formation of Fossil Assemblages, *Geological Society of America Bulletin* 71:1075–1086.

Jones, David 1985. Growth Increments and Geochemical Variations in the Molluscan Shell, in Bottjer, D., Hickman, C., and Ward, P. (eds.), *Mollusks, Notes for a Short Course* (Knoxville, Paleontological Society) 72–87.

Jones, David, Thompson, Ida, and Ambrose, William 1978. Age and Growth Rate Determinations for the Atlantic Surf Clam *Spisula solidissima* Based on Internal Growth Lines in Shell Cross-Sections, *Marine Biology* 47:63–70.

Jones, Rhys and Allen, Jim 1978. Caveat Excavator: A Sea Bird Midden on Steep Head Island, North West Tasmania, *Australian Archaeology Association Newsletter* 8:142–145.

Jones, Terry 1996. Mortars, Pestles, and Division of Labor in Prehistoric California: A View from Big Sur, *American Antiquity* 61:243–264.

Jones, Terry and Richman, Jennifer 1995. On Mussels: *Mytilus californianus* as a Prehistoric Resource, *North American Archaeologist* 16:33–58.

Keene, Arthur 1983. Biology, Behavior, and Borrowing: A Critical Examination of Optimal Foraging Theory in Archaeology, in Moore, J. and Keene, A., *Archaeological Hammers and Theories* (New York, Academic Press) 137–156.

Kent, Bretton 1988. *Making Dead Oysters Talk* (St. Mary's City, Maryland Historical Trust).

Kenward, H. 1978. The Analysis of Archaeological Insect Assemblages: a New Approach, *The Archaeology of York* 19/1.

Kerber, Jordan 1997. *Lambert Farm: Public Archaeology and Canine Burials Along Narragansett Bay* (New York, Harcourt Brace).

Kidder, J., Jr. 1959. *Japan Before Buddhism,* (London, Thames and Hudson).

Kidwell, Susan and Bosence, Daniel 1991. Taphonomy and Time-Averaging of Marine Shelly Faunas, in Allison, P. and Briggs, D. (eds.), *Releasing the Data Locked in the Fossil Record,* (New York, Plenum Press) 115–209.

Killingley, John 1981. Seasonality of Mollusk Collecting Determined from O–18 Profiles of Midden Shells, *American Antiquity* 46:152–158.

 1983. Seasonality Determination by Oxygen Isotopic Profile: A Reply to Bailey et al., *American Antiquity* 48:399–403.

Kirch, Patrick and Dye, Tom 1979. Ethno-archaeology and the Development of Polynesian Fishing Strategies, *The Journal of the Polynesia Society* 88:53–76.

Klippel, Walter, Celmer, G., and Pardue, R. 1978. The Holocene Naiad Record at Rodgers Shelter in the Western Ozark Highland of Missouri, *Plains Anthropologist* 23:157–170.

Klippel, Walter and Morey, Darcey 1986. Contextual and Nutritional Analysis of Freshwater Gastropods from Middle Archaic Deposits at the Hays Site, Middle Tennessee, *American Antiquity* 51:799–813.

Koch, Carl and Sohl, Norman 1983. Preservational Effects in Paleoecological Studies: Cretaceous Mollusc Examples, *Paleobiology* 9:26–34.

Koch, Christopher 1989. *Taphonomy: A Bibliographic Guide to the Literature,* Center for the Study of the First Americans, Institute for Quaternary Studies, University of Maine, Orono.

Koike, Hiroko 1979. Seasonal Dating and the Valve-Pairing Technique in Shell-Midden Analysis, *Journal of Archaeological Science* 6:63–74.

 1980. Seasonal Dating by Growth-Line Counting of the Clam, *Meretrix lusoria*: Towards a Reconstruction of Prehistoric Shell Collecting Activities in Japan, *University of Tokyo Bulletin* 18.

Koike, Hiroko and Okamura, Michio 1994. Time-Scaling of Successively Accumulated Shell Layers for Exploitation Dairy [sic] Analysis, *Archaeozoologia* 6(2):23–36.

Koloseike, A. 1969. On Calculating the Prehistoric Food Resource Value of Molluscs, *University of California, Los Angeles, Archaeological Survey, Annual Report* 11:143–162.

Kunz, George 1898. The Fresh-Water Pearls and Pearl Fisheries of the United States, *U.S. Fish Commission Bulletin* 17:373–426 (Washington, D.C.).

Lampert, R. 1981. The Great Kartan Mystery, *Terra Australis* 5.

Land, Lynton 1967. Diagenesis of Skeletal Carbonates, *Journal of Sedimentary Petrology* 37:914–930.

Lanning, Edward 1967. *Peru Before the Incas* (Englewood Cliffs, NJ, Prentice-Hall).

Larsen, Clark, Schoeninger, Margaret, van der Merwe, N., Moore, Katherine, and Lee-Thorp, Julia 1992. Carbon and Nitrogen Stable Isotopic Signatures of Human Dietary Change in the Georgia Bight, *American Journal of Physical Anthropology* 89:197–214.

Lasiak, Theresa 1992. Contemporary Shellfish-Gathering Practices of Indigenous Coastal People in Transkei: Some Implications for Interpretation of the Archaeological Record, *Suid-Afrikaanse Tydskrif Vir Wetenskap* 88:19–28.

Laughlin, William 1974/75. Holocene History of Nikolski Bay, Alaska, and Aleut Evolution, *Folk* 16–17:95–115.

Lee, F. and Wilson, W. 1969. Use of Chemical Composition of Freshwater Clamshells as Indicators of Paleohydrologic Conditions, *Ecology* 50:990–997.

Lewis, B. 1979. Hunter-Gatherer Foraging: Some Theoretical Explorations and Archaeological Tests, Ph.D. dissertation, Anthropology, University of Illinois.

Lewis, Thomas and Kneberg, Madeline 1946. *Hiwassee Island* (Knoxville, University of Tennessee Press).

Lima, Tania, de Mello, Elisa, and da Silva, Regina 1986. Analysis of Molluscan Remains from the Ilha de Santana Site, Macaé, Brazil, *Journal of Field Archaeology* 13:83–97.

Linck, Dana and Modreski, Peter 1983. Fluorescence of Shell Fragments as an Aid to the Study of Early American Mortars, *Journal of the Fluorescent Mineral Society* 12:6–15.

Little, Elizabeth 1993a. From the Sand Eel to the Great Auk: Potential Prehistoric Coastal Diets for Isotope Analysis, in Jamieson, R., Abonyi, S., and Mirau, N. (eds.), *Culture and Environment: A Fragile Coexistence*, Proceedings of the 24th Annual Chacmool Conference (Calgary, The Archaeological Association of the University of Calgary) 193–201.

1993b. Radiocarbon Age Calibration at Archaeological Sites of Coastal Massachusetts and Vicinity, *Journal of Archaeological Science* 20:457–471.

1995. Apples and Oranges: Radiocarbon Dates on Shell and Charcoal at Dogan Point, in Claassen, C. (ed.), *Dogan Point: A Shell Matrix Site in the Lower Hudson Valley*, Occasional Papers in Northeastern Anthropology, 14 (Bethlehem, Conn., Archaeological Services) 121–128.

Little, Elizabeth and Andrews, Clinton 1986. Prehistoric Shellfish Harvesting at Nantucket Island, *Bulletin of the Massachusetts Archaeological Society* 47:18–27.

Little, Elizabeth and Schoeninger, Margaret 1995. The Late Woodland Diet on Nantucket Island and the Problem of Maize in Coastal New England, *American Antiquity* 60:351–368.

Littler, M. 1980. Overview of the Rocky Intertidal Systems of Southern California, in Power, D. (ed.), *The California Islands* (Santa Barbara Museum of Natural History) 265–306.

Lobdell, John 1980. Prehistoric Human Populations and Resource Utilization in Kachemak Bay, Gulf of Alaska, Ph.D. dissertation, Anthropology, University of Tennessee.

Lubbock, John 1869. *Pre-historic Times* 2nd edn (London, Williams and Norgate).

Lumley, Henry de 1972. A Paleolithic Camp at Nice, in Lamberg-Karlovsky, C., *Old World Archaeology* (San Francisco, W. H. Freeman) 33–41.

Lundberg, Emily 1985. Interpreting the Cultural Associations of Aceramic Deposits in the Virgin Islands, *Journal of Field Archaeology* 12:201–215.

Lutz, Richard 1976. Annual Growth Patterns in the Inner Shell Layer of *Mytilus edulis* L., *Journal Marine Biology Association*, UK 56:723–731.

Lyell, Charles 1849. *A Second Visit to the United States of North America* (London, John Murray).

McCay, Bonnie 1981. Optimal Foragers or Political Actors: Ecological Analyses of a New Jersey Fishery, *American Ethnologist* 8:356–382.

McGovern, Thomas 1980. Site Catchments and Maritime Adaptations in Norse Greenland, *Anthroplogy UCLA* 10(1/2):193–210.

McKinney, Frank 1995. Taphonomic Effects and Preserved Overgrowth Relationships Among Encrusting Marine Organisms, *Palaios* 10:279–282.

McManamon, Francis 1984. *Chapters in the Archeology of Cape Cod*. Division of Cultural Resources, North Atlantic Regional Office, NPS, U.S. Department of Interior, Cultural Resources Management Study 8.

Mackay, Richard and White, Peter 1987. Comment: Musselling in on the NSW Coast, *Archaeology in Oceania* 22:107–111.

Madsen, Mark 1992. Lithic Manufacturing at British Camp: Evidence from Size Distributions and Microartifacts, in Stein, J. (ed.), *Deciphering a Shell Midden* (San Diego, Academic Press) 193–210.

Malek, Emile 1985. *Snail Hosts of Schistosomiasis and Other Snail-Transmitted Diseases in Tropical America: A Manual*. Publicacíon Scientífica 478, Pan American Health Organization, Washington, D.C.

Malinowski, Bronislaw 1922. *Argonauts of the Western Pacific* (New York, Dutton).

Marquardt, William 1992. Shell Artifacts from the Caloosahatchee Area, in Marquardt, W. (ed.), *Culture and Environment in the Domain of the Calusa*, Monograph No. 1, Institute of Archaeology and Paleoenvironmental Studies, University of Florida, 191–227.

Mason, J. 1957. The Age and Growth of the Scallop, *Pecten maximus* in Manx Waters, *Journal of the Marine Biological Association* 36:473–492.

Matteson, Max 1955. Studies on the Natural History of the Unionidae, *American Midland Naturalist* 53:126–145.

1960. Reconstruction of Prehistoric Environments Through the Analysis of Molluscan Collections from Shell Middens, *American Antiquity* 26:117–120.

Matthew, G. 1884. Discoveries at a Village of the Stone Age at Bocabec, N.B., *Bulletin of the Natural History Society of New Brunswick* 3:6–29.

Maxwell, David 1989a. Meat-Yield Estimates in Bivalve Shellfish. Paper presented at the 42nd Annual Northwest Anthropology Conference, Spokane, Washington.

1989b. Shellfishing Seasonality: Some Midden Sampling Requirements. Paper delivered at the Annual Meeting of the Canadian Archaeological Association, Fredericton.

Meehan, Betty 1982. *Shell Bed to Shell Midden* (Canberra, Australian National University).

Meighan, Clement 1959. The Little Harbor Site, Catalina Island: An Example of Ecological Interpretation in Archaeology, *American Antiquity* 24:383–405.

1969. Molluscs as Food Remains in Archaeological Sites, in Brothwell, D. and Higgs, E. (eds.), *Science in Archaeology* (London, Methuen) 415–422.

1989. Early Shell-Mound Dwellers on the Pacific Coast of North America. Paper delivered at the Pacific 89 Conference, Seattle.

Meldahl, Keith and Flessa, Karl 1990. Taphonomic Pathways and Comparative Biofacies and Taphofacies in a Recent Intertidal/Shallow Shelf Environment, *Lethaia* 23:43–56.

Mellars, Paul 1978. Excavation and Economic Analysis of Mesolithic Shell Middens on the Island of Oronsay (Inner Hebrides), in Mellars, P. (ed.), *The Early Postglacial Settlement of Northern Europe* (University of Pittsburgh Press) 371–396.

1987. *Excavations on Oronsay: Prehistoric Human Ecology on a Small Island* (Edinburgh, Edinburgh University Press).

Mester, Ann 1989. Marine Shell Symbolism in Andean Culture, in Hayes, C. (ed.), *Proceedings of the 1986 Shell Bead Conference*, Rochester Museum and Science Center Research Records No. 20, (New York) 157–168.

Miller, Katherine 1980. Chemical Characterization of Archeological Shell, Senior Honors Thesis, Anthropology, Harvard University.

Mills, C. 1985. Shellfish Utilization and Its Effect on Rocky Shore Biota in Transkei, M.A. Thesis, Archaeology, University of Cape Town, South Africa.

Mitchell, Peter 1996. Prehistoric Exchange and Interaction in Southeastern Southern Africa: Marine Shells and Ostrich Eggshell, *African Archaeological Review* 13:35–76.

Moholy-Nagy, Hattula 1963. Shells and Other Marine Material from Tikal, *Estudios de Cultura Maya* 3:64–83.

Monks, Gregory 1977. An Examination of Relationships between Artifact Classes and Food Resource Remains at Deep Bay, DiSe7. Ph.D. dissertation, Archaeology, University of British Columbia.

Mook, W. 1971. Palaeotemperatures and Chlorinities from Stable Carbon and Oxygen Isotopes in Shell Carbonate, *Palaeogeography, Palaeoclimatology, Palaeoecology* 9:245–263.

Moreau, Jean-François 1980. A Report on the Hunter-Robinson and Sardinal Sites, *Vinculos* 6(1–2):107–124.

Moreno, Carlos, Sutherland, John, and Jara, Fernando 1984. Man as a Predator in the Intertidal Zone of Southern Chile, *Oikos* 42:155–160.

Morlot, Adolphe 1861. General Views on Archaeology, *Smithsonian Institution Annual Report for 1860*:284–343.

Morse, Edward 1879. *Shell Mounds of Omori*, Memoirs of the Science Department, University of Tokyo, vol. I, part 1, The University of Tokyo.

Moseley, Michael 1975. *The Maritime Foundations of Andean Civilization* (Menlo Park, Cummings).

Moseley, Michael, Wagner, David, and Richardson, James III, 1992. Space Shuttle Imagery of Recent Catastrophic Change Along the Arid Andean Coast, in Johnson, L. (ed.), *Paleoshorelines and Prehistory: An Investigation of Method* (Boca Raton, CRC Press) 215–235.

Moss, Madonna 1993. Shellfish, Gender, and Status on the Northwest Coast: Reconciling Archeological, Ethnographic, and Ethnohistorical Records of the Tlingit, *American Anthropologist* 95:631–652.

Mountjoy, Joseph, Taylor, Robert, and Feldman, Lawrence 1972. Matanchén Complex: New Radiocarbon Dates on Early Coastal Adaptation in West Mexico, *Science* 175:1242–1243.

Msemwa, Paul 1994. An Ethnoarchaeological Study on Shellfish Collecting in a Complex Urban Setting, Ph.D. dissertation, Anthropology, Brown University.

Muckle, Robert 1985. Archaeological Considerations of Bivalve Shell Taphonomy, M.A. Thesis, Anthropology, Simon Fraser University.

Namio, Egami 1974. Migration of the Cowrie-Shell Culture in East Asia, *Acta Asiatica* 26:1–53.

Naydenova, N. and Zakhaleva, V. 1993. Fungal Diseases of the Shells of Black Sea Mollusks, *Hydrobiological Journal* 29(5):1–6.

Neck, Raymond 1987. Terrestrial Gastropod Succession in a Late Holocene Stream Deposit in South Texas, *Quaternary Research* 27:202–209.

Negus, C. 1966. A Quantitative Study of the Growth and Production of Unionid Mussels in the River Thames at Reading, *Journal of Animal Ecology* 35:513–532.

Neves, Richard 1986. An Overview of Recent Die-Offs of Freshwater Mussels in the United States. Ms. on file Department of Fisheries and Wildlife Sciences, Virginia Polytechnic Institute, Blacksburg.

Newell, Richard 1970. *Biology of Intertidal Animals* (London, Paul Elek Limited).

Noe-Nygaard, Nanna 1983. The Importance of Aquatic Resources to Mesolithic Man at Inland Sites in Denmark, in Grigson, C. and Clutton-Brock, J. (eds.), *Animals in Archaeology vol. 2: Shell Middens, Fishes and Birds*, British Archaeological Reports, International Series 183 (Oxford, BAR), 125–142.

Noli, Dieter and Avery, Graham 1988. Protein Poisoning and Coastal Subsistence, *Journal of Archaeological Science* 15:395–401.

O'Brien, Deborah and Peter, Deborah 1983. Preliminary Ceramic and Seasonality Analysis from the Regional Settlement Survey on St. Catherines Island. Paper delivered at the Annual Meeting of the Southeastern Archaeological Conference, Columbia.

O'Connor, Terence 1988. Slums, Puddles, and Ditches: Are Molluscs Useful Indicators?, in Murphy, P. and French, C. (eds.), *The Exploitation of Wetlands*. British Archaeological Reports, British Series 186 (Oxford, BAR), 61–68.

O'Neil, Dennis 1993. Excavation Sample Size: A Cautionary Tale, *American Antiquity* 58:423–528.

O'Sullivan, Tim, Hartley, John, Saunders, Danny, and Fiske, John 1983. *Key Concepts in Communication* (New York, Methuen and Co.).

Okaichi, Tomotoshi, Anderson, Donald, and Nemoto, Takahisa (eds.). 1989. *Red Tides: Biology, Environmental Science, and Toxicology* (New York, Elsevier).

Oliva, Doris and Castilla, Juan 1992. Guía para el Reconocimiento y Morfometria de Nueve Especies del Género *Fissurella* Comunes en la Costa y Conchales de Chile Central, *Gayana Zoologia* 56(3–4):77–108.

Onat, Astrida 1985. The Multifunctional Use of Shellfish Remains: From Garbage to Community Engineering, *Northwest Anthropological Research Notes* 19:201–207.

Ossa, Paul, and Moseley, Michael 1972. La Cumbre: A Preliminary Report on Research into the Early Lithic Occupation of the Moche Valley, Peru, *Nawpa Pacha* 9:1–16.

Ottesen, Ann 1979. Acquisition of Exotic Raw Materials by Late Woodland and Mississippian Peoples, Ph.D. dissertation, Anthropology, New York University.

Pallant, Eric 1990. Applications of Molluscan Microgrowth Analysis to Geoarchaeology; A Case Study from Costa Rica, *Geological Society of America Centennial Special Volume* 4:421–430.

Palmer, Jay and Williams, Raymond 1977. The Formation of Goethite and Calcareous Lenses in Shell Middens of Florida, *Florida Anthropologist* 30(1):24–27.

Pannella, Giorgio and MacClintock, Copeland 1968. Biological and Environmental Rhythms Reflected in Molluscan Shell Growth, *Journal of Paleontology* 42:64–80.

Parker, R. and Carriker, Melbourne 1960. Ecology and Distribution Patterns of Marine Macro-Invertebrates in Northern Gulf of Mexico, in Shepard, F. (ed.), *Recent Sediments, Northwest Gulf of Mexico* (American Association of Petroleum Geologists, Tulsa, Oklahoma) 302–337.

Parmalee, Paul and Klippel, Walter 1974. Freshwater Mussels as a Prehistoric Food Resource, *American Antiquity* 39:421–434.

Parsons, Elsie 1974 [1939]. *Pueblo Indian Religion*. Midway Reprints (University of Chicago Press).

Parsons, Karla and Brett, Carlton 1991. Taphonomic Processes and Biases in Modern Marine Environments, in Donovan, S. (ed.), *The Processes of Fossilization* (New York, Columbia University Press) 22–65.

Paul, C. 1987. Land-Snail Assemblages from the Shell-Midden Sites, in Mellars, P. (ed.), *Excavations on Oronsay: Prehistoric Human Ecology on a Small Island* (Edinburgh, Edinburgh University Press) 91–107.

Paulsen, Allison 1974. The Thorny Oyster and the Voice of God: *Spondylus* and *Strombus* in Andean Prehistory, *American Antiquity* 39:597–607.

Peacock, W. 1978. Probabilistic Sampling in Shell Middens: A Case-Study from Oronsay, Inner Hebrides, in Cherry, J., Gamble, C., and Shennan, S. (eds.), *Sampling in Contemporary British Archaeology*, British Archaeological Reports, British Series 50 (Oxford, BAR), 177–190.

Pennington, Jean 1994. *Bowes and Church's Food Values of Portions Commonly Used*. 16th edn (New York, Lippincott Co.).

Perlman, Stephen 1973. *Pecten irradians*: Growth Patterns: Their Application to Archaeological Economic Analysis, M.A. Thesis, Anthropology, University of Massachusetts.

Peterson, Charles 1976. Relative Abundances of Living and Dead Molluscs in Two California Lagoons, *Lethaia* 9:137–148.

Picha, Paul 1995. Expedient Mussel Shell-Tool Technology on the Northern Great Plains: Historical, Archaeological, and Taphonomic Considerations. Paper presented at the Annual Meeting of the Society for American Archaeology, Minneapolis, MN.

Pirrie, Duncan and Marshall, James 1990. Diagenesis of *Inoceramus* and Late Cretaceous Paleoenvironmental Geochemistry: A Case Study from James Ross Island, Antarctica, *Palaios* 5:336–345.

Post, Alan 1982. Evaluation of Freshwater Mussels (*Megalonaias gigantea*) as a New Protein Source, Ph.D. dissertation, Food Technology and Science, University of Tennessee.

Powell, Eric, King, Julie, and Boyles, S. 1991. Dating Time-Since-Death of Oyster Shells by the Rate of Decomposition of the Organic Matrix, *Archaeometry* 33:51–68.

Powers, M. 1953. A New Roundness Scale for Sedimentary Particles, *Journal of Sedimentary*

Petrology 23:117–119.

Pratt, D. and Campbell, D. 1956. Environmental Factors Affecting Growth in *Venus mercenaria. Limnology and Oceanography* 1:2–17.

Price, Doug, Johnson, Clark, Ezzo, Joseph, Ericson, Jonathan, and Burton, James 1994. Residential Mobility in the Prehistoric Southwest United States: A Preliminary Study Using Strontium Isotope Analysis, *Journal of Archaeological Science* 21:315–330.

Qian, Yaorong, Engel, Michael, Goodfriend, Glenn, and Macko, Stephen 1995. Abundance and Stable Carbon Isotope Composition of Amino Acids in Molecular Weight Fractions of Fossil and Artificially Aged Mollusk Shells, *Geochimica et Cosmochimica Acta* 59:1113–1124.

Quitmyer, Irvy 1985. Zooarchaeological Methods for the Analysis of Shell Middens at Kings Bay, in Adams, W. (ed.), *Aboriginal Subsistence and Settlement Archaeology of the Kings Bay Locality, vol.* 2: *Zooarchaeology*, Department of Anthropology Reports of Investigations No. 2. (University of Florida, Gainesville) 33–48.

Quitmyer, Irvy, Hale, Stephen, and Jones, Douglas 1985. Paleoseasonality Determination Based on Incremental Shell Growth in the Hard Clam, *Mercenaria mercenaria*, and its Implications for the Analysis of Three Southeast Georgia Coastal Shell Middens, *Southeastern Archaeology* 4:27–40.

Reese, David 1979–80. Industrial Exploitation of Murex Shells: Purple-dye and Lime Production at Sidi Khrebish, Benghazi (Berenice), *Libyan Studies* 11:79–93.

    1989. Treasures from the Sea, *Expedition* 31(2–3):80–86.

Rehder, Harald 1981. *The Audubon Society Field Guide to North American Seashells* (New York, Knopf).

Reinman, Fred 1964. Maritime Adaptation on San Nicolas Island, California: A Preliminary Speculative Evaluation, University of California, Los Angeles, Archaeological Survey Annual Report 1964, 51–73.

Reitz, Elizabeth, Newsom, Lee, and Scudder, Sylvia 1996. *Case Studies in Environmental Archaeology*, (New York, Plenum Press).

Reitz, Elizabeth and Quitmyer, Irvy 1988. Faunal Remains from Two Coastal Georgia Swift Creek Sites, *Southeastern Archaeology* 7:95–108.

Reitz, Elizabeth, Quitmyer, Irvy, Hale, Stephen, Scudder, Sylvia, and Wing, Elizabeth 1987. The Application of Allometry to Zooarchaeology, *American Antiquity* 52:304–317.

Riser, George 1987. The Quave Ceramic Collection: Mississippian Presence on the North Shore of Lake Pontchartrain. Paper delivered at the Annual Meeting of the Louisiana Archaeological Society, New Orleans.

Ritchie, Carson 1974. *Shell Carving: History and Techniques* (South Brunswick, New Jersey, A. S. Barnes and Co.).

Ritchie, Theodore 1977. *A Comprehensive Review of the Commercial Clam Industries in the United States* (Washington, D.C., National Marine Fisheries Service).

Robins, R. and Stock, E. 1990. The Burning Question: A Study of Molluscan Remains from a Midden on Moreton Island, *Tempus* 2:80–100.

Robinson, Mark 1988. Molluscan Evidence for Pasture and Meadowland on the Floodplain of the Upper Thames Basin, in Murphy, P. and French, C. (eds.), *The Exploitation of Wetlands*. British Archaeological Reports, British Series 186 (Oxford, BAR), 101–112.

Rollins, Harold, Sandweiss, Daniel, and Rollins, Judith 1990. Mollusks and Coastal Archaeology; A Review, in Lasca, N. and Donahue, J. (eds.), *Archaeological Geology of North America*, Geological Society of America, Centennial Special Volume 4, (Boulder, CO) 467–478.

Ronen, A. 1980. The Origin of the Raised Pelecypod Beds Along the Mediterranean Coast of Israel, *Paleorient* 6:165–172.

Roscoe, E. 1967. Ethnomalacology and Paleoecology of the Round Butte Archaeological Sites, Deschutes River Basin, Oregon, *University of Oregon Museum of Natural History Bulletin* 6:1–20.

Rosenberg, Gary 1980. An Ontogenetic Approach to Environmental Significance of Bivalve Shell Chemistry, in Rhoads, D. and Lutz, R. (eds.), *Skeletal Growth in Aquatic Organisms* (New York, Plenum Press) 133–168.

1990. The "Vital Effect" on Skeletal Trace Element Content as Exemplified by Magnesium, in Carter, J. (ed.), *Skeletal Biomineralization: Patterns, Processes, and Evolutionary Trends* (New York, Van Nostrand Reinhold) 567–577.

Rowland, Michael J. 1989. Population Increase, Intensification or a Result of Preservation?, Explaining Site Distribution Patterns on the Coast of Queensland, *Australian Aboriginal Studies* 1989(2):32–42.

Rowley-Conwy, Peter 1983. Sedentary Hunters: The Ertebølle Example, in Bailey, G. (ed.), *Hunter-Gatherer Economy in Prehistory* (Cambridge University Press) 111–126.

Russel-Hunter, W. 1978. Ecology of Freshwater Pulmonates, in Fretter, V. and Peake, J. (eds.), *Pulmonates*, Vol. IIA, (London, Academic Press) 335–383.

Russo, Michael 1988. A Comment on Temporal Patterns in Marine Shellfish Use in Florida and Georgia, *Southeastern Archaeology* 7:61–68.

1991. A Method for the Measurement of Season and Duration of Oyster Collection: Two Case Studies from the Prehistoric Southeast U.S. Coast, *Journal of Archaeological Science* 18:205–220.

1996. Southeastern Preceramic Archaic Ceremonial Mounds, in Sassaman, K. and Anderson, D. (eds.), *Archaeology of the Mid-Holocene Southeast* (University of Florida Press) 556–592.

Russo, Michael and Quitmyer, Irvy 1996. Sedentism in Coastal Populations of South Florida, in Reitz, E., Newson, L., and Scudder, S. (eds.), *Case Studies in Environmental Archaeology* (New York, Plenum) 215–231.

Rye, Danny and Sommer, Michael II 1980. Reconstructing Paleotemperature and Paleosalinity Regimes with Oxygen Isotopes, in Rhoads, D. and Lutz, R. (eds.), *Skeletal Growth of Aquatic Organisms* (New York, Plenum).

Safer, Jane and Gill, Frances 1982. *Spirals from the Sea: An Anthropological Look at Shell* (New York, C. N. Potter).

Salls, Roy 1988. Prehistoric Fisheries of the California Bight. Ph.D. dissertation, Anthropology, University of California, Los Angeles.

Sandweiss, Daniel 1996. Environmental Change and Its Consequences for Human Society on the Central Andean Coast: A Malacological Perspective, in Reitz, E, Newson, L., and Scudder, S. (eds.), *Case Studies in Environmental Archaeology*, (New York, Plenum) 127–146.

Sandweiss, Daniel, Richardson, James, Reitz, Elizabeth, Hsu, Jeffrey, and Feldman, Robert 1989. Early Maritime Adaptations in the Andes: Preliminary Studies at the Ring Site, Peru, in Rice, D., Stanish, C., and Scarr, P. (eds.), *Ecology, Settlement and History in the Osmore Drainage, Peru*, British Archaeological Reports, International Series 545 (Oxford, BAR) Part i, 35–84.

Sandweiss, Daniel, Richardson, James, Reitz, Elizabeth, Rollins, Harold, and Maasch, Kirk 1996. Geoarchaeological Evidence from Peru for a 5000 Years B.P. Onset of El Niño, *Science* 273:1531–1533.

Sandweiss, Daniel and Rodríguez, María 1991. Moluscos Marinos en La Prehistoria Peruana: Breve Ensayo, *Boletin de Lima* 75:55–63.

Sandweiss, Daniel, Rollins, Harold, and Richardson, James 1983. Landscape Alteration and Prehistoric Human Occupation on the North Coast of Peru, *Annals of Carnegie Museum* 52:277–298.

Sanger, David 1981. Unscrambling Messages in the Midden, *Archaeology of Eastern North America* 9:37–42.

Sassaman, Ken 1993. *Early Pottery in the Southeast: Tradition and Innovation in Cooking Technology* (Tuscaloosa, University of Alabama Press).

Schoeninger, Margaret and Peebles, Christopher 1981. Effects of Mollusc Eating on Human Bone Strontium Levels, *Journal of Archaeological Science* 8:391–397.

Schofield, J. 1937. Natal Coastal Pottery From the Durban District: A Preliminary Survey – Part II, *South African Journal of Science* 33:993–1009.

Schoute-Vanneck, C. 1960. A Chemical Aid for the Relative Dating of Coastal Shell Middens, *South African Journal of Science* 56:67–70.

Scudder, T. 1971. Gathering Among African Woodland Savannah Cultivators, *Zambian Paper* 5.

Sealy, Judy, van der Merwe, Nicholas, Sillen, Andrew, Kruger, F., and Krueger, Harold 1991. $^{87}Sr/^{86}Sr$ as a Dietary Indicator in Modern and Archaeological Bone, *Journal of Archaeological Science* 18:399–416.

Shackleton, Judith 1988. *Marine Molluscan Remains from Franchthi Cave* (Indiana University Press).

Shackleton, Nicholas 1973. Oxygen Isotope Analysis as a Means of Determining Season of Occupation of Prehistoric Midden Sites, *Archaeometry* 15:133–141.

Shackleton, Nicholas and Renfrew, Colin 1970. Neolithic Trade Routes Re-aligned by Oxygen Isotope Analyses, *Nature* 228:1062–1065.

Shawcross, Wilfred 1967. An Investigation of Prehistoric Diet and Economy on a Coastal Site at Galatea Bay, New Zealand, *Proceedings of the Prehistoric Society* 33(7):107–131.

Shenkel, J. Richard 1974. Quantitative Analysis and Population Estimates of the Shell Mounds of the Marismas Nacionales, West Mexico, in Bell, B. (ed.), *The Archaeology of West Mexico* (Sociedad de Estudio, Avanzados del Occidente de México, Ajijic, Jalisco) 57–67.

1986. An Additional Comment on Volume Calculations and a Comparison of Formulae Using Several Southeastern Mounds, *Midcontinental Journal of Archaeology* 11:201–220.

Shimoyama, Shoichi and Fujisaka, Hirokazu 1992. A New Interpretation of the Left–Right Phenomenon during Spatial Diffusion and Transport of Bivalve Shells, *Journal of Geology* 100:291–304.

Sidwell, V., Bonnett, J., and Zook, E. 1973. Chemical and Nutritive Values of Several Fresh and Canned Finfish, Crustaceans and Mollusks Part 1: Proximate Composition, Calcium, and Phosphorus, *Marine Fisheries Review* 35(12):16–19.

Sidwell, V., Foncannon, P., Moore, N., and Bonnett, J. 1974. Composition of the Edible Portion of Raw (Fresh or Frozen) Crustaceans, Finfish, and Mollusks. I. Protein, Fat, Moisture, Ash, Carbohydrate, Energy Value, and Cholesterol, *Marine Fisheries Review* 36(3):21–35.

Siegfried, W., Hockey, Philip, and Crowe, A. 1985. Exploitation and Conservation of Brown Mussel Stocks by Coastal People of Transkei, *Environmental Conservation* 12:303–307.

Sigler-Eisenberg, Brenda and Russo, Michael 1986. Seasonality and Function of Small Sites on Florida's Central-East Coast, *Southeastern Archaeology* 5:21–31.

Simenstad, Charles, Estes, James, and Kenyon, Karl 1978. Aleuts, Sea Otters, and Alternate Stable-state Communities, *Science* 200:403–411.

Sindermann, Carl 1970. *Principal Diseases of Marine Fish and Shellfish* (San Diego, Academic Press).

Singer, Ronald and Wymer, John 1982. *The Middle Stone Age at Klasies River Mouth in South Africa* (University of Chicago Press).

Skelton, Duane 1978. The Seasonal Factor of *Rangia cuneata* Clam Collecting, in Skelton, D. (ed.), *Prehistoric Archaeological Investigations at Palmetto Bend Reservoir*, Texas Archaeological Survey, Research Report 45 (Austin, University of Texas) 65–75.

Smith, Bruce 1992. *Rivers of Change*, (Washington, D.C., Smithsonian Press).

Smith, Hugh 1898. The Mussel Fishery and Pearl-Button Industry of the Mississippi River, *Bulletin of the U.S. Fisheries Commission* 18 (Washington, D.C.).

Solem, Alan 1974. *The Shell Makers: Introducing Mollusks* (New York, John Wiley and Sons).

Sorant, P. and Shenkel, Richard 1984. The Calculation of Volumes of Middens, Mounds, and Strata Having Irregular Shapes, *American Antiquity* 49:599–603.

Southon, J., Nelson, D., and Vogel, J. 1990. A Record of Past Ocean–Atmosphere Radiocarbon Differences from the Northeast Pacific, *Paleoceanography* 5:197–206.

Spanier, Ehud 1986. Cannibalism in Muricid Snails as a Possible Explanation for Archaeological Findings, *Journal of Archaeological Science* 13:463–468.

Spencer, Charles 1982. *The Cuicatlan Canada and Monte Albán: A Study of Primary State Formation* (San Diego, Academic Press).

Spennemann, Dirk 1987. Availability of Shellfish Resources on Prehistoric Tongatapu, Tonga: Effects of Human Predation and Changing Environment, *Archaeology in Oceania* 22:81–96.

Spennemann, Dirk and Colley, Sarah 1989. Fire in a Pit: the Effects of Burning on Faunal Remains, *Archaeozoologia* 3(1,2):51–64.

Spiess, Arthur and Hedden, Mark 1983. Kidder Point and Sears Island in Prehistory, *Occasional Publications in Maine Archaeology* 3.

Staff, George, Stanton, Robert, Powell, Eric, and Cummins, Hays 1986. Time-averaging, Taphonomy, and Their Impact on Paleocommunity Reconstruction: Death Assemblages in Texas Bays, *Geological Society of America Bulletin* 97:428–443.

Stansbery, David 1970. Eastern Freshwater Mollusks (I) The Mississippi and St. Lawrence River Systems, *Malacologia* 10:9–22.

Statham, E. 1892. Observations of Shell-Heaps and Shell-Beds, *Journal of the Royal Society of New South Wales* 26:304–314.

Stein, Julie 1983. Earthworm Activity: a Source of Potential Disturbance of Archaeological Sediments, *American Antiquity* 48:277–289.

1986. Coring Archaeological Sites, *American Antiquity* 51:505–527.

1992a. The Analysis of Shell Middens, in Stein, J. (ed.), *Deciphering a Shell Midden* (San Diego, Academic Press) 1–16.

1992b. Interpreting Stratification of a Shell Midden, in Stein, J. (ed.), *Deciphering a Shell Midden* (San Diego, Academic Press) 71–94.

Stein, Julie (ed.) 1992c. *Deciphering a Shell Midden* (San Diego, Academic Press).

Stein, Julie and Teltser, Patrice 1989. Size Distributions of Artifact Classes: Combining Macro- and Micro-Fractions, *Geoarchaeology* 4:1–30.

Stephenson, Lani 1987. *Impact of Helminth Infections on Human Nutrition* (London, Taylor and Francis).

Stephenson, Robert 1971. The Potts Village Site Oahe Reservoir, South Dakota, *Missouri Archaeologist* 33.

Stiner, Mary 1993. Small Animal Exploitation and its Relation to Hunting, Scavenging, and Gathering in the Italian Mousterian, in Peterkin, G., Bricker, H., and Mellars, P. (eds.), *Hunting and Animal Exploitation in the Later Paleolithic and Mesolithic of Eurasia* (Archeological Papers of the American Anthropological Association 4) 107–125.

Stix, Hugh, Stix, Marguerite and Abbott, Tucker 1984. *The Shell: Gift of the Sea* (New York, Abradale Press/Harry N. Abrams, Inc.).

Stone, Tim 1989. Origins and Environmental Significance of Shell and Earth Mounds in Northern Australia, *Archaeology in Oceania* 24:59–64.

Stuiver, Minze and Braziunas, Thomas 1993. Modeling Atmospheric ^{14}C Influences and ^{14}C Ages of Marine Samples to 10,000 BC, *Radiocarbon* 35(1):137–189.

Styles, Bonnie 1981. *Faunal Exploitation and Resource Selection: Early Late Woodland Subsis-*

tence in the Lower Illinois Valley (Evanston, IL, Northwestern University Archeological Program).

Suguio, Kenitiro, Martin, Louis, and Flexor, Jean-Marie 1992. Paleoshorelines and the Sambaquis of Brazil, in Johnson, L. (ed.), *Paleoshorelines and Prehistory: An Investigation of Method*, (Boca Raton, CRC Press) 83–99.

Sullivan, Marjorie 1984. A Shell Midden Excavation at Pambula Lake on the Far South Coast of New South Wales, *Archaeology in Oceania* 19:1–15.

Swadling, Pamela 1977. Depletion of Shellfish in the Traditional Gathering Beds of Pari, in Winslow, J. (ed.), *The Melanesian Environment* (Singapore, Angus and Robertson) 182–187.

   1980. Shellfishing in Papua New Guinea, with Special Reference to the Papuan Coast, in Morauta, L., Pernetta, J., and Heaney, W. (eds.), *Traditional Conservation in Papua New Guinea: Implications for Today*, Institute of Applied Social and Economic Research Monograph 16 (Boroko) 307–310.

Swann, C., Carriker, Melbourne, and Ewart, J. 1984. Significance of Environment and Chronology on Distribution of 16 Elements (Na to Sr) in the Shells of Living Oysters, *Nuclear Instruments and Methods in Physics Research* B3 1984:392–395.

Tartaglia, Louis 1976. Prehistoric Maritime Adaptations in Southern California. Ph.D. dissertation, Anthropology, University of California, Los Angeles.

   1980. Late Period Site Catchments in Southern California, *Anthroplogy UCLA* 10(1/2):179–192.

Teichert, C. and Serventy, D. 1947. Deposits of Shells Transported by Birds, *American Journal of Science* 245:322–329.

Tevesz, Michael and Carter, Joseph 1980. Environmental Relationship of Shell Form and Structure of Unionacean Bivalves, in Rhoads, D. and Lutz, R. (eds.), *Skeletal Growth in Aquatic Organisms* (New York, Plenum Press) 295–322.

Thomas, K. 1985. Land Snail Analysis in Archaeology: Theory and Practice, in Fieller, N., Gilbertson, D., and Ralph, N. (eds.), *Palaeobiological Investigations* British Archaeological Reports, International Series 266 (Oxford, BAR), 131–155.

Thompson, Eric 1960. *Maya Hieroglyphic Writing: An Introduction* (Norman, University of Oklahoma Press).

Tiffany, W. 1968. The Life Cycle and Ecology of the Beach Clam *Donax variabilis*. M.S. Thesis, Biology, Florida State University.

Tipper, J. C. 1979. Rarefaction and Rarefiction – The Use and Abuse of a Method in Paleoecology, *Paleobiology* 5:423–434.

Toizumi, Takeji 1994. Scasonality of the Jomon Fishery Determined from Shell Midden Deposition: a Case Study at the Ikawazu Shell Midden Site, Central Japan, *Archaeozoologia* 6(2):95–110.

Toth, Nicholas and Woods, Michael 1989. Molluscan Shell Knives and Experimental Cut-Marks on Bones, *Journal of Field Archaeology* 16:250–255.

Trigger, Bruce 1986. *Native Shell Mounds of North America: the Early Years* (New York, Garland).

   1989. *A History of American Archaeology* (Cambridge University Press).

Trinkley, Michael 1981. *Studies of Three Woodland Period Sites in Beaufort County, S.C.* (Columbia, S.C., South Carolina Department of Highways and Public Transportation).

Trinkley, Michael and Adams, Natalie 1994. *Middle and Late Woodland Life at Old House Creek, Hilton Head Island, South Carolina.* Chicora Foundation Research Series 42. Columbia, S.C.

Tucker, Maurice 1991. The Diagenesis of Fossils, in Donovan, S. (ed.), *The Processes of Fossilization* (Columbia University Press) 84–104.

Turekian, K. and Armstrong, R. 1960. Magnesium, Strontium and Barium Concentrations and

Calcite–Aragonite Ratios of Some Recent Molluscan Shells, *Journal of Marine Research* 18:133–151.

van der Merwe, Nickolas and Vogel, J. 1978. [13]C Content of Human Collagen as a Measure of Prehistoric Diet in Woodland North America, *Nature* 276:815–816.

Vanuxem, L. 1843. On the Ancient Oyster Shell Deposits Observed Near the Atlantic Coast of the U.S., *Proceedings of the Association of American Geologists and Naturalists 1840–1842* (Boston, Gould, Kendall, and Lincoln) 21–23.

Vaught, Kay 1989. *A Classification of the Living Mollusca* (Melbourne, FL, American Malacologist, Inc.).

Verger, F. 1959. Les Buttes Coquillieres de Saint-Michel-en-l'Herm, *Norois* 21:35–45.

Vermeij, Geerat 1993. *A Natural History of Shells* (Princeton, Princeton University Press).

Voigt, Elizabeth 1975. Studies of Marine Mollusca from Archaeological Sites: Dietary Preferences, Environmental Reconstructions and Ethnological Parallels, in Clason, A. (ed.), *Archaeozoological Studies* (Amsterdam, North Holland) 87–98.

1982. The Molluscan Fauna, in Singer, R. and Wymer, J. (eds.), *The Middle Stone Age at Klasies River Mouth in South Africa* (University of Chicago Press) 155–186.

Vokes, Harold, and Vokes, Emily 1983. Distribution of Shallow-Water Marine Mollusca, Yucatan Peninsula, Mexico, *Middle American Research Institute* 54, Tulane University, New Orleans.

Volman, Thomas 1978. Early Archeological Evidence for Shellfish Collecting, *Science* 201:911–913.

Voorhies, Barbara 1976. The Chantuto People: An Archaic Period Society of the Chiapas Littoral, Mexico, *Papers of the New World Archaeological Foundation*, 41 (Provo, Brigham Young University).

Voorhies, Barbara, Michaels, George, and Riser, George 1991. Ancient Shrimp Fishery, *National Geographic Research and Exploration* 7(1):20–35.

Walker, Karen 1992. The Zooarchaeology of Charlotte Harbor's Prehistoric Maritime Adaptation: Spatial and Temporal Perspectives, in Marquardt, W. (ed.), *Culture and Environment in the Domain of the Calusa* (Monograph No. 1, Institute of Archaeology and Paleoenvironmental Studies, University of Florida, Gainesville) 265–366.

Walker, S. T. 1883. The Aborigines of Florida. *Smithsonian Institution, Annual Report for 1881*: (US Government Printing Office) 677–680.

Warren, Robert 1991. Freshwater Mussels as Paleoenvironmental Indicators: A Quantitative Approach to Assemblage Analysis, in Purdue, J., Klippel, W., and Styles, B. (eds.), *Beamers, Bobwhites, and Blue-Points: Tributes to the Career of Paul W. Parmalee* (Illinois State Museum Scientific Papers, 23, Springfield) 23–66.

1997. Shell Volumetric Capacity as a Pan-Species Correlate with the Food Value of Freshwater Mussels. Paper delivered at the Annual Meeting of the Society for American Archaeology, Nashville.

Waselkov, Gregory 1987. Shellfish Gathering and Shell Midden Archaeology, in Schiffer, M. (ed.), *Advances in Archaeological Method and Theory* vol. XI (San Diego, Academic Press) 93–210.

Watters, David, Donahue, Jack, and Stuckenrath, Robert 1992. Paleoshorelines and the Prehistory of Barbuda, West Indies, in Johnson, L. (ed.), *Paleoshorelines and Prehistory: An Investigation of Method* (Boca Raton, CRC Press) 15–52.

Webb, William and DeJarnette, David 1942. An Archeological Survey of Pickwick Basin in the Adjacent Portions of the States of Alabama, Mississippi, and Tennessee. Bureau of American Ethnology, Bulletin 129. Washington, D.C.

Weide, Margaret 1969. Seasonality of Pismo Clam Collecting at Ora-82, *University of California at Los Angeles Archaeological Survey Annual Report* 1969:127–141.

Wells, F. E. and Bryce, C. W. 1985. *Seashells of Western Australia* (Western Australian Museum, Perth).

Wessen, Gary 1982. Shell Middens as Cultural Deposits: A Case Study from Ozette. Ph.D. dissertation, Anthropology, Washington State University.

Whitmer, Ann, Ramenofsky, Ann, Thomas, J., Thibodeaux, L., Field, S., and Miller, B. 1989. Stability or Instability: The Role of Diffusion in Trace Element Studies, in Schiffer, M. (ed.), *Archaeological Method and Theory*, vol. I (University of Arizona Press) 205–273.

Widmer, Randolph 1989. Archaeological Research Strategies in the Investigation of Shell-Bearing Sites, a Florida Perspective. Paper delivered at the Annual Meeting of the Society for American Archaeology, Atlanta.

Wilbur, Karl 1964. Shell Formation and Regeneration, in Wilbur, K. and Yonge, C. (eds.), *Physiology of Mollusca* (New York, Academic Press) 243–282.

1972. Shell Formation in Mollusks, in Florkin, M. and Scheer, B. (eds.), *Chemical Zoology VII* (New York, Academic Press) 103–142.

1976. Recent Studies of Invertebrate Mineralization, in Watabe, N. and Wilbur, K. (eds.), *The Mechanisms of Mineralization in the Invertebrates and Plants* (Columbia, University of South Carolina Press) 79–108.

Wild, C. and Nichol, R. 1983. Estimation of Original Numbers of Individuals from Paired Bone Counts Using Estimators of the Krantz Type, *Journal of Field Archaeology* 10:337–344.

Wilken, G. 1970. The Ecology of Gathering in a Mexican Farming Community, *Economic Botany* 24(30):286–294.

Willey, Gordon and McGimsey, Charles 1954. The Mongarillo Culture of Panama, *Papers of the Harvard University Peabody Museum of Archaeology and Ethnology* 49(2).

Williams, Mary Beth and Bendremer, Jeffrey 1997. The Archaeology of Maize, Pots, and Seashells: Gender Dynamics in Late Woodland and Contact Period New England, in Claassen, C. and Joyce, R. (eds.), *Women in Prehistory: North America and Mesoamerica* (University of Pennsylvania Press) 138–149.

Williams, Winston 1962. Twenty Fathoms Down for Mother-of-Pearl, *National Geographic* April:513–529.

Wing, Elizabeth and Brown, Antoinette 1979. *Paleonutrition: Method and Theory in Prehistoric Foodways* (Orlando, Academic Press).

Wing, Elizabeth and Quitmyer, Irvy 1985. Screen Size For Optimal Data Recovery: A Case Study, in Aboriginal Subsistence, in Adams, W. (ed.), *Aboriginal Subsistence and Settlement Archaeology of the Kings Bay Locality, vol. 2: Zooarchaeology*, Department of Anthropology Reports of Investigations No. 2 (University of Florida, Gainesville) 49–59.

1992. A Modern Midden Experiment, in Marquardt, W. (ed.), *Culture and Environment in the Domain of the Calusa*, Institute of Archaeology and Paleoenvironmental Studies, Monograph 1 (University of Florida, Gainesville) 367–373.

Wright, Thomas and Kornicker, Louis 1962. Island Transport of Marine Shells by Birds on Perez Island, Alacran Reef, Campeche Bank, Mexico, *Journal of Geology* 70:616–618.

Wyatt, T. and Reguera, B. 1989. Historical Trends in the Red Tide Phenomenon in the Rias Bajas of Northwest Spain, in Okaichi, T., Anderson, D., and Nemoto, T. (eds.), *Red Tides: Biology, Environmental Science, and Toxicology* (New York, Elsevier) 33–36.

Wyman, Jeffries 1875. Fresh-Water Shell Mounds of the St. John's River, Florida, *Peabody Academy of Science, Memoir* 1(4):1–94.

Yengoyan, Aram 1968. Demographic and Ecological Influences on Aboriginal Australian Marriage Sections, in Lee, R. and DeVore, I. (eds.), *Man the Hunter* (Chicago, University of Chicago Press).

Yesner, David 1977. Prehistoric Subsistence and Settlement in the Aleutian Islands. Ph.D. dissertation, Anthropology, University of Connecticut.

1981. Archaeological Applications of Optimal Foraging Theory: Harvest Strategies of Aleut Hunter-Gatherers, in Winterhalder, B., and Smith, E. (eds.), *Hunter-Gatherer Foraging Strategies: Ethnographic and Archaeological Analyses* (University of Chicago Press) 148–170.

Zale, Alexander 1986. Mussel Mortalities in the Neosho River System, Oklahoma, Ms. on file Department of Fisheries and Wildlife Sciences, Virginia Polytechnic Institute, Blacksburg.

Zeitlen, Robert 1978. Long-Distance Exchange and the Growth of a Regional Center on the Southern Isthmus of Tehuantepec, Mexico, in Stark, B. and Voorhies, B. (eds.), *Prehistoric Coastal Adaptations* (Academic Press, New York) 183–210.

INDEX OF TAXA

SUBJECT INDEX

263